R040572134   12/05

THE IRON HORSE AND THE WINDY CITY

The Iron Horse and the Windy City

How Railroads Shaped Chicago

DAVID M. YOUNG

NORTHERN ILLINOIS UNIVERSITY PRESS / DEKALB

Library of Congress Cataloging-in-Publication Data

Young, David, 1940 Sept. 22–

The iron horse and the windy city : how railroads shaped Chicago / David M. Young.

    p.   cm.

Includes bibliographical references and index.

ISBN-10: 0-87580-334-2

ISBN-13: 978-0-87580-334-0

(clothbound : alk. paper)

1. Railroads—Illinois—Chicago. 2. Chicago (Ill.)—Economic conditions. 3. Land use—

Illinois—Chicago. I. Title.

HE2781..C4Y68 2005

385′.09773′11—dc22

2004016972

Contents

Preface

A friend visiting from another city a few years ago was overly apologetic when he arrived late to a meeting. He explained in great detail how he had been delayed for 20 minutes by three successive freight trains at the same railroad crossing. While highway traffic jams were a common occurrence in his hometown, as they are in almost every city in America, he claimed he had never experienced such a lengthy delay because of multiple trains. His effusive apology only amused the other attendees, however—they were all Chicagoans who long ago accepted crossing delays as an inevitable consequence of living in and around the Windy City.

For the first century in the city's existence, frequent ship traffic on the Chicago River gave people who worked in the Loop iron-clad excuses for being late: because the bascule bridges were up. Then the railroads came along—not just a few railroads, but all of them—and the iron horse became a universal excuse for being late. Plodding freights slowly chugging in and out of yards were perhaps the most maddening phenomenon, but frequent intercity and commuter passenger trains contributed to the problem.

When an editor at Northern Illinois University Press suggested it was time to do a book on the history of the city's railroads as part of what has developed as a series on local transportation modes, I thought that perhaps the story that needed to be told was the influence the iron horse had had on Chicago's development. The long delays at grade crossings were only an obvious piece of a bigger picture. Chicago in the second half of the nineteenth century became the nation's largest rail junction, a factor that was to influence almost every aspect of life locally—including the law, architecture, business, industry, and population.

An enormous amount of literature has been written about railroads in America, most of it concerned with the history of individual companies, the lore of the industry, and what could be described as photographic accounts aimed at the rail-fan market. For example, there have been no less than five well-illustrated books published on the Chicago, Aurora & Elgin, a hundred-mile electric line that operated for slightly more than half a century. Railroad-related development is a topic covered in varying degrees by social historians, geographers, economists, and urbanologists, primarily concentrating on the nineteenth century. This book attempts to complement their efforts at both ends of the historical spectrum by discussing why Chicago became America's largest railroad center in the nineteenth century and why it has remained so through the twentieth despite substantial changes in traffic patterns.

The evidence used to answer both questions is largely circumstantial, something like the material gathered by a prosecutor trying a conspiracy case in which there is no smoking gun. But in the present case there was no conspiracy. Chicago attained a critical mass in railroads without the need for any plot or master plan. A wise airline president I once interviewed described the propensity of the carriers in his industry to congregate at the same hubs and match each others' discount fares as the "herd instinct," and I suspect that would be a good term to describe what happened among the railroads serving Chicago. They built lines to the Windy City in the nineteenth century to share in the developing traffic being interchanged there, and they have stayed in Chicago since then despite a contraction of the industry, because they could not afford to lose the market shares they had developed.

The book also deals with the collective effect of railroads on Chicagoland. The fact that the city is covered by railroad tracks is obvious to anyone trying to drive around it and its suburbs. An observant motorist also will notice rusting rails leading to abandoned factories or grain elevators, a vestige of the railroads' past influence, as well as vast residential projects in close proximity to Chicago's Loop. Those cities-within-a-city stand on what were once railroad passenger yards serving depots that fell to the wrecking balls. So this book does not dwell in great detail on the legendary passenger trains—the Twentieth Century Limiteds and 400s—that sped across the landscape carrying both the glitterati and unwashed immigrants. Instead, it discusses the city's hotel and tourism industry, which arose as a result of those trains, and the way that Chicago creatively reused the vast tracts of railroad land made superfluous by the decline of the passenger train after World War II.

Likewise, as the visitor whose arrival at a meeting was delayed by freight trains surmised, a motorist in Chicagoland cannot help but notice that every few miles or so he or she will pass beneath a railroad viaduct, or, if in the suburbs, will be stopped at a crossing by a slow freight. For some reason, academia—not to mention the trade press and rail-fan publications—has largely ignored the rail crossing problem in America, although some legal scholars have dealt with the issue as the origin of much of the tort litigation in this nation. A history of Chicago's railroads would be deficient without discussing the enormous grade crossing problem. That requires the examination of scores of old court cases, which helpfully included discussions of the nature of the accidents un-

der litigation, as well as city ordinances on track elevation and government reports dealing with crossing accidents.

The research for this book goes back almost 30 years and has included my travels on many passenger and freight trains when I reported on the industry for the *Chicago Tribune*. I rode on some famous trains like the Broadway Limited, Zephyr, Southern Crescent, and Super Chief, but some of the train rides that were most important for assembling knowledge for this book occurred on locomotives pulling fast intermodal freight trains. A trip from Houston to Chicago aboard a Missouri Pacific chemical train with highly toxic cargo was particularly memorable. There were also reconnaissance trips on a number of branch lines and rides on virtually all of Chicago's commuter railroads.

Because most railroads in America resulted from the continuing consolidation of smaller railroads, describing those carriers in a book of this nature provides a maddening problem for the historian, not to mention the reader. Over the course of half a century a railroad might have had a dozen different names. Thus the Chicago & Eastern Illinois Railroad, which was initially proposed in Illinois as the Chicago & Vincennes, in part has been known variously as the Evansville & Illinois; Evansville & Crawfordsville; Evansville, Indianapolis & Terre Haute; Big Four; Chicago, Attica & Southern; Evansville, Terre Haute & Chicago; and Chicago, Danville & Vincennes to name a few. More recently it became part of the Missouri Pacific and then the Union Pacific.

Since this book is more concerned with railroad routes than individual railroad companies, wherever possible I have tried to use the railroad names popular in the twentieth century.

A number of organizations were generous with their time and energy in helping me assemble this book and its photographs. Railroad historian H. Roger

Grant not only shared his insight into the industry but some of his extensive photo collection as well. Michael Ebner's comments on urban affairs were helpful too, as were the observations of John McCarron, one of my former editors at the *Chicago Tribune*. M. J. Grandinetti, editor of the newspaper's transportation section, also indulged my curiosity to pursue some arcane stories on railroading.

Officials of various railroads I covered for the newspaper were also helpful in catering to my intellectual whims about railroads. They include Jim Macdonald and Jerry Conlan of the North Western, Pete Briggs of the Burlington, Joe Beckman of the C&EI and CSX, Chris Knapton of the Rock Island and Metra, Bill Burk and Bob Gehrt of the Santa Fe, Tom Hoppin of Conrail, Ed Edel of Amtrak and CSX, Bob O'Brien and Frank Malone of the IC, and Wally Abby of the Milwaukee Road. A number of railroad presidents were also willing to spend time educating me about their business. They included Larry Cena of the Santa Fe, Tom Lamphier of the Burlington Northern, Larry Provo and Jim

Wolfe of the North Western, John Ingram of the Rock Island, Harry Bruce of the Illinois Central, and Stan Crane of Conrail.

Robert W. McKnight shared his extensive knowledge of grade crossings, and in her spare time my lawyer daughter, Darcee, culled legal records for accident cases I needed in my research. The staff of Chicago's Municipal Reference Library and the Chicago Historical Society were never too busy to dig up this or that document. The late George Krambles shared both his extensive knowledge of the region's interurban system and his numerous photos. Lois Wille, a former colleague on the *Tribune* editorial board, provided many helpful tips on urban affairs.

Others who opened their private photo collections include Norm Carlson, Art Peterson, Al Lind, Mike Brown, and Steve Smedley. Two erudite rail fans—Bob Goldsborough and Fritz Plous—read the manuscript and made a number of helpful suggestions. Retired newspaper editor Bob Rockafield also read the text and corrected a number of grammatical problems.

Tom Willcockson did the maps.

THE IRON HORSE AND THE WINDY CITY

Introduction

Chicago owes its existence to geography and its greatness to railroads. Its location at the southwest corner of Lake Michigan, where the Great Lakes and Mississippi River watersheds come within a few miles of each other, was its strongest geographic asset before the Industrial Revolution, when people and goods traveled primarily by water. Thus Chicago developed as a modest but thriving maritime center in the first half of the nineteenth century. Before then the local Indians and colonial French and British sporadically used the area as a canoe portage for the fur trade. But the expansion-minded citizens of the new American nation developed it as an east-west gateway for waterborne commerce, first as a jumping off place for the settlers headed west and after that as a center where manufactured goods from the East could be distributed to the settlers in the West and the products of those settlers' labors could be collected for shipment in the other direction.

Even as the Fort Dearborn settlement that became Chicago was developing as a trading post in the opening years of the nineteenth century, the British were applying the concept of mounting a steam engine on a wheeled platform that could run on an iron-railed tramway to pull coal from mine heads to the nearest canal. Fort Dearborn was built in 1803, and the next year Richard Trevithick conducted his first successful test of a steam locomotive on the Pennydarren Tramroad, a horse railway in South Wales. The idea eventually occurred to the British promoters of the new rail roads that if they could be used to haul coal and stone from mines, they could also be adapted as common carriers to transport people and manufactured goods to places where the rivers and canals did not run.

Chicago's earliest transportation projects for the most part were maritime-oriented—essentially publicly funded schemes to improve the city as a port, such as building lighthouses, dredging the Chicago River, and building a canal to connect the Great Lakes with the Mississippi River. Not surprisingly, the city's first two rail roads were designed and built to function as an overland extension of the Great Lakes for hauling people and goods to and from ships. The concept proved so successful that within a decade more rail roads were built, fanning out west across the plains, north to the woodlands, south to the plantations, and east to the manufacturing centers. It was not long before the public shortened the name of the new technology: they were not rail roads—roads on which rails had been laid—but became simply railroads.

At some point in the middle of the nineteenth century, perhaps earlier than 1860 but certainly no later than 1870, Chicago attained a "critical mass" as a transportation center, to borrow a term from a century later when nuclear power was developed in Chicago. Not only did the city become a giant magnet for railroads from all over the country, but railroads that attempted to bypass Chicago did so at their own peril. Railroads with general offices in such distant locations as Baltimore, Topeka, and Minneapolis decided they had to have lines to Chicago, and some eventually moved their headquarters there as well. Small local railroads, or belts, were built in Chicago simply to haul freight cars around the city between the major railroads.

There is no grand document, no master plan or congressional enactment, that designated Chicago as the nation's primary railroad center. The story of how Chicago attained its critical mass in railroads is gleaned not from a single pronouncement but circumstantially from the individual histories of scores of railroads. It was a matter of following the money trail. The organizers of railroads from around the country spent considerable sums to build lines to the Windy City, and many of those that did not have the money to do so added Chicago to their corporate names because they had connections to that city over other railroads.

It would be interesting to speculate about what would have happened had government built the U.S. railroad system. Would the local political pressures in highly sectional America in the 1850s have forced the building of a system that did not favor any particular region over another? The political debate in the 1850s over the building of the first transcontinental railroad offers a clue, as does the emergence of the government-subsidized and -controlled Amtrak system more than a century later. Antebellum politicians in cities and states around the nation squabbled over whether the eastern terminal of the transcontinental line would or would not favor their constituencies. More than a century later, Amtrak was designed for political reasons to run passenger trains through as many congressional districts as possible to ensure its continuing subsidy, but the policy diluted its effectiveness as a transportation system.

The American railroad system was built largely by private enterprise in the middle of the nineteenth century. It is true that cities and states attempted to influence the decisions about where railroads would run, even to the point of granting subsidies, and local merchants built short railroads to benefit their small communities across the landscape, but for the most part entrepreneurs and speculators built America's railroad system.

They were a competitive bunch, and as the local railroads increasingly fell under their control, the moneymen, usually for competitive reasons, decreed that their railroads had to have a line to Chicago where all the other railroads were headed. Perhaps it was the herd instinct, but more likely it was the realization that to compete, their individual railroads needed to interchange traffic with as many other railroads as possible. Thus Chicago became the place where the western railroads swapped passengers and freight with the eastern lines. It is a role that persists into the twenty-first century.

It is something of an irony that the city fathers of Chicago, the nation's emerging railroad center, did very little to promote the industry from which the city ultimately derived so much benefit. The citizens and governments of rival cities actively solicited railroads even to the point of providing them subsidies, but Chicago did not have to. In fact, only one of the city's major railroad systems, its first, can claim Chicago as its birthplace. All the others were organized somewhere else and gravitated to Chicago.

It can be speculated that had railroads not been invented, Chicago by virtue of its maritime trade would still have become a large city. But the railroads built it into the metropolis of the American interior—a manufacturing center as well as a trade emporium. Entire industries arose in or moved to Chicago because of the railroad system. That included more than just the railroad supply industry, which grew up to provide such things as brake shoes and Pullman cars; there were steelmaking and wholesale distribution. The city's location at the center of the national railroad network made it an ideal site for such companies as Sears Roebuck and Montgomery Ward.

The railroads also gave the city (and the nation) a modern system for commercial governance—the incorporated joint-stock company. The railroads made possible the assembly-line mass-production techniques used at the Union Stock Yards long before Henry Ford adapted them to production of his Model T. The miscreancy of the railroads in Chicago also resulted in the nation's first system for economic regulation of private industry. The hotel industry and its allied convention and tourism business was a direct result of the passenger transportation system the railroads provided.

The railroads' influence on Chicago extended far beyond their obvious roles as transportation providers and the impact their payrolls had on the local economy. Their ubiquitous tracks carved up the city into neighborhoods, and the public grade crossings created issues of safety and traffic congestion as wagons and later motor vehicles waited for long freight trains to pass. The railroads gave Chicago (and the nation) its standard time system, a taste for steaks, and catalogues from which to order tools and fashions. They helped it rebuild after the great fire of 1871. In the form of the great Victorian depots they gave the city its first public architecture. The railroads also created the suburbs.

The vast transportation emporium the railroads created carried over into the twentieth century even after they lost their monopoly on transportation. The wholesale distribution industry that remained in Chicago created a huge demand for interstate trucking as the railroads waned and other industries moved to locations in the Sun Belt. Chicago as the twenty-first century commenced was the third busiest city in the world in intermodal traffic (containers and trucks carried on flatcars), behind only the seaports of Hong Kong and Singapore. The critical mass that the railroads had created extended not only to motor trucks and interstate highways but to the airlines as well. It is no coincidence that Chicago for most of the twentieth century was successively home to the two busiest airports in the nation even as it continued in its role as America's biggest rail freight junction.

1 Before the Iron Horse

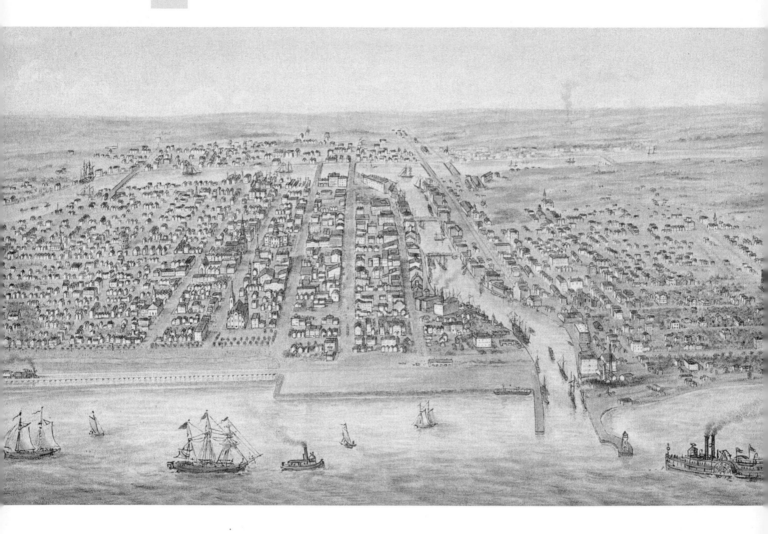

This bird's-eye view of Chicago in 1853 shows plenty of maritime commerce but only two railroads. The Galena & Chicago Union is barely visible just north of and parallel to the main stem of the river, and the Illinois Central is shown with a train chugging along the lakeshore. Notably absent is the city's third railroad of the time, the Rock Island. (Historic Urban Plans, Ithaca, N.Y.)

When sixteen-year-old Gurdon S. Hubbard traveled from Montreal to Fort Dearborn in 1818 as part of a team of traders employed by John Jacob Astor's American Fur Company, he did so by *bateaux*, the French term used interchangeably for a variety of small craft.[1] Canoes, bateaux, and variations of them were the preferred method of travel on the North American inland waters since the French began exploring them in the 1600s. The fort at the southwestern end of Lake Michigan and the small outpost that surrounded it was also the nexus of a number of meandering Indian trails fanning out in every direction, but the trails became quagmires in the spring and autumn, and their frozen ruts were difficult to negotiate in the winter. So the favored mode of travel by pioneers of European ancestry was by water.

Except for a relatively short canoe portage connecting the watersheds of the St. Lawrence and Mississippi rivers, there was little to commend the site of the future city of Chicago to anyone but fur traders like Hubbard. The Chicago River meandered for a few miles through a marshland that was not considered suitable for permanent habitation even by the Illiniwek, Wea (Miami), and Potawatomi who had successively controlled the area for centuries before Europeans began settling there. The village of 10 cabins that were scattered around Fort Dearborn in 1818 was home to perhaps 40 residents.

Yet when Hubbard died 68 years later, his adopted hometown of Chicago had become one of the nation's largest cities, its inland transportation center, and an industrial complex. His lifetime spanned the arrival of the Industrial Revolution in the Midwest. When he was born on August 22, 1802, in Windsor, Vermont, the mechanical device that would revolutionize transportation—the high pressure steam engine—had already been developed, but its practical application to traction took several decades to accomplish. By the time Hubbard arrived in Chicago in 1818 the era of the canoe, keelboat, and flatboat on the inland rivers and lakes was in decline: there were 17 steamboats operating on the Mississippi and Ohio rivers and 4 steamships on the Great Lakes.

Little of that mattered to the occupants of the Fort Dearborn outpost on the edge of the American frontier in the first two decades of the nineteenth century. Their links to the outside world were by canoe or occasionally by a sailing ship, or by a long ride over Indian trails. In fact, it was not until the opening of the Erie Canal linking the Hudson River with Lake Erie in 1825 that Fort Dearborn had a continuous water route to New York City. Although the two places are 713 miles apart as the crow flies, the waterway wandered for 1,400 miles. A person traveling west from New York went north by steamboat on the Hudson River to Albany, west over the 363-mile Erie Canal by canal boat to Buffalo, then over Lakes Erie, Huron, and Michigan for 893 miles by steamship or schooner to Chicago—a journey measured in weeks. West of Chicago, the journey was by stagecoach as far as the head of navigation of

the Illinois River at La Salle, Illinois, where steamboats connecting with the Mississippi River system were available. Freight went by lumbering and expensive drays.

Illinois early in its existence, even before the Erie Canal was opened, decided to extend the New York–Fort Dearborn waterway farther west by the expedient method of digging a canal 97 miles to connect the Illinois and Chicago rivers. It would have the effect of connecting New York (and Fort Dearborn) with the Mississippi-Missouri River system and extending the waterway another 1,000 miles west, almost to the Rocky Mountains, and south to New Orleans. It took more than two decades to plan, finance, and dig the canal, and in the 1830s the Fort Dearborn settlement, by then known as Chicago, experienced its first boom in anticipation of the project even before construction had begun.

Not surprisingly, the transportation schemes proposed for the future site of Chicago in the 1820s were maritime projects. The first was the development of the Chicago River as a port, essentially done by dredging a hole on the bar that sporadically blocked access from the lake to the river by all but the smallest craft. The second was the digging of a canal to connect the Chicago River and the Great Lakes with the head of navigation of the Illinois River, a Mississippi tributary 97 miles to the southwest. Those efforts occupied the new state of Illinois and city of Chicago for most of the second quarter of the century.

However, before both projects were completed a new technology appeared on the scene. As early as 1831 it was suggested that a railroad between Chicago and La Salle, Illinois, would be a cheaper alternative to the Illinois and Michigan Canal then on the drawing boards but which the state was having trouble financing. James M. Bucklin, chief engineer for the canal commission, estimated that a railroad could be built for a fourth the cost of the canal. The state proceeded with the canal anyway.[2]

Hubbard, perhaps the last person to use the Chicago portage on a large scale,

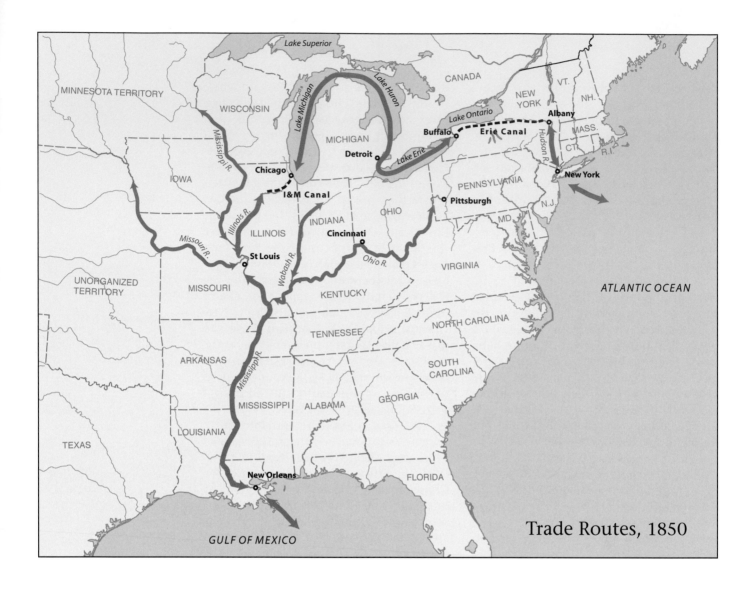

Trade Routes, 1850

The principal trade routes to and from Chicago in the first half of the nineteenth century followed the waterways. States like New York and Illinois built canals to connect their rivers with the Great Lakes.

shortly after the canal was proposed in 1818 had concluded the portage was no longer adequate for the fur trade. Low water in autumn forced the American Fur Company crews to drag their boats through the quagmire of Mud Lake connecting the Chicago and Des Plaines rivers or to portage for six miles around the lake, and low water in the Des Plaines meant the canoes and bateaux had to be dragged by ropes rather than paddled for much of the journey. Hubbard urged his superiors to abandon the portage in favor of trains of pack animals, and he did just that in 1825 after he was promoted to superintendent of the Illinois River trade. He also began to develop a fur trade using packhorses between Fort Dearborn and the lands of Miami In-

dian tribes along the Vincennes Trace (later also known as Hubbard's Trail), a trail connecting the outpost with east-central Illinois and western Indiana.[3]

It was that route that Hubbard decided a few years later would be better served by the new technology then emerging in the East—the railroad. As early as January 17, 1835, when the fur trade was dead and Hubbard was looking for other investments, he signed on as an incorporator of the 200-mile Chicago & Vincennes (Indiana) Railroad. The idea was that the railroad could capture the growing wagon traffic between Chicago, eastern Illinois, and the Wabash River valley. Unfortunately there was little private capital available for railroads in the American interior in those days, a factor that forced the state of Illinois to finance with public funds the first common carrier railroad within its borders a few years later. Hubbard's Chicago & Vincennes Railroad was not completed under different charters and corporations until 1872 as what became the Chicago & Eastern Illinois Railroad.[4]

Hubbard went on to invest in various enterprises in Chicago, including several steamships on the Great Lakes, a warehouse, real estate, a hotel, and an insurance agency. He also was elected at different times to various political offices and served on the Illinois and Michigan Canal Commission. Although he was nearly wiped out financially in the Chicago Fire of 1871, he survived to rebuild at least part of his fortune. When he died in 1886 the sparsely settled outpost he first visited in 1818 had grown into a city of three quarters of a million people and was the transportation center of the American interior.[5]

Although not as well known as Hubbard, John Frink was another Chicago transportation pioneer whose life spanned the beginning of the Industrial Revolution and who made the transition from the horse to the iron horse. Frink, the son of a stagecoach inn operator, was born in Ash-ford, Connecticut, in 1797. He got into the stagecoach business as a young man, first as a driver, and for a time operated lines serving Boston, Albany, New York, and Montreal. When it became obvious to him in the mid-1830s that the railroads then being built in the East were likely to put the stagecoaches out of business, Frink migrated west to Chicago. At the time, four of the six railroads in the United States were in New York and Massachusetts—three linking Boston to Lowell and Worchester in Massachusetts and to Providence, Rhode Island, and one connecting Albany with Schenectady in New York.[6]

Frink began acquiring existing stagecoach lines after his arrival in Chicago, succeeded in obtaining mail contracts that were necessary to subsidize them, and took in Martin O. Walker as a partner. By the end of the 1840s, Frink & Walker was the largest stagecoach operator in the Midwest, with 2,000 to 3,000 miles of lines stretching through Illinois, Indiana, Missouri, Iowa, Wisconsin, and Michigan. By 1850, it was estimated Frink had a near monopoly on postal routes in the Midwest, which produced $158,000 annually.[7]

However, by then it was obvious to him that the railroads were coming. The

In the two decades prior to the arrival of the railroads in Chicago, the stagecoach was the principal mode of overland passenger transport. Frink & Walker, subsisting primarily upon mail contracts, became the dominant carrier operating out of Chicago.

Galena & Chicago Union had been built in 1848–1849 between Chicago and Elgin, two railroads were heading toward Chicago from the east, and plans were under way for three other railroads from Chicago to the west and south. Frink, after a falling-out with Walker, began putting his money into the new technology, investing in assorted railroads that would be consolidated into the Chicago, Burlington & Quincy system. As early as 1849 he was one of the incorporators of and a director of the Aurora Branch Railroad, the first of the CB&Q predecessors, and by some accounts had put some money into the Galena Railroad that was the CB&Q's connecting line to Chicago. Frink had invested in other earlier ventures with J. Young Scammon and Walter R. Newberry, who were two of the Galena's founders. When Frink died in 1858 Chicago was already served by 10 railroads stretching 3,000 miles in almost every direction.[8]

Early Railroad Schemes

Frink and Hubbard were not the only residents of Illinois to quickly notice the comparative advantages the railroads in the East had over other forms of transportation. In 1831 the residents Vermillion County in east-central Illinois petitioned Congress for a land grant for a railroad between Chicago and Vincennes, Indiana—a project that would have connected east-central Illinois with navigation on both the Great Lakes and Wabash River. Abraham Lincoln, campaigning for the state General Assembly in early 1832, publicly suggested that a $290,000 "rail road" could be built from Alton to Springfield to operate in weather conditions unsuitable for steamboats, especially the seasonable problems of high and low water, although he concluded navigation improvements to the Sangamon River would be a cheaper alternative. Joseph Duncan, who had served in the U.S. House of Representatives in the 1826–1834 period when railroads were being built in the East, in his inaugural address as Illinois governor

on November 3, 1834, urged the state to build both railroads and canals to encourage development.[9]

The speed with which news of the new technology spread to what was then still the American frontier was surprising. The earliest steam engines developed by Thomas Savery in 1698 and Thomas Newcomen in 1712 were intended to power mine pumps and were not very efficient because they relied on alternate heating and cooling of the cylinder, so James Watt in 1769 improved Newcomen's engine by separating the condenser from the cylinder, greatly reducing fuel consumption. The next leap forward, and the one that would have the most profound influence on transportation, occurred in 1800 when Richard Trevithick in England and Oliver Evans in America independently developed the high-pressure steam engine capable of producing a pressure of 30 pounds per square inch, twice that of the Watt engine. Successive refinements led to an engine capable of 200 pounds per square inch of pressure, which could drive a riverboat upstream against a current or a land vehicle over hills.[10]

Although he built a steam-powered dredge in Philadelphia and tried to interest assorted governments in subsidizing a steam road vehicle, Evans's main interest in his invention was as a stationary power source for industry. After an unsuccessful attempt to build a steamboat in New Orleans in 1802, he left that task to others. On the other hand, Trevithick began developing his engine as a prime mover for traction vehicles, a steam-powered road carriage in 1801 and a railroad locomotive in 1804. The earliest such locomotive was used on a mine tramway.

The practical steamboat perfected by Robert Fulton and Robert Livingston in New York in 1807 didn't appear in appreciable numbers on the Mississippi River system until the 1820s, after the legal dispute over their patent was resolved and high-pressure engines became available. Although the first steamers on the Great

Lakes were launched after the War of 1812, they were not common on those inland seas until the Erie Canal opened the lakes for commerce in 1825. As late as 1848, steamboats constituted only 15 percent of the merchant marine on the lakes.

However, frontier entrepreneurs and politicians were talking about building railroads six years after the first train ran on the other side of the Atlantic Ocean in England. As noted by Ludwig Klein, an Austrian civil engineer, in his preface to German colleague Franz Anton von Gerstner's epic 1842 study of the American transportation system, the development of the railroad in America was far more rapid than in Europe, where the technology first had been developed.[11]

George Stephenson by 1825 had perfected the steam locomotive for the world's first railroad in England, but the first common carrier railroad in the United States, the Baltimore & Ohio, used horses to pull its first train on January 1, 1830. The South Carolina Canal and Railroad later the same year began service out of Charleston with a steam engine, and the Albany & Schenectady in New York used steam power when it opened in 1831. Although steam locomotives were in common use on eastern lines by then, the difficulty of obtaining such machines in the Midwest meant that the first railroad in Illinois used horse power when it commenced operations and the second had to resort to mule power when its locomotive wore out.

The Illinois Railroad, a private venture serving a coal mine in St. Clair County near St. Louis, used horses to pull its cars when it opened on December 7, 1837. The state-financed Northern Cross Railroad between Springfield and Meredosia used a steam engine when it began service in mid-1839 at Meredosia but replaced it with mules and oxen when the locomotive wore out. The railroad's first engine had to be shipped by sea from Philadelphia to New Orleans and put on a steamboat for the long trip upriver to Illinois. Two other engines destined for the Northern Cross were lost at sea on January 1, 1838.[12]

The first American railroads for the most part were conceived as portages between waterways, but within a few years port cities on the East Coast realized that the new technology could be used to extend their economic influence inland to places where the tidal rivers did not run and canals were too expensive to build. Thus railroads in America quickly became an instrument of development in the untamed interior and the device used by such ports as Charleston, South Carolina; Baltimore; Philadelphia; New York; Boston; and Portland, Maine, to extend their economic hegemonies into the developing wilderness. That pattern was quickly copied in the Midwest. It is no coincidence that the first five railroads proposed to serve Chicago beginning in 1835 were intended as extensions of that port into the interior of Illinois. The same pattern was evident in Detroit and St. Louis.[13]

Development of the interior was the primary impetus behind the canal-building craze that gripped the nation after the War of 1812 and the railroad-building mania that followed and overlapped it. In 1836 Illinois, which had committed itself to building the I&M Canal in the 1820s, launched an even more ambitious program to build railroads to every corner of the state. A total of 16 privately held railroad companies were chartered in 1835–1836, including Hubbard's Vincennes line and a railway from Chicago to Galena in the northwestern corner of the state. But after their organizers were unable to raise the necessary capital, the General Assembly on February 27, 1837, committed the state's credit to building eight railroads to all corners of the state but Chicago, which it considered would be adequately served by the proposed I&M Canal that was also part of the state program.

At the time it was not entirely clear to the political community that railroads were superior to river steamboats, canals, and highways. It was generally understood

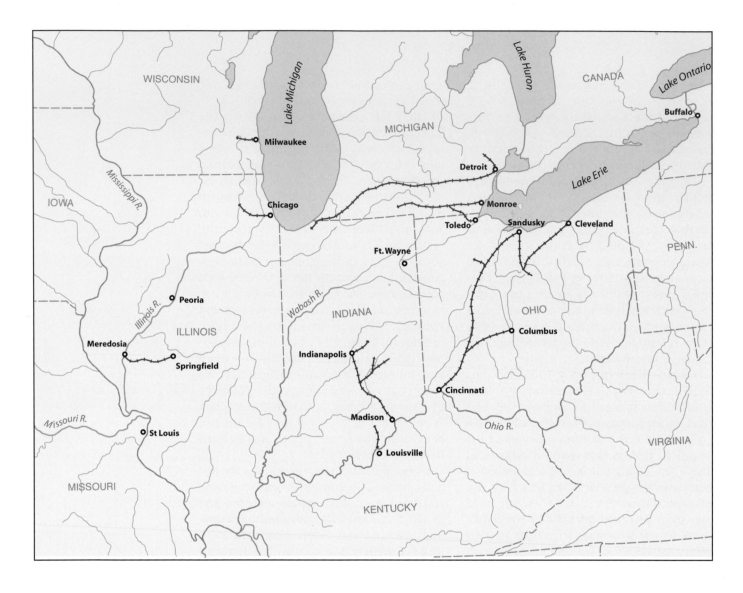

Chicago in 1850 was served by only one railroad. The Galena & Chicago Union connected Elgin with Lake Michigan, the principal transportation artery at the time.

that railroads were cheaper to build, had more direct routes, and could be operated year-round; the lakes, rivers, and canals were often closed in winter, and the marginally navigable rivers were especially vulnerable to periods of low water. Highways became impassable in the spring rains and were deeply rutted in winter.[14]

However, railroads had an enormous up-front appetite for capital that had to be acquired before the first train could run. The Northern Cross in 1838–1839 cost $3,571 per mile to build on level ground, but a seven-mile section between Springfield and the Sangamon River cost more than $100,000—$14,285 per mile—because of the necessary bridges and excavation. The Illinois Railroad built at about

the same time cost an average of $6,000 per mile, and the Galena & Chicago Union a decade later cost $9,538 per mile for its first 42.5 miles between Chicago and Elgin. That was an up-front cost of $405,382. On the other hand, a group of entrepreneurs could build a Great Lakes steamship in 1840 for an average of $50,000, a river steamboat for $20,000, and a canal packet for $2,000. A Great Lakes sailing schooner had an average replacement cost of $6,352.[15]

As early as 1831, chief canal engineer James M. Bucklin estimated that a 100-mile railroad from Chicago to La Salle could be built for $1 million, less than a quarter of the projected $4.1 million cost of a canal, although his lowest estimate for construction of a canal was $1.6 million. Based on his calculations, the Canal Commission in 1833 recommended a railroad instead, but Joseph Duncan, an ardent canal supporter, was elected governor in 1834 and nothing immediately came of the idea.

On the other hand, the January 16, 1836, charter for the privately organized Galena & Chicago Union stipulated that the project could be built as either a railroad or a toll highway. Its organizers chose the former, but construction ended after only four miles had been built when the organizers ran out of money in 1838, and the project languished for a decade. The Galena Railroad, like the state-subsidized Internal Improvements Program that followed it, illustrated that Illinois in the 1830s had neither the capital to build railroads nor a population sufficient to support their operation, a reality Gerstner recognized in 1839: "The population of the northern part of Illinois, through which this railroad is to pass, is still so small at the present time that construction of this road would be much too premature." At the time, the 168-mile Chicago-Galena route was able to support stagecoach service only three days a week.[16]

Railroad Mania

John Reynolds, who served as governor from 1830 to 1834 before being elected to Congress, described Illinois's early infatuation with railroads as a "mania" and blamed the phenomenon more on the general populace than the politicians. "When I returned home [from Congress] in 1837 I found the people perfectly insane on the subject of improvements. No reason or argument could reach them," Reynolds wrote with hindsight in his 1879 memoirs.[17]

In fact, the only railroad in the state in the 1830s to be built with private funds was the state's first—the Illinois Railroad (also known as the New Pittsburgh & Mississippi), in which Reynolds had invested.

The seven-mile line was built for $42,000 in 1837 to haul coal from some mines in Illinois to St. Louis. The track ended at the Mississippi River, and the coal was hauled across it by ferry. The railroad was primitive even by the standards of the day; it was built with strap iron rails in which flat straps of iron were secured to the top of wooden stringers, or rails, and it had only 8 cars that were pulled by a stable of 20 horses. Although the partners sold the enterprise in 1838 for $20,000 less than it had cost to build, the line survived under several reorganizations into the twentieth century to become part of the Southern Railway.[18]

The state's Internal Improvements Program of 1837 called for no less than eight railroads collectively covering 1,327 miles and expected to cost $9.4 million. The program also included improvements to navigation on five rivers and a post road across the south-central part of the state between Vincennes and St. Louis. Financial provisions for the I&M Canal were contained in a separate act in 1838. The rail segment of the program included proposed lines between Vincennes, Indiana, and Alton, and between Cairo, La Salle, and Galena (the eventual Illinois Central); the Southern Cross from Alton to Mt. Carmel and Shawneetown; the Northern Cross from Quincy to Springfield and Lafayette, Indiana; an Illinois Central branch to Terre Haute, Indiana; a Southern Cross branch to Belleville; a line from Peoria to Warsaw on the Mississippi River; and a route from Bloomington to Mackinaw with a branch to Pekin. None of them came closer than 100 miles from Chicago.[19]

The Internal Improvements railroads not only were premature but were an example of the problems associated with applying political solutions to transportation problems: the pork barrel took precedence over economic reality. The state plan called for four east-west railways to bisect the southern two-thirds of the state, but none in the northern tier; the only railway there was to be a north-south line. Neither

Illinois's Internal Improvements Program, a state-financed boondoggle initiated in 1837, called for railroads to be built to every corner of the state but the northeast—the site of Chicago.

Chicago, the growing lake port in the northeast, nor St. Louis, the busy river port in the southwest, was to have a rail line, although they would ultimately become the nation's two busiest inland rail centers. Alton, St. Louis's Illinois rival 20 miles north, was, under the Internal Improvements plan, to get three rail lines linking it to Shawneetown on the Ohio River and the Indiana state line near both Danville and Paris. Chicago's only connection to the proposed rail system was to be at La Salle, where the Illinois Central Railroad on its journey from Galena in the northwest corner of the state to Cairo at the southern tip crossed the Illinois & Michigan Canal.

However, the failure of the Internal Improvements Program had nothing to do with the planned railroad lines. It was simply too ambitious a project to be undertaken by what was still a frontier state. Only one 59-mile section of the eight proposed railways, the Northern Cross line from Springfield to Meredosia on the Illinois River, was ever built before the financial Panic of 1837, as the depression of that time was known, and the subsequent failure of the state's credit doomed the rest of the ambitious rail-building project, leaving the state $1,561,000 in the red on the railroad projects alone. The Northern Cross, which had cost $1 million to build, by 1842 was not producing enough revenue to cover operating expenses and was reduced to using mules to pull its trains after its single locomotive wore out. The railroad was sold at auction in 1847 for $21,000 but survived to be incorporated into the Wabash Railroad system.[20]

The collapse of the Internal Improvements Program not only got the state out of the business of planning and financing railroads until well into the twentieth century, and then only to protect itself during a period of railroad contraction, but it caused a 10-year hiatus on railroad building. Construction on the I&M Canal proceeded, and in the late 1840s various plank toll highways were built in northern Illinois. Even before the canal was completed in 1848 and the plank roads were appearing, there was a renewed interest in railroad building because of the growth of the ports of Chicago and St. Louis. Capitalists in the East and Europe were aware of the success of the railroads along the Atlantic seaboard and began to conclude that inland railroads could be good investments.

Equally important, a market was beginning to develop for inland transportation. In the 1830s and 1840s Chicago's communication with the rest of the world was slow and to some extent seasonal. For the most part the Great Lakes were closed to shipping in the winter months, river steamboats could get no closer to Chicago than 100 miles on the Wabash and Illinois rivers, and land transport was arduous, slow, and expensive. In 1800 it took more than a month to travel between Chicago and New York by foot and water. Forty years later the same trip could be made entirely by water in about two weeks, and in a great deal more comfort, using the lakes, the Erie Canal, and the Hudson River. Land transportation west of Chicago was even slower. A loaded freight wagon under the best of circumstances could make an average of 30 miles a day, usually a lot less, and charged 30¢ per mile per ton. Stagecoaches of the time averaged four to five miles an hour over the crude midwestern roads. Understandably, people traveled or shipped goods by water whenever possible.[21]

It was the primitive condition of land transport that caused midwesterners to look to railroads as instruments of internal improvement. Water travel was an entirely acceptable mode of transportation where it

It took more than a month to travel by water and foot between New York and Chicago in 1830. By the end of the century the journey had been compressed into an overnight trip on the railroads.

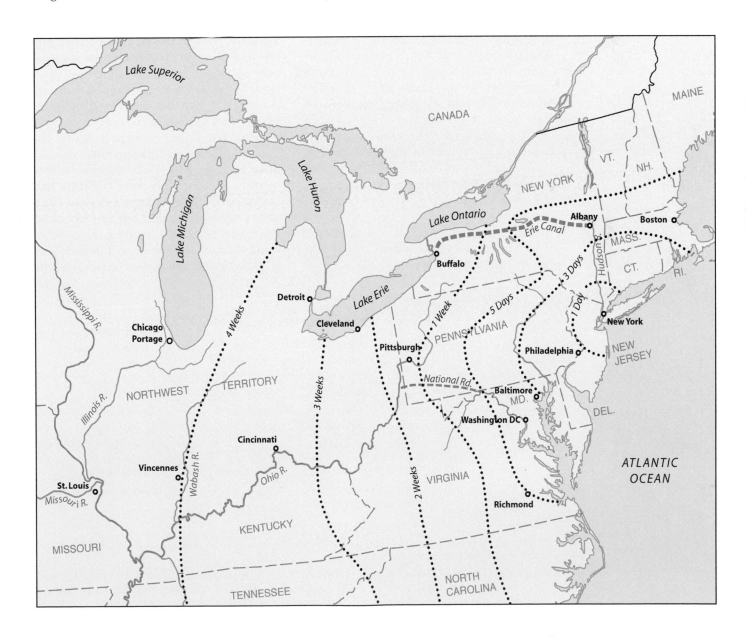

existed, and some of the steamboats on the rivers and passenger ships on the lakes were floating palaces. But getting to one's destination from a lake port or head of navigation on a river could be an ordeal that belied the modern movie image of a stagecoach gently rolling at high speed across the western plains. The Concord coaches that dominated overland passenger transport in the first half of the nineteenth century were dusty, drafty, bumpy, hot in summer, and cold in winter. Abraham Lincoln was known to have taken circuitous routes to avoid stagecoach travel, including, in 1852, a 100-mile detour to the Illinois River at Naples to travel by train (from Springfield to Naples) and steamboat (from Naples to La Salle) instead of a 71-mile stagecoach ride between Springfield and Peoria.[22]

The limitations of horse-drawn vehicles were more obvious in the freight trade, however. A single overnight Concord coach under optimal circumstances might be able to carry 9 passengers and 200 pounds of baggage 100 miles in 24 hours (including stops for meals and to change teams), and a freight wagon might take the better part of 4 days to carry 2.5 tons of cargo the same distance. By the late 1830s, the early 4-2-0 locomotives then popular on American railroads were capable of pulling 200-ton trains, about half of which was cargo, at speeds of 15 miles an hour. That would enable a railroad to move 100 tons of cargo 100 miles in just over 5 hours, although as a practical matter the average speed was much slower because of the necessity to stop for fuel, water, passengers, and freight at settlements along the route.[23]

Stagecoaches often traveled through the night, stopping only to change teams and allow the passengers and driver to eat, but the teamsters on freight wagons stopped overnight to allow themselves and their teams to rest. Overland wagons were an extremely expensive way to get crops to market, and farmers often found it cheaper to herd their hogs down the roads to the slaughterhouses in Chicago than to ship them in drays. As a result, the first victims of the early railroads were typically the overland freight wagons, because they were unable to compete with the trains in either cost or time. They were relegated to being short-haul distributors and collectors of traffic for the railroads. The next victims

TABLE 1-1 **Speed of Travel**   (Chicago to New Orleans)

Year	Mode	Distance (miles)*	Elapsed Time	Event
1682	Canoe	1,400	ca. 70 days	LaSalle voyage
1855	Steamboat	1,400	ca. 8 days	Various
1874	Rail	912	48:30 hours	ICRR Schedule
1942	Air	920	6:20 hours	C&S Schedule
1950	Rail	912	15:30 hours	ICRR Schedule
1976	Auto	929	19:40 hours	Rand McNally est.**
1992	Air	920	2:15 hours	UAL Schedule

*The differences between water, land, and air distances are based on the meandering of the rivers, highway and rail routes, and air route estimates by the carriers.

**The estimate is from the *Rand McNally Road Atlas* (Skokie, Ill., 1976), United States Mileage and Driving Time Map, based on the speed limit of 55 mph then in force. The *Rand McNally Travel Atlas* (Skokie, Ill., 2000), North American Mileage and Driving Time Map, published after federal speed limits had been removed, estimates the driving time as 15:05.

were the stagecoaches and finally the river steamboats. The railroads, at least in the nineteenth century, never put much of a dent in Great Lakes freight traffic, especially the bulk commodities.[24]

Chicago fortuitously emerged as a city just as the steam engine was adapted to mechanical traction, and it benefited enormously from the innovation. By the time Chicago was platted as a city less than 30 years after its settlement, it was being visited regularly by steam-powered ships. Within two decades railroads were fanning out from the city in every direction, and by the end of the century electrical traction and internal combustion engines, which would eventually relegate most steam engines to museums, were being developed.

All that would remain of the horse as a traction engine was its name: the term *horsepower* used to describe increments of 746 watts or 550 foot-pounds of work per second. The big, articulated steam locomotives and the stationary engines that powered electrical dynamos to operate municipal transit systems both appeared at the end of the nineteenth century and were measured in thousands of horsepower, as were the marine engines that drove the 7,000-ton steel freighters that appeared on the lakes before the end of the century.

Nowhere was the impact of the steam engine and its successor, the internal combustion engine, more obvious than on the speed of travel. For a nation always on the move, the steam engine cut travel times from weeks to days and then to hours. By the end of the century a journey between New York and Chicago that had taken more than a month by foot or canoe now was an overnight trip by train. The data for New Orleans were comparable (see Table 1-1).

Chicago's Early Development

The steam engine used as a stationary power source also proved critically important to the eventual industrialization of Chicago, though not at first. The city's river was too sluggish to drive water wheels to power factories as had been done in the East, so Chicago's earliest development was not as a manufacturing center but as a transportation node, a break-bulk center where cargo was transferred between ships and wagons, and a gateway to the West for pioneers. In fact, for a few years in the 1830s after the fur trade died, Chicago's principal industry was real estate speculation. That was the business in which such men as Gurdon Hubbard and William B. Ogden made their fortunes.

In its first half century of settlement (1800 to 1850), Chicago underwent no less than three transformations that reflected the changing technology of transportation as well as the march of the American frontier westward. In 1800 the site of Chicago was a vestigial remnant of the colonial system that had persisted since the French first visited the area in 1672. Its primary link to the outside world was by means of the canoe that generations of voyageurs, first under the French flag and after 1763 under the British, had used in their travels over the rivers and lakes between Montreal and the wilderness. Even after the United States won its independence in 1783, the British retained effective control of the Great Lakes until the new nation built Fort Dearborn at the mouth of the Chicago River in 1803. Overland travel between Chicago and other wilderness outposts was largely by foot using the meandering trails radiating from the south end of Lake Michigan that had served the local Indian tribes for centuries.[25]

Although sailing vessels in military service began to appear at the mouth of the Chicago River to support the Fort Dearborn garrison and the small settlement of houses that grew up around it, the canoe and its close relative, the bateau, remained the primary means of travel in and around Chicago until after 1821, when the merged Northwest and Hudson Bay fur trading companies began replacing their flotillas of canoes with sailing ships. The settlement, which probably never exceeded a permanent population of 50, was as wild as anything on the frontier: pioneer trader John Kinzie in 1812 stabbed to death Indian interpreter John Lalime in a fight, and later in the year some of the military garrison and many of the civilian residents were killed by Indians in the Fort Dearborn Massacre while trying to evacuate to Detroit.[26]

The community's second transformation began in 1830 when the I&M Canal Commission platted a town there and began to sell lots from a federal land grant to finance construction of the proposed waterway. A canal connecting Mississippi River tributaries with the Great Lakes at Chicago had been suggested as early as 1673 by explorer Louis Jolliet, and it became one of the primary goals of Illinois when that state entered the union in 1818. The project took on increased urgency after 1825 when the Erie Canal across upstate New York opened, giving New York City access to the Great Lakes. Thus Chicago in the 1830s became a Wild West boomtown in anticipation of the digging of a canal linking it to the vast Mississippi River system, a settlement of hastily built frame structures and board sidewalks lining mud streets. Sailing ships anchored offshore to transfer cargos to bateaux to cross the shallow bar at the mouth of the Chicago River, and stagecoaches lumbered up and down the streets bound to and from such places as Detroit, La Salle, and Galena.

Preindustrial Chicago in the 1830s was primarily a small retail center at the western end of a 1,400-mile waterway that began in New York City, and, aside from its role as a gateway for settlers heading west, the city primarily served a local market that did not extend inland much more than 50 miles. Most traffic on the Hudson-Erie–Great Lakes waterway was westbound. The census of structures in Chicago in 1837 indicated the extent of the city's commerce: 4 warehouses, 29 dry-goods stores, 5 hardware stores, 3 drugstores, 19 grocery and provisions stores, 10 taverns, 26 groceries, 17 lawyers offices, 5 churches, and 398 dwellings. The city's population in 1837 was 4,170.[27]

Within a few years, enough of the wilderness around Chicago had been settled and converted to farms that the farmers found they had produced a surplus above what the local market could consume. By the fall of 1839 they turned to the local merchants to ship surplus wheat and pork east to New York, and Chicago's role as a consolidator and exporter of agricultural products began. As the agricultural trade increased in the 1840s, warehouses sprang up along the Chicago River and its branches, adding a new dimension to the cityscape. The river became choked with sailing schooners delivering commodities like lumber and coal and loading grain, flour, and pork for the trip back east.[28]

The backhaul rates on otherwise empty Great Lakes ships headed east were considerably lower than rates at river ports that sent their cargo on steamboats downriver to New Orleans and then by ship to New York—a journey of more than 3,400 miles, or considerably more than double the length of the Chicago–New York route. The trip from Chicago to Buffalo typically took 10 days but was a relatively economical form of transportation because schooners could be manned by crews as small as 5 persons, in contrast to the average crew size of 21 on western river steamboats in 1843 and 40 on the Great Lakes steamship *Illinois* in 1839. Obviously, larger crews meant correspondingly higher operating costs and tariffs. For example, the river steamboat rate for 100 pounds of flour between St. Louis and New Orleans in the 1840s fluctuated between 15¢ and $1.25 depending upon river conditions and the market. The rate for the same commodity on a Great Lakes steamship between Chicago and Buffalo in 1840 was 50¢, less by sail. By wagon, the rate between Chicago and Buffalo would have been about $15 for 100 pounds of flour.[29]

The problem with Chicago's lower

freight rates in the 1830s and 1840s was that they were inaccessible to most farmers. The early settlement of Illinois and its neighboring states was along the navigable rivers that gave farmers access to cheap water transport. The Illinois and Michigan Canal was built not only to develop the interior of the state but to interdict that river-based market and connect the Great Lakes at Chicago with the western river system. But by the time it was completed in 1848, the new settlers in areas far from the rivers, the speculators who wanted to sell land there, and the business community in places like Chicago were agitating for a better system of overland transport to get people and crops from farm to market cheaply. Thus a market for the new technology of railroads emerged in the Midwest in the 1840s. A number of entrepreneurs tried building planked toll roads in that decade, but they deteriorated rapidly in Chicago's climate and proved to be inferior to railroads in every way. The plank road craze lasted barely a decade.[30]

The steam engine arrived in Chicago in the 1830s. Chartered steamships brought General Winfield Scott's army to Chicago in 1832 to fight in the Black Hawk War, and two years later George E. Walker and George Hickling imported a stationary steam engine to operate a sawmill on the north branch of the Chicago River near Clybourn Avenue. On the American frontier, sawmills and gristmills were more likely to be operated by water power, using a water wheel and mill race to power the machinery, an impossibility on the sluggish Chicago River. By the 1840s, steam engines, used both as stationary power plants for industry and as prime movers on ships, were so important to the growing city's economy that they were being manufactured locally.[31]

Thus began Chicago's third transformation—the arrival of the Industrial Revolution—which may be conveniently dated at 1848. By then Chicago had grown from an abandoned military fort surrounded by a fur trading outpost whose population had declined by 1829 to only about 30 inhabitants, to a bustling lake port of 20,000 residents. Over the next 52 years the steam engine powered Chicago's emergence as the midcontinent's largest industrial and transportation center, a metropolis of 1,698,575 inhabitants. Of course, the most important single use of the steam engine was to power the railroad locomotive.

2 Arrival of the Railroads

Early Illinois railroads were built quickly and cheaply across the flat prairies by large gangs of workmen. George I. Parrish, Jr.'s, painting of a crew building the Illinois Central Railroad at Mason, Illinois, in 1856 was commissioned for the state's sesquicentennial. (SBC Archives and History Center)

Chicago's first railroads were built not with any transcontinental pretensions in mind but as extensions of the Great Lakes to serve the pioneers who were settling the prairies and woodlands of the upper Midwest. They needed a way to get their crops to market and the manufactures from the East to their homesteads. There was some forethought as to where the railroads would go, but the plans were often changed. Chicago's first railroads at times wriggled across the landscape like a garter snake, frequently changing their direction

to take advantage of a donation of land by a farmer or a stock subscription by a hamlet hungry for train service, or to gain some competitive advantage over the other railroads racing into the hinterlands.

There were boosters in the Windy City as well as pioneers who had crossed the shifting frontier, wanted a reliable connection with civilization, and were willing to promote railroads. Towns fought towns for tracks. But for the most part eastern and European money built the railroads west of Chicago or quickly bought and consolidated local lines. The new common carriers they funded were intensely competitive, building lines into territory occupied by other railroads and to cities that for one reason or another became common destinations of the railroad industry, whether they were called gateways, ports, junctions, break-bulk points, or loci.

Chicago became one of those places in a matter of six years, 1847–1852. Before then it was a bustling Great Lakes port; afterwards it was also the largest single rail junction in the United States. Over the next quarter of a century it grew into a gigantic railroad center—probably the largest in the world—a city covered by railroad tracks.

By then the railroads had spread so far so fast that they began to attract traffic from both steamboats on the Mississippi River and packets on the Great Lakes. They spread across the Great Plains to the Rocky Mountains and through the forests of the Old Northwest and bayous of the South.

Ultimately Chicago's granger railroads, as they were called because they served the agricultural cornucopia of midcontinental America, became the bridges over which traffic moved from coast to coast between the transcontinental railroads in the West and the trunk lines in the East.

Somewhat surprisingly, Chicago made very little investment in the railroads from which it benefited. The first railroad, the Galena & Chicago Union, raised from Chicago investors only a fraction of the money needed to get construction under way. The Illinois Central, originally a state project, subsisted on federal land grants, and when revenues from their sale proved inadequate, on eastern investors. The original 12-mile Aurora Branch Railroad was a strictly homegrown affair but was quickly acquired by a Boston-based investment group headed by John Murray Forbes, and the Rock Island Line early in its existence came under the control of his rivals in New York.[1]

The earliest railroad locomotives used in the Midwest were predominantly wood burners. Note the cordwood stacked for this North Western American-style locomotive at the railroad's Baraboo, Wisconsin, roundhouse in 1871. (H. Roger Grant Collection)

Beginning in the 1850s, the Illinois Central was one of the first to convert its steam engines from wood to coal. The railroad was built through the middle of the state's rather substantial coal deposits. (Chicago Historical Society)

The Great Lakes in the middle of the nineteenth century not only provided Chicago with an avenue of maritime commerce to the East but acted as a barrier to land transport. Lakes Huron and Michigan form a natural barrier to east-west transport across the northern tier of the United States, so railroad builders were forced to skirt the south end of the lakes at the place called Chicago. At the time, the lakes provided a cheaper form of transportation than either the railroads or rivers, resulting in a constant downward pressure on freight rates to and from Chicago and further enhancing the city's attractiveness to shippers who determined the routes their cargo would take. The lakes thus developed a synergy with the railroads at Chicago, feeding westbound traffic to them and carrying eastbound traffic from them.[2]

The Galena Railroad

The focus of three of Chicago's first four railroads was to the west, but there were a couple of ventures proposed in the 1830s to build railroads in other directions. The fact that they did not succeed set the stage two decades later for the meeting of eastern and western railroads at what became the great Chicago junction. During the railroad craze of 1835–1836, Illinois chartered no less than 16 private railroads, including 1 between Chicago and Vincennes, 2 between Chicago and Galena, and a central railroad between Galena and Cairo. However, the promoters of all but one of the railroads were unable to raise the capital necessary to get construction started, and in 1836 the state stepped in and adopted its Internal Improvements

Program. The only private railroad built in Illinois in that decade was a six-mile coal line in St. Clair County in 1837.[3]

Another private charter approved in 1835–1836 was the result of a proposal by a group of businessmen and professionals in Chicago headed by Theophilis W. Smith, a justice of the state Supreme Court, and his lawyer friend, Ebenezer Peck, to build either a railroad or a turnpike or a combination of both from Chicago to Galena, a booming lead-mining center about four miles up the Fever River from its confluence with the Mississippi River. The venture languished for lack of capital and ultimately fell victim to the Panic of 1837, although not until after a 10-mile route west had been surveyed and some land on the banks of the Des Plaines River had been purchased.[4]

The Galena & Chicago Union Railroad project remained dormant for a decade until another group of Chicago businessmen led by land speculator and former mayor William B. Ogden obtained the charter and assets from a New York investment house in return for 200 shares of stock in the reorganized company. Although Ogden's partners included Walter Newberry, a merchant and banker; Thomas Dyer, a meatpacker; and Charles Walker, a commodities broker, they needed to raise a considerable amount of capital to get the project under way. Buying a charter for a song was one thing, but coming up with the estimated $2,648,727 that Richard P. Morgan, the engineer hired to plan the line, estimated it would cost to build the 182-mile railway was quite another. No one in Chicago in 1847 had that kind of money.[5]

To make matters even more expensive, Morgan proposed that the Galena Railroad be built east from Chicago around the southern end of Lake Michigan to New Buffalo, Michigan, to meet the Michigan Central Railroad from Detroit. The cost of that project was estimated at $328,000, and it required obtaining a dormant charter in Indiana. The railroad's organizers went to work and by early 1847 had stock

subscriptions, or promises to buy stock, valued at $351,800 but only $20,817 in cash, so Ogden and his partners decided to drop the eastern extension and stick with their original plans to build to the west. The Indiana charter ultimately was acquired by the Michigan Central Railroad to get to Chicago.[6] (See Chapter 3.)

Even the scaled-down western line taxed their fund-raising abilities. The bulk of the Chicago business community, apparently satisfied with transportation provided on the Great Lakes and with the imminent opening of the I&M Canal, took a pass on railroad stock. The organizers of the railroad, principally Ogden and J. Young Scammon, had been able to raise only $20,000 from Chicagoans of the initial stock subscription of $365,000. On the other hand, residents of rural Winnebago County subscribed to $250,000 to $300,000 in stock.[7]

Since their railroad also was unable to get financing from eastern or European sources and Illinois subscribers were slow to back their stock subscriptions with cash, Ogden and his group decided to take an audacious gamble and build the line entirely as a pay-as-you-go system. By the end of 1847 when he made the decision to proceed with construction, Ogden had only $106,000 in cash from the sale of stock and pledges for an additional $249,000. That meant it was necessary to extend the railroad in sections across the partially settled northern tier of Illinois and hope that as each stage opened it would generate enough revenue not only to cover operating costs but to build the next section. Ogden's initial goal was a 41-mile section west as far as Elgin on the Fox River, a project that would cost $341,000 to build.[8]

By the autumn of 1848 Ogden and his group had completed the first 10 miles as far as the Des Plaines River. It was then that Ogden's skills as a promoter paid off. He decided to stage an inaugural trip for editors and dignitaries to publicize the imminent opening of the line and hopefully entice additional investors. On November

Chicago's first railroad locomotive in 1848 was a hand-me-down dubbed the "Pioneer," but it continued in service on the Galena & Chicago Union for decades. The post-retirement engine was used as a prop for this photograph, taken in 1878, of the Chicago & North Western roundhouse employees in suburban West Chicago. (West Chicago Historical Society)

20, 1848, the train consisted of a couple of baggage cars fitted with seats for 100 guests and was pulled by a small, second-hand locomotive that a month earlier had been brought to Chicago by ship because at the time there was no rail connection to the East.

However, there does not seem to be agreement as to when the railroad officially commenced operation. Chicago historians A. T. Andreas and Bessie Louise Pierce place the inaugural run on November 20, and the railroad reported on October 26, 1848, that a test run had been made the previous day. In its annual report of 1849, the railroad said that revenue service began on December 15, 1848. On the return trip of the November 20 publicity run to Oak Park, the train picked up a load of wheat and hides from a farm wagon, apparently to demonstrate the freight capability of the new mode of transportation.

Before the year was out, the railroad hauled 30 loads of wheat from the Des Plaines River to Chicago.[9]

Ogden's gamble was successful. The railroad was profitable from the beginning. The fact that it was able to pay a 10 percent dividend from earnings of $29,812 on revenues of $48,331 during its first full year of operation attracted the notice of eastern investors, who began to plow money not only into the Galena but into several other Chicago-based rail ventures. In 1847 the organizers of the Galena Railroad had projected the following as first-year sources of revenue for the completed 181-mile line: $35,000 (8.9%) from lead, $100,000 (25.4%) from wheat, $12,000 (3%) from lumber, and $180,000 (nearly 49%) from passengers and mail. Eastbound traffic in that report had been projected at almost 78 percent of the total. However, westbound traffic turned out to be considerably stronger than expected and by 1856 surpassed eastbound. By 1860 the westbound passenger traffic constituted almost 52 percent of the total of more than 330,000 persons carried.[10]

The immediate success of the Galena turned the drought in capital that had plagued Illinois railroad projects in the 1830s and 1840s into a speculative craze in the 1850s. Capital from Europe, Boston, and New York poured into the Chicago-based granger railroads then on the drawing boards, enabling them within a few years to build lines to the Mississippi and Ohio rivers. The Illinois Central Railroad, for example, had so many investors in the United Kingdom that they regularly held alternative annual meetings there, and Dutch investors were able to elect two members to the board of the North Western Railway. American investors in the early days of railroading generally favored stocks, or equity, which by virtue of the stockholders' election of the boards of directors gave them some say in the operation of the railroads. However, European investors for the most part preferred buying railroad bonds, which were secured by a mortgage on the property.[11]

Railroads' appetite for capital was enormous by the standards of that day. The U.S. through 1860 spent $188 million on its canal system, 73 percent of which was supplied by state and local government, but the railroads through 1859 consumed $1.1 billion, of which $700 million was raised in the 1850s. In the case of the conservatively managed Galena & Chicago Union, as the railroad continued to expand westward its directors found it increasingly difficult to finance such extensions with local stock subscriptions, so they were forced to sell stock in the developing financial markets in New York and the traditional markets in Europe. Increasingly, as investors demanded greater security, the successor North Western sold bonds to finance expansion.[12]

By 1854 only $3 million of the $8.3 million in capital the Galena had raised to build the railroad was attributable to bonds, and by 1864 when the Galena merged into the Chicago & North Western, it had $6 million in capital stock and $3.5 million in bonds on its books. By 1880 the North Western's common stock had a face value of $36.5 million, but its bonded indebtedness exceeded $50.1 million.[13]

Within two years of the Galena's startup, promoters of the Illinois Central, Aurora Branch, and Chicago & Rock Island railroads, who had struggled to raise funds prior to 1850, found eastern investors interested in their stocks. By the middle of that decade and until the Panic of 1857, the developers of other Chicago-based lines had a relatively easy time raising money for projects that were not always well conceived. The Chicago, St. Charles & Mississippi Air Line Railroad intended to parallel the Galena between Chicago and the Mississippi River and by 1854 had gotten $1.25 million in stock subscriptions, most of it from eastern capitalists. The Galena Railroad bought out that potential rival in 1856. Beginning in 1851, eastern investors also backed the Illinois & Wisconsin, a railroad to run from Cary in McHenry County, where it connected with the Galena to Chicago, to Beloit in southern Wisconsin. Likewise the organizers of the Chicago & Milwaukee were able to get financing and begin operation for 40 miles between Chicago and Waukegan in less than two years after obtaining a charter. On the other hand it had taken the organizers of the Galena Railroad more than 14 years from its inception in 1835 to raise the capital necessary to build and get into operation a 42 1/2–mile line between Chicago and Elgin.[14]

The Chicago, Burlington & Quincy

Chicago's second railroad was another strictly local project that owed its inception to rivalry between communities west of Chicago. The Galena Railroad had been operating less than two weeks and was still an unproven venture when some residents of communities along the Fox River, a non-navigable stream running north and south about 38 miles west of Chicago, met to discuss the possibility of building another railroad. The Galena's destination on the Fox was Elgin, not the rival communities of Batavia and Aurora 7–12 miles to the south on the same stream, and the leaders of those towns were concerned about the economic disadvantage they would suffer as a result. The Galena Railroad's organizers had originally considered the more southerly route favoring Aurora, but they abandoned the idea after the civic leaders of Naperville to the east spurned their proposal because they had already invested in a plank road to Chicago.[15]

The Aurora-Batavia group was fortunate in having among its members John Van Nortwick, a resident of Batavia and civil engineer who was building the Galena Railroad. The group in 1849 made a very pragmatic decision, in view of the difficulty in raising capital, to build a modest 12-mile line. This would run from Aurora and connect with the Galena Railroad then being built westward toward a place that would become known as Junction (the future suburb of West Chicago). However, their February 12, 1849, charter contained a provision allowing them to acquire or merge with other railroads, a measure that would enable the Aurora Branch Railroad, as it was originally named, to quickly extend itself beyond the Chicago area.[16]

The railroad was slapped together very quickly using secondhand rail, locomotives, and rolling stock, and it began service with a borrowed locomotive on October 21, 1850, just 10 months after its first organizational meeting. However, it was too small to generate the kind of revenues needed for expansion as the Galena Railroad had done, so in July 1851 the directors voted to make a secondary stock offering in the hope that it would bring in more capital. Within four months they noticed the stock was being bought up by the investment group that controlled the Michigan Central Railroad then being built west toward Chicago.[17]

The investment group was headed by Boston shipping magnate John Murray Forbes, whose associate, James F. Joy, was looking for an outlet for their railroad system somewhere on the Mississippi River. Thus by the end of 1851, barely three years after the first train chugged out of Chicago and months before the first railroad would connect the Windy City to the East, a race commenced between railroads to get to the Mississippi and beyond. Besides the Aurora Branch and Galena railroads, the participants in the race included the newly chartered Chicago & Rock Island and the Illinois Central.

The Rock Island Line

The Rock Island Line as originally proposed in 1837 by a group of civic leaders in the Quad Cities, primarily Rock Island and Moline on the western border of Illinois and Davenport across the Mississippi River in Iowa, was to serve as an extension of the Illinois & Michigan Canal to their area from its western terminal on the Illinois River at La Salle. The canal had effectively extended the reach of the Great Lakes inland 97 miles to the head of navigation of the Illinois River, and as early as 1834, when the I&M was still on the drawing boards, residents of western Illinois were agitating to have it extended another 86 miles west to the Mississippi. When the canal was opened in 1848 water travel from the Quad Cities to Chicago was by a circuitous 607-mile route down the Mississippi to Grafton, up the Illinois to La Salle, and on the canal to the Chicago River. A railroad-canal route would reduce the distance to 183 miles. The canal proponents finally got their canal as the result of a federal pork barrel program, but the Illinois & Mississippi Canal, better known as the Hennepin Canal, was not completed between the Illinois River at Bureau and Rock Island until 1907 and was never able to compete with the railroads built half a century earlier.[18]

The financial malaise following the Panic of 1837 delayed the La Salle & Rock Island Railroad for a decade, and even after it was chartered in 1847 its proponents had difficulty raising money to start construction. By late 1850, only $128,300 of the needed $300,000 had been raised, but the promoters approached New York financier Henry Farnam, who was then building the Michigan Southern and Northern Indiana Railroad (later known as the Lake Shore) west toward Chicago, to see if he was interested in their venture. Farnam told them the railroad would not make any sense unless it was built all the way to Chicago. His ulterior motive was that the New York investors behind the Michigan Southern project needed an Illinois railroad to gain access to Chicago; their charter extended only to the state line, and at the time Illinois was dubious about granting "foreign" railroads charters within its borders.[19]

The deal cut between Farnam and the Rock Island's organizers in 1851 was for the New York investors to put up the money to build the rechartered Chicago & Rock Island, which would run 181 miles across northern Illinois. They would also pay for trackage rights over the new railroad to enable the Michigan Southern to enter Chicago and would get four seats on the Rock Island's new board. Farnam then rushed completion of the Chicago section of the Rock Island line to enable the Michigan Southern to get into Chicago in 1852. The new railroad was completed to Rock Island in 1854. Two years later, to assuage the railroad's original promoters from Davenport, the Rock Island Lines completed the first bridge across the Mississippi.

The speed with which the Farnam group worked spurred the new railroads' rivals to get to the Mississippi as well. Beginning in 1852 Forbes's group began its westward march using the tried and true strategy of buying up small railroads and where necessary building connections between them. The Chicago, Burlington & Quincy, as their railroad had been renamed, reached the Mississippi at both Burlington and Quincy in 1856. Even before that had happened, Forbes leaped the river and acquired control of the Hannibal & St. Joseph Railroad being built across northern Missouri.[20]

The Galena & Chicago Union reacted in early 1853 when the Rock Island's intentions became obvious. Its directors abandoned their plans to build to Galena and decided instead to build a more direct route to Iowa, reaching Fulton on the Illinois bank of the Mississippi in late 1855. The Illinois Central got to Galena in 1854, although it had to rely on friendly connections to get to Chicago until it completed its own line across northern Illinois to the Windy City in 1888.[21]

The most immediate effect on all that railroad building in the northern tier of the state was in the Illinois River valley and on the Illinois and Michigan Canal that connected it to Chicago. Traffic on the Upper Mississippi River between St. Louis and St. Paul actually increased for a few years after the railroads arrived in that area as the newcomers used steamboats to extend their markets, but it began to decline after the Civil War. However, the decline in traffic on the Illinois River was immediate and devastating. From an average of 741 steamboats a year reaching St. Louis from the Illinois River in the years preceding the railroad-building spurt, river traffic declined to slightly more than a third of that level in the period 1871–1875.[22]

The effect of the Chicago & Rock Island on the I&M Canal also was immediate, though not nearly so devastating as on the Illinois River. The railroad for about half its length ran parallel to the canal, and passengers deserted the canal for the railroad virtually overnight, followed by high cost package freight. Such merchandise and sundries carried on the canal declined precipitously between 1852 and 1859, from more than 14.8 million pounds to just over 1 million pounds. By 1865, canal

This Galena & Chicago Union Railroad locomotive, shown on a culvert in Rockford just after the Civil War, was built in 1853 and was rebuilt twice in its long career, which lasted until 1893. (H. Roger Grant Collection)

traffic in merchandise was down to 512,000 pounds. The Rock Island, which did not exist in 1952, carried 40.8 million pounds of merchandise by 1859 and 159 million pounds by 1871. However, the railroad had less of an impact on canal traffic in grain and other bulk commodities, and the canal through much of the rest of the nineteenth century acted as a competitive control on railroad freight rates.[23]

Iowa and the Transcontinental Connection

The race to the Mississippi had hardly begun when the owners of Chicago's new railroads began thinking in terms of cross-

ing the river into Iowa. The fertile Iowa land and the agricultural traffic it would generate was one attraction, but so was the possibility of connecting with a transcontinental railroad that the United States government had begun to contemplate to connect California with the rest of the nation. The traffic west of Chicago was so great that although the IC was primarily a north-south railway, its busiest station in 1855 handled east-west traffic. That was at Freeport, in northwestern Illinois, where its line to the Mississippi River near Galena connected with the Galena & Chicago Union's line to Chicago. Freeport in 1855 handled 73,590 passengers; the I.C. station in Chicago handled only 22,135.[24]

The Rock Island was first to cross the river, but it was followed in rapid succession by the other railroads. The issue of whether the railroads could bridge the Mississippi River had been settled in the 1850s after a court fight. The Rock Island in 1855 completed a structure opposed by the steamboat industry as a hazard to navigation. The matter wound up in court after the steamboat *Effie Afton* slammed into the bridge, causing a fire that destroyed the vessel and heavily damaged the bridge. Lawyers for James Ward, the boat owner, contended that the bridge was an obstruction to river traffic. Abraham Lincoln represented the railroad and got a hung jury in Federal District Court in Chicago, and the U.S. Supreme Court in 1862 ruled the bridge was legal.[25]

Not to be outdone, the North Western crossed the river at Clinton, Iowa, in 1865. The Illinois Central completed its bridge across the river at Dubuque, Iowa, in 1868, the same year that the CB&Q completed spans at both Burlington and Quincy. However, even before the bridges were completed, Chicago's railroads had begun their push westward across Iowa by buying up local lines and using ferry boats to cross the river.[26]

In 1860, within 12 years of the start of construction of Chicago's first railroad, granger lines radiated from the city into Wisconsin, Iowa, and Missouri and to the Kentucky border.

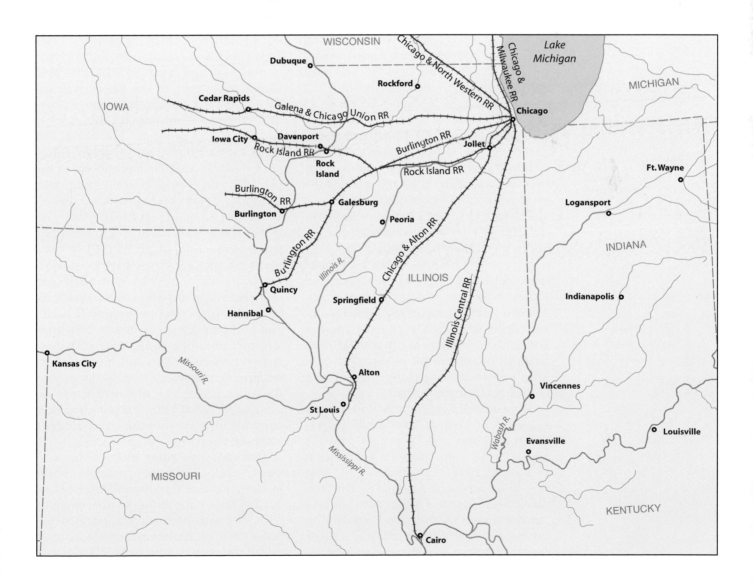

For example, the Galena got into Iowa in 1862 by the quick and expedient method of leasing the undercapitalized Chicago, Iowa & Nebraska Railroad, which despite its name ran for only 78 miles from Clinton on the Mississippi River to Cedar Rapids. The Cedar Rapids & Missouri Railroad, a line built with federal land grants, was leased to the Galena later the same year. The Galena's successor Chicago & North Western bought both lines outright in 1884.[27]

The rapid expansion of Chicago railroads into Iowa brought that state into Chicago's economic sphere. The types of crops grown on Iowa's farms were done to the dictates of Chicago's markets, Chicago drummers fanned out across Iowa hawking their wares, Chicago banks loaned money for projects in Iowa, and Iowans who wanted to travel to the "big city" caught a train for Chicago. It is no coincidence, as William Cronon has noted, that Iowa, unlike the other neighboring states dominated by the Chicago-based railroad system, never developed a regional metropolis of its own. "Chicago remains the chief metropolis of Iowa to this day."[28]

The race to Council Bluffs on the western edge of Iowa attained greater urgency in the 1860s after the decision to build the transcontinental railroad west from there. Iowa cooperated by giving the Rock Island a charter for the Mississippi & Missouri Railroad from Davenport to Council Bluffs, and the CB&Q got a charter for the Burlington & Missouri River Railroad across the southern tier of the state. Both Iowa lines were eventually merged into their larger Chicago partners.

Missouri senator Thomas Hart Benton suggested as early as 1848 a railroad between St. Louis and California, and the mayor of St. Louis called a convention with other states for October 15 of that year to discuss such a proposal. The convention turned into a debate between Benton and Illinois's Stephen A. Douglas, who successfully argued that endorsing a single eastern terminus would erode support for

the project in a then highly sectionalized Congress. An 1854 survey by the U.S. Bureau of Topographical Engineers indicated that no less than five potential transcontinental routes were feasible. However, Secretary of War Jefferson Davis, a former senator from Mississippi and later president of the Confederacy, recommended using the southernmost transcontinental route along the 32nd parallel, through El Paso and the Gadsden Purchase to Los Angeles. Davis's recommendation was interpreted in the North as a highly partisan decision favoring the South and ensured that Congress would not reach a decision on the route anytime soon.[29]

Once the southern delegation walked out of Congress at the beginning of the Civil War, the major rivals for a transcontinental railroad became St. Louis and Chicago. Congress in the Pacific Railroad Act of 1862 left it to the president to determine the transcontinental line's eastern terminus, and Abraham Lincoln chose Omaha, a site that favored Chicago. Historians have assigned various motives to explain Lincoln's decision, everything from favoritism toward his home state to uncertainty over Missouri's southern sympathies in the Civil War. Historical geographer James E. Vance, Jr., suggested the latter was the prime motive: "There have been theories concerning Lincoln's motivation, but only the overly suspicious mind need look beyond fairly direct geographical logic. The terminus obviously had to be within territory fully loyal to the union. That effectively ruled out St. Louis, not so much because of the sympathies of the city as the country lying west of it, which was appropriately called Little Dixie with cotton cultivation, slave holding, and evident southern sympathies."[30]

However, contrasting with that opinion was Lincoln's sometimes parochial record in Congress and the General Assembly in dealing with such things as the move of Illinois's capital from Vandalia to his hometown of Springfield, which also received the only rail line built in the state's abortive Internal Improvements Program. Lincoln also supported a then-unprecedented federal land grant for the Illinois Central, for which he later served as attorney, and represented the Rock Island in its Mississippi River bridge case, which pitted Chicago's railroad interests against St. Louis's steamboat lobby. However, Lincoln's choice of Omaha as the eastern terminus of the transcontinental line clearly favored Chicago's railroads over those of St. Louis, although at the time Omaha was beyond the lines of any Chicago railroad.

By the time that Lincoln in 1863 made his selection of Omaha, no less than four Chicago railroads were already racing west across Iowa in the general direction of Omaha. The North Western got there first in 1867, followed by the Rock Island in 1869, the Burlington in 1870, and the Illinois Central in 1888 via a connection over the North Western branch line. The North Western had been extending its way west at the rather leisurely pace of 13 miles a year in the 1862–1865 period when the war claimed priority over capital and construction material, but accelerated its rate to 149 miles per annum in 1866–1867.

Illinois Central

The Illinois Central Railroad, perhaps more than any other in the state, was a creature of politics. The rather abrupt shift of its northern terminus to Chicago within a few months in 1850–1851 was a clear indication of how Chicago's rapid growth was influencing the body politic in Illinois that, 15 years earlier, had rejected the city's inclusion in the state rail network. The concept of a central railroad originated with the state's Internal Improvements Program in 1836 as a way to link the interior of the state with two of its largest river ports—Galena in the northwestern corner near the Mississippi River and Cairo at the junction of the Ohio and Mississippi rivers at the southern tip of the state. The central railroad was to come no closer to Chicago than La

Salle, Illinois, 97 miles to the southwest where a connection to Chicago was to be provided by the I&M Canal.[31]

Both the canal and the railroad were predicated upon substantial subsidies from government in the form of land grants, not only for the rights-of-way but for selling surplus land to generate cash for construction. The assumption was that such government endorsements would also attract private capital to the projects. The canal received substantial federal land grants in 1822 and 1827, but the sale of that land produced less than half of the necessary funds, and the state was ultimately forced to guarantee repayment of the bonds sold to raise additional money. Despite all that support the Panic of 1837 jeopardized the private funding needed to complete construction, and the state had to yield a substantial amount of control over the project to the bondholders, an arrangement that has continued on public works projects to the present day.[32]

The central railroad was another state-financed project that fell victim to the Panic of 1837. The project ground to a halt for lack of money after only 40 miles of the right-of-way had been graded. It languished for more than a decade until rescued by a combination of a federal land grant and the renaissance of investments in American transportation schemes. In the meantime, interest in the railroad was kept alive by Colonel Sidney Breese, a land speculator from southern Illinois who sought the railroad as a way to enhance the value of his holdings. The central railroad was also favored by Darius B. Holbrook, another southern Illinois land speculator of dubious reputation, who attempted to build the railroad as a private project, the Great Western Railway, after the Internal Improvements Program collapsed. However, the state revoked the Great Western's two-year-old charter in 1845 after Holbrook's sources of capital in England dried up.[33]

Meanwhile, Breese got himself elected to the United States Senate in 1842 and spent the next six years trying to obtain federal funding for the project. As a state legislator, Abraham Lincoln backed the railroad as part of the Internal Improvements Program, and by 1847, as a member of the U.S. House of Representatives, he urged a federal land grant for the central railroad in his home state. But it was Stephen A. Douglas, a member of the Senate that included Daniel Webster, Henry Clay, and John Calhoun, who engineered the successful compromise that got the land grant approved.

To get southern votes, Douglas negotiated a deal in which the Mobile & Ohio Railroad would get a similar grant. Although federal land grants for transportation date from the National Road extension into Ohio in 1806, Douglas's 1850 bill to allow private railroad companies to get federal land grants was modeled on the 1827 act by Congress for land grants to build both the I&M Canal in Illinois and the Wabash-Erie Canal in neighboring Indiana. The huge IC grant included not only land for the right-of-way but alternate sections six miles wide on either side of the right-of-way (an area of more than 2.5 million acres) to be sold to generate cash for construction.[34]

As late as 1848, Breese's plan for a central railroad still did not include a line to Chicago. But Douglas slipped into his land grant bill introduced that year a provision for a branch line from Effingham County 200 miles north to Chicago. Douglas had moved to Chicago in 1847 and began to speculate in land south of the city. He owned the lakefront property from 22nd Street to 35th Street and ultimately sold the railroad 16.37 acres for a 200-foot-wide right-of-way for $21,310. He later bought 6,000 acres of the railroad's land grant near Lake Calumet for industrial development.[35]

His land grant act, which failed to pass the U.S. House in 1848 but was approved by both houses of Congress in 1850, became the model for similar railroad land grant laws across the nation during the second half of the nineteenth century. Ul-

timately, the federal government between 1850 and 1871 granted 223 million acres to private railroads to encourage them to build lines, although grants of 35 million acres were revoked before the end of the century because the railroads had failed to build the specified lines.[36]

Breese, who had lost his Senate seat in 1849 to James Shields, tried to assemble a local group of investors to finance the railroad, but Douglas successfully steered the contract to an eastern group that included Robert Rantoul of Massachusetts. He was a law associate of Webster, who also speculated in land in Illinois and was an ardent supporter of the railroad land grant act. The group of eastern investors moved quickly; on December 28, 1850—just three months after Congress passed the act—they presented their proposal to build the railroad to the Illinois General Assembly for a charter. Three months later, on March 22, 1851, they hired engineer Roswell B. Mason to start construction.[37]

Mason arrived in Chicago on May 19, 1851, and spent a month touring the route of the proposed railroad and the rest of the year putting together the plans. By then it had become obvious that the Michigan Central Railroad would reach Chicago from the east sometime in 1852 and would need trackage rights into the city over the Illinois Central. The Forbes group that controlled the railroad was willing to buy $2 million in IC bonds to secure the deal. In March 1852, while in Washington conferring with federal officials, Mason ordered that construction begin on the Chicago section of the line to accommodate the Michigan Central. Thus the railroad, which three years earlier had not been contemplated to come any closer to Chicago than 97 miles, opened its first 14 miles of track in the Windy City on May 21, 1852, to allow Michigan Central service to Detroit to begin. The rest of the 705.5-mile railroad, at the time the world's longest, was not completed until 1856.[38]

The Illinois Central's entrance into Chicago was a controversy that beset the

This Edwin Whitefield lithograph shows the joint Illinois Central–Michigan Central depot in 1860. The freight yard beyond the station facilitated the interchange of traffic with ships on the Great Lakes. (Chicago Historical Society)

city for more than a century. Although Chicago's boosters generally favored building railroads to their city instead of bypassing it, there was considerable opposition to having the railroad build a line along the lakeshore to reach the mouth of the Chicago River. Railroad officials originally wanted access to the river west of the city's business district because the bulk of the city's port district stretched along the south branch of the river, where Great Lakes ships interchanged traffic with the canal and other railroads. But supporters of the Chicago & Rock Island then under construction were opposed to IC access to that area, and in 1851 Mason had to change his plans to get to downtown Chicago and its port with a route along the lakefront. In 1852 the original IC terminal was at 12th Street, south of the downtown area.[39]

Use of the lakefront precipitated a political brouhaha because wealthy landowners there did not want a railroad in their front yards. So the IC's managers proposed building a trestle in the lake that would serve not only as the railroad's access to the mouth of the Chicago River but as a much-needed breakwater that the city did not have the funds to build. The railroad paid the federal government $45,000 for a portion of the abandoned Fort Dearborn military reservation at the river's mouth,

but Mayor Walter S. Gurnee vetoed the December 29, 1851, ordinance to allow the railroad trestle, which had been passed by the Chicago Common Council.[40]

More controversy followed as factions favoring the Illinois Central–Michigan Central railroads, including Douglas and U.S. Representative John Wentworth, fought with factions favoring the Rock Island–Michigan Southern railroads, until the Common Council in June 1852 passed the ordinance with sufficient votes to override another veto. The railroad built a stone causeway in the lake and filled the lake for 1,000 feet east for freight and passenger yards. In the twentieth century, long after the city had filled an additional lake-bottom lane on either side of the causeway to create Grant Park, the railroad right-of-way was the focus of more controversy when the Illinois Central sold air rights over it for development (see Chapter 14).

Railroads to the North

As early as 1851 the promoters of railroads in Chicago were beginning to think strategically. Before then the railroads chartered by the state with Chicago as a terminal had for the most part been intended for the internal development of Illinois, although it was assumed they would ultimately reach the borders of the state where connections with other carriers were possible. Since Illinois's borders were primarily rivers—the Mississippi, Ohio, and Wabash—it was also assumed the railroads would interdict river traffic controlled from Cincinnati, Louisville, St.Louis, and New Orleans.

After 1851, the state began to charter railroads intended to tap markets in other states. The stated goal of two railroads chartered in Illinois that year was to reach the developing hinterlands of Wisconsin, which cooperated by chartering its own railroads south to meet them at the border. The Illinois & Wisconsin chartered by the Illinois General Assembly on February 12, 1851, and the Chicago & Milwaukee chartered five days later both had that as their goal. The Illinois & Wisconsin was planned to run northwest from Cary across McHenry County to connect with another railroad to Janesville, Wisconsin. The Chicago & Milwaukee was planned as a line north from Chicago to the state line, where it would connect with the Milwaukee & Chicago. This would give Wisconsin's largest city access to the eastern railroads then approaching the Windy City.[41]

The Illinois & Wisconsin was a mess from the beginning. It was underfunded, the victim of financial shenanigans, and built to a nonstandard gauge. By 1853 it was forced to merge with its connecting line, the Rock River Valley Union, and reorganized as the Chicago, St. Paul & Fond du Lac Railroad, with William B. Ogden as president. It had a broadened strategic goal of building all the way to the developing iron and copper mines on the shores of Lake Superior. Not even Ogden and some heavy backers like New York attorney Samuel J. Tilden, the future presidential candidate, were able to save the venture after the Panic of 1857. The line was sold in foreclosure in 1859 and reorganized as the Chicago & North Western Railway. Ogden's considerable skills enabled the railroad to reach the mines of Michigan's upper peninsula during the Civil War and eventually absorb its Wisconsin vassal

lines. In 1864 Ogden merged the North Western with his original railroad, the Galena, in what was one of the largest railroad consolidations up to that time—an 860-mile network stretching north and west from Chicago into Iowa, Wisconsin, and Michigan.[42]

Wisconsin was exceedingly cooperative in the charter of a proposed railroad between Milwaukee and Chicago. On February 11, 1851, Illinois chartered the Chicago & Milwaukee to be built along the lakeshore north to the state line, and on March 13 the Wisconsin legislature chartered the Milwaukee & Chicago to be built south to the same point. Wisconsin's charter was valid only to its border but contained a provision allowing the Chicago & Milwaukee Railroad being built north from Chicago to acquire its Wisconsin connection, an event that occurred in 1863.[43]

A major backer of the Chicago & Milwaukee railroad was former Chicago mayor Walter S. Gurnee, who like many politicians of the time speculated in land, in this case on the North Shore, and invested in railroads to enhance the value of their real estate holdings for development. Judge Henry W. Blodgett, of Waukegan, was another backer. With the help of Wisconsin investor-politicians, he engineered the merger of the two lines. In 1866 the Chicago & Milwaukee railroad was leased in perpetuity by the North Western and merged into that system.[44]

At the same time Chicago's railroads were racing north, west, and south from the city, a similar race toward the Windy City was taking place from the east. Some of the eastern lines had financial connections with the western roads. But all of the eastern trunks sometime after 1850, and in a few instances before, felt a need to reach the port city at the foot of Lake Michigan to obtain rail connections to the west. Thus Chicago almost by accident, but certainly not due to any grand scheme by its civic and political leaders, became the nation's great railroad junction.

Critical Mass 3

By the late 1840s when Chicago was still predominantly a lake port and stagecoach stop with fewer than 30,000 inhabitants, it began to attract the attention of the men who were building railroad systems in the East as well as the moneyed men who were financing them. Since the end of the War of 1812, the principal cities on the eastern seaboard—Boston, New York, Philadelphia, Baltimore, and Charleston—had been in a race to reap the economic rewards the developing American interior would certainly yield and to prevent their rivals from becoming dominant in that market. Chicago was a dot on the map that sometime after 1835 began to elicit the interest of some of those railroad builders.

At about the same time the new states of the Old Northwest Territory began to dabble in transportation schemes to encourage development within their borders. That required a symbiotic relationship with the speculators, politicians, and merchants in the East, often the same individuals, who hoped to profit from the growth in the interior. The midwestern pioneers needed

Not long after shipping magnate John Murray Forbes acquired the financially foundering Michigan Central in 1846, he realized that Chicago should be its western terminus. To get into the Windy City the Michigan Central used Illinois Central tracks, shown here near Michigan Avenue and Randolph Street ca. 1870. (Chicago Historical Society) eastern money to build transportation corridors that would ultimately provide both groups a return on their investments.

The eastern speculators, politicians, and merchants first built canals to gain access to the interior, but after they proved to be too expensive and too limited in scope, they turned to railroads. Canals for the most part were built to connect existing navigable waterways—the coastal rivers of the East with the rivers and lakes west of the Allegheny range. The movers and shakers in the eastern ports focused their schemes on reaching the Ohio River in the case of Maryland and Pennsylvania and the Great Lakes in the case of New York and Pennsylvania. At first it was assumed that either Cincinnati on the Ohio River or St. Louis on the Mississippi River would become the metropolis of the interior, but New York had a prospective interest in developing the western border of the Great Lakes basin.

However, the waterways were circuitous transportation routes vulnerable to seasonal interruptions because of weather. The steaming distance on the lakes from Buffalo to Chicago was 893 miles because of the necessity of sailing around Michigan's lower peninsula, but by rail the route could be shortened to only about 550 miles by cutting across northern Indiana. Much of the Great Lakes froze in winter, as did some of the rivers, which were plagued by low water that hampered navigation during droughts. The railroads could go almost anywhere on nearly straight routes and in all weather.[1]

At some time around the midpoint of the nineteenth century, certainly before the Civil War, the nation's railroad men began to aim their lines toward Chicago. The strategic redirection affected not just the builders and backers of what were to become the eastern trunk lines out of New York, Philadelphia, and Baltimore, but the promoters of local railroads in Indiana, Michigan, Illinois, and Wisconsin. Local railroads that reached such lake ports as Toledo; Milwaukee; New Buffalo, Michigan; and Michigan City, Indiana, found it necessary to lay track to Chicago as well. Little railroads that would not own rails within a hundred miles of that Lake Michigan port began using the word *Chicago* in their corporate names as if it gave them some legitimacy as a common carrier.

The geography of the Midwest was certainly a major factor in the ascendancy of Chicago as a rail center. The same Great Lakes that provided a transportation corridor inland also formed a barrier to transcontinental land transportation. It was a relatively easy matter to skirt Lake Erie to the north and south through Ontario or Ohio, but Lakes Superior, Huron and Michigan were a formidable barrier to land transport that stretched for almost 500 miles from north to south. The only place where it was relatively easy to bridge that barrier given the technology of the day was far to the north at Sault Ste. Marie. The other alternative for railroad builders was to flank the lakes to the south through Indiana, where there was no natural harbor of any consequence.

However, there was a harbor along the banks of the Chicago River around the corner of the lake a few miles to the northwest in Illinois. By 1850 the city that had arisen at the mouth of the river was a busy port interchanging traffic between the lakes and the I&M Canal as well as a single railroad, although several rail lines were in the planning stage.

Geography aside, perhaps the most important single reason that city became a railroad junction was the intense competition between eastern cities and their railroads. Once the first eastern railroads, or trunk lines as they are often called, reached Chicago and obtained connections to the western railroads, the other trunks had to follow. It was a conclusion reached independently within a few years by railroad builders and financiers in cities from Montreal to Baltimore. Competition was also a factor in the decision of various local railroads' organizers in the Midwest to build to Chicago or at least to add *Chicago* to their corporate name.

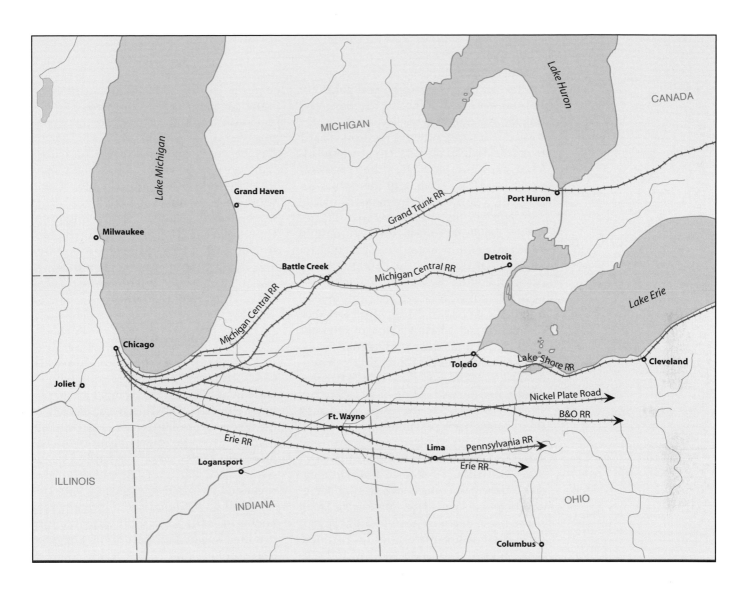

As early as 1836, proponents of expansion of the then-115-mile Baltimore & Ohio Railroad, America's first, suggested Chicago might be a good western terminus for an extension of their line. A decade later John W. Brooks, a Bostonian, concluded the railroad he was building west from Detroit across Michigan should continue to Chicago. Francis Hincks, controller-general of the British province of Canada, became convinced a few years later that a rail line to Chicago would make more sense than a transcontinental line across Canada from the Atlantic to the Pacific.

The arrival of two Michigan railroads in Chicago in 1852 quickly attracted the attention of other eastern trunk lines. The Michigan railroads were linked, or soon would be, with other railroads that had New York City as their eastern terminus. The railroads serving such ports as Philadelphia and Baltimore did not want their more northern rival, which ultimately under Cornelius Vanderbilt's control became the New York Central system, to have a competitive advantage. Other railroads serving the New York area also wanted competitive access to the Windy City, especially since a railroad-building boom was occurring south, west, and north of that city. Thus Chicago at some indefinite point before the Civil War attained what could be described as critical mass—becoming a magnet for railroads in all directions of the compass that needed access to its growing rail hub to be competitive.

The eastern trunk lines, in this map of the region in the 1880s, converged on Chicago in a very narrow corridor around the southern tip of Lake Michigan and made the industrial development of northern Indiana possible.

The northern, western, and southern railroads wanted access to the East, and the eastern railroads needed access to the traffic from the other directions as the frontier spread across the continent. Chicago, more than the other east-west gateways of St. Louis and Memphis, became the place where the railroads met to exchange traffic. Chicago, which did not have a single railroad at the beginning of 1848, was within 6 years the terminal for 10 of them stretching for 3,000 miles in every direction. By 1856, those railroads were operating 58 passenger trains and 38 freights a day to and from Chicago. The city continued to attract eastern railroads through the end of the century.[2]

In the first century and a half of railroading in Chicago, more than 110 standard railroads (excluding interurban and street railways) had the word *Chicago* in their name. Some existed only on incorporation documents or state charters; some did not come within hundreds of miles of Chicago but used the name because they had connections to it or someday hoped to get there; some were small short lines, terminal companies, or belt railroads; some were gobbled up and amalgamated into larger systems; and others failed and disappeared. A few, like the Monon (Chicago, Indianapolis & Louisville) and Nickel Plate Road (New York, Chicago & St. Louis) had *Chicago* in their official titles but were commonly known by their nicknames. The names of quite a few railroads, like the Pittsburgh, Ft. Wayne & Chicago (Pennsylvania Railroad) and Michigan Central (New York Central System), existed on legal documents, but their public identities were subsumed by their larger owners. By the end of the twentieth century only one Class I railroad (an industry classification defining the largest railroads) in the United States—the Kansas City Southern—did not own tracks to Chicago.[3]

Several historical geographers have noted the phenomenon that D. W. Meinig described as the "great Chicago focus."

James E. Vance, Jr., in his book *The North American Railroad,* elaborated: "As the American rail net expanded to encompass the West, Chicago took on a role that no city before it had assumed. Companies that had restlessly sought to project short intercity links into regional systems, and those in turn into subcontinental lines reaching well across the settled interior to the last cities before the settlement frontier—St. Louis, Chicago, Memphis, and New Orleans—seemed to find first in Chicago, and later in the other three, a natural frontier of their own."[4]

The Route from Baltimore

Aside from the debate in Illinois in 1831–1834 over the wisdom of building a railroad or a canal west from Chicago, perhaps the first substantive mention of Chicago as a possible terminal for any railroad occurred in Maryland in 1836. The promoters of a westward extension of the six-year-old Baltimore & Ohio Railroad suggested the carrier ultimately could be extended to "Chicago at the head of Lake Michigan." The suggestion was contained in a March 9, 1836, report to the Maryland legislature by John H. B. Latrobe, a lawyer for the railroad as well as a promoter of it. At the time, the B&O's promoters were simply trying to raise capital to extend the line west from Harper's Ferry, Virginia, to the Ohio River to gain a toehold in the developing American interior. New York City had gained an advantage in that respect with the completion of the Erie Canal in 1825, and Baltimore's canal to the Ohio (the Chesapeake & Ohio Canal) was proving to be too expensive to build over the mountains, a problem that also plagued rival Philadelphia.[5]

Building a railroad through the mountains also proved expensive and difficult. The B&O did not get to Wheeling on the Ohio River in the northwestern corner of what would become West Virginia until early 1853 and to Parkersburg further south until 1856. By that time the two

Michigan railroads that were destined to act as a link in the rail connection between New York City and the central Midwest had already reached Chicago. From those two Ohio River towns the B&O had jumping-off points—from Parkersburg to Cincinnati and St. Louis, and from Wheeling to Chicago. The Civil War delayed any major extensions, but B&O president John W. Garrett began late in the war to make plans for both projects.[6]

The two lines the B&O ultimately acquired were an interesting contrast to the important St. Louis and Chicago rail gateways in the second half of the nineteenth century. Both were created by the method of assemblage—acquiring financial interests in some existing local railroads, leasing others, and building new track to fill in the gaps and create a continuous rail line. The Parkersburg-Cincinnati–St. Louis assemblage completed in 1857 faced tough competition from the river steamboat and never lived up to its proponents' expectations, so much so that Garrett was unwilling to buy it outright, although his successors later did. The Wheeling-Chicago connection, completed in 1874 only after the B&O built a new 263-mile line from what is today Willard, Ohio, south of Sandusky, across northern Indiana to Chicago, showed a profit in its second year of operation.[7]

Interest in Chicago as a western rail terminal was less focused and somewhat slower to develop among Baltimore's rivals, New York City and Philadelphia. Probably because of the success of the Erie Canal in opening the Great Lakes to trade, New York's early interest in the new railroad technology was only a complement to the canal. Beginning in the 1830s, some of New York's railroad projects, such as what became the New York Central, were intended as ventures to augment the state's successful canal by feeding it traffic and providing service in the winter (when maritime operations came to a halt). Others, like the Erie Railroad across the southern tier of the state, were meant to stimulate development where the canal did not

run and to connect various cities along that route. Only later did the railroads become a land bridge between New York City and the Great Lakes; and only after the Civil War when the robber barons fought for control of the railroads did the two New York trunk lines buy or build routes to Chicago to protect their markets.

The state's first railroad, incorporated in 1826 and completed in 1831, was the Mohawk & Hudson, a 16-mile connection parallel to the canal between the Albany on the Hudson River and Schenectady on the Mohawk River. Between 1831 and 1842 six more railroads were built, end-to-end and parallel to the canal, across upstate New York to Buffalo. They gradually combined into what became the New York Central. Shortly after the Mohawk & Hudson began service, promoters in New York City and several rural counties announced plans in 1832 for a second railroad. The New York & Erie, as it was originally called, would run for 483 miles across the southern tier of the state from the west bank of the Hudson River about 25 miles north of New York City to Dunkirk on Lake Erie—a destination it did not reach until 1851.[8]

It was only a matter of time before the railroad routes built to parallel the Erie Canal were extended the entire length of the Chicago–New York waterway as well. New lines were built or existing lines acquired across the states of Michigan, Ohio, and Indiana, and around the southern tip of Lake Michigan. Only later did the eastern trunk railroads build or buy lines to St. Louis to create a second western gateway. The first continuous route involving 18 independent, end-to-end railroads was completed in 1853. Commodore Cornelius Vanderbilt, the New York shipping magnate who began dabbling in railroads in the 1840s, began assembling those railroads into his New York Central system in 1863 and completed the task six years later.[9]

Like its New York City and Baltimore rivals, Philadelphia also became interested in establishing an economic suzerainty in the Middle West but was somewhat slower to identify Chicago as a potential western terminal. As early as 1818, Colonel John Stevens, a year after construction started on New York's Erie Canal, proposed a railroad between Philadelphia and Pittsburgh, but in 1824 the state finally opted to build a canal instead. By the time the Main Line of Public Works, as the canal was called, finally was completed a decade later, Pennsylvania's rivals had already built railroads.[10]

Thus when construction on the Pennsylvania Railroad began in 1847, its directors were contemplating the necessity of having to finance friendly rail connections from Pittsburgh west to Cincinnati. However, within a few years the railroad's strategic focus began to shift northward, and by 1853, the railroad's board was also considering investing in a railroad line from Ft. Wayne, Indiana, west to Peoria, Illinois, and Burlington, Iowa, with a secondary spur to Chicago. Within three years the Pennsylvania Railroad's managers realized that Chicago, not Burlington, would have to be its major focus. The Pennsy renamed its consolidated western subsidiaries the Pittsburgh, Ft. Wayne & Chicago and began a crash program to get the line to the Windy City, a task completed in 1858.[11]

The Erie Railroad, from its inception plagued with financial troubles that were made worse when it was looted by the robber barons, as late as 1870 was still strictly a New York railroad dependent upon other carriers for traffic to and from the rapidly growing Midwest. The Erie Wars between Danial Drew, James Fisk, Jay Gould, and Vanderbilt; Vanderbilt's acquisition of a route to Chicago; and the appearance of another New York syndicate intent on building a third railroad between Buffalo and Chicago finally forced the Erie to change strategic direction. Despite its burdensome debt load, the railroad was forced to buy and build its own Chicago route, which was finished in 1880.

Gould had realized that for competitive

reasons it was necessary for the railroad to reach Chicago, but his tenure at the Erie was too short and stormy to accomplish that goal. He was ousted in 1872 just four years after taking control, and his successors moved slowly. They had earlier obtained control of the Atlantic & Great Western, which began as a local carrier in Pennsylvania and Ohio and eventually developed as a bridge line between the Erie and Pennsylvania railroads and St. Louis. Within a few years the regime in control of the Erie realized that Chicago, not St. Louis, had to be the railroad's primary western connection and built a 250-mile line from the Atlantic & Great Western at Marion, Ohio, to Chicago.[12]

Yet another syndicate of railroad builders, this one headed by George I. Seney, a New York banker, appeared on the scene in 1880 with the intention of assembling a group of existing railroads into another interstate system connecting Buffalo with the Midwest. The result was the 353-mile-long Lake Erie & Western Railway between Fremont in north-central Ohio and Bloomington, Illinois, with St. Louis as its intended western destination. However, within two years of its inception the syndicate realized that Chicago would be a preferable terminus to St. Louis. The projected railroad became the New York, Chicago & St. Louis, better known by its nickname, the Nickel Plate Road. Construction was rushed to finish the 523-mile Buffalo-Chicago line, and service began in the autumn of 1882. The railroad never did build its proposed line to St. Louis.[13]

Michigan

The railroad situation in Michigan in the nineteenth century illustrated perhaps better than any other the magnet Chicago became for railroads within a few years after they appeared in the Midwest. The territorial government of Michigan began plotting railroad lines in the 1830s as a way to encourage development of what was soon to become a state, and very soon after the first Michigan legislature met in January 1837, it adopted an internal improvement program similar to what was being done in neighboring states, including Illinois. However, the Michigan program concentrated on railroads because of the high cost of building canals. As in the other states, politics and local interests soon became a factor that diluted the state's strategic plan.[14]

Detroit, which had been founded in 1701 and was the state's largest city and port, was the obvious choice for the eastern terminus of such developmental rail lines, and a group of Detroit boosters in 1832 secured a charter for a line from that city across the state to Lake Michigan at St. Joseph—the Michigan Central Railroad, as it would later be called. However, the group was not able to raise enough capital to get the project under way, and by the time the state legislature intervened in 1837 to provide public funds, regional interests were agitating for a second line between Lakes Erie and Michigan across the southern tier of the state—the Michigan Southern Railroad.[15]

The Panic of 1837 doomed the Michigan railroad scheme just as it did the state public works programs throughout the Midwest. By the end of 1845 the construction crews on the Michigan Central were slowly approaching Battle Creek, only 115 miles west of Detroit, and the building of the Michigan Southern had been halted after only 68 miles of track had been laid west from Monroe, Michigan, on Lake Erie just north of Toledo. At that time, railroad passengers continuing west to Chicago had to spend 20 hours in a dusty coach bouncing over mud roads and an additional 6 hours on a steamship across the lake.[16]

The nearly bankrupt state was ready to give up on both projects and look for buyers who could complete them. John Woods Brooks, a civil engineer from Boston who was visiting Michigan at the time, and James Frederick Joy, a Harvard-educated lawyer practicing in Detroit, put together a proposal early in 1846 to buy the Michigan Central for $2 million (with $500,000 down) and went to Boston to find the money. Brooks knew John Murray Forbes, a Bostonian who had made his fortune in the China trade just as the railroad boom took off in America. Forbes had enough wealthy acquaintances to raise the down payment.[17]

Brooks also had a radical suggestion: move the proposed western terminal of the railroad 28 miles to the south from St. Joseph, a good lake port, to New Buffalo, to make for a closer stagecoach or rail connection to Chicago. At first Forbes did not consider extending the rail line beyond the eastern shore of Lake Michigan as the state legislature had envisioned in 1837, but when he visited Michigan in 1847 to look over his new investment, he wound up in Chicago to begin his return trip east. The sprawling boomtown he saw convinced him it ultimately would be the western terminus of the Michigan Central.[18]

Brooks had realized years earlier that the railroads then being built in Michigan would prosper because of overland traffic, not local, and access to Chicago as well as the East was the key to their success. Forbes eventually became sufficiently convinced of the wisdom of Brooks's prophecy that even before the Michigan Central reached Chicago he had his associate, James F. Joy, looking to buy railroads in Illinois that could link Chicago with the Mississippi.[19]

What finally spurred Forbes into action was the appearance of competition. The Michigan Southern had been purchased by a group of Michigan investors with New York connections. They accelerated the westward extension of the railroad and in 1850 acquired the long dormant charter of the Northern Indiana Railroad. The race was on. Forbes was forced to lease, for the exorbitant price of $500,000, the rights of the New Albany & Salem Railroad to cross northwestern Indiana, and he worked his construction crews all winter to reach the Illinois state line ahead of the rival Michigan Southern.

The problem was getting across the Illinois state line. Since neither railroad could get a charter from Illinois, and the political position of the Chicago Common Council and U.S. senator Stephen A. Douglas was that no eastern railroad would have a monopoly on access to Chicago, the rival lines had to resort to acquiring trackage rights over existing Illinois charters to get into the Windy City. Henry Farnam, one of the principals in the Michigan Southern, was in Chicago late in 1851 trying to get access to that city when he was approached for financing by some proponents of a railway to connect Rock Island on the Mississippi River with La Salle on the Illinois River. Farnam thought the proposed railroad ought to go all the way east to Chicago, and he interested his New York backers in investing in that project in return for trackage rights for the Michigan Southern to Chicago over the proposed Rock Island.[20]

Forbes at the Michigan Central employed similar tactics a few months later. In return for the purchase of $2 million in Illinois Central Railroad bonds, he got access to Chicago by means of trackage rights over the IC. However, he had to illegally extend the Michigan Central for six miles into Illinois without a charter from the state to reach the IC. The Michigan Central entered Chicago on May 21, 1852—one day ahead of the Michigan Southern.[21]

Soon after the two lines reached Chicago, Michigan was awash in railroad schemes involving that city, which was 60 miles beyond its borders. Even before the Michigan state legislature in 1855 passed a general railroad incorporation act, effectively abolishing the monopoly on railroad construction it had conferred on the two original state-owned lines that were by then in private hands, the applications for new charters poured in. The influence of Chicago as the emerging railroad center in the Midwest became obvious as the charters for new lines were issued. Many of them contained the name *Chicago* in their charters even though they did not own tracks to or near the Windy City. The Chicago & Lake Shore (later Chicago & West Michigan) had its terminal in New Buffalo; the Chicago, Detroit & Canada Grand Trunk Junction ran from Detroit to Port Huron; the Chicago & Northeastern ran from Flint, Michigan, to the state capital in Lansing; the Chicago & Lake Huron was built from Port Huron to Durand, Michigan, and from Lansing to Valparaiso, Indiana. The name *Chicago* was used because all four railroads planned and eventually obtained connections over other railroads to that city.[22]

The Grand Trunk Railway, a Canadian line originally built between Toronto and Montreal beginning in 1852 and later extended to Portland, Maine, to give Canada access to an ice-free winter port, by 1859 had been extended west to Sarnia, Ontario, just across the river from Port Huron, Michigan. To get a western connection, the Grand Trunk then leased the Chicago, Detroit & Canada to get to Detroit where it could exchange traffic with the Michigan Central. That arrangement worked well for years, and the Grand Trunk remained competitive in the rate wars being fought between railroads serving various East Coast ports and Chicago. But officials in Montreal decided on some added insurance for their Chicago connection by routing some traffic over the Chicago & Lake Huron when it completed its line to Valparaiso, Indiana, connecting to Chicago over the Pennsylvania Railroad.[23]

The decision inevitably led to a war for control of the lines between William K. Vanderbilt, the commodore's son who by then controlled the Michigan Central as well as the Grand Trunk's principal rival, the New York Central, and Sir Henry Tyler, the Englishman who served as president of the Grand Trunk. Vanderbilt got control of the Chicago & Lake Huron in 1878 and denied the Grand Trunk access to it. Tyler vowed to Grand Trunk stockholders at their annual meeting on April 29, 1879, that he was going to fight for an independent route to Chicago. He then dashed west to Detroit and Chicago to conduct secret negotiations with bondholders of the Chicago & Lake Huron, which enabled him to gain control of the railroad from Vanderbilt. The commodore's son then sold the Grand Trunk his controlling interest in the Chicago & Northeastern bridge line for $450,000. Tyler had assembled a rail line that was to get no closer to Chicago than Valparaiso, so he rushed construction of a line from there across northwestern Indiana to south suburban Thornton, Illinois, and acquired another railroad from there into Chicago. The first Grand Trunk train ran out of Chicago on February 7, 1880.[24]

Pere Marquette

The last Michigan railroad to get to Chicago was the Pere Marquette—a late amalgamation of what had been about 150 companies serving the timber market in Michigan. One of the three surviving companies that merged in 1900 to form the Pere Marquette was the Chicago & West Michigan, the line that had begun on February 1, 1870, as the 28-mile Chicago & Lake Shore between New Buffalo and St. Joseph in the southwest corner of the state. By the end of the century, the timber market was in serious decline. The management of the new Pere Marquette Railroad (later renamed Railway) attempted to reposition that railroad as a bridge between eastern and western railroads by operating railroad car ferries across Lakes Erie and Michigan and building its own route to Chicago to provide a connection between that city and Buffalo.

The Chicago connection was made possible by the simple expediency of building a 28-mile line from New Buffalo, Michigan, to Porter, Indiana, and arranging for trackage rights over other railroads from there into Chicago, a task completed by the end of 1903. The railroad was never successful financially, and after passing through several different owners and a couple of receiverships was acquired by the Chesapeake & Ohio in 1947.[25]

Indiana Railroads

Although many of the railroads in Indiana were built as through lines to either the St. Louis or Chicago gateways, a number of north-south railroads built to develop the state found in the late 1800s that they could not avoid Chicago. The movement of agricultural goods from southern and central Indiana had begun to shift from the Ohio River on the state's southern border to Chicago on its northern border even before the railroads appeared. By the 1830s "Hoosier wagons" driven by Indiana farmers on the 200-mile trip from the Wabash River valley over the Vincennes Trace began to appear in Chicago, and they increased in number in the 1840s.[26]

Indiana, like Ohio, concentrated its efforts in the 1830s on building canals to encourage development, specifically the 468-mile Wabash and Erie Canal connecting the Ohio River at Evansville with Lake Erie at Toledo. The canal was built between 1832 and 1853, running along the western border of the state to Lafayette, then cutting diagonally across the northern tier of Indiana to the Maumee River at Ft. Wayne to connect with an Ohio canal to Lake Erie, but bypassing by a wide margin both Indianapolis and Indiana's Lake Michigan shoreline. Although it generated some traffic from the interior to Evansville and gave Lafayette an alternative to the Wabash River trade dominated by New Orleans steamboats, the canal is generally considered to have been a folly. By the time it was completed, railroads had appeared on the scene and were competing for traffic.[27]

A midstate railroad linking the interior of Indiana with the Ohio River steamboats and the Great Lakes schooners was the idea behind the Monon (Chicago, Indianapolis & Louisville) Railroad, which began in 1847 as the New Albany & Salem and by 1854 connected New Albany on the Ohio River across from Louisville, Kentucky, and Michigan City on Lake Michigan 54 miles east of Chicago. James Brooks, the railroad's founder and a believer in the superiority of steamboats over railroads, mistakenly presumed Michigan City would develop into a major port because it provided cheaper and more direct access to the lake for his railroad than did Chicago. However, traffic failed to develop, the railroad fell victim to the Panic of 1857, and Brooks was replaced the following year by Dowd Williamson as receiver. In 1859 Williamson had the name of their railroad changed to Louisville, New Albany & Chicago in a belated recognition that it would have to find tracks to the Windy City. The LNA&C finally acquired the moribund Chicago & South Atlantic—a railroad that was originally intended go all the way from Chicago to Charleston, South Carolina, and in 1883 completed it to Chicago. The Monon, as it was later called, survived as the state's unofficial lifeline until it was absorbed in 1971 by the Louisville & Nashville railroad to gain its own connection to Chicago.[28]

The Big Four, or Cleveland, Cincinnati, Chicago & St. Louis Railway, was an x-shaped amalgamation of many short-line railroads that marched across the landscape between those four midwestern cities. The Cincinnati, Indianapolis, St. Louis & Chicago, one of the many railroads in the 1889 assemblage into the Big Four, had gained a somewhat tenuous line to Chicago when it leased in 1874 the 56-mile Kankakee & Indiana line to connect to the Illinois Central Railroad in Kankakee about 56 miles south of the Windy City. The Big Four was acquired by the New York Central in 1891, and in 1977 much of what had been the Kankakee & Indiana was taken over by the Kankakee, Beaverville & Southern short line.[29]

The Chicago & Eastern Illinois Railway began in 1849 as the Evansville & Illinois to serve western Indiana along the Wabash River as far north as Terre Haute from the Ohio River steamboat port of Evansville. Steamboat traffic on the Wabash, which was navigable only three or four months a year as far north as Lafayette, was likely to bypass Evansville in favor of other Ohio River ports, like Louisville and Cincinnati. In fact, of the 29 Wabash steamboats calling at Terre Haute and the 99 calling at Lafayette in 1852, only about a third were bound to or from Evansville. Evansville's leaders hoped the new railroad, which reached Terre Haute in 1854, would correct that imbalance.[30]

After the Civil War, the railroad's directors decided to make Chicago its ultimate destination by crossing the state line and continuing northward on the Illinois side of the border. By building north from Terre Haute the railroad reached Danville, Illinois, in 1871, and by building south from suburban Dolton, Illinois, it connected the system in a continuous route the following year. The railroad was renamed Chicago & Eastern Illinois in 1877 after a foreclosure. In 1888 is was merged with the Chicago, Attica & Southern, an Indiana coal-hauling line that despite its name bypassed Chicago by a substantial margin. The C&EI also acquired lines to Thebes in southern Illinois and St. Louis, and in turn was acquired and split up by the Missouri Pacific and L&N beginning in 1965.[31]

The last Indiana line to arrive in Chicago was the Chicago, Terre Haute & Southeastern, which had been chartered in 1886 as the Evansville & Richmond and early in the twentieth century began looking for additional markets for the coal it was hauling from assorted mines in southern Indiana. After several name changes it incorporated as the Chicago & Southern to build a line from Terre Haute north just inside the eastern border of Illinois to Chicago Heights, where it connected over a belt line to Chicago. The railroad was leased by the Milwaukee Road in 1921 as a

"handy bypass around the Chicago terminal area congestion," one of several unfortunate expansion projects of that railroad in the early twentieth century.[32]

Wisconsin

The railroad builders in Wisconsin, with a few notable exceptions, realized from the beginning that they could not avoid Chicago. The two biggest railroads chartered in that state, the Milwaukee Road and the Wisconsin Central, both tried to avoid Chicago for a while but found the task impossible. As mentioned in the previous chapter, several Wisconsin railroads were chartered primarily as extensions of lines being built north from Chicago.

As early as 1836 when Wisconsin was still part of the Michigan Territory, a railroad was proposed across the southern tier of the state from Lake Michigan to the Mississippi River. A canal was considered in the 1840s but proved to be too expensive, and finally in 1847 a railroad was chartered. Its prime promoter was Milwaukee mayor and

booster Byron Kilbourn, who identified Chicago as his city's biggest rival and predicted that if Milwaukee were to be the first to reach the Mississippi with a railroad, Chicago would be foreclosed from that market. The railroad originally was intended to run only 20 miles inland to Waukesha, but there was no doubt in Kilbourn's mind as to its eventual destination.[33]

As in the case of Chicago's Galena Railroad, which got its start about the same time, raising capital was a problem for the Milwaukee & Mississippi (the eventual Milwaukee Road) promoters, and the railroad did not begin service on the first 20 miles to Waukesha, Wisconsin, until 1851. The M&M finally reached Prairie du Chien on the Mississippi River in 1857 and began building and acquiring lines into northern Illinois to expand its markets. The Chicago & North Western Railway, meanwhile, began expanding into Wisconsin, and even before the Civil War, Wisconsin newspapers were complaining that the M&M was catering to Chicago traffic at the expense of Wisconsin shippers.[34]

Southern Indiana Railway, which was nicknamed the "Bedford Route" because it served that hamlet, was one of many Hoosier railroads that later found it could not bypass the great rail junction growing in Chicago. It kept extending to the north and was eventually renamed the Chicago, Terre Haute & Southeastern. In 1921 it came under the control of the Chicago-based Milwaukee Road. (Krambles-Peterson Archive)

Because space was at a premium in downtown Chicago, freight and passenger yards were often built adjacent to one another and freight cars were stored on every available side track. The arched Baltimore & Ohio passenger train shed can be seen in the distance. The railroad's freight house at the left obscures a view of the Chicago River. (Krambles-Peterson Archive)

Within a few years competition with the North Western had become so intense that Milwaukee & Mississippi president Alexander Mitchell realized his railroad would have to build its own line to Chicago. At the time, the North Western had connections in Chicago with three eastern railroads, but the M&M was forced to rely on another railroad, the Chicago & Milwaukee, to get its freight to and from Chicago. When William B. Ogden's North Western absorbed that line through a perpetual lease in 1866, Mitchell was forced to act. In 1872 he organized the Chicago, Milwaukee & St. Paul Railroad (commonly called the "St. Paul" until the nickname

Milwaukee Road came into use after World War I) in Illinois and began building north to the state line to meet a line he had built the previous year south from Milwaukee. Then in 1873 he acquired a bankrupt charter and began building a line west from Chicago across the northern tier of Illinois to the Mississippi River at Savannah, with the intention of connecting with the transcontinental railroad at Omaha, a goal reached in 1882.[35]

The Milwaukee Road's two new lines converging on Chicago from the north and west effectively shifted the center of operations of the Wisconsin railroad to Chicago from Milwaukee. Its name was changed to Chicago, Milwaukee & St. Paul in 1872 to reflect that reality, and by the end of the century it had moved its headquarters to Chicago as well. By then financial control of the railroad had shifted from Wisconsin investors to a group that included Chicago meatpacker Philip D. Armour, William Rockefeller of Standard Oil, and financier Charles W. Harness.[36]

The other Wisconsin railroad that found it was necessary to get to Chicago for competitive reasons was the Wisconsin Central, an 1871 amalgamation of northern Wisconsin lumber lines that by 1880 went no farther south than Menasha, Wisconsin, on the shores of Lake Winnebago about 265 miles from the Windy City. Competition from the North Western and Milwaukee Road, both of which had their own tracks to Chicago, was the most important factor in the Wisconsin Central's extension southward. From 1882 onward the Wisconsin Central used the Milwaukee Road as its connection to both Milwaukee and Chicago, but after a dispute over passenger service in 1885, Wisconsin Central management decided it needed to build its own line. That was completed to Chicago's western suburbs in 1886, but it was not for another two years that the railroad got access to downtown Chicago, eventually at Grand Central Station at Harrison and Wells streets. The Wisconsin Central was later leased beginning in 1909 by the Minneapolis, St. Paul & Sault Ste. Marie Railway (Soo Line), since 1887 a subsidiary of the Canadian Pacific, giving that giant system access to Chicago.[37]

The Transcontinentals

Inevitably as the nineteenth century progressed, Chicago became a magnet for the transcontinental lines both in the United States and Canada. The city's granger railroads for the most part provided the link between the four U.S. transcontinental railroads built late in the nineteenth century and the rest of the nation's railroad system, but two of the

transcontinentals decided they needed their own lines to Chicago, and one of the granger railroads, the Milwaukee Road, decided in the early twentieth century to build its own transcontinental extension.

James J. Hill, the "empire builder," when he discovered that a northern route bypassing Chicago was infeasible for his Great Northern and Northern Pacific railroads (which came no further east than the Twin Cities), got to Chicago with financier J. P. Morgan's help by the simple expediency of acquiring the Chicago, Burlington & Quincy Railroad in 1901. He outbid Edward Harriman, who controlled the Union Pacific and also wanted to get it to Chicago. The Q was finally merged into what became Burlington Northern in 1970.[38]

Both Canadian transcontinental railroads gained access to Chicago by means of American subsidiaries. The Canadian National arrived in 1880 over the Grand Trunk. The Canadian Pacific, which got financial control over the Soo Line in 1888, got to Chicago in 1909 when the Soo leased the Wisconsin Central.

Of the other transcontinentals, the Union Pacific did not get its own line to Chicago until it acquired the Missouri Pacific in 1982 and the Southern Pacific, which was by then controlled by the Denver & Rio Grande Western, got access by means of leased trackage rights from Kansas City in 1990. Somewhat later it bought the former Chicago & Alton line between St. Louis and Chicago. The fourth transcontinental, the Atchison, Topeka & Santa Fe, beat the rest to Chicago in the 1880s.[39]

The Santa Fe was conceived before the Civil War as a 45-mile local railroad between Atchison, Kansas, on the Missouri River to Topeka in the interior, but the war and the usual problems in raising money delayed the start of construction until 1868. However, promoter and developer Cyrus K. Holliday had grand designs for his line, which he pushed west across Kansas, Colorado, New Mexico, and Arizona, reaching California in 1882. Although Holliday as early as March 1869 predicted the railroad would eventually reach Chicago, the Santa Fe's organizers initially believed its eastern connections would be through other railroads at Hannibal, Missouri, and Kansas City. Incursions into his territory from railroads based in St. Louis and Chicago convinced then–Santa Fe president William Barstow Strong in 1884 to proceed with the Chicago line.[40]

Three years later he acquired the dilapidated Chicago & St. Louis Railway to get its 65-mile right-of-way from downstate Streator to the outskirts of Chicago. Beginning in 1887 he built a 350-mile connecting line between Atchison and Streator, a project completed on April 28, 1888. In 1890 then-ATSF president Allen Manvel moved his offices to Chicago, which remained the railroad's corporate headquarters until 1995 when it merged with the Burlington Northern.[41]

By the 1880s, Chicago's critical mass had made it exceedingly difficult for a railroad crossing the Midwest to bypass the city, although as the rail junction became increasingly congested a number of attempts were made to do just that. Many of the trunk systems built mainlines to St. Louis as well as the Windy City, but independent railroads trying to carry bridge traffic between east and west without using the Chicago junction had limited success, whether they used more southerly routes or ferries to cross Lake Michigan. Some ultimately were forced to build lines to Chicago, others were gobbled by larger carriers, some failed, and a few survived in limited roles.

Bypassing Chicago

4

Assorted railroads trying to bypass Chicago built ships to ferry trains across Lake Michigan. The *Badger* was the last such vessel in service, but when this photo was taken in 1999, it hauled automobiles and motor trucks, not railroad cars, between Ludington, Michigan, and Manitowoc, Wisconsin.

From the beginning of the railroad era in the Midwest there were a number of attempts to bypass Chicago. At least initially, some of the proposed bypasses were planned to act as a catalyst for development in other areas of Illinois. Others were planned on the assumption that rival cities, like St. Louis or Alton, were more important than the port at the foot of Lake Michigan, or that they offered potentially more lucrative markets. After the midpoint of the nineteenth century some railroads were built for the specific purpose of avoiding the rapidly congesting Chicago rail maze. Others were assembled from local railroads into east and west connectors that did not happen to go anywhere near Chicago but later tried to capitalize on their ability to bypass it. A few were built as belt lines girding the city in an effort to avoid most of the congestion that plagued the downtown area.

The belt lines were successful; indeed they thrived because of the city's railroad congestion. However, the non-belt lines were a mixed bag. A few of the these bypass lines survived into the twenty-first century, if not as independent railroads at least as branches of major railroads. Most simply disappeared, gobbled up in mergers, abandoned, or both. The fact that the bypasses collectively attained only very limited success is a clear, if understudied, indication of the importance the Chicago rail junction had attained in the second half of the nineteenth century.

The major eastern trunk railroads with lines to Chicago found they could afford to build bypasses to places like St. Louis and Kansas City, but the smaller midwestern railroads had an especially difficult time attracting sufficient traffic if they avoided Chicago. Many of the organizers of such independent midwestern lines,

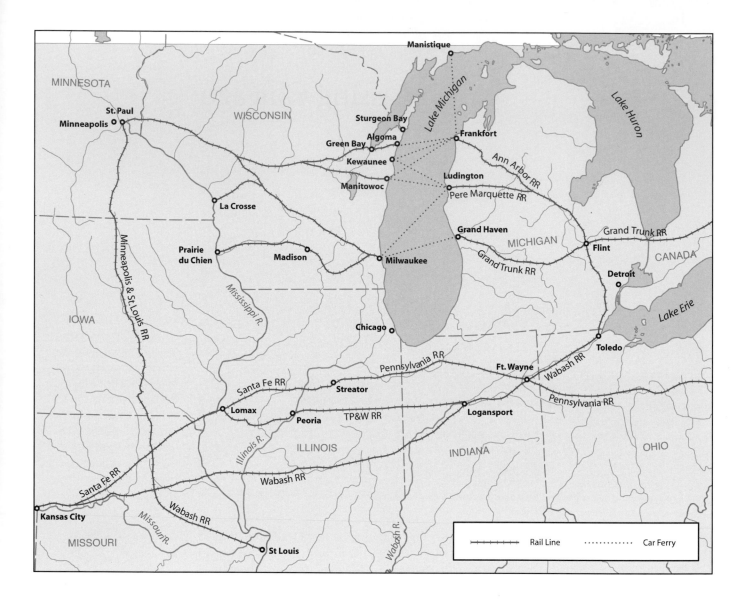

Various attempts to build railroads bypassing Chicago to the north, south, and west were never particularly successful. Often the bypasses, like those shown in this map of the region in 1900, were engineered by railroads like the Pennsylvania, Wabash, and Grand Trunk that also had lines to the Windy City.

especially in areas far removed from the waterways, built their railroads as a stimulus to local development without a lot of thought as to where the tracks would ultimately lead. This was the case for railroads serving places like Springfield, Illinois's new state capital, and Indianapolis, which by virtue of its railroads turned out to be the largest city in the Midwest not located along a waterway. Cities like Peoria on a marginally navigable waterway, the Illinois River, also promoted railroads as a way to increase their economic influence over the hinterlands and spur development.

For a time, major lake and river ports like Cincinnati, Toledo, St. Louis, and Milwaukee promoted railroads to feed traffic

to their ports, and developing communities in the interior agitated for rail lines to connect to those cities. By the late 1850s, Chicago's transportation rivals realized that the city was developing as the region's major rail center. They accelerated their own efforts to encourage rail lines to their municipal limits. The state of Missouri and the cities of St. Louis and Cincinnati made substantial investments of public funds in railroads.[1]

In 1850, the states of Ohio, Indiana, and Illinois combined had 914 miles of railroad in operation, only 90 miles of which had Chicago as a terminus. Missouri had no mileage. However, by 1860 the railroad network in those three states had grown to 7,899 miles—2,533 miles, or approximately a third of it, either terminating in Chicago or having that city as its announced destination.[2]

The major eastern trunks that acquired lines to places like St. Louis and Cincinnati also built lines to Chicago. Because of the Lake Michigan barrier, Milwaukee's eastern connections were through Chicago, as were Minneapolis–St. Paul's. The final blows to St. Louis and to a lesser extent Cincinnati were the Civil War, which disrupted Mississippi River traffic as well as Missouri's new railroad system, and the selection of Omaha as the eastern terminus of the transcontinental railway, a decision that favored Chicago over St. Louis.

In the 1870s, when rail congestion in Chicago became a serious problem, rail systems built across Illinois, Wisconsin, and Michigan began to promote themselves specifically as bypasses to the traffic jam that had developed in the Windy City. For the most part their efforts were too little too late. The predecessors of the Wabash and the Milwaukee Road in the 1870s were forced to build lines to Chicago. A decade later the organizers of the system that became the Chicago Great Western in Minnesota (Minnesota & Northwestern and later the Chicago, St. Paul & Kansas City) made no attempt to avoid Chicago in building their principal east-west mainline despite considerable competition from existing railroads. A system of railroad car ferries launched on Lake Michigan beginning in the 1890s with the intention of bypassing Chicago to the north proved inadequate for the task in the twentieth century and one by one they were abandoned. The Toledo, Peoria & Western, which was promoted as a southern bypass around Chicago for much of its existence, never made much of a dent in traffic serving that big junction.

As the eastern trunk lines had discovered earlier, the midwestern roads found that the competitive nature of the new railroad industry required them to obtain Chicago connections. Within the space of a few

decades, the city had become the largest rail junction in the world, one in which traffic was exchanged between carriers and in which shippers could shop for the best rates. A railroad bypassing Chicago might connect with one or two railroads west of the Mississippi River and one in the East, but any railroad serving Chicago by the early 1880s had available five eastern connections and six to the west.

Chicago's Rivals

Perhaps the most concerted efforts to develop midwestern railroad gateways in a place other than Chicago occurred in both Cincinnati and St. Louis in the decades before the Civil War. Although both cities were river ports with considerable steamboat traffic to and from New Orleans, the leaders of both cities by the 1840s realized they would need railroads to maintain and expand their economies. They were quite willing to use the public treasury and promote local stock subscriptions to augment the financing necessary to build railroads. Chicago, on the other hand, did none of that.

Cincinnati by 1840 had obtained an outlet to the Great Lakes to augment its river route to New Orleans by means of a series of publicly financed canals emptying into Lake Erie at Toledo. As early as 1836 Cincinnati also contemplated a railroad link to the Great Lakes and loaned the Little Miami Railroad $200,000 for that purpose. A decade later residents of the city subscribed to $750,000 in stock to build the Cincinnati, Hamilton & Dayton Railroad and give the city another Great Lakes connection at Toledo. In 1851 Cincinnati made a $600,000 loan and its residents subscribed to $500,000 in stock to build a line west to St. Louis, which received $500,000 from that city and a like amount from its residents in stock purchases.

The Ohio & Mississippi, completed in 1857, was built to a six-foot-gauge that enabled it to connect to the Atlantic & Great Western and Erie railroads. This connected St. Louis and Cincinnati with New York in a circuitous bypass of Chicago. However, the nonstandard gauge, which was adopted to give the line a monopoly on traffic in its territory, made interchanging traffic with other railroads difficult. In 1876–1877 Cincinnati built a bridge over the Ohio River and leased it to a railroad to obtain better access to southern markets. All that railroad building enabled Cincinnati by the end of the century to become the largest railroad center in Ohio, trailing only Chicago and St. Louis in volume of railroad cars handled.[3]

Perhaps because its transportation system was dominated by the steamboat industry, St. Louis was somewhat slower than Cincinnati to embrace the railroad. However, by 1847 both St. Louis and the state of Missouri had become interested in the new technology. A National Railroad Convention was held in St. Louis in 1849, but it devolved into a political struggle between Senators Thomas Hart Benton of Missouri and Stephen A. Douglas of Illinois over whether a proposed transcontinental railroad route would favor Chicago or St. Louis. This issue was decided in Chicago's favor 15 years later by another Illinois resident, President Abraham Lincoln. St. Louis hosted a second national railroad convention in 1852.[4]

Missouri's early railroad schemes, with one exception, generally favored St. Louis as their eastern terminal. As a result, the state for the most part concentrated on western railroads that would feed traffic to the Mississippi River levee. Those projects were also plagued by the lack of private capital, which by then was heavily invested in Chicago's railroads, forcing the state of Missouri to plan and finance its own railroads. The resulting political interference in a state with strong antebellum sectional differences hampered completion of the system. The projects were also plagued by corruption, sabotage by sappers during the Civil War, and shoddy construction. In 1855, four years after construction of the Missouri Pacific railroad began, a bridge over the Gasconade River

collapsed as it was being crossed by a trainload of dignitaries. Among the 31 persons killed was the railroad's chief construction engineer. The railroad did not reach Kansas City until 1865, and three years later the state sold its $11 million investment in the railroad for only $5 million.[5]

Missouri did not have much luck with its other railroad projects, either. The North Missouri Railroad was chartered in 1851 with the intention to run from St. Louis north into Iowa to interdict railroads being built west from Chicago. But construction did not begin until 1854, and the first 157 miles between St. Louis and Macon—still 61 miles short of the Iowa line—did not open until 1859, after which construction was halted until after the Civil War. By then three Chicago-based railroads were already crossing Iowa. A second proposal in 1852 to build a line on the west side of the Mississippi between New Orleans, St. Louis, and the Twin Cities never got beyond the talking stage.[6]

Missouri's most successful early railroad turned out to be its biggest transportation policy failure. The Hannibal & St. Joseph Railroad was chartered in 1847 to build a line across the northern tier of the state between those two cities, and in 1851 it got a $1.5 million loan subsidy from the state as part of a political compromise to permit subsidies to the Missouri Pacific. Construction started in 1853 and was completed in 1859, but by then Boston financier John Murray Forbes had gotten financial control of the railroad and used it as a western extension of his Chicago, Burlington & Quincy. So the railroad the state of Missouri subsidized became a vassal of Chicago, diverting traffic to the city on the Great Lakes and away from St. Louis.[7]

Southern Bypasses

Because the early settlement of Illinois was along the rivers and the Great Lakes did not become a factor in commerce for several years after completion of the Erie Canal in 1825, most of the earliest railroads in Illinois were proposed to join river towns that were in existence years before Chicago was developed. There was nothing there to bypass. It became obvious as the century progressed that a major city was emerging at the foot of Lake Michigan, so some of the early railroads had to change their plans to include Chicago as a terminal. The Chicago & Alton was originally envisioned as a route from Springfield, Illinois, to St. Louis, but even before construction was completed, its organizers realized they had to extend it to Chicago. The original promoters of the Northern Cross, which later became the Wabash Railroad, never intended it to come closer than 110 miles to Chicago, but later owners realized that they needed the Chicago junction to interchange traffic.

As a lawyer, Abraham Lincoln represented a number of railroads, and as an Illinois politician, he was constantly promoting programs favoring his hometown, including the shifting of the state capital from Vandalia to Springfield and the dredging of the Sangamon River for navigation. As early as 1832 he suggested that a 72-mile north-south railroad be built between Springfield and Alton on the Mississippi River about 20 (river) miles north of St. Louis. But the plan that ultimately emerged from the state's 1836 Internal Improvements Program was the Northern Cross spanning the central part of the state from east to west from Danville through Springfield to Quincy on the Mississippi. However, Lincoln had not given up on his idea for a north-south line. On February 4, 1841, he introduced a bill in the General Assembly calling for state subsidies for an Alton-Springfield line. After the railroad was finally chartered in 1847, Lincoln not only bought six shares of stock in it but publicly promoted its stock sale in a letter to the *Sangamo Journal*.[8]

The future president's horizons were widened considerably when he attended the national River and Harbor Convention in Chicago in July 1847 and, with other delegates from downstate Illinois, was im-

pressed with the city's rapid growth. The following month he and nine other railroad promoters signed a letter to the *Sangamo Journal* suggesting the Springfield & Alton would be "but a link in a great chain of railroad communication which shall unite Boston and New York with the Mississippi."[9]

Construction on the railroad did not begin until 1850, and within a year the railroad's major promoters realized it should be extended from Springfield to Chicago. The railroad's name was changed to the Chicago & Mississippi in 1852, and the race to Chicago was on. It began running trains as far north as suburban Joliet in 1854, connecting to Chicago over other lines, and four years later as the Chicago, Alton & St. Louis finally completed its own line into the Windy City.[10]

What became the Wabash Railroad originated in 1836 as the Northern Cross segment of Illinois's abortive Internal Improvements Program. Its principal proponents included Lincoln and some of his political colleagues. Of course, the railroad was planned to run through their hometown of Springfield, although there has been a healthy disagreement among Illinois historians as to whether the Long Nine, as the group was called, engaged in political logrolling to get the railroad. Chicago at the time had already started to boom but had a population estimated at only 3,820, contrasted to approximately 2,500 residents in Springfield, and it did not figure in the railroad's plans.[11]

The Northern Cross was completed in 1842 between Meredosia on the Illinois River and Springfield, but by 1955 had been renamed the Great Western Railway of Illinois and extended to Danville on the state's eastern border. A series of amalgamations followed, and by the Civil War the Wabash had emerged as a St. Louis–Toledo carrier—the only St. Louis railroad reaching the Great Lakes and trunk lines east of Chicago. Businessmen in the port of Toledo were interested in attracting traffic from the rich agricultural lands of central Illinois that were coming under Chicago's influence, and St. Louis businessmen were amenable to rail links to the East that bypassed Chicago.[12]

However, the strategy did not result in a particularly healthy railroad financially. Cornelius K. Garrison, a San Francisco banker who had acquired the Missouri Pacific and Kansas City Northern to gain a monopoly on traffic between Kansas City and St. Louis, became interested in the Wabash in 1878 after the Chicago & Alton refused him a connection to Chicago. His strategy was to buy the Wabash relatively cheaply after one of its reorganizations and have it build a link to Chicago. He got the project started by buying an existing railroad under construction and extending it 90 miles from Streator to Chicago. New York railroad magnate Jay Gould bought him out in 1879 and completed the project.[13]

The Wabash did provide a bypass around Chicago, connecting with many western railroads in Omaha, Kansas City, and St. Louis and various eastern lines between Ft. Wayne and Toledo. But most of the railroads to which it offered connecting service already owned lines to Chicago and could reap more in revenue by hauling goods an extra 200 miles to Chicago than by turning them over to a bridge line in Toledo. In 1893 the Wabash was forced for competitive reasons to obtain a second line to Chicago, this time from the east. The Wabash in 1925 also acquired a northern bypass of Chicago when it absorbed the Ann Arbor Railroad and its fleet of ferries to haul freight cars back and forth across Lake Michigan.

The Wabash had an added advantage in that it provided its shippers with a bypass of St. Louis, which in the twentieth century became a rail center as congested as Chicago. This was because most lines from the east converged in East St. Louis (formerly Illinoistown) on the Illinois side of the Mississippi River, and traffic had to be sent by ferry across the Mississippi River or funneled over a single railroad bridge. The

Interstate Commerce Commission as late as 1941 noted in its report on yet another bankruptcy reorganization of the Wabash that its line from Toledo to Kansas City provided the Pennsylvania Railroad with a route avoiding the congestion of both Chicago and St. Louis.[14]

The Pennsy had become involved because as a defensive maneuver in 1928 it had acquired a major bloc of Wabash stock, ostensibly as an investment but in reality to prevent the Wabash from completing its ambitious plans to become the nation's fifth trunk line railroad between the East Coast and the Midwest. The Wabash had pursued those plans despite, or perhaps because of, its inability to prosper primarily as a bypass carrier. It suffered bankruptcies in both 1911 and 1931.[15]

Despite its periodic financial problems, the Wabash provided competition for the railroads serving Chicago, which helped keep freight rates lower. For example, rate cutting in the late nineteenth century helped the Wabash undermine the Iowa Pool, a conspiracy of granger railroads (Burlington, North Western, and Rock Island) intended to split the traffic equally and to keep rates higher than they would have been with competition. But it could not sustain such an effort forever, and the Wabash was in receivership again by 1885.[16]

To cut expenses and raise funds, the Wabash was forced to sell off various earlier acquisitions and cancel the leases on others. One such leased line was the Toledo, Peoria & Western, another Chicago bypass railroad operating no more than 60 miles north of the Wabash. The TP&W was not only the longest lived of the bypasses, surviving as an independent railroad into the twenty-first century, but it had one of the most colorful histories of any carrier in the nation. It had Illinois's worst train wreck, endured the longest rail strike in U.S. history, and was the only American railroad to suffer the assassination of its chief executive. It was in financial difficulty almost from its inception.

Like the Wabash, the TP&W was built

over a route that originated as part of the Internal Improvements Program—a line from Bloomington, where it would connect with the Illinois Central, to Peoria on the Illinois River and Warsaw on the Mississippi River. Some grading of the western section was completed before the state ran out of money and the project collapsed, but the graded section was incorporated into the line of one of the TP&W's predecessors.

The revival of the line as a private enterprise began with a state charter in 1849 for a railroad between Peoria and Oquawka on the Mississippi River. Over the next 20 years additional short railroads were chartered to become an end-to-end system from Warsaw, a hamlet 50 miles downstream on the Mississippi from Oquawka,

to Sheldon on the Indiana-Illinois state line, where it would connect with an eastern railroad network.[17]

By the end of the Civil War, the various railroads built along the route had been consolidated into the Toledo, Peoria & Warsaw, but in its first four decades of existence it suffered three foreclosures (1864, 1880, and 1886), had several name changes, was extended into Iowa and Indiana, and at one time connected with 17 different railroads. It was also the site of the worst accident in Illinois railroad history at Chatsworth in 1887 (see Appendix C). The Toledo, Peoria & Western, as the railroad was called beginning in 1880, was also acquired over the years by a succession of railroads intent on exploiting it as a bypass, and in at least one instance by a

Ferries were used by railroads to cross rivers until traffic could justify the building of expensive bridges. This painting shows a ferry that carried trains across the Missouri at Council Bluffs, Iowa, as well as a railroad bridge built at the site later. The painting was done for the Union Pacific's centennial.

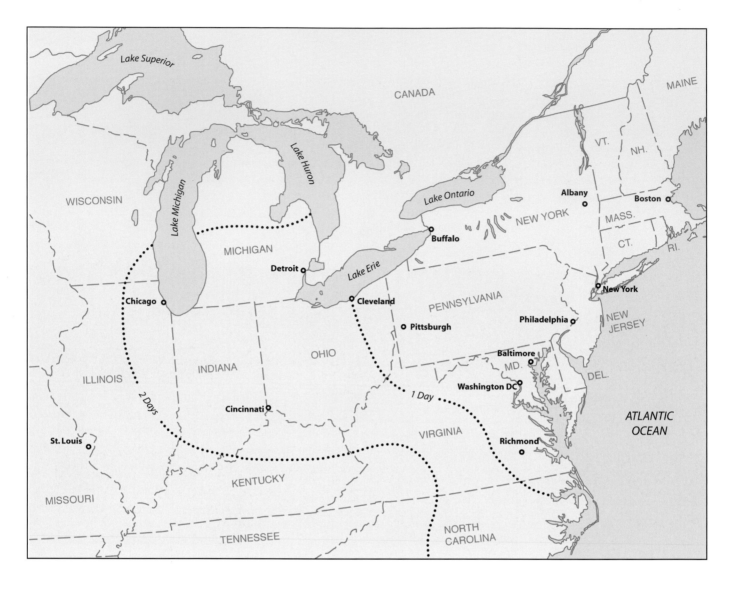

By the time of the Civil War, the travel time between New York and Chicago had been reduced to only two days.

railroad intent on precluding it from developing that role—the Wabash by lease in 1880, the Burlington and Pennsylvania with stock in 1893, and the Santa Fe and Pennsylvania (again) with cash in 1955. The acquisition agreement between the Burlington and Pennsylvania in 1893 stipulated the TP&W could only handle local, not bypass, traffic.[18]

At least two individuals also sought to get control of the TP&W to exploit it as a bypass—George P. McNear, Jr., who bought it at yet another of its foreclosures in 1926, and Ben Heineman, a Chicago lawyer and investor, who unsuccessfully tried to buy it in 1955. McNear's tenure was clouded by a long and bitter labor dispute that began in 1941, forcing the federal government to

take over and operate the railroad during World War II, and his unsolved assassination in Peoria on March 10, 1947, during another outbreak of labor unrest.[19]

In 1954 Heineman, who would later gain control of the Chicago & North Western, bought stock in the Minneapolis & St. Louis Railroad, which, despite its name, never got to St. Louis but did have nearly 1,400 miles of track wandering around the Midwest from Akaska in central South Dakota through the Twin Cities to Peoria. He then tried to acquire both the TP&W and Monon to create a Chicago rail bypass stretching from central Iowa through north-central Illinois and Indiana. The Santa Fe, which used the TP&W as a bypass to connect with the Pennsylvania Railroad, became alarmed at that prospect, bought the TP&W to block Heineman, and then sold a half interest to the Pennsylvania.[20]

That arrangement worked until the successor Penn Central collapsed into bankruptcy and the Consolidated Rail Corporation, its successor, sold its half interest back to the Santa Fe. The general pressure on the railroad industry to shed underperforming branches caused the Santa Fe in early 1989 to sell the TP&W to an investment group.

The new owner was Gordon Fuller, who had intended to develop the line as a Chicago bypass for time-sensitive container traffic, but the revenues from that traffic were insufficient to keep the track in condition for high-speed service. Fuller then sold control of the railroad to an eastern railroad holding company called Delaware Otsego Corporation, which also was interested in using the railroad as an intermodal bypass. At that time CSX Transportation and the Norfolk Southern each bought 10 percent of the TP&W stock. However, Delaware Otsego also had problems developing intermodal bypass traffic and sold the railroad in 1999.[21]

The new buyer was RailAmerica Inc., a Florida holding company of short-line

Chicago, which did not have a single railroad until 1848, was the nation's railroad capital by 1860.

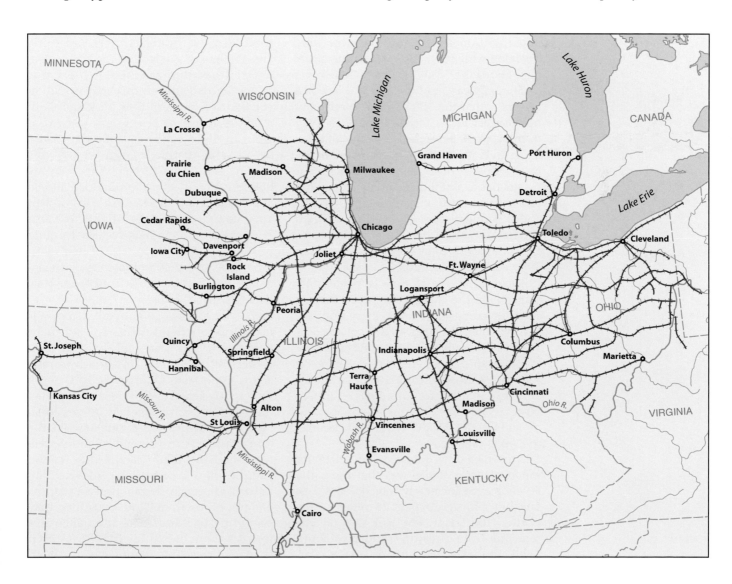

railroads scattered around the nation. That company quickly found itself in financial difficulty as the result of its purchase of 17 railroads just as the economy slumped into a recession. To generate cash to pay off its debt, it began selling many of its recent acquisitions. One sale for $2,179,878 was 71.5 miles of the TP&W mainline from Peoria west to La Harpe to a subsidiary of A&K Materials, a firm that sold railroad scrap. When another connecting short line (Keokuk Junction Railway) protested that A&K intended to eventually downgrade, abandon, and scrap the line, the U.S. Surface Transportation Board, the successor to the Interstate Commerce Commission as regulator of railroads, in 2002 annulled the sale and ordered RailAmerica to take back the line. Abandonment of the line would effectively have ended the TP&W's role as a bypass.[22]

The implication of its long and troubled history is that the TP&W could survive but not prosper as a Chicago bypass. In 1955 from 80 to 90 percent of the railroad's revenues were produced by overhead traffic exchanged with other railroads, much of it bypass traffic. But it carried only 3.6 million tons and operated only 12 line locomotives and 254 freight cars. The railroad suffered financially when the Minneapolis & St. Louis was acquired by the North Western in 1960 and rerouted traffic over that line to Chicago; when the Norfolk & Western absorbed both the Wabash and Nickel Plate in 1964, diverting more traffic away from the TP&W; when the Rock Island collapsed in 1980; and again when Conrail began diverting traffic elsewhere in 1981. Traffic on the TP&W dropped from 105,524 carloads annually in 1961 to only 66,042 carloads 20 years later. In 1999 when it was acquired by RailAmerica, TP&W traffic had declined to 59,000 carloads.[23]

A problem that plagued the TP&W for much of its existence was that the Santa Fe, its parent for nearly four decades, had another Chicago bypass 25 miles to the north. That was a New York Central System line from Streator, Illinois, to South Bend, Indiana. That line, originally char-

tered in 1881 as the Indiana, Illinois & Iowa Railroad, or "Three I," made the TP&W redundant when the New York Central and Pennsylvania railroads merged into the ill-fated Penn Central. The combined railroad did not need two parallel bypasses a few miles apart. The Three I passed from the Penn Central's bankruptcy estate to the successor Consolidated Rail Corporation (Conrail) and finally the Norfolk Southern Railroad.[24]

One of the grander bypass schemes, at least in name, was the Atlantic & Great Western Railroad alluded to earlier. Fortunately the memoirs of one of its promoters survive and give some insight into the motivation behind the routing of the railroad. Because interests in Philadelphia and Pittsburgh controlled the Pennsylvania Railroad and attempted to exclude routes across Pennsylvania that would favor the rival ports of New York and Baltimore, a group of promoters in central Ohio in 1851 conceived of what would become the Atlantic & Great Western as a way to get access to New York City by building a connection to the Erie Railroad at Salamanca on the western edge of New York State. By 1856, the Atlantic & Great Western promoters had decided to build west to Dayton, Ohio, to connect with other railroads that would create a broad-gauge rail system stretching from New York City to St. Louis.[25]

The six-foot-gauge railroad system was intended to extend across the southern tier of New York State, cut south through western Pennsylvania, run southwesterly across Ohio from Orangeville to Dayton, turn south again to Cincinnati, and then run west across Indiana and Illinois to St. Louis. Besides the Erie and A&GW, the other railroads in the end-to-end system were the Cincinnati, Hamilton & Dayton and the Ohio & Mississippi. All were built to the wide gauge, despite the fact that the nation's northern railroads even then were beginning to standardize at a gauge of 4 feet 8 1/2 inches to facilitate the interchange of cars. The Atlantic & Great Western, which traversed some sparsely populated and largely rural areas, suffered from anemic traffic from its inception, wound up in receivership several times, and was leased to the Erie Railroad. By then the Erie was intent on building a line to Chicago, however.[26]

Local Bypasses

Several short bypasses built around the Chicago metropolitan area failed to attain the success their promoters had hoped, most probably because they served only a few railroads and were boycotted by the others. The competitive situation in the Chicago junction was such that any railroad that tried to bypass it and connect to another railroad ran the substantial risk of losing traffic to and from the railroads that remained in Chicago. Several belt lines were built in the metropolitan area in the late 1800s to bypass the most congested parts of the Chicago rail plant, but they were usually owned by a consortium of major railroads.

The independently owned Elgin, Joliet & Eastern belt line to some extent functioned as a bypass, although not to any great extent until the late twentieth century. A group of cheaply constructed interurban railroads built in an arc in the fringe of suburbia after 1900 never generated any significant bypass traffic and were out of business by the middle of the Depression.

The Joliet & Northern Indiana and the Chicago, Milwaukee & Gary railroads were two failed bypasses owned by major railroads. Although Chicago successfully blocked an attempt by Forbes's Michigan Central to build what at the time was called the "Joliet cutoff" to bypass the Windy City to the south, a railroad was later constructed over the route. The Joliet & Northern Indiana was originally built between 1849 and 1853 as a wooden plank highway from far southwest suburban Oswego, Illinois, through Joliet to the Indiana state line. But in 1854–1855 the own-

ers converted the highway to the 44-mile Joliet & Northern Indiana Railroad connecting the Chicago & Rock Island in Joliet with the Michigan Central at Lake Junction (East Gary), Indiana, in a line that never came closer than 20 miles to downtown Chicago. Perhaps because of Rock Island's financial woes, the "Joliet cutoff" was never particularly successful, even under the control of the New York Central System (1890–1968), and by the end of 1972 it had deteriorated to the point that train speeds were limited to 10 miles an hour. The line was abandoned in 1976 by Consolidated Rail Corporation.[27]

A bigger failure was the Chicago, Milwaukee & Gary, organized in 1908 to build a 95-mile route around Chicago passing through Joliet, Aurora, and Rockford. The line was heavily in debt by 1922 when the Milwaukee Road, which itself was in weak financial condition, bought it as a bypass of the Chicago terminal congestion and as a way to get to the Chicago, Terre Haute & Southeastern Railway for access to the coal mines of southern Indiana and as a connection to railroads there. Between 1978 and the end of 1980, the Interstate Commerce Commission approved the fragmentary abandonment of the line that Milwaukee Road critic Thomas Ploss described as the "Louisville Sluggard."[28]

During the electric interurban railroad-building craze of 1901–1909, four ill-conceived and independently owned electric railways were built almost end-to-end in an arc from 79th Street in Chicago around the metropolitan area to Chicago Heights, Joliet, Aurora, and Elgin. Running alongside highways in suburban areas and on streets in towns, the railroads never developed sufficient passenger or freight traffic to survive. One went out of business as early as 1924, and the other three were gone by 1935. The last—the Aurora, Elgin & Fox River—survived mainly as a streetcar line until its owners replaced the trains with buses in 1935.[29]

The 400-mile Illinois Traction (later the Illinois Terminal Railroad), one of the longest railroads in Illinois and the second largest interurban railroad in the United States after the Pacific Electric in Los Angeles, never made a serious attempt to reach Chicago or operate as a Chicago bypass. The railroad ran between St. Louis and Springfield, then split into lines east to Danville and north to Peoria, subsisting on passenger and freight traffic in communities poorly served by the steam railroads. William B. McKinley, the downstate Illinois traction magnate who had assembled the system beginning in 1890, bought the Chicago & Illinois Valley line just after the turn of the century and pushed its construction east to Joliet on the fringe of the Chicago metropolitan area. It reached Joliet in 1912, but the railroad's management never built a line between Bureau and Peoria to connect the two systems. McKinley's interest in interurban railroads began to wane during his long political career that began in 1904 when he was elected to Congress. By 1923 he had essentially retired from railroading after utilities moguls Clement Studebaker and Samuel Insull had gained control of the Illinois Traction through the Illinois Light and Power Company. The Chicago & Illinois Valley was abandoned during the Depression, and the remainder of Illinois Terminal, as it was by then called, was acquired by the Norfolk & Western in 1981.[30]

Western Bypasses

The idea of a western bypass of Chicago occurred not only in the river city of St. Louis but in Minneapolis as well. Shortly after the Civil War some businessmen in Minneapolis decided they needed a rail connection to both the Great Lakes and the navigable section of the Mississippi River. They originally chose Duluth on Lake Superior as the northern terminal, albeit briefly, and St. Louis as the southern, to give them year-round access to navigable water when the Great Lakes were frozen over. Access to Chicago was a tertiary consideration, to be accomplished by

interchanging traffic in Iowa with granger lines to Chicago.[31]

The Minneapolis & St. Louis, as the resulting railroad was called, got to the Iowa-Missouri state line but never to St. Louis. It also reached Peoria, Illinois, in 1912 by acquiring the Iowa Central and was nicknamed "Peoria Gateway Line," but it never made a serious effort to get to Chicago although for a short time after 1910 it maintained its headquarters there. But in 1882 the M&St.L hired an aggressive railroad man named A. B. Stickney, a St. Paul lawyer who decided to take up railroading in the 1860s, as a vice president and director. He had somewhat different ideas as to where the railroad should run, and perhaps because of his ambition to run his own railroad, he lasted only a year at the M&St.L. Stickney believed that Chicago, not St. Louis, was the logical terminal for a railroad from the Twin Cities.[32]

Shortly after leaving the M&St.L he acquired the dormant 1854 charter for a line to run from the shore of Lake Superior through St. Paul to Dubuque, Iowa. There it could connect with the Illinois Central for a through route to Chicago before its own line was built there. Thus was born the last of the granger railroads into the Windy City, and the only one built to the Chicago area from the west—the Chicago Great Western. At first the new railroad used the IC as its Chicago connection, but Stickney in 1888 completed his own line that included a half-mile tunnel through the rough terrain near Galena. The railroad, although profitable, was not particularly successful in competition for overland traffic with the other granger lines out of Chicago. In 1968 it was acquired by the Chicago & North Western, which promptly abandoned much of the CGW's Chicago mainline. Meanwhile, the M&St.L could not find a buyer and languished in bankruptcy for 20 years after 1923, but it was in somewhat better financial shape when it was finally gobbled up by the North Western in 1960.[33]

Perhaps Stickney's greatest legacy to Chicago was his promotion in 1889 of a

giant consolidated freight yard on the Southwest Side. His idea was to build a classification yard large enough to serve as a clearinghouse for all freight cars moving through Chicago. Because of intense competition between railroads in the metropolitan area, many of which built their own classification yards, Stickney's 786-acre, 5.5-mile-long clearing yard just south of Midway Airport never attained its progenitor's goals of being the central yard for all freight traffic.[34]

Bypasses to the North

The Great Lakes presented the biggest obstacle to bypassing Chicago to the north, but several smaller midwestern railroads attempted to avoid the Chicago bottleneck by routing traffic across Lake Michigan instead of around it. To do that they built small fleets of specialized ships called car ferries to carry their rail cars. Milwaukee especially was interested in such ferries as a way to capture some rail

traffic, which had been dominated by its neighbor 90 miles to the south. However, none of the attempts to bypass Chicago by sea was very successful, and the problem of the bottleneck continued into the twenty-first century despite assorted attempts to correct it.[35]

Although the railroad car ferries on the lakes originated in 1857 in Buffalo, they did not appear on Lake Michigan for another 30 years, and then only as a device to connect the isolated upper peninsula of Michigan to the rest of the state without having to route the trains around the southern end of the lake and through Chicago. Three small railroads serving both peninsulas of Michigan in 1887 ordered and put into service the *St. Ignace*, an ice-breaking, single-ended wooden ferry fitted with railroad tracks, to haul freight cars across the Straits of Mackinac in what was essentially a local service connecting the two halves of the state.

The Toledo, Ann Arbor & North Michigan Railway in 1892 began cross-lake

This photograph, taken ca. 1910 in suburban West Chicago, shows the pattern of development typical in towns along the early railroads. The freight train on the left apparently was waiting for a commuter train shown on the right to begin its run to Chicago. Note the livestock pens along the tracks. The siding on the left containing two boxcars was part of the original line of the former Aurora Branch Railroad, later the Burlington Route. (West Chicago City Museum) regional ferry service in 1892 between Michigan's lower peninsula and points on its upper peninsula and in northern Wisconsin. Its initial vessel had four tracks and could carry 24 freight cars. It was the direct ancestor of the fleets of car ferries that plied the lake until 1983.[36]

The possibility of using even larger vessels to haul trains across the lake attracted the attention of several railroads interested in creating a bypass for through freight to avoid Chicago. The Flint & Pere Marquette Railroad, one of the Pere Marquette's predecessors, made arrangements in 1896 to connect with the Wisconsin Central at Manitowoc, Wisconsin, and built a 337-foot steel ferry capable of handling 30 cars. The vessel, the *Pere Marquette*, went into service the following year, and by the end of 1903 the railroad had five more ferries in service on routes to Kewaunee, Manitowoc, and Milwaukee.[37]

Officials of the Grand Trunk Railway noticed the success of the Ann Arbor and Pere Marquette ferries and got into that business in 1903 between Grand Haven, Michigan, and Milwaukee. The services, at least in the beginning, were considered successful because the trains were relatively short and would fit nicely on a single ferry: the Ann Arbor in the early 1900s was hauling 26,000 cars a year across the lake and claiming to make a profit on it. However, by the 1920s trains had grown to such a length that six voyages requiring two or three days were needed to get one long freight across the lake. The last surviving car ferry line, which was operated by the Chesapeake & Ohio Railroad, successor to the Pere Marquette, began a program of "controlled withdrawal" from the lakes completed in 1983. The C&O in 1963 had acquired the Baltimore & Ohio and its substantial rail plant in Chicago.[38]

Despite the attempted bypasses, the railroad stampede to Chicago continued in the second half of the nineteenth century and was transforming the city itself. Much of the fertile farmland south and west of the city was developed as railroad yards.

There were no less than 22 yards built in the city and suburbs in a 12-mile swath south of the Loop and 11 yards to the west—just for freight. None were built to the north.

The impact on Chicago's central business district was even greater as the century progressed. South of the downtown area a swath nearly a mile wide and a mile long covered with railroad yards extended from Clinton Street to the lake, interrupted only by a two-block corridor between State Street and Michigan Avenue that gave the city access to its South Side. Much of the land was used for passenger yards, but the Illinois Central maintained a large freight yard on the old Fort Dearborn military property on the south bank of the river at its mouth.

To the west of downtown as a number of western railroads moved their operations to Union and North Western stations, a similar two-mile-long swath of railroad yards appeared just west of the Chicago River's south branch, hampering ingress and egress to the Loop from the West Side. In the second half of the nineteenth century and until it built North Western station in 1911 on Canal Street west of the river, the North Western had freight and passenger tracks north of the main stem of the river as far east as the lake.

As the railroads' push to Chicago continued in the second half of the nineteenth century, the resulting development of their facilities and those of industries dependent upon them for transportation was largely unplanned. The city, which originally had a policy of discouraging railroad access to land within its municipal limits, responded on a piecemeal basis to successive appeals for more space for railroads. The collective impact of the railroads was greater than anyone in the growing port city in 1840 could have imagined. The railroads and their interface with each other and with shipping on the Great Lakes transformed Chicago into an industrial giant within a period of only 50 years.

Shaping Chicago

The railroads did not transform the Fort Dearborn outpost into a city—the waterways did that—but the iron horse accelerated Chicago's growth into one of the world's major metropolises within half a century. Chicago began 1848 as a bustling lake port with a population estimated at something over 20,000 persons. In 1893 it celebrated its emergence as a metropolis of more than a million inhabitants with the World's Columbian Exposition, an elaborate world's fair held in Jackson Park. The fair, which attracted more than 12 million people, was ostensibly a celebration, albeit a year late, of the four hundredth anniversary of Columbus's voyage of discovery to America in 1492, but in fact it was the host city's coming-out party.

The year of 1848 is a convenient, if not entirely accurate, boundary between preindustrial and industrial Chicago. Industrialization began somewhat earlier, but 1848 was the year the Illinois and Michigan Canal opened, the telegraph arrived, the city's first steam-powered grain elevator was completed, and the first railroad

McCormick's second factory, built on the Southwest Side, was dependent upon the railroads for transportation. (Wisconsin Historical Society)

commenced operation. The city in the nineteenth century before the arrival of the iron horse was primarily a destination for goods, although some local grain was shipped east beginning in the late 1830s. Ships that anchored beyond the mouth of the Chicago River, which at the time was not navigable for deep-water vessels, off-loaded pioneers from the East, their belongings, and an assortment of manufactures—clothing, lumber, and tools—that they would need to build homes and survive on the frontier. The earliest vessels also hauled such foodstuffs as pork, flour, whiskey, and tobacco.[1]

After 1848, Chicago became what transportation professionals call a break-bulk center, a place where commodities are transferred between modes and shipments are broken down into consignments or assembled for bulk movement. Although some modest manufacturing operations had already sprung up or moved to the city, the largest single source of employment in Chicago at midcentury involved the transfer of goods between ships, trains, and canal boats. As a result, the city's industry in 1850 lined the Chicago River and its branches. Its retail stores were further inland and its residences beyond that.

Along the river that served as the city's harbor, there were warehouses to break down for distribution the bulk cargos that arrived from the East on ships and grain elevators to assemble the cargos, primarily crops, harvested in the Middle West but destined to fill hungry stomachs on the Atlantic seaboard and in Europe. Cargo ships in the middle 1900s generally sailed only when they had a full hold; schedules were something for the passenger trade. Eastbound commodities in 1850 arrived in Chicago by canal boat, the city's sole railroad, and covered wagon. They, in turn, hauled back into the interior the manufactured goods that had come to Chicago aboard schooners and a few steamships.

Although it is a topic rarely covered in the historical literature, the existence and growth of what is known within the trans-portation industry as back haul contributed mightily to Chicago's ultimate growth and its ascendancy over assorted rivals as the transportation center of the American interior. Transportation systems work most efficiently and cheaply if they have cargo moving in relatively equal proportions in both directions. Thus the master of a tramp steamer or a gypsy trucker is always looking for a back haul to absorb the cost of a return trip with an empty hull or rig, and mass transit operators continually wrestle with the inherent inefficiencies of systems designed to move masses of people in one direction twice a day—rush hour.[2]

Chicago was in a considerably better position geographically than its rivals to develop multidirectional traffic. Cleveland, Detroit, and Toledo, although they developed as regional transportation centers, were situated too far east on the Great Lakes to take advantage of the settlement of the lush farming areas in Kansas, Nebraska, Iowa, Wisconsin, southern Minnesota, and Illinois in the 1850s and 1860s when the railroad-building boom began in those states. Cincinnati, Memphis, and St. Louis were river towns more dependent on the north-south steamboat trade in the Mississippi Valley than railroads during the same period. The territory that could be expected to fall under their economic suzerainty—southern Illinois and Indiana, Missouri, Arkansas, Kansas, and Oklahoma—was somewhat less fertile than the region that became linked by rail to Chicago. The Civil War not only disrupted river traffic to the port of New Orleans but had a dampening effect on railroad development in the border states. By the time the war ended and reconstruction got under way, Chicago had already attained a critical mass in the nation's railroad system.

Thus the development of Chicago was not only the result of the convergence of such factors as favorable geography, eastern and European capital, entrepreneurial spirit and boosterism, competition between rail and sail that kept rates below that of rival

Many of Chicago's earliest railroads were built as overland extensions of the Great Lakes maritime trade. This photograph, taken ca. 1880, shows a sail-to-rail interchange. Note the schooner masts in the background and ventilated cars for livestock at right. (Chicago Historical Society)

cities, and the arrival of the Industrial Revolution in the form of the steam engine, but also of the existence of a potential back haul that caused people who were building railroads to make sure their plans included a mainline to the southwestern corner of the Great Lakes. It was the back haul that in the third quarter of the nineteenth century gave Chicago its greatest advantage over its rivals in attracting railroads. Other cities had to induce railroads to build to their municipal limits; Chicago shortly after 1850 had begun to try to regulate, and in some cases discourage, railroad development.[3]

The city's efforts were for the most part unsuccessful as the railroads rolled into Chicago in the second half of the nineteenth century, resulting in unplanned development or development in which the municipal interests of Chicago took a back seat to the economic interests of the railroads. Much of the railroad building after the Civil War was in unincorporated areas beyond the city limits and annexed to Chicago during the great expansion of 1889, which increased the size of the city from almost 36 square miles to more than 179 square miles. For the most part the city responded to railroad proposals on a piecemeal basis, and where consolidations of railroad facilities occurred they were frequently the result of economic, not political, considerations.[4]

To a large extent the city's industrialization in the second half of the century can be measured by the availability of raw materials and the existence of a transportation system to move them. The grain and lumber trade moved through Chicago, but meat and steel were processed there, arriving as raw materials and leaving as semifinished products—sides of beef for the butcher shops in the East and pig iron or steel for the development of the West. Again, the synergy between rail and water that existed in Chicago was an important factor, as was the city's emergence as a rail junction. The Great Lakes allowed the cheap transportation of such heavy raw materials as iron ore and coal for hundreds of miles from mine to mill, and the railroads enabled the relatively inexpensive distribution of the finished products for a thousand miles or more. In the case of meat, the railroads were both the gatherers of the raw materials, and after a stop in Chicago for processing, their distributors. So both the meat-processing and steel industries gravitated to Chicago in the second half of the nineteenth century.

The volume and nature of Chicago's rail and maritime traffic to a large extent determined the pattern of the city's development. In 1846 before the Industrial Revolution occurred in the Midwest or at least while it was in its very early stages, Chicago's manufacturing industry was for the most part preoccupied with the local and regional markets. There were in Chicago that year 177 manufacturing businesses employing 1,400 persons, or 10 percent of the population, including 71 in foundries; 50 in tanneries; 46 in barrel-making operations; 61 in wagon shops; 190 in shoe shops; 59 in saddle and harness shops; 44 in cap and fur factories; 121 in tailor shops; 83 in furniture shops; 16 in candle, soap, and oil factories; and 250 in

packing houses. Within a decade, manufacturing employment exceeded 10,000, and by 1890 it was in excess of 203,000.[5]

By 1857 when Chicago was served by 10 railroads, a census of industrial employment indicated that twice as many people—2,866—worked in foundries making such things as iron, steam engines, and machinery, as had been in the entire industrial workforce in 1846. There were still plenty of factories geared to the local market, but plants making agricultural implements—a market extending hundreds of miles in every direction—employed 575 workers, and 351 people worked making brass and tin ware. By 1886, the city's iron and steel industry alone employed more than 19,000, and the agricultural implement industry employed 2,750.[6]

The Back Haul

Successful trading centers whether they were in ancient Mesopotamia, on the China coast, or on the nineteenth-century American frontier, were dependent upon two-way traffic. Cities often develop at the terminals of unilateral trade routes—mining towns, for example—but rarely survive for very long on a one-dish diet. The Near East and American West are smattered with ghost towns that died with their mines or because of a shift in trade routes in ancient or modern times, but Chicago survived the loss of its lumber trade in the nineteenth century and the demise of its grain trade and stockyards in the twentieth century. A major reason for its survival and continued prosperity was the network of man-made steel rails that radiated from the city in every direction. No rival city possessed such a network; so as the pattern of trade in commodities shifted over the years—the loss of export grain to the port of New Orleans in the late twentieth century, the exhaustion of the forests of Michigan and Wisconsin in the nineteenth century, and the migration of the meatpacking industry to small towns to be closer to the source of beef, for example—the railroads adapted to new commodities. Their tracks still pointed to Chicago, however.

Though it was (and still is) possible for an individual carrier, whether a caravan of camels or a railroad, to exist and prosper on traffic in one direction, its tariffs had to be relatively higher than a carrier that hauled goods in both directions. The one-way operator had to cover his fixed costs whether or not he had a back haul; the camels, ships, or locomotives had to be purchased in advance. When standing idle for lack of traffic or being ferried empty, they were not earning their owners any money or repaying the loans that had been used to buy them. The cost of building and maintaining track was the same whether a railroad had traffic in one direction or two, but it could be amortized in lower tariffs if the railroad hauled coal in one direction and lumber in the other. On the other hand, a one-way railroad had to amortize the entire cost of its track with the tariffs on the coal it hauled from mine to mill.

The railroads were a considerably more capital-intensive industry than their competitors on the water or stages and drays on land. A railroad in the middle of the nineteenth century could be built for as cheaply as $9,500 per mile if the land was flat and few river crossings were needed, but a schooner could be bought for $6,300 and a river steamboat for $9,073.[7] High fixed costs for such things as track, rights-of-way, locomotives, and cars that may have accounted for roughly two-thirds of a railroad's total transportation expenses had to be covered whether the railroad ran 1 train or 40 and whether the traffic ran in one direction or both. Although railroads with traffic that are concentrated in one direction, like the coal-hauling lines in the United States and England, have been successful, obviously it also is better for the railroad to run full trains in both directions than have half its trains run empty.[8]

Since financially successful trade routes are predicated on some sort of back haul, the voyageurs who in colonial times visited the Chicago portage in their canoes to trade with the Indian tribes carried manufactured wares and trinkets west and returned to Montreal with furs. As the fur trade declined in the early nineteenth century, trade with Fort Dearborn became a one-way proposition, with pioneers and their necessities, even foodstuffs, moving west but very little returning. However, by the late 1830s enough farmers had settled in the Chicago area that a trade in grain with eastern markets developed.

By midcentury Chicago was exporting to the East a considerable quantity of grain, giving the sailing and steamships on the Great Lakes a substantial back haul. The I&M Canal in 1850 was responsible for the transit of 417,000 bushels of wheat, 318,000 bushels of corn, and 5.7 million pounds of sugar, all primarily eastbound. Westbound canal traffic that year consisted of 10.4 million pounds of merchandise and 38.7 million board feet of lumber.[9]

Two years later, canal boats hauled almost 2.8 million bushels of grain to Chicago, and the city's only railroad, the Galena & Chicago Union, hauled an additional 1.9 million bushels. The two carriers combined also carried east nearly 800,000 pounds of wool, nearly 1.3 million pounds of hides, and considerable quantities of pork products and cured meats. They collectively hauled west more than 70 million board feet of lumber, 48 million pounds of merchandise, and 3.9 million pounds of iron. Thus Chicago by 1852 had become the city that historian William Cronon more than a century later dubbed "nature's metropolis"—a trading center dependent for the most part on harvests.[10]

The extent of the traffic in both directions on the Galena Railroad was something of a surprise. Richard P. Morgan, the engineer hired in 1847 to plan the city's first railroad, estimated that in its first year of operation a 182-mile line between Chicago and Galena would generate only about a quarter of its revenues from westbound traffic. However, by 1852 when the railroad had been built only as far as Rockford 92 miles west of Chicago, the railroad carried eastbound 1.9 million bushels of grain, 715,000 pounds of lead, and substantial quantities of wool, hides, pork, and cured meats. The westbound traffic included 21.6 million feet of lumber, 34 million pounds of manufactured merchandise, and 3.9 million pounds of iron.[11]

The bilateral traffic made the Galena Railroad profitable from its inception, and its early financial success undoubtedly influenced the organizers of the other railroads to make Chicago their terminal. Those included the trunk lines from the east as well as the granger lines fanning out to the south, north, and west. Again, the prospective back haul was a factor.

By 1859 when 10 railroads already were serving Chicago, 3 from the east and 7 from the other compass points, traffic was heavy in both directions. The canal and 7 granger lines hauled more than 15 million bushels of grain to Chicago that year—more than 12 million of them continuing east on the Great Lakes fleet. More than 297 million board feet of lumber arrived on ships, and 153 million feet of it continued inland on the granger railroads. By then Chicago, because of its rail network, was becoming a distribution center, and manufactured merchandise poured into (213.7 million pounds) and left (359.4 million pounds) the city in all directions. The city was also becoming an iron-making center, shipping 6.8 million pounds east on the lakes and 47.6 million pounds inland on the granger lines.[12]

Trading centers in ancient and modern times also reflected the nature of the commodities shipped through their gates. Since cargos on caravans, ships, or trains from one direction had to be broken down, sorted, and distributed to carriers heading in the other directions—the "breaking of bulk" as it is known in the transportation trade—markets developed in the trading centers. A cargo from one direction was sold piecemeal or in total to merchants intending to ship it elsewhere. In Chicago, grain from the hinterlands was assembled for bulk shipment to the east and lumber arriving in bulk from the north was sold, broken down, and sent to the hinterlands. The towering grain elevators along the river became the signature structures on Chicago's skyline, and lumberyards lined the riverbanks.

Because of the system of lakes, canals, and railroads that served the city, it soon became more economical and practical to haul raw materials to Chicago and turn them into manufactured products. The railroads provided the city with an excellent distribution system. The meatpacking, manufacturing, and distribution industries that developed on a large scale in Chicago later in the century did so to a great extent because by then, the city's well-developed railroad network offered them wide and fast access to both raw materials and markets. Dressed and processed meats gained in importance as the railroads fanned out to the west. Ultimately, steel, machinery, an array of manufactured wares, package freight, and dry goods became major railroad shippers as new industries moved to Chicago or, in the case of distributors and catalogue merchandise, evolved in the Windy City.

The railroads also contributed significantly to the rise of modern electronic communications by providing not only a major market for the new telegraph but the rights-of-way for its lines. The telegraph in the mid-nineteenth century not only provided a method for the instantaneous transmittal of information crucial to the growing stock and commodities markets but made it possible for average citizens to send short but urgent, albeit expensive, messages to business associates or relatives in far-flung places, including such things as purchase orders, the wiring of funds, news dispatches, and announcements of births and deaths. The local railroad station in many towns functioned as the telegraph office.[13]

Golden Grain

Passengers, mail, merchandise, and grain were the most important early cargos hauled by railroads in Chicago, a factor that put pressure on the early lines to operate with greater speed and on tighter schedules than their competitors on land or water. Coal was the cargo most responsible for the development of earliest railroads in Britain, but grain was the most important commodity to Chicago's first railroads, built as they were as extensions of the Great Lakes maritime routes. Lumber, the other major commodity important to Chicago's early economy, was somewhat less time sensitive than grain because it had to be cut and dried before it could be used for construction. But wheat, the principal grain grown in the central Midwest before it was displaced by corn and soybeans, would rot if improperly stored or stored too long. On the eve of the Civil War wheat accounted for 60 percent of the four major grains (also including corn, oats, and barley) hauled to Chicago on the western railroads.[14]

Grains were also subject to wide fluctuations in price, so their shippers were far more demanding than were shippers of minerals, for which the cost of transportation, not time of transit, was the major consideration. Grains' transportation in bulk from farm to market gave rise to a whole new industry to regulate that market. Chicago's Board of Trade was founded in 1848, although it did not assume its roles as the trader and regulator of grains until later.

Before the advent of railroads, grain was typically sold by a farmer to a local general merchant, who had it bagged and sent by flatboat or steamboat to the grain market in the nearest city. The bags were then opened for inspection, and, if the grain was not intended for the local market it was turned over to commission brokers to arrange for shipment to New York or New Orleans. On the rivers, bags were used because they made for easy, if inefficient, transfer between boats and ships on the long journey. On the lakes, grain was not bagged but loaded and unloaded in bulk, using boxes with handles for easier carrying and shovels.[15]

The system changed very quickly in the 1850s after the railroad appeared. Shippers began to think in terms of railroad carloads of 325 bushels instead of bags, and the development of powered elevators to handle grain in bulk meant that the products of many different farms had to be mixed together, requiring weight and grading standards. That was developed by the Board of Trade to eliminate frequent reinspections and to enable transmission by long-distance telegraph to the sight-unseen sale of known measures of grain. By 1856 the Board of Trade began arranging long-distance contracts between buyers and sellers, permitting the speculation that has persisted in commodities markets into the twenty-first century.

Within a few years in the 1850s, the development of the railroad transformed Chicago into what was the world's most efficient grain market. By 1954, Chicago, with 3 million bushels handled annually, had surpassed St. Louis (at 2.1 million bushels) as the principal grain market of the interior. By 1856, due largely to the combined efficiencies of the railroads, Chicago's 12 grain elevators, and the relatively large hold capacities of Great Lakes ships, wheat could be handled at a cost of a half cent a bushel, contrasted to the nickel-per-bushel cost of the hand transfer of bags still in use along the St. Louis levy.[16]

Lumber

The grain market alone would have sustained a railroad network radiating from Chicago but probably not much larger than those of any of the other midwestern cities. The development of the back haul in lumber made those radiating lines almost instantly profitable and erased much of the reluctance, evident since the Panic of 1837, of eastern and European investors to finance them. Grain was hauled east-ward to port, and lumber flowed west across the prairie.

In the case of the new railroads radiat-ing west from Chicago, the principal source of their freight revenue was ex-pected to be grain, a highly seasonal com-modity that moved from west to east. There was some westbound movement of passengers and manufactured goods, but not enough to offset the excess capacity the railroads would have if they built and maintained their physical plant and rolling stock solely for the autumnal grain trade. Because Chicago sat on the bound-ary of the great American prairie that stretched for more than a thousand miles west to the Rocky Mountains and the for-est that stretched east almost that far to the Atlantic Ocean, the city's railroads be-came the vehicle for a westbound lumber trade. The forests of Michigan and Wiscon-sin were cut, shipped to Chicago's huge lumber market on Great Lakes schooners, and sent west by rail to build the settle-ments on the treeless prairies. In fact, rail-road historian Albro Martin has argued that settlement of the prairie would have been impossible without an inexpensive form of transportation like the railroad.[17]

The westbound lumber trade from Chicago during the second half of the nineteenth century before the forests were exhausted was substantial. Chicago shipped 220 million board feet of lumber by 1860, a total of 580 million board feet by 1870, and more than a billion board feet by 1880—95 percent of it by rail.

Meat

The rise of the meatpacking industry in Chicago after the Civil War was attribut-able largely to the rail junction that had emerged there a decade earlier. The west-ern railroads fanned out from Chicago across the Great Plains, gathering the har-vest in beef and hogs, which were shipped to the Windy City's giant Southwest Side abattoirs. Their dressed carcasses were then shipped to market on the railroad network that fanned out to the east. It was a rail-road monopoly because the waterways, which provided a competitive downward pressure on rates of other commodities, were too slow to compete and did not have the facilities to feed and water the livestock on their journey to Chicago or refrigerate the carcasses on the trip east. However, it was competition among the railroads themselves that held down the rate tariffs on meat.[18]

There is no clearer indication of Chicago's emergence as the principal rail junction and manufacturing center of the interior than the 1864 decision by nine railroads and the Chicago Pork Packer's As-sociation to form the Union Stock Yard and Terminal Company to consolidate all of the city's stockyards into a $1 million, half-mile-square livestock interchange south-west of the city limits. The stockyards as originally designed had little to do with Chicago's then-evolving meatpacking in-dustry but were intended to be a giant transfer center between eastern and west-ern railroads for livestock moving across the country. However, the development of the refrigerated railroad car within a few years made possible the development of the city's meatpacking industry around the stockyards. Live animals arrived in Chicago in stock cars, were slaughtered in the pack-ing houses, and were sent east as dressed meat in insulated cars cooled by ice. In 1871, 530,544 cattle and 2.3 million hogs arrived in Chicago by train, and 169.5 mil-lion pounds of fresh and cured meat was shipped by rail, primarily to the East. By the end of the century, Chicago's abattoirs were slaughtering more than 3 million cat-tle annually and the packing industry's trade in beef, cattle, and hogs required a fleet of nearly 300,000 stock cars.[19]

The meatpacking industry did not de-velop in Chicago, but it moved there to be at the epicenter of what was develop-ing as the nation's freight transportation center. Because pork could be preserved by salting and pickling before refrigera-

Chicago's Union Stock Yards, shown here ca. 1909, was a joint venture between the railroads. It was a giant rail yard surrounded by live-stock pens and, somewhat later, abattoirs. Note the train in the background.

tion was developed, Chicago became a regional pork-packing center that by the time of the Civil War surpassed Cincinnati in production. The mass disassembly techniques developed for pork-butchering in Cincinnati were quickly adopted in Chicago, and by 1858 Chicago firms were using ice cut from ponds in winter to preserve some fresh pork for local consumption in summer.[20]

However, beef was not as easily preserved and was usually driven in herds or shipped live by railroad to be slaughtered for regional markets in the East. The toll on cattle in terms of death and weight loss was substantial despite the development of ventilated livestock cars, however. Detroit packer George H. Hammond shipped dressed beef carcasses by refrigerated rail car to Boston as early as 1868, and shortly thereafter he moved his operations to what is today Chicago's southern suburb of Hammond, Indiana, to be closer to the supply of live cattle. Philip D. Armour arrived in Chicago in 1875, moving his meat business from Milwaukee, and the same

year Gustavus F. Swift shifted his meat-packing operation from Boston.[21]

By the time Hammond arrived, Chicago's Union Stock Yard was in operation as a rail transfer station, but as late as 1871 only about 4 percent of the cattle that were received by the stockyards were slaughtered in Chicago. However, Hammond was already dabbling with ice-cooled rail cars, and within four years Swift was experimenting with the shipment of refrigerated, dressed beef from Chicago slaughterhouses to eastern cities. The vehicle he used was an adaptation by Arnold W. Zimmerman, of Zimmerman Ventilated Car Co. of Chicago. It was a railway boxcar that was equipped with insulation, an internal ventilation system, and chambers at either end for the storage of ice.[22]

Swift successfully overcame resistance by eastern packers by underselling them, primarily because he could mass-produce beef and eliminate the shipping charge on the 45 percent of every carcass, primarily bone, that was inedible. By building his own fleet of refrigerator cars and icehouses along the route, he also overcame the reluctance of the railroads to haul dressed beef because they had already invested in stockcars for live cattle. The extremely competitive nature of the railroad industry was his ally. When the eastern railroads conspired to charge a differential rate at which live beef traveled at 57 percent of the rate for dressed beef, the Grand Trunk (formerly Great Western) Railroad unilaterally reduced its dressed beef charges to get Swift's business, and a rate war ensued. By the late 1880s, Chicago, by virtue of its position at the nucleus of the nation's railroad network, dominated eastern consumer markets for both dressed beef and live western cattle.[23]

Manufacturing

By then, the developing Industrial Revolution had also turned the city into a manufacturing center in which the railroads played an important, though not dominant, role. Cyrus McCormick relocated his mechanical harvester manufacturing operation from Virginia to Chicago in 1845 to be closer to the developing agricultural markets. A significant factor in McCormick's selection of Chicago was its water and impending rail transportation. The railroad network that developed enabled him to establish a distribution system that within a few years made him one of the dominant manufacturers in the farm machinery industry.[24]

Before the Civil War the Chicago rail junction had become a center for the nation's emerging agricultural manufacturing industry although its plants were scattered across the nation. The city in 1859 was selected by the U.S. Agricultural Society as the site for the Seventh Annual United States Fair and Agricultural Convention, an event best remembered because it featured a plowing contest between two huge steam-powered plows.[25]

The rapid expansion of railroads in all directions from Chicago also created a market for steel rail that helped establish Chicago as a steelmaking center after the Civil War. The iron industry in Chicago originally consisted principally of importers and distributors. Joseph T. Ryerson in 1842 set up shop in a building along the Chicago River as an agent for a Pennsylvania iron master. He later broke away, forming his own company, and it became a major steel distributor before the end of the century. Seeing a developing market for iron rails because of the railroad-building boom, Eber B. Ward in 1857 moved to Chicago from Detroit and established the Chicago Rolling Mills to reroll iron bars into rail. Finally, the discovery of deposits of iron ore on the shores of Lake Superior in the 1850s, the availability of cheap transportation for both ore and coal, and the expanding market for rail combined to create the city's steel industry.[26]

A group of businessmen in 1868 organized Chicago Iron Company with blast furnaces capable of producing 40 tons of pig iron a day, and two years later Chicago Rolling Mills built two furnaces. The rolling mills ultimately became the Illinois Steel Corporation, which in 1901 was assembled into the giant United States Steel Company by financier J. P. Morgan. In 1880, the predecessor company had outgrown its local facilities and built on the banks of the Calumet River a huge mill that ultimately employed 20,000 people. By then, Illinois ranked fourth in the nation in iron and steel production with almost 418,000 tons, and the city had more than 600 companies employing 17,000 persons involved in some sort of iron or steel manufacture.

The principal fuel for industry in the second half of the nineteenth century in America was coal; without it, manufacturing plants were relegated to sites along rivers where water power could be used, an option that was not available to marshy Chicago. In fact, it has been argued that the Industrial Revolution in the United States was delayed until the middle of the nineteenth century by the lack of adequate fuel and lack of an effective market for goods because the primitive state of inland transportation limited markets to a regional or a local nature. Wood was burned in early steam engines but was not very efficient. As the development of anthracite mines in the East led to the Industrial Revolution there, vast soft coal deposits under Illinois provided industrializing Chicago with a source of fuel for heating, and its location on the Great Lakes enabled it to receive eastern industrial coal at reasonable expense. By 1871, the city was consuming nearly a million tons of coal, nearly half of it arriving by ship, and within 14 years it was consuming almost 6 million tons and shipping nearly a million tons elsewhere.[27]

The Illinois Central, which in its earliest years was principally a grain-hauling granger railroad, by 1860 was hauling 61,000 tons of coal, the soft Illinois variety suitable for heating and steam generation but not steelmaking. The railroad also converted its fleet of wood-burning locomotives to coal in the 1860s. Coal traffic on the IC had tripled by 1870, and by 1900 it hauled 5.7 million tons. The other granger roads were not so blessed. The North Western, successor to the Galena & Chicago Union, as late as 1875 owned only 84 coal cars in its fleet of nearly 7,800 vehicles.[28]

The manufacture of finished products, especially heavy machinery, also grew with the city's rail system. When Cyrus McCormick moved his agricultural machinery manufacturing operation to Chicago in mid-1847, the site he selected for his first factory was on the banks of the Chicago

Cyrus McCormick's original reaper works on the north side of the Chicago River at Lake Michigan obtained rail service shortly after it was built in 1847. (Wisconsin Historical Society)

River near its mouth. Water transport, not water power, seems to have been the primary consideration in picking the site. McCormick bought a 10-horsepower steam engine to run his machinery. The Chicago River was too sluggish to drive water wheels, and the marshland on which the city was built obviated the building of mill races.[29]

McCormick's first plant employed 33 persons and had a capacity for building 500 mechanical reapers per year for the growing market in the Midwest. The problem of getting his reapers from factory to farm became easier the following year when the I&M Canal opened and somewhat later when Galena & Chicago Union built a branch line to the plant. However, after the Chicago Fire of 1871, McCormick built his replacement plant employing 8,000 workers and capable of producing 55,000 machines a year on a site on the Southwest Side of Chicago that was served predominantly by railroads.[30]

Possibly the most dramatic growth of any Chicago industry that can be traced directly to the emergence of the railroad system is what is known today as distribution and wholesaling but in the mid-nineteenth century was known as jobbing. Before 1850, frontier merchants had to travel once a year to wholesalers on the East Coast to restock, but jobbers began to move west with the railroad and telegraph. Again, Chicago's development as a railroad terminal made it an excellent site for distributors of manufactured goods—everything from clothing to tools and machinery—and by 1866 Chicago had 59 jobbers each with sales of more than $1 million a year, contrasted to 15 apiece in St. Louis and Cincinnati. Among the largest were the partnership of Marshall Field, Levi Leiter, and Potter Palmer, which had $9.1 million in sales in 1867, and James V. Farrell and Company, which had a sales volume of $7.1 million that year.[31]

Eventually in the 1880s mail-order houses, which were almost totally dependent upon rail transportation, emerged. Instead of going to a local store to order

goods, farm families in Iowa and Nebraska could peruse a catalogue sent to their door, place an order by mail, and have the goods delivered to their home. The nation's catalogue house giants—Montgomery Ward & Company and Sears, Roebuck & Company—both originated in Chicago in 1872 and 1887, respectively. The furniture store founded in the city in 1865 by Joseph Spiegel began in 1905 to transform itself into a catalogue house specializing in women's fashions.

The Outward Migration

The industrial growth, especially after the fire of 1871, resulted in an expansion of industry to outlying parts of the city and into some suburbs. Industrial decentralization along railroad lines began after the fire. Land along the downtown river and its branches had become premium and for the most part was taken up by the existing businesses—such things as lumberyards, grain elevators, and warehouses—dependent upon the rail-water interchange. Companies building huge new factories looked to cheap land in outlying areas. Although the new factories generally clung to the waterways like the Calumet River and I&M Canal, the simultaneous growth of the railroad network gave industry greater flexibility as to where to locate. The development late in the century of electric motors to drive machinery also freed factories from the reliance on large stationary steam engines and the need to have water transport for coal deliveries.[32]

Thus the steel industry migrated to the Calumet River 11 miles south of downtown Chicago to build its new mills, and McCormick rebuilt his reaper plant to a site at 22nd Street and Western Avenue, about 4 1/2 miles southwest of the original factory near the mouth of Chicago River. The new plant was north of the canal and was served mainly by railroads. Even industries that were not affected by the fire chose outlying sites. The meatpacking plants were built around the rail-

By the end of the nineteenth century the major railroad lines in Chicago were lined with industry as the railroads supplemented ships and canal boats as the major carriers of all but bulk commodities. Industrial decentralization along the tracks began after the Chicago Fire.

dominated stockyards four miles southwest of downtown, and George Pullman chose the area just west of Lake Calumet for his rail car–manufacturing operation. The Central Manufacturing District was organized in 1890 on land north of the stockyards, and lumber magnate Turlington Harvey developed the industrial south suburb that bears his name in the last decade of the century.[33] By the end of the nineteenth century the major rail lines radiating from downtown Chicago were lined with industry.

The Corporation

One of the railroad industry's strongest influences on Chicago, although it was not so obvious because there was no brick and mortar involved, was on corporate governance: it was the prototype of the modern corporation. The incorporated stock company was devised by the British in the sixteenth century to promote overseas trade and colonization. However, except for John Jacob Astor's American Fur Company, which maintained an outlet at the Fort Dearborn settlement, that corporate form of governance was essentially unknown in Chicago before William B. Ogden and his partners settled on it as a way to finance the revival of the moribund Galena & Chicago Union charter. Chicago's first railroad was also its first important corporation and became the model for those that followed.[34]

Until the advent of the railroads, the typical business organization was the partnership, or, more commonly, the family enterprise. The building of high-cost transportation systems, such as the canal network, was typically arranged by government, although the boats that used them were owned individually or in partnership, as were the steamboats on the rivers, the ships on the lakes, and the stagecoaches and drays on the highways. However, the high up-front capital costs required to build railroads and the organizations necessary to manage them required something new. Thus the incorporated stock company came into widespread use to build and run railroads.[35]

The railroads, which required a substantial amount of start-up capital for acquisition of right-of-way, construction of track, and purchase of locomotives and rolling stock a year or more before the first revenues began to flow, at first were treated as state-financed public works projects. When that system proved infeasible after the Panic of 1837, the states resorted to issuing charters to private promoters of railroads. The railroads in turn formed corporations to sell stocks and bonds to the public to raise capital. Ultimately as companies in other industries grew beyond the capability of their individual owners to finance expansion, they adopted the railroad model and incorporated as stock companies.

The very nature of corporate organization in which a board or committee was required to oversee the interests of investors, but did not have the time or expertise to run a complex business scattered over hundreds of miles, required railroads very early in their existence to develop professional managers. The separation of directors and professional staff in publicly held corporations is considered commonplace in the twentieth century, but in the first half of the nineteenth century companies were typically run by their owners and members of their family.[36]

The evolution of the corporate professional staff typically started with an engineer hired to build the railroad, a legacy from the canal era. He was very quickly joined by someone hired to operate the new railroad, and in short order was joined by specialists in freight and passenger service, traffic, maintenance of way, cars and locomotives, finance, law, and marketing.

One of the most obvious influences the railroads had on the Chicago area was in the creation of the suburbs. Chicago was a port and managed to attract population and some industry before the rails reached it, but except for the canal towns of Lemont and Lockport, the suburbs that arose in the second half of the nineteenth century were almost totally creatures of the railroads. The suburban sprawl that dominated the metropolitan area in the twentieth century is in the public's mind the result of the automobile, but nearly a century before it became an effective and widely used method of commuting, the railroads began to develop settlements at outlying mileposts along their lines, or in many cases houses began to spring up near the train depots in farm communities. As the speed and efficiency of train travel increased, those settlements evolved into suburbs.

The Suburbs

The desire by those who could afford it to escape the crowded industrial port city to cottages in the country began very early in Chicago's existence, and within a few years the arrival of the railroads made daily commuting possible. The immigrant laborers who crowded into bungalows and three-flats in the city tolerated the smells and pollution of the stockyards and steel mills because that is where they earned their living. But the emerging middle class—the accountants who kept the books and managers who ran the factories—left the city to more pleasant surroundings in which to raise their families as soon as it became possible to do so.

Suburbanization began along the steam railroads. However, within a few years the building of street railways encouraged suburban growth along their lines, as did the erection of the elevated railways toward the end of the century. At first, much of the travel on the suburban lines was to weekend and summer resorts, such as Hyde Park. Somewhat later commercial parks like Ravinia on the North Shore and

Almost from their inception in Chicago, passenger trains were popular for excursions in the countryside, and some railroads ran their own amusement parks. This North Western picnic train was photographed in 1898 in Austin, then a suburb, which was later annexed to Chicago. (Krambles-Peterson Archive)

The Dunes Beaches

By the
SOUTH SHORE LINE

Trains from Chicago operated over Illinois Central R.R.
from Randolph, Van Buren, 12 TH, 43 RD, 53 RD & 63 RD St. Stations.

Commuter railroads often promoted the recreational amenities available in the suburbs. This 1925 poster promoted the South Shore's trips to the Indiana Dunes along the Lake Michigan shore.

sanitation at times seemed to influence outward migration. These were interrupted by periodic economic downturns that put the brakes on suburban growth. Suburbanization ground to a standstill during the Great Depression and World War II, for example. Some suburban corridors—primarily those in which railroads were built before the Civil War—were developing by the 1880s, but off-railroad suburbs did not blossom until the 1960s after a network of express highways had been built.

The region had a well-developed system of 10 railroads radiating from downtown Chicago before the advent of the Civil War, and that infrastructure was the nucleus of a commuter railroad system that persisted into the twenty-first century. The first spurt in the development of Chicago's suburbs occurred in the 30-year period following the Civil War and was related to the existence of the city's street and steam railroad lines. The second suburban migration followed the building of electric railways, both elevated and interurban, for a 30-year period after the turn of the century. Following a 15-year interruption during the Depression and World War II, the third wave occurred in the 50 years following the war and was primarily influenced by the automobile and highways. It tended to fill in the gaps between the rail corridors.

Finally in the late twentieth century suburbanization had devolved into a decentralized, largely unplanned suburban sprawl into rural areas. However, as the difficulty of commuting by automobile increased due to highway congestion, the old railroad suburbs enjoyed something of a revival, erecting multistory apartment buildings in their central business districts near the depots to concentrate a captive market along their transit lines.

Although a few suburbs, primarily Hyde Park and Evanston, traced their origins to the 1850s, the first notable suburban growth began shortly after the Civil War in an eight-mile radius of downtown Chicago. It gradually radiated outward

Batavia on the Fox River attracted daytime excursions from the city. However, as the speed, reliability, and comfort of railroad travel increased, Chicagoans found it possible to live year-round in the suburbs and commute to and from work.

The development of Chicago's suburbs was not a continuous phenomenon but one punctuated by events that encouraged or retarded outward migrations. Cataclysmic events such as the rash of devastating fires in Chicago in the early 1870s and sporadic epidemics attributed to poor principally along five steam railroad lines—three operated by the Chicago & North Western System to the north, northwest, and west of Chicago; one operated by the Chicago, Burlington & Quincy to the west; and the Illinois Central line to the south. Development along the Rock Island line to the southwest of Chicago; the Milwaukee Road lines to the north and northwest; the Chicago & Alton line parallel to the Illinois and Michigan Canal; and the Wabash line to the southwest occurred at a somewhat slower pace. Several other railroads operated commuter service on a smaller scale, including the New York Central to Elkhart, Indiana; the Pennsylvania Railroad to Valparaiso, Indiana; the Erie Railroad to Rochester, Indiana; the Illinois Central on a line west to Addison; and the Chicago Great Western to Ingleton. But they never generated sufficient traffic to continue in operation and eventually were abandoned.

The first wave of suburban growth just after the Civil War involved many communities—Oakland, Kenwood, and Hyde Park along the Illinois Central and Rosehill and Wright's Grove on the Chicago & Milwaukee—that originally were suburbs but eventually were annexed to Chicago. Except for their early development, they more properly belong in a history of the city's street and elevated railway system. By the end of the twentieth century, only the steam railroad stations at Hyde Park on the Illinois Central and Ravenswood and Rogers Park on the former Chicago & Milwaukee had sizeable ridership. Ridership at the other six IC stations on Chicago's south lakefront between 18th and 83rd streets was negligible.[1]

Excluding the towns along the I&M Canal, like Lockport, and the satellite cities more than 30 miles from Chicago (Joliet, Aurora, Elgin, and Waukegan), on the eve of the Civil War there were only two

The Wabash Railroad, pictured here at Palos Park in 1934, used hand-me-down locomotives from mainline service to pull commuter trains. (Krambles-Peterson Archive)

incorporated communities situated more than eight miles from Chicago along rail lines. Those towns of Evanston and Wheaton combined had a population of about 3,000. There were many more small settlements scattered along the railroads, but they would not grow large enough to incorporate for decades. An 1874 atlas of DuPage County, for example, showed 19 settled communities along the 3 railroad lines from Chicago, only 4 of which were incorporated.[2]

By 1880, there were 20 incorporated municipalities 8 miles or more from Chicago along 7 rail lines, and they had a combined population approaching 20,000. Suburbs within an eight-mile ring around Chicago, with the possible exception of those along the Illinois Central Railroad, were more influenced by the explosion in street and elevated railway construction in the second half of the century than they were by anything the steam railroads did. Nevertheless, the railroad suburbs more than doubled in size in the next decade and then doubled again before the end of the century. The number of municipalities in the steam railroad corridors increased to 26 with a combined population of 42,157 by 1890, and at the turn of the century there were 37 municipalities with a combined population of more than 89,000.[3]

Everett Chamberlin's 1874 book *Chicago and Its Suburbs* contains brief profiles of a number of outlying towns—actually a motley collection of summer resorts, farm towns, exurbs, true suburbs, and satellite cities lumped together and categorized by the term *suburbia.* More important, railroad passenger schedules in the 1880s show a pattern of short-distance trains timed to carry people into the city in the morning and out in the afternoon.

Historian Ann Durkin Keating exhaustively traced the development of suburbs in Cook County in her 1988 book *Building Chicago,* and further refinement of her maps and tables, as well as census data and state incorporation records, shows a pattern of development as it relates to the re-

gion's transportation network. Keating identified 10 major Cook County settlements outside of Chicago from the arrival of the first pioneers in 1831 until 1840—Blue Island, Calumet, and Thornton to the south; Brighton, Summit, Lyons, and Willow Springs to the southwest; Niles and Wheeling to the northwest; and Gross Point (the future Wilmette) to the north.[4]

The 10 communities were predominantly agricultural in nature, located along trails leading to and from Chicago, and with one exception were widely scattered. The only pattern of development that even remotely could be called a corridor existed to the southwest, where Brighton, Lyons, Summit, and Willow Springs were strung out along the old Checagou canoe portage and future (by then platted) route of the Illinois and Michigan Canal. None of the communities attained sufficient population to seek incorporation until 1872, and two (Brighton near the site of the future Union Stock Yards and Calumet on the lake by that name) were eventually annexed to Chicago.[5]

The first railroads began arriving between 1848 and 1860, and within a few years had indelibly stamped their influence on the pattern of suburban development. By 1860, 22 new suburban communities had sprung up in what would become suburban Cook County, and although agriculture was still the predominant economic base, accounting for nearly 55 percent of the discernible firms in those communities, a category Keating identified as "commuter services" accounted for almost a third of the businesses in the new towns. That category included such things as offices specializing in real estate, insurance, legal services, architecture, and engineering; tradesmen and contractors; and specialty shops dealing in such things as dry goods. Industry—primarily foundries, building materials, and manufacturing—accounted for slightly less than 10 percent of the development in the suburbs.[6]

The development pattern of those new communities was clearly along corridors

Some suburbs were developed as residential communities from the start. Others, like Mount Prospect, pictured here in 1882, began as farm towns and eventually developed into suburbs. (Mount Prospect Historical Society)

formed by the railroad lines to the north, northwest, and south of the city. In fact, 16 of the 22 communities had sprung up along three rail corridors. Oakland, Kenwood, Hyde Park, and Grand Crossing, all later annexed to Chicago, as well as Homewood and Matteson, had emerged along the Illinois Central Railroad to the south of Chicago. Wright's Grove (the future Lincoln Park neighborhood of Chicago), Rose Hill (the future Rogers Park neighborhood), Evanston, and Winnetka had appeared along what would become the Chicago & North Western's north division but was then called the Chicago & Milwaukee Railroad. The North Western's northwest division included the new suburbs of Jefferson (later Jefferson Park in Chicago), Des Plaines, Arlington Heights, Palatine, and Barrington. Settlement had begun in Oak Park, then part of Cicero Township but later an independent village, along the Galena & Chicago Union Railroad that later would be merged into the North Western system. Although the future northwestern suburbs were predominantly agricultural, commuter-related businesses were clearly evident in the

northern and southern corridors. Grand Crossing, where the Illinois Central crossed a number of other railroads, was primarily industrial.[7]

After the Civil War the development and growth of the suburbs of Chicago occurred in several distinct waves influenced by such factors as improvement in railroad technology—faster locomotives and bigger coaches that made commuting longer distances quicker and more comfortable. A series of major fires in Chicago in the autumn of 1871, which destroyed much of the city's housing and created a market for cottages in the country away from the urban congestion; aggressive marketing by assorted suburban land developers; and industrial development that resulted in the creation of a middle class with the financial wherewithal to afford the suburban lifestyle were also factors.[8]

Kenneth T. Jackson and Robert Fishman, two historians who have written extensively on the suburban phenomenon, traced the concept of the suburb as a bedroom community of cottages to eighteenth-century England before the advent of railroads. The appearance of the suburb in the United States before the Civil War was influenced primarily by four individuals, two of whom wrote extensively on the virtues of living in a cottage in the country and two who designed such villages. Catharine Beecher, sister of famed nineteenth-century clergyman Henry Ward Beecher and author Harriet Beecher Stowe *(Uncle Tom's Cabin)*, was a feminist who in 1841 wrote *Treatise on Domestic Economy, For the Use of Young Ladies at Home and School.* In that book she extolled the virtues of family life in a semi-rural cottage. Andrew Jackson Downing, a landscape gardener and editor of the *Horticulturist* periodical also wrote of such an idyllic lifestyle. Calvert Vaux, a landscape architect and Downing disciple, and Frederick Law Olmsted, Vaux's partner, began in the 1850s to design planned suburbs that were dominated by detached, single-family homes built on landscaped lots that surrounded a commuter railroad station. Riverside on the Chicago, Burlington & Quincy Railroad 11 miles west of Chicago[9] was perhaps their most influential suburb.[10]

Although the development of other suburbs in the region showed some degree of planning, none was laid out from scratch with the degree of forethought that went into Riverside. From its inception, Riverside was intended as a bedroom of Chicago—a community of cottages in the country that would have pleased Beecher and Downing. Fishman described it as the "ultimate bourgeois utopia." Instead of having the usual grid pattern of streets typical of most suburbs, Riverside was designed by Olmsted with curved streets from which the single-family homes were set back at least 30 feet. More than 40 percent of the community was set aside for open or common space.[11]

The project that developer E. E. Childs and his partners picked Olmsted to plan just after the Civil War was a 1,600-acre tract of low-lying land along the banks of the Des Plaines River. The site was not conveniently accessible to Chicago except by

the Burlington Railroad; the old stagecoach route along Ogden Avenue skirted Riverside to the south and was little more than a dirt road following the course of the Potawatomi Indian trail that forded the Des Plaines River. The I&M Canal was to the south of that. The key to the success of the Riverside project was getting the Burlington to build a depot, which the railroad dutifully did. By 1869 it had begun to put on suburban trains, the primary purpose of which was to carry commuters to Chicago in the morning and home at night.[12]

However, the Riverside Land Improvement Company's project was not immediately successful. The company built a hotel on the banks of the river to serve as both a resort and a place for potential customers to stay, and although the Riverside Hotel was filled to capacity with refugees after the Chicago Fire in 1871, land sales lagged and the company that had spent $3 million on developing the suburb slipped into bankruptcy after the Panic of 1873. Keating notes that Chicagoans looking for a more suburban setting after the fire tended to buy homes in the suburb of Ravenswood (annexed to Chicago in 1889) 6.5 miles north of downtown rather than in Riverside, nearly twice that distance. Riverside in 1880 had a population of only 450, and by 1900 that had grown to only 1,551.[13]

More typical of the suburbs that sprang up around Chicago were the industrial satellites that developed almost contemporaneously with the big city, summer resort communities that eventually acquired a year-round commuting population, farm towns that gradually evolved into suburbs by virtue of their locations along railroads, and largely unplanned subdivisions that developers and land speculators hurriedly built in rail corridors to take advantage of the outward migration of the middle class after the Chicago Fire. Most such suburbs were largely unplanned, laid out like Chicago on a grid pattern, and contained a *(right)* Suburban depots varied considerably in style. This simple structure was photographed in 1874 in what is today Park Ridge. (Krambles-Peterson Archive)

(left) The Illinois Central's suburban station at Bryn Mawr, shown in 1896, was a rather elaborate structure with a mansard roof.

(below) The North Western's Woodstock depot was a wood-frame structure in 1913, typical of railroad stations across the nation. Note the Auburn touring car in the foreground. (Michael Brown)

When they appeared on the suburban scene after 1900, the electric interurban railroads sometimes used storefront stations. This Aurora, Elgin & Chicago (later Chicago, Aurora & Elgin) station occupied part of the Elgin Opera House. (Chicago Historical Society)

mixture of commuter-oriented, agricultural, industrial, and local market-based businesses. Few were strictly bedroom communities.[14]

The satellite cities included Joliet, Aurora, Elgin, and Waukegan, which developed along waterways because of the availability of either water power, in the case of Aurora and Elgin on the Fox River, or waterborne transportation, in the case of Joliet on the I&M Canal, and Waukegan, a lake port. All of the satellites eventually were absorbed into Chicago's suburban sphere by virtue of their rail connections. Waukegan and Joliet embraced the con-

struction of the Chicago & Milwaukee and Rock Island lines, respectively, to serve them. Aurora promoters built their own railroad to get access to Chicago. Elgin was a stop on the Galena Railroad.[15]

The emergence of a group of adjacent communities in DuPage County about twenty-five miles west of Chicago is a good example of the influence of the railroads on suburban development in the nineteenth century. Naperville was originally settled by several pioneer families in 1831 along the west branch of the DuPage River, which was not navigable and was little more than a creek with sufficient wa-

ter flow to power gristmills like that of set-
tler Joseph Naper. Within the decade
Naperville had become a prosperous farm
town of 180 inhabitants, a stop on the
stagecoach lines leading west from
Chicago, and the county seat. The community's leaders in the 1840s invested in
the construction of a plank road west from
Chicago to Naperville, and the existence of
that road was a factor in the decision by
Naper to decline a request of the organizers of the Galena & Chicago Union Railroad in 1847–1848 to route their line
through the town.[16]

The adjacent community of Warrenville a few miles north of Naperville on
the west DuPage River began in 1833 with
a sawmill operated by Julius Warren, another investor in plank roads. It also developed into a small agricultural community and stagecoach stop. Like Naper,
Warren also forsook the railroad in favor
of plank roads.[17]

The brothers Warren and Jesse Wheaton
in 1837 began farming tracts a few miles
north and east of Warrenville. After Naper
and Warren to the south and homesteaders
to the north rejected overtures from the
railroad's organizers in 1847, the Wheaton
brothers offered the Galena Railroad a strip
of their land 3 1/2 miles long for a right-of-
way. It was the intention of the Wheaton
brothers, who were a carpenter and school-
teacher by profession, not farmers, to plat a
town alongside the tracks.[18]

The arrival of the railroad had a dramatic effect on the development of the
three communities. Naperville, which had
2,599 residents in 1860, declined to 1,713
in 1870 and only began to grow again
when the Chicago, Burlington & Quincy
was built through it between Aurora and
Chicago. Warrenville declined into a back-
water until the Chicago, Aurora & Elgin
electric interurban railway was built
through it between Wheaton and Aurora
after 1900. Wheaton, which did not exist
in 1849 when the Galena Railroad arrived,
had grown to 645 residents by 1860 and
nearly 1,000 by 1870, supplanting

Naperville as the county seat. Within a few
years of the start of service on the Galena
Railroad, the plank road had been driven
out of business, and both Warrenville and
Naperville were actively seeking a railroad
of their own.[19]

Although agriculture had declined in
importance relative to other occupations
as early as 1860, none of the three communities evolved into predominantly bedroom suburbs until after 1900, by which
time Naperville's population at 2,629 had
finally surpassed what it had been in 1860
and Wheaton's had grown to 2,345. In Du-
Page County as a whole, the percentage of
the workforce listing farming as an occu-
pation declined from 60.3 percent in 1850
to 37.9 percent 10 years later; the percentage of people listing their occupations as
professional, service, tradesmen, or skilled
workers—jobs that might be associated
with suburbanization—increased only
slightly over the same span, from 15.5 percent in 1850 to 17 percent in 1860. The
population of Warrenville, which did not
incorporate until 1967, was not recorded
in 1900.[20]

However, the influence of the railroads
on the corridors in which Naperville and
Wheaton were located, as well as a rail corridor that was developed somewhat later
by the Milwaukee Road across western
Cook County and the northern tier of Du-
Page County, clearly shows the effect the
railroads had on growth. In 1860 before
the Burlington Route built its direct line
from Aurora to Chicago, the corridor it
was to serve had one incorporated municipality (Naperville, population 2,599). Prior
to the completion of that line in 1864, Aurora's rail connection to Chicago had been
by means of the Aurora Branch (later the
Aurora & Chicago and after 1855 the
Burlington), a 12-mile line from Aurora
northeast to Turner Junction and for the
remaining 30 miles to Chicago over the
Galena Railroad. By 1880 when fast, reliable commuter service was available on
the Burlington's direct line to Chicago, the
27.9-mile corridor between Cicero and

Aurora had five incorporated municipalities with a combined population of 4,459. The Burlington timetable of 1883 shows that of the 15 weekday westbound passenger trains the railroad operated from Chicago, 8 were clearly commuter operations terminating at either Downers Grove 21 miles west of Chicago (5 trains) or in Aurora (3 trains). Included among the commuter trains clearly intended for suburban patronage was the Theater Train, which left Union Depot in Chicago at 11:30 p.m. after the last curtain calls six nights a week and dropped off passengers at 14 stations all the way to Aurora. By 1900, the number of suburbs in the Burlington corridor had grown to seven with a combined population of 14,603.[21]

The 25.8-mile North Western (Galena Railroad prior to 1864) corridor between River Forest and Geneva experienced similar growth, although, for reasons that are not entirely clear, at a somewhat slower pace. Though the North Western rail line predated that of the Burlington by 16 years, the population of the three incorporated municipalities in the corridor had reached only 2,777 in 1880. However, within 20 years the number of North Western suburbs had grown to seven with a combined population of 15,974.[22]

The third western commuter railroad corridor traces its origins to the Chicago & Pacific Railroad built from Chicago to Elgin in 1873–1874 and actively promoted by Frederick Lester in Addison Township and Roselle Hough in neighboring Bloomingdale Township. Both townships were sparsely populated jurisdictions at the time, and the two men could clearly see the growth occurring on the North Western and Burlington lines further south. Perhaps because their new railroad lapsed into insolvency in 1879 and was acquired by the Chicago, Milwaukee & St. Paul Railroad, a carrier at the time more oriented to Wisconsin than Illinois, suburban growth did not occur in the 20-mile corridor between Elmwood Park and Bartlett until the final decade of the nineteenth century.

Even then growth lagged considerably behind that in the other two western corridors until after World War II. As late as 1900, only 4 of the 10 suburbs that would eventually emerge in the corridor had incorporated, and their combined population was only 1,446.[23]

A fourth potential commuter railroad corridor in the western suburbs failed to develop probably because it was patched together late in the nineteenth century. To compete in the transcontinental market from Chicago west, the Illinois Central Railroad beginning in 1888 completed a line through the western suburbs as part of an intended route from Chicago to Iowa. Because of the lateness of its entry into the market, there was no direct route available into the city, so the IC pieced together a patchwork of trackage rights over other railroads for the 15 miles between Elmhurst and downtown Chicago—an arrangement that was not particularly satisfactory for freight operations and was abominable for commuters. The railroad began operating commuter trains over the line for 24 miles between Chicago and Addison Township in 1892 in anticipation of the Columbian Exposition but abandoned the service for lack of ridership in 1931. Of the two suburbs of note on the line, Elmhurst was already served by the North Western, and Addison, which was incorporated in 1884, had a population of less than 600 in 1900. There was little settlement west of Addison until after the automobile became a factor in commuting in the second half of the twentieth century and the communities of Glendale Heights, Bloomingdale, and Carol Stream sprang up.[24]

The Northern Suburbs

A similar pattern evolved in the northern suburbs where development occurred first along the earliest steam rail line, and the last such carriers to appear were failures at least as commuter operators. As was the case in the western suburbs, the early-arriving railroads were the most successful as commuter operations. Although the North Western prospered with its lakeshore route dating from the 1850s, the corridors served by the late-arriving Milwaukee Road and Wisconsin Central failed to encourage sufficient population density to support good commuter service until well into the twentieth century. The Chicago & Milwaukee (later Chicago & North Western) in the early 1850s picked off the prime route along the northern shoreline about one-half mile inland from Lake Michigan, followed by the Milwaukee Road three miles further inland in 1873 and the Wisconsin Central nine miles further inland in 1886. Between 1882 and 1889 a second Milwaukee Road line adjacent to the North Western was built as far north as Winnetka.

Although the Illinois Central commuter operation was booming in inner suburbs that later became the South Side of Chicago, the North Western's predecessor was the first commuter line to show any appreciable commuter traffic and population growth beyond eight miles from its downtown terminal. This corridor of suburbs stretching from Evanston, about 10 miles from downtown Chicago, to Kenosha, Wisconsin, about 40 miles further north, is collectively known as the North Shore, and it ranges in economic status from such extremely wealthy suburbs as Lake Forest and Kenilworth to relatively modest areas like North Chicago and Highwood and industrial satellite cities like Waukegan and North Chicago.

Although Evanston began to develop in the 1850s, the growth of the corridor in a 23-mile section from the Chicago city limits through North Chicago increased in the 1870s. Evanston with a population of 3,062 was the only incorporated municipality along that section of the rail line as late as 1870, but within a decade there were six suburbs with a combined population of 11,833, and by 1900 the combined population of the corridor had quadrupled[25] (see Appendix A).

A single developer and politician was responsible for much of the early development along the North Shore. Just as U.S. senator Stephen A. Douglas influenced the routing of the Illinois Central to favor his real estate holdings on Chicago's South Side and former Chicago Mayor William B. Ogden, who made his fortune speculating in land, became president successively of the Galena & Chicago Union and North Western railroads, Walter S. Gurnee used the Chicago & Milwaukee railroad to further his financial interests. A former mayor of Chicago (1851–1852), Gurnee began dabbling in real estate speculation in the areas that would become the suburbs of Highland Park, Glencoe, Lake Bluff, and Winnetka just as the Chicago & Milwaukee Railroad was being planned. After being denied renomination for mayor of Chicago, he became president of the railroad and began plotting suburban stations to benefit his landholdings.[26]

The second northern suburban corridor to develop, albeit more slowly than the North Western's, began in 1873 when the Milwaukee Road's predecessor built a line to Chicago from Milwaukee about 3 1/2 miles inland from the lake. Although Libertyville, 35.5 miles north of downtown Chicago, began to develop earlier, the rest of the corridor did not show any appreciable development until the 1890s. The corridor, which in 1890 had only one incorporated municipality, Libertyville, with a population of 550, by the turn of the century had four municipalities with a combined population of 2,392. By way of contrast, the more developed North Western corridor further east had nine incorporated suburbs and a combined population of 31,412 by 1900.[27]

The third railroad line to enter Chicago from the north was the Wisconsin Central, which completed its connection in 1886 on a right-of-way approximately 9 1/2 miles east of the lake. Because of its relatively late arrival when all the prime routes downtown were already taken by other railroads that opposed its entry, the Wisconsin Central was forced to acquire a right-of-way over a more circuitous route beyond the western limits of Chicago and entering the city over a patchwork of trackage rights granted by other friendly railroads. A temporary passenger depot was built at 15th and Canal streets some distance from the central business district. Despite the geographic disadvantages of its route and the existence of established competitors, the Wisconsin Central decided to get into the commuter business. In 1887 it started running commuter trains as far as Thatcher Park (River Forest) in the western suburbs, although four daily through trains stopped at north suburban stations as far north as Antioch 52.8 miles from downtown Chicago.[28]

Despite the fact that Henry Villard's Northern Pacific Railroad acquired control of the Wisconsin Central to gain access to Chicago, giving the WC somewhat deeper pockets than it had as an independent railroad, and in 1890 built Grand Central Station, competition from the North Western and assorted street and elevated lines in the western suburbs prevented the Wisconsin Central's commuter operation (renamed Chicago & Northern Pacific) from being profitable. The railroad, which also operated a branch to south suburban Blue Island in competition with the Illinois Central and Rock Island, in its best year of 1893 reported revenues of only $153,000 from hauling 1,948,000 passengers. The financial collapse of the Northern Pacific in the Panic of 1893 doomed the commuter operation, which was shut down in 1897.[29]

The passenger market in the sparsely populated northern leg of the WC line was limited to summer resort traffic to Lake County and Wisconsin and never developed any year-round commuter passengers. A major problem was the traveling distances involved because of the Wisconsin Central's circuitous route. The more direct, 17-mile North Western route from Chicago to Des Plaines was three miles shorter than the Wisconsin Central's, for example.

The same year the Wisconsin Central arrived in Chicago, the Milwaukee Road

decided to go into direct competition with the North Western's lakeshore route by acquiring the dormant franchise of the Chicago, Evanston & Lake Superior Railway and building a line parallel and in some cases adjacent to the existing railroad. At the time there were numerous complaints about the quality of North Western service. The project quickly ran into opposition from the North Western and some local officials, and land acquisition proceeded at a glacial place. By the end of 1889—seven years after construction was started—the Milwaukee Road's Evanston division tracks had progressed only as far north as the Wilmette municipal limits about 14 miles north of downtown Chicago.[30]

The line was a money loser from the start, although as late as 1895 the Milwaukee Road operated 55 trains in both directions. The problem was that it was a steam railroad operated as a rapid transit line with 20 stations, 7 of them in Evanston, on a railroad that was only 13 miles long. The expansion of Chicago's street, cable, and elevated railways doomed the Evanston division within a few years of its inception, and the combined Evanston-Wilmette population of only 21,559 was hardly sufficient to support one electric interurban and two steam railroads even at the dawn of the auto age.[31]

In 1899 the Milwaukee Road agreed to sell a portion of the line to the predecessor of the Chicago, North Shore & Milwaukee electric interurban then under construction. The balance of the Milwaukee Road's right-of-way into Chicago ultimately became part of the Northwestern Elevated Railway (now Chicago Transit Authority) as far north as the Wilmette-Evanston border. The last steam train ran in 1908.[32]

Noncommuter Operations

Commuter traffic was not the sole influence the railroads had on the suburbs. Although the availability of transportation is not a factor usually associated with higher

CHICAGO · HAMMOND · GARY · MICHIGAN CITY · SOUTH BEND

education, the availability of railroad transportation as well as large tracts of cheap land in developing suburbia also acted as a magnet for educational institutions during church organizations' college-building spree in the second half of the nineteenth century. Besides Northwestern University and Lake Forest College on the Chicago & Milwaukee line, the Illinois Institute (later Wheaton College) was located on a site along the Galena Railroad in Wheaton in 1854, and Elmhurst College was incorporated along the same railroad. Plainfield College (later North Central College), founded in 1861 in that rural town, moved to Naperville on the Burlington Railroad in 1870, and St. Procopius College (later Benedictine University), founded by Benedictine monks in Chicago in 1887,

moved to Lisle adjacent to the Burlington Railroad in 1901. Aurora University started in downstate Mendota in 1893 and moved to Aurora on the Burlington in 1911.[33]

Local freight traffic was relatively more important on suburban lines in the late nineteenth century before the suburbs developed as predominantly residential communities, even along the North Shore. The railroads of the time encouraged local freight although they typically considered overland freight traffic to have the largest profit potential. The lack of good, hard roads until after World War I meant that local farmers were largely dependent upon the railroads for supplies—everything from lumber for building to cultivating machinery—and for moving their crops to market. A 25-mile trip by farm wagon to and from

In 1908 the South Shore Line's first car to South Bend, Indiana, made it clear from its name board above the windows what communities it served. (Norm Carlson Collection)

the lake port at Chicago could take the better part of three days, but after the trains began running a farmer could get his harvest to market in Chicago in as little as three hours.[34]

Although other industries developed in pockets around suburbia, the railroads for the most part reduced those communities to economic satrapies of Chicago within a few years. In the case of the North Shore, the communities of Racine and Kenosha in Wisconsin and Waukegan in Illinois developed as lake ports as well as manufacturing centers. Waukegan, 36 miles north of Chicago, had been platted in 1841 as a community known as Little Fort and within eight years had boomed to a port community serving 1,000 ships a year, a manufacturing center, and a regional market center of more than 3,000 inhabitants. Its residents eagerly supported the arrival of the railroad to broaden its economic reach, but after the trains began running in 1855, they discovered, like the inhabitants of so many other communities in the Midwest, that their town was quickly eclipsed by Chicago.[35]

Manufacturing industry sprang up in western Cook County along rail lines but not to any extent in northwestern Cook and DuPage counties. In Kane and Will counties, manufacturing was concentrated in cities that had developed along waterways, places like Joliet, Aurora, and Elgin. The arrival of the railroads simply enhanced their positions as factory towns.

In the nonindustrial suburbs a boom in residential development displaced farms after 1900, so the importance of local freight traffic in most suburban areas declined relative to railroad commuter operations. The introduction of the motor truck and hard roads in the first decades of the twentieth century also resulted in an erosion of the suburban freight market, especially in agricultural products, although the surviving local freight sidings handled increased amounts of such things as lumber for the building boom and coal to heat the growing number of buildings. However, the commuter train increasingly dominated local rail operations in suburbia.

The commuter trains even before the turn of the century were responsible for a substantial majority of the passengers who passed through Chicago's downtown rail depots. By 1913 commuters accounted for almost two-thirds of the railroad passengers entering and leaving the city. However, the great architectural palaces that served as depots for the most part had been built to serve intercity passengers. Commuters were an afterthought, a secondary market.

Travelers and Terminals

7

Within a decade of the railroads' arrival in Chicago, they proved to be such a formidable and efficient competitor that they had driven most of the other passenger carriers out of business. The overland stagecoaches were gone, reduced to the role of omnibuses hauling passengers between railroad depots, as were the Great Lakes passenger steamers. The 2,002-ton steamer *Western World,* a ship as opulent as anything that sailed the oceans, was laid up for lack of passenger traffic within three years of her launching, as were the steam-

ers *Buffalo, Plymouth,* and *Mississippi.* Only the cross-lake packet ships survived as passenger carriers into the twentieth century.

The Illinois and Michigan Canal lost virtually all of its passenger traffic within six years of its opening when the Chicago & Rock Island Railroad completed a line parallel to it. The number of passengers on the canal declined by almost 26,000 in 1853 when the Rock Island was opened as far west as Joliet, and most of the rest of its passengers switched to the railroad in the following years when the Rock Island

Chicago's first railroad depot—the Galena & Chicago Union station just west of the Chicago River— was a rather plain frame structure dating from 1848. It served both passengers and freight shippers and housed the railroad's offices on the second floor. (H. Roger Grant Collection)

reached the I&M terminal at La Salle. The impact of railroads on steamboat passenger traffic on the western rivers—the Ohio, Illinois, Mississippi, and Missouri—occurred a few years later as tracks reached them from Chicago. But by the time the Civil War shut down most of the civilian traffic on the rivers, travelers had already switched their allegiance from steamboats to trains.[1]

As the railroads monopolized passenger travel and the city attained a critical mass in railroads in the second half of the nineteenth century, what would later be called the travel industry became one of the most important enterprises in Chicago. It in turned fueled the growth of the city's hotel and convention businesses. Drummers from Chicago's wholesale houses fanned out across the landscape to hawk their wares, delegates from Cleveland and Denver arrived to attend political or business conventions, and people journeying between the Atlantic and Pacific coasts spent a few hours or a night between trains in Chicago. By 1889, an estimated 18 million intercity passengers were handled by Chicago's stations—drovers accompanying their herds to the stockyards, European immigrants headed west to farm a plot of land on the Great Plains, newly freed blacks seeking a new life in the North, and down-on-their-luck professionals seeking their fortunes in the booming American interior.

Chicago at the time had no public architecture to speak of and no great museums or concert halls, so the railroads began building palaces to serve as depots, the hoteliers began erecting huge inns, and entrepreneurs threw up convention halls. The railroads began catering to the passenger travel market by introducing such things as express trains, sleeping cars, diners, and immigrant cars with cheap fares. They also added to their trains such innovations as knuckle couplers, air brakes, steam heating, and electric lights to make travel safer, more efficient, and more comfortable. The depots became cities unto themselves with an as-

sortment of restaurants and stores to serve travelers. In the age of the steam engine, they were drafty, noisy, and sooty places, but they were very busy. A local industry arose to transfer people and their luggage between those depots.[2]

The issue of safety of the traveling public also arose, but not with the political intensity it had earlier during the era of the steamboat and later in the air age. Despite the often inflammatory, anti-railroad publicity following spectacular train wrecks, the public in the second half of the nineteenth century apparently considered the railroads a relatively safe way to travel, or at least was willing to accept the risk. Given the monopoly the railroads had on travel there was no groundswell of support to have Congress regulate rail safety the way it had the steamboats in 1838 and 1852. Perhaps because the railroads never suffered a calamity approaching the disasters that befell steamships on the oceans, lakes, and rivers, which claimed anywhere from a hundred to more than a thousand lives, the federal government did not impose any meaningful safety regulation on railroads until late in the nineteenth century.[3]

The worst train wreck in Illinois history claimed perhaps 85 lives in 1887, and the worst train wreck in Chicago caused 45 fatalities in 1972, contrasted to the 1860 *Lady Elgin* disaster on Lake Michigan (279 dead), the 1915 *Eastland's* capsizing on the Chicago River (844 dead), and the 1865 *Sultana* explosion on the Mississippi River (more than 1,500 dead). In fact, the greatest toll in human life caused by the railroads was at crossings and along the railroad tracks, where pedestrians and equestrians died singly or in pairs when hit by trains. Of the 166 persons killed in Chicago on railroads during the first half of 1892, only 13 were railroad passengers, and the bulk of them died while trying to board or alight from trains.[4]

Surprisingly, economic regulation of the railroads was a stronger political issue in the late nineteenth century than was safety regulation. Almost as an afterthought Illinois empowered its Railroad and Warehouse Commission, created in 1871 for economic regulation of the industry, to investigate railroad accidents as well. The federal government did not get around to empowering the Interstate Commerce Commission to do likewise until 1901, although Congress in 1893 had mandated that railroads use air brakes and couplers for safety.[5]

Influence on Mass Transit

Perhaps the first effect, albeit unintended, of the arrival of the railroads in Chicago in the 1850s and the resulting construction of passenger depots was the creation of the city's mass transit system. The stagecoach companies were one of the first competitive victims of railroads, and as steel rails were stretched farther across the landscape, the role of the stagecoach line became that of a feeder and distributor of mail and passenger traffic to and from communities that the tracks had not yet reached. Stagecoach operators who were losing long-distance travelers to the railroads began compensating by hauling transfer passengers between railroad depots in Chicago, and that business very quickly evolved into omnibus services carrying the general public. Although the omnibuses were supplanted by street railways within a decade, they survived in Chicago to serve the market of people transferring between railroad depots. The price of a through train ticket included the transfer of a person and his baggage between stations on a Parmelee omnibus.[6]

Although streetcar lines in Chicago were predominantly horse-powered until after the cable car was introduced in 1880, the lone local survivor from the horse-and-buggy era in passenger transport was the depot transfer service. It was finally motorized in the twentieth century. The company founded in 1853 by Franklin Parmelee, one of the city's pioneers in omnibuses and street railways, successfully operated a depot transfer business well into the second half of the twentieth century and eventually wound up as an operator of express transfer buses between downtown Chicago and its airports.[7]

The problem of multiple depots and the necessity of hauling transfer passengers between them arose abruptly in 1852 when four railroads arrived in the city within a couple of months of each other. Another pair of railroads arrived in 1858. Chicago, at the time a lake and canal port with no master plan for accommodating the new transportation technology, dealt individually with each railroad as it applied to enter the city. However, examination of the various railroad ordinances passed between 1848 and 1896 by the Common Council, as the city council was then called, indicates that a strategy evolved to deal with the railroads even if it was not written as part of a formal plan. Lacking a master ordinance, the Common Council simply imposed conditions on each railroad when it applied for a franchise to operate on public streets, a common occurrence in the 1850s, or to acquire a private right-of-way.

The various railroad franchise ordinances passed between 1848 and 1862 show that the city was guided by several general considerations. First, each railroad was granted the authority to build a line to the Chicago River to enable it to interchange traffic with the Great Lakes and Illinois and Michigan Canal. Since the early railroads west of Chicago were built as overland extensions of Great Lakes maritime routes, access to the lakes by means of the Chicago River was critical. The massive railroad yards on the west side of the Chicago River, still used in the twenty-first century by Amtrak and several commuter railroads, are the remnant of what was an even larger system that extended south of the Loop and along the lakeshore.[8]

The second common characteristic of the early franchises was that they generally authorized the railroads to build tracks only to what was the fringe of the settled areas of the city. That was where the railroads were allowed to build their terminal depots, and the survivors of those original depots to this day roughly define the boundaries of the Chicago settlement in 1855. The city in 1850 was less than 10 square miles in area although only about half the land had been developed into anything other than farms. As the city grew, the depots somewhat later came to define the city's central business district. The term *Loop* came into common use after the elevated railway system was built, initially to describe the mile square area the L circled and only later to identify downtown Chicago in general. But the railroad depots, not the Loop L, for the most part defined the boundaries of downtown Chicago until the second half of twentieth century.[9]

A third factor that came into play was that the state and city, at least initially, were adverse to allowing non-Illinois railroads to enter those jurisdictions over their own tracks, forcing the eastern railroads to contract with local railroads for trackage rights and depot space. This policy had the effect of consolidating rail passenger terminals into fewer giant depots than would have occurred had each railroad had to build its own train station and accompanying yards, although the existence of six depots in downtown Chicago was a controversy that continued until 1970.[10]

Chicago's first eight railroads paired up to use new depots built far apart on all four sides of the city. The Galena & Chicago Union's 1848 franchise, which also accommodated the Aurora Branch Railroad, resulted in a route along North Water Street just north of the Chicago River; the Illinois Central and Michigan Central jointly built a depot on the east side along the lake at Lake Street on what had been the Fort Dearborn military reservation; and the Rock Island and Michigan Southern built their joint passenger terminal on Van Buren Street south of the downtown area. On the west side of the river, the Pittsburgh, Ft. Wayne & Chicago

and Chicago & Alton railroads shared a right-of-way as far north as Madison Street, where they built their depot.[11]

Many of the early stations were modest structures, often one- or two-story frame buildings. But within a few years as traffic increased they became larger and more substantial structures. The Illinois Central and Michigan Central in 1856, just four years after their joint arrival in Chicago, built a three-story stone station with turrets, and after the Chicago Fire of 1871 the stations became grand structures with clock towers and huge train sheds, reflecting the dominance the railroads had attained over the American transportation system. The depots became individual gateways to Chicago, cities unto themselves with shops, restaurants, clothing stores, apothecaries, newsstands that sold books, and giant waiting rooms in which travelers could catch naps between trains. Grand Central Station boasted a waiting room with seats for 1,800 persons.[12]

The phenomenon was not unique to Chicago; it just had more stations than other American cities. The growth in size of train stations began earlier in Europe and spread to the United States in the second half of the nineteenth century as escalating land values in the central business districts forced railroads to build taller station structures just as it forced them to move their freight facilities to the fringes of the city where land was cheaper. By the 1890s, the railroads across the nation were building urban architectural monuments, not just train stations. At the end of the maritime era in the third quarter of the nineteenth century the city's skyline was dominated by grain elevators and ship's masts; in the fourth quarter of the century, before skyscrapers obscured them, the railroad station towers dominated the skyline.[13]

Collectively, the four original permanent stations in Chicago formed the corners of a tetragon approximately one mile to one-half mile apart. As other railroads arrived later in the century, they built two more depots immediately south of the downtown area, which promptly expanded south to meet them. By the time the last passenger terminal was completed in 1890, terminals and the massive yards that supported them ringed downtown Chicago. Although the North Western in 1912 moved to a new depot west of the downtown area, the railroads' passenger facilities were an effective damper on the expansion of the central business district to the east, south, and west until well into the twentieth century. The main stem of the Chicago River was a barrier to commercial growth northward until the 1920s.[14]

The railroads' original temporary stations were somewhat remote. The Galena Railroad's first depot in 1848 was a modest, one-story frame structure west of the Chicago River at Canal and Kinzie streets. The Illinois Central in March 1852 put a temporary station at 22nd Street along the lake to accommodate its Michigan Central partner, and in late 1853 it opened a new temporary terminal at 12th Street and the lake. The Rock Island in early 1852, under pressure from its Michigan Southern partner, opened a temporary terminal at 22nd Street even though it had not yet completed the western segment of its own line to Joliet. Both eastern railroads were

The Galena Railroad built its second depot at Dearborn and Kinzie streets north of the Chicago River. It burned in the Chicago Fire of 1871 and was replaced by the ornate Romanesque structure shown here. Note the omnibuses. (H. Roger Grant Collection)

engaged in an intense competition to reach Chicago and were unwilling to wait for their Illinois partners to complete their tracks elsewhere.[15]

Those original depots were primitive, hurriedly erected frame structures, typical of the architecture of pre-fire Chicago. The grand Victorian depots familiar to millions of American travelers during the golden age of railway travel were not built until after the Chicago Fire razed the earlier structures. By that time passenger traffic had increased to the point where the railroads needed larger stations. The city's post-fire renaissance was a major stimulus for the elaborate new depots, as was the 1893 Columbian Exposition and competition between railroads for business. In an age when almost everyone and everything traveled by rail, elaborate terminals were architectural advertisements for the railroads that occupied them.[16]

The progression of depots built by the Galena Railroad and its successor, the Chicago & North Western, illustrate how the growth in passenger traffic dictated ever-larger and more elaborate terminal stations. The original 1848 station west of the river was only one-story, but within a year the company added a second story for offices and a cupola on the third floor for observation of train operations by railroad officers. In its first full fiscal year of operation (April 30, 1849 to May 1, 1850), the railroad carried only 37,524 passengers on its two coaches (see Table 7-1). Two years later traffic had more than doubled to 91,920, and the railroad acquired a large tract north of the main stem of the Chicago River, bridged the north branch of the river on pontoons, and built a brick and stone freight station at Dearborn and Kinzie streets. A year later when it was handling more than 140,000 passengers, the Galena Railroad completed a two-story brick passenger terminal nearby at Wells and North Water streets on the north bank of the river. The new station not surprisingly was the busiest on the railroad's 122.5-mile mainline that by the end of the

1856 fiscal year extended as far west as Freeport. Of the 553,777 passengers the railroad hauled that year, almost 60 percent began or ended their trip in Chicago. The railroad added a third story to the depot in 1863 to house its general offices.[17]

TABLE 7-1 **Galena & Chicago Union Railroad Passenger Traffic**
1851–1856 fiscal years

Year	Passengers
1851/2	91,920
1852/3	140,016
1853/4	238,296
1854/5	471,325
1855/6	553,777

Source: Galena & Chicago Union Railroad Company, Ninth Annual Report to Stockholders (Chicago, June 4, 1856), 21 (Table F).

The pattern on the Illinois Central was similar. The railroad's organizers originally had hoped to enter the city on the West Side, where there was plenty of land along the river for an interchange with lake ships and canal boats, but the Rock Island and Galena railroads beat them to the prime sites. Besides, the railroad was under some pressure from U.S. senator Stephen A. Douglas, the man who had engineered its federal land grant and had insisted on a branch to Chicago, to provide rail service to the sizeable tract of lakefront property he owned between 22nd and 35th streets. Douglas sold the IC a total of 16.37 acres for $21,310 and bought a 6,000-acre parcel of its land grant near Lake Calumet because he hoped to develop it for industry.[18]

The IC, which ran its first passenger train on May 22, 1852, on what was then a 14-mile railroad between the Chicago city limits and the Lake Calumet station (later Kensington), by the end of 1856 was, at more than 700 miles, the longest railroad in the nation. The railroad, although it had

extended its line as far north as 12th Street by the end of 1853, still lacked direct access to the Chicago River to interchange freight traffic with lake ships. When it got to the river three years later by means of a causeway in the lake, it moved its passenger depot north to Lake Street, adjacent to its new freight house. In that year it hauled 62,351 passengers on its Chicago branch—more than a third of them (22,135) beginning or ending their trip in the Windy City. The four-story station on more than two acres of land at Lake and South Water streets, although it was heavily damaged in the 1871 fire, served the IC until 1892, when it was torn down and converted into a commuter station.

The third of Chicago's original three train stations was built by the Rock Island at the south end of what was to become the Loop and was somewhat less nomadic than the other depots. Like the Illinois Central, the Chicago & Rock Island was still under construction in 1852 when the Michigan Southern arrived from the East and hurriedly negotiated trackage rights into the city to beat the rival Michigan Central. Thus the first section of the Rock Island Line to be completed and put into service was a five-mile stretch between a place called Englewood, where the Michigan Southern hurriedly built a junction, and

Although the Chicago Fire of 1871 did not devastate the railroads as seriously as some other industries, the new LaSalle Street station was a victim of the conflagration. The depot the Chicago & Rock Island shared with the Michigan Southern and Northern Indiana had been built in 1866–67 and was typical of the first evolutionary stages of the trend toward the giant downtown depots characteristic of the later years of the Victorian Era. (Chicago Historical Society) the city limits at 22nd Street. The Michigan Southern service began there on February 20, 1852, although the Rock Island did not operate its first public train from the 22nd Street depot until the following October 10 on a two-hour run to Joliet.[19]

The highly competitive and ultimately tragic race between the two eastern railroads to reach Chicago was not over. With terminals at 22nd Street, both railroads had to haul passengers by stagecoach or omnibus almost three miles to reach the city's central business district, and both railroad groups clearly wanted their depots as close to downtown Chicago as the city would allow. The Rock Island–Michigan Southern had a slight advantage, having obtained a charter on May 26, 1851, to build tracks as far north as Van Buren Street. The Illinois Central, because of dif-

ficulties in obtaining a franchise to build a line along the lake, did not obtain its franchise from the Common Council until June 7, 1852.[20]

Soon after opening the 22nd Street depot, the Rock Island began extending its tracks northward. In 1853 it opened a new terminal with the Michigan Southern at 12th and Clark streets. Even as that station began serving trains, the two railroads started construction a new, $60,000 terminal farther north at Clark and Van Buren streets. In 1866 that facility was expanded to include waiting rooms, a dining room, a baggage room, and five tracks for trains and was renamed Union Depot. It burned in the Chicago Fire of 1871 but was rebuilt at a cost of $500,000 in 1873 as a larger facility commonly known as either LaSalle Street or Van Buren station. By the end of

Prior to 1871, the Chicago, Burlington & Quincy and Michigan Central used this building on South Water Street for their offices. (Chicago Historical Society)

the century, the station served about 8,000 passengers a day, 4,500 from the Rock Island and the remainder on the Lake Shore (as the Michigan Southern was by then called) on 52 Rock Island and 56 Lake Shore trains.[21]

The fourth of the city's original train stations was a temporary structure erected in 1858 jointly by the Pittsburgh, Ft. Wayne & Chicago (a Pennsylvania Railroad subsidiary) and the Chicago & Alton railroads at Van Buren and Canal streets west of the river. The Chicago & Alton, which began running trains to Chicago before the station was completed, at first used the Rock Island's station, but because of friction between the two carriers, it switched to the Illinois Central station along the lake. In 1863, the Pennsy and Alton railroads built a replacement station—a modest frame structure—a few blocks north at Madison Street. That structure survived the 1871 fire and remained in use until 1881 when the two original railroads and the Chicago, Milwaukee & St. Paul Railroad built a new brick Union Station at Adams and Canal. They were soon joined as tenants by the Chicago, Burlington & Quincy, which had been using the Illinois Central station since arriving in Chicago over its own tracks in 1864.[22]

Safety

In addition to the relative speed, comfort, and reliability of travel by railroad when contrasted to its competitors on land and water, the explosive growth in train travel in the nineteenth century may also have been influenced by its relative

The city's second Union Station, shown here ca. 1905, was built in 1881 west of the river at Canal and Adams streets as a joint project by several railroads. (Chicago Historical Society)

safety—or the public perception that it was a safe way to travel. Contrasted to the spectacular boiler explosions and fires on steamships that often claimed hundreds of lives in a single incident and forced the federal government as early as 1838 to attempt to impose safety regulations, railroad accidents rarely had death tolls as high as the more spectacular maritime disasters. The Chicago region's two major train wrecks in the 1850s, at Grand Crossing and South Bend, claimed 20 and 34 lives, respectively. However, the death toll of 279 persons resulting from the sinking of the lake steamship *Lady Elgin* after a collision north of Chicago in 1860 equals the combined toll of the 10 worst mainline railroad disasters in Chicago history. Two months after the *Lady Elgin* calamity, a boiler on the steamship *Globe* blew up in the Chicago River, killing 16, and in 1868 a fire aboard the Chicago-bound steamship *Seabird* killed all but 3 of the estimated 73 to 100 persons aboard. The Chicago railroads during that period were disaster-free.[23]

The nation's first railroad disaster occurred near Chicago barely a year after four new railroads built their tracks there and to some extent because of the race by two of them to get to the Windy City. A collision between trains at a diamond crossing of the Michigan Central and Michigan Southern killed an estimated 20 passengers, mostly German immigrants, on April 25, 1853. In the 23 years since the first American railroad began operating, there had been 35 documented accidents (excluding highway crossing accidents) resulting in a combined total of 82 fatalities, but none in which more than 7 persons had died.[24] (See Appendix C for a description of the 1853 disaster and its causes.)

Although the Michigan Southern suffered another disaster on June 28, 1859, when a washout destroyed some track in South Bend, Indiana, and 34 persons were killed in the resulting train wreck, the area within a 150-mile radius of Chicago was relatively free of major train wrecks for the next three decades, a somewhat surprising record in view of the intensive railroad development that occurred in that period. Between the Michigan Southern accident in 1859 and the Toledo, Peoria & Western disaster in Chatsworth, Illinois, in 1887, there were 71 major train wrecks in the United States that resulted in 1,215 deaths—none of them in the region around Chicago.[25]

The Chatsworth crash, which killed 85 on August 10, 1887, is notable not only because it was the worst rail disaster in Illinois history in terms of loss of life but because it demonstrated that the greatest threat to the traveling public was the flimsy wooden coaches in which they rode.[26] Wooden coaches tended to splinter and disintegrate upon impact and catch fire afterward with disastrous results to their occupants—a factor in the death toll at Grand Crossing as well. The splintered wooden coaches were often ignited by illuminating lamps and became pyres that roasted victims who otherwise would have survived the impact, a danger noted by British author Rudyard Kipling in his book on his 1889 journey through America.[27]

Despite the fragility of wooden cars, the public accepted them as one of the risks of travel in the nineteenth century. It was the railroad industry that finally decided, beginning in 1904 with the Interborough Rapid Transit, a New York subway line, to convert to steel cars. The last order for wooden cars by a U.S. railroad was in 1913, although substantial numbers remained in service for years.[28]

The speed and reliability of railroad travel far outweighed any perceived risks, and the railroad industry relatively early began developing specialized cars to cater to the long-distance traveler. The typical passenger car of 1840 was a 35-foot-long wooden coach—an open room with rows of seats on either side of a center aisle—that seated 50 persons in no great comfort. It was suitable for day trips, and passengers ate when the trains stopped at restaurant-equipped depots along the route. Among the most famous were the restaurants of the

Fred Harvey chain along the Santa Fe Railroad beginning in 1876. Railroads in the 1840s began adding parlor cars and sleeping cars for long-distance passengers, although it was not until 1859 that George Pullman got into the business of building sleeping cars in Chicago. By the time the government broke up his company's monopoly on the business of building, owning, and operating them in the 1940s, the name Pullman was synonymous with the railroad sleeping car. Although some food service was available on earlier rail vehicles, the first dining car designed as such was by Pullman. Dubbed *Delmonico* after New York's famous restaurant, it entered service in 1868. Although diners were money losers for the railroads, the public demanded them and the industry complied.[29]

The Great Fire and Station Renaissance

The worst disaster to befall the city's railroads occurred not on the mainlines but in downtown Chicago—the great fire of 1871 that razed or severely damaged three of the four main terminals. They were quickly rebuilt or replaced in even grander fashion, reflecting not only the city's determination to rise from the ashes but the fact that the railroads were the city's and the nation's dominant form of passenger transportation. Some historians have attributed the fact that the city's economy grew faster after the fire than it had before to a great boom in railroad construction nationwide. It was a renaissance celebrated slightly more than 20 years later when the city was host to an audience from around the world at its Columbian Exposition.[30]

Although the fire had destroyed many of the depots, most of the city's rail plant was untouched. That not only enabled emergency relief trains from throughout the nation to reach Chicago but provided access for materials for the city's relatively quick rebuilding. Joe Tucker, the IC's freight agent, saved much of his railroad's rolling stock in yards in the path of the conflagration by recruiting anyone who could operate an engine to successfully move the trains before the fire got that far. Other railroads closer to the West Side where the fire originated did not have time to save their equipment: the North Western lost 133 freight cars and the Chicago & Alton lost 113. The Chicago & Alton ordered by telegraph all trains on its mainline onto sidings so a special train carrying fire equipment could highball the 126 miles from Bloomington to Chicago in just 150 minutes. Fire engines were also shipped by rail from Indianapolis, Detroit, Milwaukee, and Quincy, Illinois. Lt. Gen. Philip H. Sheridan, the Civil War hero who since 1867 had lived in Chicago as commander of the Military District of the Missouri, ordered several companies of infantry sent by rail to Chicago from Omaha and Fort Leavenworth, Kansas, to preserve order after martial law was declared.[31]

The North Western's Wells Street station burned during the fire and was replaced in situ by a temporary wooden structure. Its successor, a massive brick structure with turrets and a clock tower typical of the grand stations of the late nineteenth century, was completed in 1882. It was abandoned and demolished in 1911 and replaced with a massive station dominated by doric columns on its façade and an interior vaulted ceiling. The new depot was west of the river at Madison and Canal streets. It in turn was replaced in 1984 by a steel and glass office tower that contained the station on its lower floors. By then, the North Western no longer ran intercity trains and the station handled only commuters.[32]

The IC rebuilt its heavily damaged Lake Street station, but in 1892 in preparation for the Columbian Exposition it opened a grand intercity terminal at 12th Street. The depot, sometimes called Central Station, handled trains operated by the IC, New York Central (successor to the Michigan Central), and Big Four. The suburban commuter terminal remained on the site of the original IC station more than a mile to the

The IC's Central Depot at 12th Street (Roosevelt Road) served from 1892 until the railroad turned its intercity passenger operations over to Amtrak in the 1970s. It was subsequently razed for redevelopment. (Chicago Historical Society)

north. Ultimately the 12th Street station simply disappeared. It was closed in 1972 after the railroads turned their intercity trains over to Amtrak, and it was demolished two years later.[33]

The Van Buren Street station was rebuilt in situ in 1873 but was replaced at the same location in 1901 by an even larger facility, LaSalle Street Station. Besides the Rock Island and New York Central, successor to the Lake Shore, it served for a time as the Chicago terminal for the Nickel Plate Road. The depot was demolished in 1981 to make room for a stock exchange. By then Amtrak had consolidated its intercity train operations at Union Station, and a small commuter station was built to the

south of the stock exchange to serve the former Rock Island commuter operations, which were by then under the control of Metra, the public commuter rail agency.[34]

Increased traffic just before World War I forced the four railroads that owned Union Station to replace it with an even larger structure, a project that took a decade to complete. By 1913, Union Station had been handling more than 35,000 suburban and intercity passengers a day on 279 trains (see Table 7-2). The new structure covered two city blocks on either side of Canal Street, opened in 1925, and within six years was handling 53,000 daily passengers. The station's head house was demolished in 1969, and an office building was erected above it, although train operations remained in the basement.[35]

Two large depots built in the last quarter of the century to handle late-arriving railroads in Chicago never attained the importance of their earlier counterparts. Both were built south of the central business district. As can be seen in Table 7-2, both Dearborn and Grand Central stations had very little commuter traffic and intercity passenger counts somewhat below those of the other stations. Dearborn Station was built in 1885 at Dearborn and Polk streets to give access to a number of railroads using the Chicago & Western Indiana terminal railroad tracks. At one time it handled more railroads than any other Chicago depot although it ranked only fifth in numbers of passengers handled. Its tenants included the Atchison, Topeka & Santa Fe; the Wabash; the Grand Trunk Western; the Chicago & Eastern Illinois; the Monon; and the Chesapeake & Ohio. It shut down after Amtrak moved its surviving trains to Union Station and was redeveloped as a shopping and office center—the only one of Chicago's Victorian era stations to survive the wrecking ball.[36]

The least successful of the major stations, although it may have been the most significant architecturally, was the last to be built. Completed in 1890 in Romanesque style with a giant, 242-foot-high clock tower, Grand Central Station at Harrison Street and the river had the misfortune of serving a group of late-arriving and very marginal railroads. The Baltimore & Ohio was the strongest carrier, but the Chicago Great Western, Soo Line, and Pere Marquette did not have particularly strong passenger routes. Although it was supposed to have handled as many as 10,000 passengers a day just after opening, by 1913 it handled less than a third of the intercity traffic of its busiest competitors and only a fraction of their commuters. In the depths of the Great Depression in 1931, Grand Central Station handled only 3,300 passengers daily. The depot was abandoned and demolished in 1971 despite the efforts of preservationists to save it.[37]

Hotels and Conventions

Although Chicago or its site had been an occasional gathering place for Indians and armies since the early eighteenth century, the city's role as a convention center dates from 1847, the year before its first railroad and canal opened for business. Once the city became a railroad center in the 1850s it began attracting such mass meetings with increasing frequency, and by the late nineteenth century it had emerged as one of the nation's convention centers, hosting no less than 9 of the nation's 22 presidential nominating conventions between 1860 and the end of the century. Once the first transcontinental

The original Union Station was replaced with a new structure in 1925 and survived into the twenty-first century as the home to Amtrak intercity trains as well as Burlington and Milwaukee Road commuter operations.

TABLE 7-2 **Daily Chicago Railroad Passenger Traffic, 1913**

| *Station* | *INTERCITY* | | *COMMUTER* | | *Total* |
	Trains	*Passengers*	*Trains*	*Passengers*	*Passengers*
Union	167	19,145	112	16,323	35,468
Grand Central	34	3,175	4	470	3,645
North Western	121	16,311	189	32,583	48,894
LaSalle	80	10,334	111	24,718	35,052
Dearborn	104	9,968	42	3,337	13,305
Illinois Central	85	10,140	288	40,767	50,907

Source: Bion J. Arnold, "Report on the Re-arrangement of the Steam Railroad Terminals in the City of Chicago" (Chicago, 1913), total daily train, car, and passenger movements at Chicago railway stations in 1913.

railroad was completed in 1869 it was possible to travel from the West Coast to attend a convention in Chicago in about a week instead of a month as required by stagecoach or ship.[38]

Chicago's location made it a convenient gathering place for Indians and their enemies even before it became a municipality. A small army of French and Indian allies had been assembled there in the summer of 1715 in a campaign against the Fox tribe, and federal Indian agents held various conferences with assorted tribal chiefs in the early nineteenth century. In 1821 an estimated 3,000 members of the Potawatomi, Chippewa, and Ottawa confederacies met in Chicago to negotiate a land treaty with Michigan governor Lewis Cass and other government commissioners. General Winfield Scott used it as a staging point for his army in the campaign against Black Hawk in 1832—the short war that finally ended the threat of Indian uprisings in Illinois and made the state safe for settlement.[39]

In preindustrial Chicago when seasonal lake shipping was the predominant form of transportation, the city's hotel industry was rather modest in size. The first inn— Wolf Point Tavern operated by James Kinzie—dates from 1828, and within the next 20 years another 20 hotels and inns were opened. Most had only a few rooms. In fact, it was common for inns of the day to have a dormitory on the second floor in which the guests slept. One English traveler described the Sauganash Hotel, the first hotel built in Chicago (1830), as a "vile, two-story barrack." The tavern and kitchen were on the first floor. Such limited facilities could handle the normal maritime traffic in the 1840s but were hopelessly inadequate when there was a large convention or when the railroad began dumping thousands of passengers in the city who were transferring between eastern and western trains.[40]

That became painfully clear in July of 1847 when an estimated 20,000 persons from around the nation descended on Chicago for the Rivers and Harbors Convention. President James Polk's veto of the River and Harbor Bill in 1846 had caused a furor in cities hoping to get federal money for maritime improvements, so much so that a convention was scheduled in Chicago to drum up support for their cause. However, Chicago's hotel facilities were inadequate. The meetings were held in a tent in a park, and the city was forced to requisition private homes and ships in the harbor to provide accommodations.[41]

The situation improved somewhat in the 1850s with the addition of four new

Grand Central Station at the south end of the Loop was the last of the city's Victorian era depots. It never lived up to its name, except perhaps as an architectural monument. It was chronically underutilized and suffered the wrecking ball before its centennial. (Chicago Historical Society)

multistory brick hotels, but the city's inventory of rooms in its 42 hotels was still inadequate for conventions in 1859 and 1860. The Seventh Annual United States Fair and Agriculture Exhibition, which was notable in that it featured a contest between steam-powered tractors, attracted an estimated 60,000 persons to a site just south of the city in September 1859. In 1860 when the supporters of Abraham Lincoln arranged for Chicago to be the site of the Republican National Convention, the city still had no convention center. To attract the convention, the city's business leaders hurriedly raised $6,000 to finance and build in just five weeks a two-story frame structure known as The Wigwam on the site of the former Sauganash Hotel. The structure could hold 10,000 persons, sufficient for the convention, but the city had to resort to bedding some convention visitors in private homes and on billiard tables in several taverns.[42]

Despite the war, the growing travel market resulted in the construction of six major hotels and more than a score of minor ones in the city in the 1860s. By then Chicago hotels were becoming large and opulent to cater to a growing railroad-travel–induced market that included business travelers. Perhaps the best known new hotel of that era, because it survived into the twenty-first century, was Potter Palmer's seven-story Palmer House on State Street. It cost $200,000 to build and $100,000 to furnish and contained 225 rooms. When it burned in the Chicago Fire of 1871 barely a year after opening its doors, Palmer rebuilt it as a larger "fireproof" hotel.[43]

After the fire that leveled the city's entire business district, the hotel industry rebuilt, and within a few years the city had become one of the nation's largest convention and tourism centers largely as a result of the access that the growing railroad network provided. By then, the railroads had driven steamboat passenger traffic on the western rivers into an irreversible decline and had put Great Lakes passenger steamers out of business, although some cross-lake packet traffic existed into the twentieth century. Just two years after the fire, the city was host to the Inter-State Industrial Exposition.[44]

The Democrats held their national conventions in Chicago in 1864, 1884, 1892, and 1896, and the Republicans in 1868, 1880, 1884, and 1888. The railroad industry understandably was a major user of Chicago as a convention center. Although various technical conferences were held, the most famous of the railroad meetings was the General Time Convention on October 11, 1883, in the Grand Pacific Hotel, during which the railroads adopted a standard time system with five zones. The railroad industry also held national railroad fairs for the public along the lakefront in 1948–1950. The grandest of the tourist attractions in Chicago in the nineteenth century was the Columbian Exposition of 1893. It attracted 27 million visitors, 14 million from outside the United States— the bulk of the nonlocal visitors arriving by railroad. The Illinois Central Railroad commuter line between May 1 and October 31, 1893, hauled 8,780,616 passengers between downtown Chicago and the fairgrounds in Jackson Park.[45]

The railroads established Chicago as a convention center, but the business continued to grow long after the railroads lost most of their passenger traffic to private automobiles and the airlines in the second half of the twentieth century. By 1990, Amtrak, the sole surviving intercity rail passenger carrier, had less than 1 percent of the national market as measured in billions of passenger miles. The private automobile had 80.2 percent of the market, the airlines 17.3 percent, and buses 1.2 percent. However, in Chicago the hotel industry had grown to the point that by 2003 it provided 28,495 rooms in the central business district—more than enough to house the entire population of Chicago in 1847 when the River and Harbor Convention was held—and 85,127 rooms in the entire metropolitan area.[46]

In the second half of the nineteenth century, Chicago's increasingly concentrated railroad plant surrounding the downtown area began to show the strain of too many trains trying to serve too small an area. The city was becoming as much of a bottleneck for the railroads as its river was for maritime traffic; the Chicago River branches were choked with schooners, steamers, and canal boats, and its banks in many places were lined with railroad yards holding hundreds of freight cars. As more railroads arrived to find there was no more space available along the river, they began building yards wherever they could find cheap land in relative proximity to the city.

Farms became railroad yards almost overnight. There were no fewer than 22 yards built in the city and suburbs in a 12-mile swath south of the Loop, and 11 to the west. The North Side was largely spared. Their collective impact was to isolate Chicago's central business district. A swath of railroad yards south of the Loop extended from Clinton Street to the lake, interrupted only by a two-block corridor between State Street and Michigan Avenue that gave the city access to its South Side. A similar two-mile-long swath of steel rails developed west of the Loop, hampering ingress and egress from the West Side.

As more railroads arrived, the newcomers were forced to create an entirely new system of relatively short belt lines girding the city to allow the interchange of traffic. The passenger traffic might have been able to survive with shared access to a handful of depots, but the hundreds of freight trains that entered the city could not.

8 The Bottleneck

The sheer number of railroad lines in the metropolitan area has resulted in a number of diamond (rail-to-rail) crossings. Here a Union Pacific freight train (seen between the CWEX coal cars) waits for an Elgin, Joliet & Eastern coal train to pass in the western suburbs.

Chicago in the 1880s was being transformed into a gigantic railroad yard. Within 25 years of the operation of the first train from Chicago, the city had become such a bottleneck for the nation's railroad system that both the railroad industry and city were struggling for solutions. In 1858 the city was already the nation's largest rail center with 58 daily freight trains arriving and departing on 3,000 miles of rail lines. By the turn of the century the volume of daily freight trains had increased to 650, and the city was a terminal for 54,000 miles of railroads.

Over the same span the number of railroads serving the city had tripled to 30 despite periodic consolidations within the industry. Traffic at the Union Stock Yards alone increased from 223,757 cars in 1884 to 557,752 in 1890. By some calculations as many as 1,750,000 railroad cars annually were simply being shuttled around the city without ever leaving its corporate limits. Another 4,250,000—12,000 a day—arrived or departed the city.[1]

Chicago, quite simply, was choking on railroad traffic.

As the rail traffic problem intensified in

the last three decades of the nineteenth century, the city made various attempts to ameliorate the problem by studying the possibility of consolidating passenger terminals and by requiring the railroads to elevate their tracks above street level, two issues which will be discussed in later chapters. The railroad industry for its part began to build belt and terminal railroads to divert through traffic away from the downtown Chicago bottleneck.[2]

The fire of 1871 was a catalyst in the individual decisions by railroads to move as much as possible of their freight operations away from downtown Chicago. The fire destroyed most of the passenger terminals and warehouses along the river but not the more distant freight depots and track infrastructure. After the fire the downtown port began to diminish in importance as heavy industry dependent upon maritime transportation began to move southward to the city's second port along the Calumet River, and downtown land values began to increase as the city began rebuilding. Railroads needing additional land for larger freight yards to handle increased traffic began to look outward at the cheap farmland surrounding the city. Much of the outward expansion and the industrial relocation that accompanied it would have occurred regardless of whether there had been a fire. Manufacturing companies needed larger sites for expansion, and the late-arriving railroads needed space for yards and freight facilities.[3]

Increasingly the railroads were forced to build not only yards on the fringes of the metropolitan area but circumferential belt lines to serve them. The names of these small railroads were virtually unknown outside of Chicagoland; even in the metropolitan area they were commonly called "the belt" regardless of their corporate names. The outward growth of the city's railway plant may have been the result of changes in transportation patterns then occurring, or it may have helped cause them. The symbiotic relationship between water and rail in

Chicago was changing. The Illinois and Michigan Canal was in decline, as was the relative importance of Chicago's port, although lake tonnage remained high through the end of the century because of the growth of the steel industry and its dependence upon the lake for raw materials. In the final years of the century railroads increasingly interchanged freight among themselves, bypassing the Great Lakes. The rate wars between railroads undermined some maritime commerce, as did the interchange agreements that allowed the through routing of freight cars between railroads. Freight cars began to move through Chicago without ever coming close to the Loop.[4]

By 1889, 6 million freight cars passed through Chicago, pushed and pulled by 300 switch engines and another 100 locomotives assigned to interline transfers. The congestion was such that the movement of freight cars through the Chicago maze was measured in days, not hours. Despite a century of efforts to improve traffic flow, the average stay of a freight car in Chicago in the late 1900s, including switching, waiting time, loading, and unloading, was 9 to 10 days, and on average it took 48 hours for a freight car just to pass through Chicago.[5]

The effect of the congestion on the railroads caused them to attempt to engineer some solutions. This led to the often piecemeal creation in the second half of the nineteenth century of a complex terminal system of belt lines, yards, and interchange tracks. At its height before World War II, the Chicago Switching District, as the city's rail complex was called, contained 5,710 miles of railroad, 160 freight yards, and 76 freight stations and served 5,000 industries in a 400-square-mile area—perhaps the greatest concentration of railroad tracks on the planet.[6]

Because of Chicago's relative dominance as the principal rail interchange point in the central United States, congestion there could affect most of the nation's rail system. Cars tied up on sidings awaiting transfer in Chicago, for example, were not available to shippers in California. Because of the bottlenecks that rail yards had become by the end of the century, it was estimated that cars spent 18 out of every 24 hours in yards and the average speed of a freight car on a trip to New York was only about two miles an hour.[7]

The First Joint-Use Railroads

From the onset of Chicago's emergence as a rail junction, political and economic expediency dictated that the newly arriving carriers find some way to consolidate facilities to avoid building duplicate and expensive lines into the increasingly congested port area that also served as the city's central business district. The earliest solution was to share mainlines by means of negotiated trackage rights. Thus by 1852 three pairs of railroads (Michigan Southern–Rock Island, Michigan Central–Illinois Central, and Galena–Aurora Branch) shared tracks downtown.

The method of using trackage rights over another railroad to obtain access to Chicago had been pioneered a year earlier by Van Nortwick to get his under-capitalized Aurora Branch Railroad into the Windy City on the tracks of the Galena Railroad, an expediency it used for its first 14 years of existence. The December 1851 agreement between the two railroads stipulated that the Aurora Branch could operate its own trains with its own crews over the Galena but had to pay 70 percent of any revenues it earned on that 30-mile section from Junction to Chicago. It kept all revenues from its 12-mile line between Aurora and Junction. In 1864, the successor Chicago, Burlington & Quincy completed its own line to Chicago after the Galena cancelled the trackage rights.[8]

Within a few years of the inception of trackage rights, the railroads began cooperating to finance and build jointly owned connecting lines, which gained in popularity as the century progressed and eventually evolved into the region's extensive belt line railway system. The first such joint-use line dates from 1856 when a one-mile railroad called the St. Charles Air Line was built by the Illinois Central to connect its lakeshore facilities shared by the Michigan Central with the Galena & Chicago Union and Burlington lines from the west. The Michigan Southern and Rock Island had their own east-west connection.

The Air Line project, which included bridging the south branch of the Chicago River at North Street (now 16th Street), was approved by both the city and state in 1852, but didn't get started until 1855 when the IC acquired the right-of-way. Construction began immediately and the line was opened to traffic in May 1856. Its tracks were elevated in 1899 and continued to operate into the twenty-first century despite efforts by Chicago developers at that time to acquire and demolish the line to make way for their own projects in the area south of the Loop.[9]

The St. Charles Air Line was dwarfed in scale a few years later by a cooperative project to consolidate small stockyards scattered throughout Chicago into one giant facility. In the fall of 1864 the Chicago Pork Packers Association and nine railroads jointly proposed the Union Stock Yard and Terminal Co. to build a consolidated yard on a site half a mile square just southwest of the city. The Union Stock Yard, served by 100 miles of track jointly available to the member railroads, opened in late 1865. Within five years it was handling almost 2.6 million head of cattle, hogs, and sheep annually, a number that grew to almost 10 million in 1885.[10]

The stockyards were a project begun at the end of the period in which the first wave of railroads reached the city. Between 1848 and the Civil War, 10 railroads arrived and in paired track-sharing arrangements occupied most of the prime access routes and portside land along the Chicago River. They were followed in 1864 by the Chicago, Burlington & Quincy, which until that time had

The surge in the number of railroads to Chicago after 1850 soon forced the various lines to cooperate to build such things as belt lines, yards, and depots. The St. Charles Air Line—a mile-long railroad just south of the Loop that connected the lakefront railroads with those west of the Chicago River—was the first such joint venture. It is still in operation in the twenty-first century. (Alan R. Lind, Transport History Press)

operated over the Galena Railroad; the Milwaukee Road in 1872; and the Baltimore & Ohio in 1874.[11]

The second rush began in 1880. The Grand Trunk and the New York–based Erie arrived from the east that year, and the Wabash (Wabash, St. Louis & Pacific) came from the southeast. The Nickel Plate Road (New York, Chicago & St.Louis) and the Monon (Louisville, New Albany & Chicago) in 1881 reached Chicago from the east and south, respectively; the Atchison, Topeka & Santa Fe came from the southwest in 1888; and the Chicago Great Western came from the west in 1892. Before the end of the century the Wisconsin Central (later Soo Line); the Chicago & Eastern Illinois; and the Cleveland, Cincinnati, Chicago & St. Louis (Big Four) arrived. Bringing up the rear were the Pere Marquette Railway, which reached Chicago in 1903, and the Chesapeake & Ohio, which got to Chicago in 1906. A third wave of railroads—the electric interurban lines—arrived after the turn of the century, but they were principally passenger and package freight carriers serving small and relatively short-haul markets.

The Belt Lines

It was the second wave of railroads arriving in the 1880s that caused the spurt of belt line railway building in Chicago as the latecomers struggled to find access not only to downtown Chicago for their passenger depots but also to the docks along the Chicago River and connections to other railroads. Ultimately the original belts were expanded by merger and acquisition into four major systems—the Belt Railway of Chicago; the Indiana Harbor Belt; the Baltimore & Ohio Chicago Junction; and the Elgin, Joliet & Eastern—that collectively operate 323 miles of railroad lines and 1,377 miles of track in the metropolitan area. An additional 14 terminal and switching-company railroads were built between 1897 and 1928, and by the end of the twentieth century they oper-

ated an additional 109 miles of lines, essentially to serve local industry rather than to connect the major railroads.[12]

The first belt railroad built as such was a predecessor of the Belt Railway of Chicago (BRC). The Chicago & Western Indiana Belt Railway Company was chartered in 1879 with the encouragement of the Chicago & Eastern Illinois, Erie, Grand Trunk Western, Monon, and Wabash to build Dearborn Station and get them access to it. But even before they completed the station in 1882, the belt's owners decided they needed a connection with the western railroads and began building a circumferential line circling the city from 74th Street on the South Side parallel to Cicero Avenue on the West Side and as far as Belmont Avenue on the North Side, although the northern leg was never built. The five railroads also organized a corporation called the Belt Railroad of Chicago to operate the new line.

Meanwhile, 11 other railroads in 1888 organized the Chicago Union Transfer Railroad Company to build a 60-mile circumferential belt parallel to the BRC as well as a giant, joint-use rail yard on the Southwest Side south of 65th Street and stretching for miles between Cicero and Harlem avenues. The project languished for years until the Clearing Yard was completed in 1902, and then it suffered from a dearth of traffic. Finally the railroads decided to merge BRC and the Clearing Yard, add additional owners, and expand the yard into the world's largest such facility. Despite financial problems and a dropoff in traffic during a recession after the railroad industry was deregulated in 1980, the BRC survived into the twenty-first century and as late as 2000 handled 2.4 million freight cars.[13]

The Baltimore & Ohio Chicago Terminal was another belt line originally built to give late-coming railroads a passenger depot in Chicago—Grand Central Station. What finally emerged was an assemblage of short railroads known as the Chicago Terminal Transfer Company, which the

The B&OCT, or Baltimore & Ohio Chicago Terminal, is a line virtually unknown outside the railroad industry. It winds through the metropolitan area and is used by a number of other railroads, including this Belt Railway of Chicago train shown crossing the Cal Sag Channel near Blue Island. (Steve Smedley)

The proliferation of rail lines and traffic to the Chicago metropolitan area resulted in a commensurate growth in the size and number of yards. The Clearing Yard on the Southwest Side, built and owned by a number of railroads, was one of the largest and busiest. (Belt Railway of Chicago)

B&O acquired and renamed in 1910. But the roots of the byzantine project go back to a charter approved by the state in 1867 to build the La Salle and Chicago Railroad between those two cities that were already served by the Illinois & Michigan Canal and the Rock Island Railroad. Although the name of the unbuilt railroad was grandiosely changed to Chicago & Great Western (not to be confused with the later and unrelated Chicago Great Western), the project languished until 1885. It was then that a couple of railroads approaching Chicago from the north began looking for a way to get into the central city with their passenger trains and decided on the expedient process of buying up existing but dormant charters. The Wisconsin Central that year acquired the Chicago & Great Western and exercised its charter by building a nine-mile line from the western suburb of Forest Park to a modest depot on Polk Street just south of downtown.[14]

But it was Henry Villard, the financier who controlled the Northern Pacific Railroad, who gave the project impetus. He wanted access to Chicago for the NP, so he acquired the Wisconsin Central, bought a coal yard at Harrison and Wells streets, and erected Grand Central Station on that site. Villard then began actively recruiting other tenants to help share the cost. The Baltimore & Ohio moved there from the IC depot in 1891, followed by the Chicago Great Western the following year. Villard, meanwhile, began building and adding other local terminal companies, primarily on the South and Southwest sides of the city, to feed traffic to his system and gain access to the Union Stock Yards.

Although Villard lost control of the Wisconsin Central and access to Chicago during the Panic of 1893, his assemblage survived and in 1897 was reorganized as the Chicago Terminal Transfer Railroad. The new company sought an alliance with another large trunk railroad with deep pockets to complete a belt around the city about 20 miles from the Loop from the northwest suburb of Franklin Park to the southeast suburb of Whiting, Indiana. With the help of the Baltimore & Ohio and trackage agreements with another belt line, the project was completed before the turn of the century. However, the continual financial troubles at the Terminal Transfer Railroad eventually forced the B&O to acquire it.[15]

The other two Chicago-area belt lines were built strictly for freight service with no intention of entering downtown Chicago. The incentive for Indiana Harbor Belt was to link rapidly industrializing northwest Indiana to the railroads north and west of Chicago without having to go through the city's increasingly congested downtown bottleneck. The Elgin, Joliet & Eastern was planned as an outer belt to bypass Chicago roughly 35 miles from the Loop.

The Indiana Harbor Belt began in 1896 as the Chicago, Hammond & Western Railroad with the backing of G. H. Hammond and Company, one of the nation's largest meatpackers and the first firm in that industry to use ice-cooled refrigerator cars. Another firm with an interest in the line was Standard Oil Company, which had just built a refinery in adjacent Whiting, Indiana. The railroad got 14 miles from Whiting to southwest suburban Blue Island, Illinois, before reaching an agreement with the Chicago Terminal Transfer Railroad to jointly build and share track on the rest of the belt to Franklin Park.

The eastern trunk railroads with an interest in the project were the Michigan Central and Lake Shore, both by then subsidiaries of the New York Central System. Since 1852 they had been dependent upon Illinois Central and Rock Island for access to Chicago, but the New York Central wanted greater access to the growing Chicago metropolis, including the Union Stock Yards, than their original hosts could provide. So the New York Central became the financial backer of the Chicago, Hammond & Western and its acquisition of other small terminal lines in the city. The New York Central in 1907 took financial control of the belt line, renamed it Indiana

Harbor Belt, and in 1911 sold minority shares to two other railroads.[16]

The Elgin, Joliet & Eastern began as a homegrown project in the southwest suburban satellite city of Joliet in 1884. The project's purpose was to have a line between Indiana and the Mississippi River that could bring raw materials to the home city's steel industry and serve as an outlet for its production. Although Joliet was or was soon to be served by several railroads, including the Rock Island and Santa Fe, as well as the Illinois and Michigan Canal, the promoters wanted wider rail coverage. The undercapitalized project limped along with the construction of a 22-mile section between Joliet and Aurora until the promoters approached J. P. Morgan's banking house in New York for financing.

Morgan bought out the other investors in 1887, took over the project, and began pouring money into it to extend the tracks north to Elgin and east to Indiana. Within the year Morgan also agreed to extend the Elgin, Joliet & Eastern, as it was by then called (it is also sometimes referred to as "the J" or "the outer belt"), to the Lake Michigan port of Waukegan 35 miles north of Chicago to give the Joliet steel industry access to lake ore boats. In the back of the minds of Morgan's subalterns was the possibility that virtually all the other railroads could use the belt as an interchange line to avoid the Chicago bottleneck. In 1898 the EJ&E was bought by a subsidiary of Illinois Steel, a predecessor of U.S. Steel, in which Morgan also had a financial interest.[17]

Chicago's four major belt railroads continued in operation through the twentieth century despite dips in the economy that caused traffic to fall off, the bankruptcies of a number of mainline railroads, and consolidations in the industry that reduced the number of major railroads in the U.S. from 100 in 1950 to only 6 by 2000. The belts at the turn of the millennium still handled the lion's share of the 3,000 freight trains and 200,000 cars that rumbled through Chicago each week and continued their role not only as sorters and interchangers of freight cars but as distributors to local industries as well. In that role they were augmented by seven terminal and switching railroads.[18]

Switching and Terminal Railroads

The switching and terminal companies, collectively comprising 109 miles of railroad, for the most part came into existence between 1900 and 1910 to serve specific factories or industrial districts by connecting with other railroads—markets the big railroads were unwilling or unable to profitably serve. Some, like the 10-mile Chicago, West Pullman & Southern, apparently were built as speculative ventures by industrial land developers. Others, including the Pullman Railroad and the 17-mile Illinois Northern Railroad, were built by specific industries, in these instances the Pullman Car and Manufacturing Corporation on the far South Side and the giant McCormick Harvester Company plant along 26th Street and California Avenue on the Southwest Side, respectively. Chicago Union Station Company was created in 1913 to build the facility that bears its name and the giant passenger yards to the south. The Chicago Produce Terminal Company was formed to operate a fruit and vegetable facility at 27th Street and Ashland Avenue.

Although some of the terminal lines disappeared with the industries they served, including Pullman and McCormick Harvester, or were swallowed up by the larger belt lines, a few found a niche and survived the twentieth century. The history of the railroad industry in America has been one of almost continual consolidation into ever-larger corporations. Several of Chicago's little railroads survived as independent carriers long enough to be used as models when the U.S. railroad industry began to shrink.

A wave of bankruptcies swept the railroad industry in the 1970s, the most famous being the Penn Central, and the big railroads began shucking marginal branch lines. Scores of independent short-line companies were formed around the nation between 1976 and 1986 to take over and operate those lines with enough traffic to justify their existence. Among the Chicago survivors that were still around to be used as models were the Chicago Short Line Railroad Company, a 28-mile steel-hauling line in the south suburbs; the Chicago, West Pullman & Southern, a 30.6-mile switching railroad on the South Side and in the southern suburbs; and the Manufacturers' Junction Railway, a 1.78-mile switching line serving assorted industries on the West Side.[19]

The Freight Subway

One of the strangest railroads built in Chicago in the early twentieth century, and one which did not survive the shake-out, was in fact a 60-mile freight subway system. By the 1890s the distribution of freight and mail from the railroad terminals to customers in downtown Chicago not directly served by rail lines had become such a problem that some promoters came up with the innovative solution of building a freight subway system. Originally proposed as a tunnel system for telephone cables, the Chicago Tunnel Co. got permission from the city by 1903 to haul freight and mail in their system and with the backing of Edward H. Harriman, who by then controlled a number of the nation's major railroads, including the Illinois Central, Union Pacific, and Chicago & Alton, dug subway lines to various railroad freight terminals on the fringe of the downtown area. In 1905 plans were announced to build a line to the Union Stock Yards, possibly due to the Armours' influence, but the project never progressed far beyond the talking stage before being cancelled for lack of funds.[20]

The system more nearly approximated a narrow-gauge mine railroad than the steam lines of the day. Trains of as many

as 15 cars were pulled by squat electric mine locomotives on which the motor-man and sole crewman rode in the open. The track gauge was only two feet wide, less than half that of steam railroads, and the curves had a tight 20-foot radius, less than half that of the Loop elevated structure also known for its tight turns.

Despite the fact that the freight sub-way system at its apex consisted of 60 miles of lines, 149 electric locomotives, and 3,243 freight cars and was being extended as late as 1954 to serve the new Prudential Building, it was never particularly successful financially. The Tunnel Company was in bankruptcy in 1909 shortly after Harriman died, nearly failed again during the Depression, and was terminally ill by 1959 when it was sold for scrap in bankruptcy court.

Although the post office used the subway for mail distribution in 1907–1908, it declined an invitation to do so again in the 1950s despite some internal cost estimates indicating the federal agency could save $3 million to $4 million a year by removing 300 to 400 trucks from the street. As a result, the Tunnel Company had to subsist on a mixture of package freight bound for downtown department stores, coal for furnaces throughout the downtown area, ash residue from the furnaces and an assortment of trash.[21]

Trucks eventually took most of the package freight and coal, leaving the freight subway with ash and trash at three cents a ton. When construction of the passenger subways beneath Dearborn and State streets in the early 1940s interrupted service on 11 Tunnel Co. routes downtown, the system was doomed even though it continued to limp along for nearly two decades. It extracted a measure of revenge on Chicago on April 13, 1992, when a crew drilling holes for piles in the north branch of the Chicago River bed poked a hole into an abandoned Tunnel Company bore and water poured through the empty tunnels to flood most of the basements in the Loop.[22]

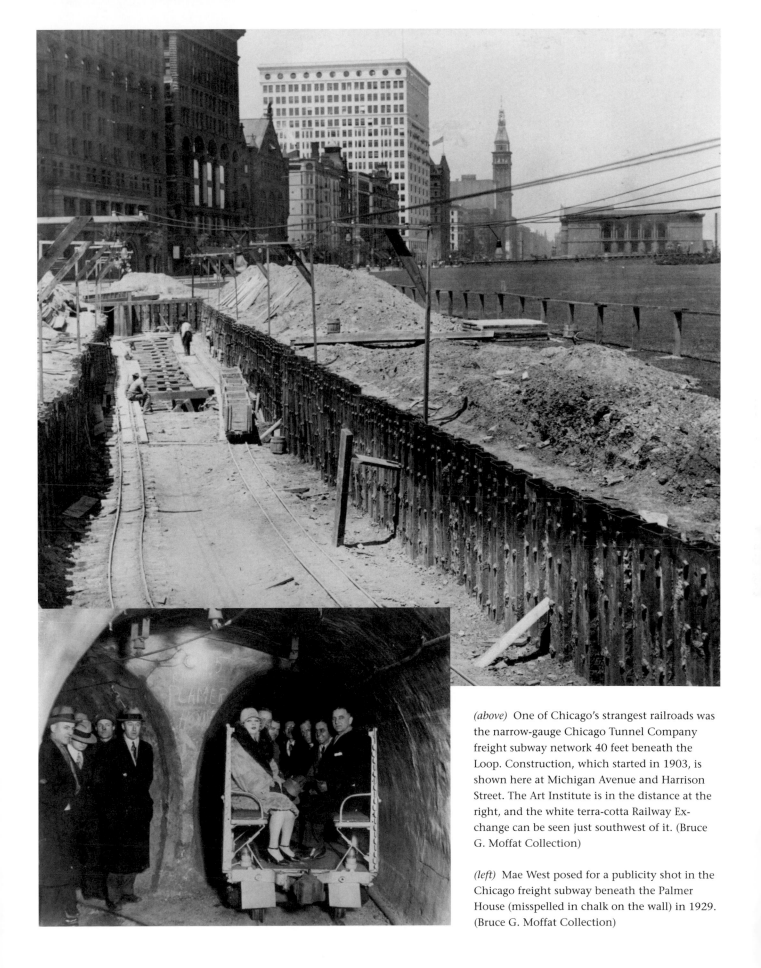

(above) One of Chicago's strangest railroads was the narrow-gauge Chicago Tunnel Company freight subway network 40 feet beneath the Loop. Construction, which started in 1903, is shown here at Michigan Avenue and Harrison Street. The Art Institute is in the distance at the right, and the white terra-cotta Railway Exchange can be seen just southwest of it. (Bruce G. Moffat Collection)

(left) Mae West posed for a publicity shot in the Chicago freight subway beneath the Palmer House (misspelled in chalk on the wall) in 1929. (Bruce G. Moffat Collection)

The Interurban Railways

Shortly after the belt railways were built, yet another type of railroad appeared on the scene as a result of technological advances with electric traction late in the nineteenth century. This was the so-called interurban, consisting for the most part of cheaply built electric railways running alongside major roads in the country and on city streets in towns and serving smaller rural markets unsuitable for mainline railroad service. However, in the Chicago area in the first half of the twentieth century several interurban railroads emerged as and are best remembered as major commuter carriers.

They also were able to develop some freight traffic, which may have helped them to survive the national shakeout of the interurban industry during the Great Depression. Aside from the fact that much of the interurban railroad industry in America was undercapitalized and in many instances poorly conceived, its decline is usually attributed to the emergence of the automobile, the motor truck, and the national hard-road building program following World War I. The Depression a few years later finished off most of the rest of the electric railroads.[23]

The absence of significant freight traffic was a major factor in the industry's demise. Despite an effort after World War I to increase freight traffic, which as late as 1920 accounted for only 9 percent of gross revenues, in 1925 the nation's interurban industry as a whole reported freight revenues of only $65 million or 15 percent of their total income. Conversely the steam railroads in 1903, at the beginning of the interurban-building boom, depended upon freight for 73 percent of their total revenues. Baggage, mail, express commodities, and small lots of packaged merchandise were the extent of the freight on most interurbans.[24]

It is no coincidence that the only two interurbans to survive the demise of the rest of the industry—the Chicago, South Shore & South Bend in the Chicago area and the Illinois Terminal downstate—both handled significant amounts of freight. The other two Chicago-area interurbans to survive the Depression but not the postwar period—the Chicago, Aurora & Elgin and the Chicago, North Shore & Milwaukee—were predominantly commuter carriers, although they handled some freight.

The Chicago, Aurora & Elgin was an example of the difficulties most metropolitan interurbans had in obtaining freight traffic. It operated on the West Side of Chicago over the West Side Metropolitan Elevated, which restricted its ability to haul freight, and at grade through the largely residential western suburbs. Only in its terminal cities of Aurora and Elgin was there any industry to speak of, and those satellite cities had been served for years by various steam railroads and the Elgin, Joliet & Eastern belt line.

In 1905 just after it began operating, freight accounted for only a fraction of total revenues. The bulk of the 2,069 tons carried was soft coal, although the railroad also hauled some lumber (101 tons), machinery (58 tons), and livestock (10 tons). The railroad at the time reported passenger revenues of $467,892, or 92.6 percent of the total, and freight revenues of only $1,869. By 1920, mail, express packages, milk, and newspapers were also providing some income, although freight revenues still accounted for less than 5 percent of operating revenues.[25]

It was in 1920 that the electric railroad, then in reorganization, purchased its first freight locomotive to complement its three box motor cars, as the self-propelled freight cars used on interurbans were called. The locomotives allowed the railroad to haul freight cars interchanged with steam railroads instead of using the expensive process of switching loads between boxcars and the box motor cars. A second electric locomotive was purchased in 1922 and two more in 1926. With little online industry, the railroad attempted to develop freight traffic by switching cars between steam railroads anxious to avoid the delays inevitable in the Chicago terminals.

However, freight, even in its peak year of 1930, never accounted for more than 17.7 percent of total revenues, and three years later in the Depression when the CA&E was once again in bankruptcy, freight revenues had fallen to 5.5 percent of the total, or about $82,930 annually. Even during World War II when traffic was heavy on U.S. railroads, freight on the CA&E never reached more than half of what it had been in the late 1920s when freight revenues had averaged about $400,000 a year.[26]

An attempt by the CA&E's post-reorganization managers to elicit more freight to offset declining passenger traffic was moderately successful, and for a time the railroad was forced to bring its three old box motors out of retirement to augment its four freight locomotives. However, it operated as a freight railroad for only two years after abandoning passenger service in 1957.

The Chicago, North Shore & Milwaukee similarly was unable to subsidize its commuter operation despite some heroic attempts to develop sufficient freight traffic. Although the North Shore was primarily a commuter railroad, it also served as an intercity carrier that provided service to industrial areas of Milwaukee, Racine, Kenosha, and Waukegan alongside and in competition with the established Chicago & North Western Railway. For most of its route in Illinois south of Waukegan, the North Shore ran through affluent residential suburbs and in the predominantly residential North Side of Chicago. To offer North Shore commuters a one-seat ride to the Loop, the railroad's owners in 1919 negotiated trackage rights over the Northwestern Elevated's rapid transit line.

The connection over the L was sufficient for passenger cars, but the lack of a good freight connection downtown caused the railroad to embark on an innovative program that would be adopted more than three decades later by the rest of the U.S. railroad industry as a way to compete with highway motor trucks. Since the North Shore's freight terminal was six miles from the Loop, the railroad had to find a way to get freight the final leg of its journey without having to use

The Chicago, North Shore & Milwaukee electric interurban line pioneered the use of piggyback truck trailers on railroad flatcars in the 1920s. The railroad, which operated over the Chicago Rapid Transit elevated structure for 10 miles north of the Loop, could not use freight cars on the L, so it trucked cargo on that leg to provide through service to downtown Chicago. (Norm Carlson Collection)

other railroads. In 1926 it developed what later became known as piggyback, or TOFC (trailers on freight cars), service in which truck trailers were carried on railroad flatcars between two destination cities. At the terminals the trailers were delivered or hauled away by motor truck.[27] In the second half of the twentieth century piggyback truck trailers became big business for railroads serving Chicago.

Despite its piggyback service, the North Shore was never able to develop much freight traffic. In 1916 freight accounted for only about 4.4 percent of revenues, and despite a concerted effort to increase freight business after utilities magnate Samuel Insull gained control of the line in 1916, the railroad was not able to induce enough industry to locate along its track to support it. In 1930, freight accounted for only 21 percent of revenues.[28] The railroad's owners finally shut it down in 1963.

The South Shore Line, which was in financial difficulty from its inception in 1908, by 1916 began to pursue freight traffic in rapidly industrializing northwest Indiana to offset its poor performance as a passenger carrier. It operated its first freight train that year and acquired its first freight locomotives. By the end of 1917 freight revenues reached $27,000. Emphasis on freight accelerated after Insull acquired the line in 1925. In the following years Insull's managers bought 10 electric freight locomotives, improved track by adding freight sidings, built freight stations, and successfully pressured other railroads and shippers for business. Working with other Insull subsidiaries, it helped establish a $200,000 loan fund to induce industries to locate in Northern Indiana. Following the lead of its North Shore sibling, it started piggyback service. By 1930, freight revenues were $1.5 million, having increased sixfold over what they were six years earlier when Insull had bought the line.[29]

By 1955 when the other two surviving interurbans were mired in financial difficulties from which they would not escape, the South Shore's freight traffic accounted for more than half of its revenues. By the end of 1975 the railroad was subsisting on freight, which accounted for three-fourths of all revenue; in fact, passenger revenue during the 20-year period 1952–1971 remained flat while freight revenues increased from $3.7 million per annum to $9.2 million.[30]

The Beginning of Decentralization

Although decentralization of the Chicago metropolitan area is a phenomenon usually associated with the expressway-building program in the second half of the twentieth century, Chicago's railroad industry began the industrial decentralization process more than 70 years earlier in an effort to cope with the congestion it had created in the central city. The belt railroads, yards, and industrial spurs built on the fringes of Chicago and in its suburbs not only helped the railroads handle the increase in freight traffic but also made it possible for other industries to migrate outward onto cheaper sites. When the expressways finally appeared, they simply accelerated the trend toward industrial decentralization.

As the city's passenger terminals expanded in size and number to handle that growing business, there was a commensurate growth in the coach yards serving them. That in turn began to squeeze out the freight yards that originally had been built along the river to enable an easy interchange of traffic with ships. For logistical reasons the passenger and commuter yards could never get very far from the downtown stations, but the freight yards could be moved, especially as the need arose to expand them.

The original railroads in the 1850s could make due with very small flat yards of three to five tracks near downtown or alongside the river docks, but toward the end of the nineteenth century they moved operations to somewhat larger yards farther from downtown. As rail traffic and the resulting congestion increased, the railroads responded by building giant classification yards in the suburbs, and by the end of the century they were acquiring sites on the fringe of the metropolitan area or beyond for intermodal yards that could handle the explosive growth of piggyback and container traffic.[31]

The incentive for building bigger yards farther from downtown Chicago was largely economic. Not only was the downtown area becoming too expensive for freight yards, but the cost of switching traffic between the small, inefficient downtown yards was becoming prohibitive. In 1889, it was calculated that it cost $12 just to move a 20-ton boxcar through the switching process in Chicago, and by 1912, yard delays cost railroads in Chicago an estimated $6 million.[32]

The Chicago & North Western was one of the first to move its freight operations out of downtown Chicago. Beginning in 1873 it moved its principal freight yard five miles west from its original site just along the Chicago River junction at Wolf Point to Crawford Avenue (now Pulaski Road) and finally, in 1903, to Proviso Township on the western edge of Cook County. Even that yard, which was built to handle 2,000 cars, had to be enlarged to handle 26,000 cars in the 1920s.

The Chicago, Milwaukee, St. Paul & Pacific in slightly more than a decade outgrew Galewood yard in Chicago and in 1918 completed a new 8,730-car yard in suburban Bensenville. The IC's lakefront yard south of Congress Street was replaced in 1926 by the Fordham yard at 87th Street and later by the Markham yard in suburban Homewood 20 miles south of the Loop.

The Clearing Yard, which opened in 1902 on the far Southwest Side, was a cooperative effort ultimately by seven railroads to build a big yard they could jointly use. It was proposed in 1889 by A. B. Stickney, who at the time was assembling the Great Western Railway and saw the possibility of a great yard that would serve as a clearinghouse for all freight cars moving through Chicago. The yard, complete with the new technology of a gravity hump for switching, was finally finished in 1902 but for most of its history never attained the importance its proponents had hoped and suffered occasional desertions even by its owning partners.[33]

Clearing and another yard like it, the Chicago Junction Railway's (later Indiana Harbor Belt) huge yard along Ashland Avenue north of the stockyards, both became magnets for substantial industrial manufacturing developments on their borders. The Junction Railway was in fact a creature of the Central Manufacturing District, which had been organized as one of the prototypical industrial development districts in the United States.[34]

The organizers planned to develop a manufacturing complex on one square mile of land north of the stockyards, which a few years earlier in the 1870s had acted as a magnet for the city's growing meatpacking industry. The Central Manufacturing District not only assembled the land, built streets, and installed utilities but offered architectural, engineering, and financial services as well as access to railroad lines. The Clearing District on the Southwest Side did much the same thing a little later.[35]

The pattern of the industrial out-migration was determined largely by the railroad network. Thus the areas with the greatest concentration of railroad lines also tended to act as the greatest magnets of industry. This was especially true of the South Side of Chicago and the southern suburbs that were crossed not only by the trunk lines from the east but railroads from the south and some from the west. At least before the advent of the motor truck, the Southwest and West sides of the city and their suburbs had somewhat fewer rail lines and industry. The Northwest and North sides of the city, and the suburbs in those directions, had in the nineteenth century the lightest concentration of railroads and industry—a pattern still evident.

One of the largest and most important of those industries that arose in the region in the second half of the century, although relatively little has been written about it, developed not only because of the transportation opportunities the Chicago rail junction provided but because that junction was, in fact, its market. The city's rail boom gave rise to factories built to supply the railroads with everything from locomotives and cars to rail and track spikes. For some industries, like big steel, the railroads accounted for only a portion of their output, but the railroads were the only customers for other companies, the transfer firms that hauled passengers between stations and factories that built freight cars. Although many of the rail supply companies were relatively unknown outside their industry, some, like Rand McNally and Pullman, became famous.

The Railroad Supply Industry

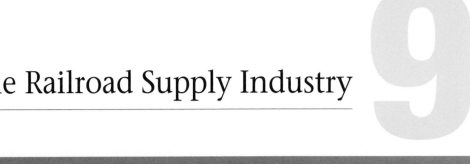

The railroads' economic influence on Chicago included not only the carriers themselves and the industries that relied on them for transportation but a new industry that grew up to supply the railroads with equipment, including everything from rail cars to signal systems. Pullman's role as a car builder is well known, but the map-making firm of Rand McNally got its start printing railroad tickets and schedules, and Nalco, an international manufacturer of water treatment systems, began in business by treating steam boilers on loco-

motives. Scores of smaller and less well-known firms manufactured a variety of components from switch frogs to crossing gates. A number of local companies, like Parmelee in the passenger business and Willett in freight, provided the railroad industry with local transportation between depots and freight houses.

Chicago early in the twenty-first century was still the epicenter of the nation's shrunken railroad supply industry, although much of the manufacturing had shifted elsewhere and many companies

General Motors–built diesels have been a fixture on Chicago-area commuter railroads since the 1950s. The locomotive on the right is representative of the earlier period when GM auto styling was more evident on its railroad equipment. The locomotives built later in the century were boxier, indicating that cost efficiency had triumphed over styling.

Railroads often built their own rolling stock but frequently went to outside suppliers for specialized equipment, like this early Illinois Central sleeping car. This gave rise to a huge railroad supply industry that was largely concentrated in Chicago. The IC car was built in 1856 by Buffalo Car Company before George Pullman got his start in that business. (Alan R. Lind, Transport History Press)

had disappeared through consolidation, had branched into other endeavors, or simply had gone out of business as the nation's railroad system declined in size in the second half of the twentieth century. As a result, the rail supply industry's impact on the local economy in 2000 was a fraction of what it had been a century earlier.

A few of the companies were giants and well known to the public, but most were small, relatively unknown, and privately held firms that specialized in the manufacture of components used to build trains, signal equipment, and track. George Pullman's name became synonymous with sleeping cars and was typically applied even to those his company had not built, but the rail supply industry included scores of other large companies. Firms like GATX, Union Tank Car, and North American Car Company leased railway cars and were relatively well known in Chicago and the railroad industry. The Electro-Motive Division of General Motors Corporation manufactured diesel-electric locomotives and for a time was dominant in North America in that business. Companies obscure outside the railroad industry included Western Railroad Supply Company (later Western-Cullen-Hayes), which built

signal systems, and Thrall Car Manufacturing Company, a freight car builder.

The effect of the rail supply industry on Chicago in the nineteenth century is difficult to quantify due to the fragmentary nature of available data and the difficulty of determining what proportion of other industries, like steel, meatpacking, and manufacturing, was rail related. Chicago in 1890 had 360,000 wage earners, almost a third of them (125,000) employed by 3,000 large firms. Pullman's Chicago factory alone employed 12,000 workers in times of peak production, and Haskell & Barker, another rail car builder in the region, had more than 2,000 workers on its payroll. The Union Stock Yards at the turn of the century had 45,000 employees, but the bulk of them were in meatpacking, not rail transportation. Most rail supply companies had only a few hundred employees, if that, but collectively they employed thousands of persons.

Pullman's Empire

Pullman for much of its corporate existence (1867–1984) was the nation's best-known and largest manufacturer of both passenger and freight cars and deserves a book unto itself, as does its founder, George Mortimer Pullman. His legacy was such that his name survived into the twenty-first century in the South Side neighborhood where he built his rail car factory and adjacent company town, and as a synonym for railroad sleeping cars. He also emerged as the villain to the American labor movement in the national railroad strike of 1894. He did not invent the railroad sleeper and dining cars that revolutionized rail travel after the Civil War, but he assembled a company to build them. Then he and his successors, through acquisitions of other companies, effectively monopolized the sleeping-car business in America by operating those vehicles under contract with almost every railroad in the nation.

Pullman, a Chatauqua County, New York, native, initially made his living by elevating and moving buildings along the Erie Canal and came to Chicago around 1856 to help raise Chicago's buildings above the marsh on which they had been built. He got his start building railroad passenger cars in 1859 when a friend and financier who had a franchise from sleeping car innovator Theodore J. Woodruff and contracts with several Chicago-based railroads to provide them with sleepers induced Pullman to join the faltering operation. In 1859 he had the Chicago & Alton Railroad shops remodel two coaches into sleepers using designs patented by Woodruff, but he did not get into the car-building business as a full-time pursuit until 1863. In the interim he made a fortune in Colorado speculating in land, mining, storekeeping, running a wagon line, and investing in such things as a shirt factory and a bank. In 1863 he and a partner bought a sleeping car for service on the Chicago & Alton and the following year leased a shed from that railroad to build a car he dubbed "Pioneer."[1]

Railroad legend has it that the use of "Pioneer" in President Abraham Lincoln's funeral train between Chicago and Springfield in 1865 attracted considerable atten-

tion in the railroad industry and gave Pullman's new company some needed prestige. According to the legend later spread by Pullman officials, the Chicago & Alton Railroad had to hurriedly modify stations and other obstructions to accommodate the oversized car. However, that legend has been largely debunked in recent years. A Pullman-built car apparently was used in the train, but it did not receive any notoriety until years later when the company was already a giant.[2]

Although Pullman by 1865 had signed up all the major railroads operating out of Chicago to use his sleepers, in fact, it was Pullman's encounter with steel magnate Andrew Carnegie during some contract negotiations in 1867 that set Pullman on the path to greatness. At the time there were perhaps a dozen sleeping-car builders in the nation with operations larger than Pullman's, but none of their owners had the organizational and capital-raising skills of Pullman, a characteristic that impressed Carnegie. Pullman had already successfully solicited the support of Chicago millionaires John Crerar and Marshall Field.

Carnegie somewhat earlier had invested in a Pullman rival—Central Transportation Company—but promptly switched alliances and engineered Pullman's takeover of Central in 1870 by the expedient and relatively cheap method of having Pullman lease the other company, including its contracts for 4,400 route-miles of service on 16 railroads. Other acquisitions quickly followed, so that by the end of the nineteenth century 14 of the 25 largest sleeping-car manufacturers in the United States had wound up in the Pullman empire.[3]

The 1870 Central Transportation acquisition forced Pullman, who had incorporated his own Pullman Palace Car Company in 1867, to consider building his own cars. Until then Pullman, like most sleeping-car companies of the time, contracted out the construction of its vehicles and made its money by operating its sleepers under contract with the railroads. Most railroads, though not all, were only too happy to avoid the problem of staffing and maintaining the cars. Soon after the Central Transportation takeover, Pullman acquired the Detroit Car & Manufacturing Company's old plant in Detroit, modernized it, and began building his own cars to create the base on which he would build his vertical monopoly. Within a few years Pullman had developed dining and lounge cars as well as sleepers and employed 2,000 persons building and operating his fleet of 400 cars. He had put his first dining car in operation in 1868.[4]

The Detroit factory did not have the capacity to match Pullman's designs for expansion; however, within a few years he began planning for a giant new plant in Chicago. The resulting Pullman Car Works near Lake Calumet south of Chicago opened in 1881 to be close to the steel industry and suppliers of components like wheels and trucks. He built a model town nearby to house and serve workers. The factory was the largest railroad car plant in existence, initially employing more than 3,000 and at peak times as many as 12,000.[5]

As the company continued to grow, it acquired the Haskell & Barker plant in Michigan City, Indiana, in 1922; the Osgood Bradley Car Company plant in Worcester, Massachusetts, in 1920; and the Chickasaw Shipbuilding and Car Company in Bessemer, Alabama, in 1929. The Standard Steel Car Company with plants in Butler, Pennsylvania, and Hammond, Indiana, was merged into Pullman in 1930. By then the company controlled an estimated 90 percent of the sleeping-car business in the United States, and the federal government after the Democrats took control in 1933 began to look into whether the company was violating antitrust laws.[6]

Almost 40 years earlier the federal government had intervened on Pullman's behalf in the 1894 strike, a clear indication of how influential the railroad industry and Pullman had become in the late nineteenth century. Before the general railroad strike of 1877 and in addition to troops as-

signed to Camp Douglas during the Civil War, federal troops had been sent to Chicago in force only twice before in peacetime. General Winfield Scott's army had arrived by ship from the East in 1832 to fight Black Hawk, and General Philip Sheridan had summoned troops to maintain order after the fire of 1871.[7]

However, both Democratic and Republican administrations committed federal troops in Chicago during the 1877 and 1894 strikes, and Illinois sent in the militia in 1877. The commitment of troops in the first strike was an effort to put an end to rioting, but in the Pullman strike of 1894 the role of the troops was more to quash the strike and get the trains rolling again. The 1877 strike was begun by firemen and brakemen in the East after the Baltimore & Ohio Railroad announced wage cuts and an increase in train sizes without a commensurate increase in crews, and it quickly spread to Pittsburgh, Buffalo, Chicago, St. Louis, and St. Paul. The strike erupted spontaneously in Chicago and quickly devolved into street riots, forcing Mayor Monroe Heath to request federal troops and call out the national guard to preserve order. Chicago accounted for 30 of the 100 laborers killed nationally in the riots.[8]

Rail labor unrest continued to erupt sporadically over a decade and a half, culminating in the Pullman strike of 1894. There were strikes against several of Jay Gould's railroads, including the Wabash, in 1885–1886; one against the Chicago, Burlington & Quincy in 1888; and another against the New York Central in 1890. The 1894 strike began at Pullman Car Works in Chicago and was precipitated by George Pullman's decisions during the Panic of 1893 to cut wages by a third and reduce his workforce, as well as by his refusal to reduce rents on company-owned housing and retail prices at his company stores.[9]

Labor leader Eugene V. Debs organized the Pullman workers, and a strike was called on May 11, 1894. It spread to much of the rest of the nation, especially the western railroads, the following month when the fledgling American Railway Union sympathetically refused to handle Pullman cars and the railroads' General Managers Association based in Chicago threatened to fire anyone who went along with the boycott. Richard Olney, Democratic President Grover Cleveland's attorney general and a former railroad lawyer, then appointed Edwin Walker, the General Managers Association's legal adviser, as the special U.S. attorney in Chicago.

Walker, after a couple of minor disturbances and labor confrontations with the state militia on July 2, 1894, obtained an injunction against the strikers for violation of the Sherman Anti-Trust Act. The next day Olney persuaded President Cleveland to send in federal troops despite the objections of Illinois governor John Peter Altgeld. The troops enabled the railroads using strikebreakers to get the trains rolling again by July 9; Debs was arrested for violating the injunction; and the strike collapsed the following August 2.[10]

Freight Cars

Although the locomotive builders remained in the East where they had gotten their start before Chicago's ascendancy as a rail center, a situation that would not change until General Motors began building diesel electric locomotives in the Chicago area in the 1930s, much of the freight car–building industry became centered in the Windy City and its environs during the second half of the nineteenth century primarily because of the concentration of railroads there and the large local markets for cars. The steel industry required large numbers of hopper cars for raw materials, like coal and ore, and gondolas for finished products. Meatpacking needed specialized refrigerator and cattle cars, and the oil industry used tank cars.

Although many railroads initially built their own cars in company shops, the growth of the railroads occurred so quickly in the last half of the nineteenth century that private companies sprang up because

the railroads were unable to build freight cars fast enough. Simultaneously with the arrival of the Northern Indiana (Lake Shore) Railroad in Michigan City, Indiana, Frederick Haskell and Mason C. Sherman opened a small car shop there. After a few lean years, the resulting Haskell & Barker Car Company grew fat on Civil War orders and by 1869 was one of the nation's largest freight car builders, producing two cars per day. By 1910 the company was churning out 15,000 cars annually and was the largest manufacturing operation in Indiana.[11]

Wells, French & Company, Chicago bridge builders, decided in 1871 to expand into railcar construction and hired Charles F. Scoville from the Illinois Central Railroad's car department to run the operation. After filling building orders for a number of railroads, the company was acquired in 1899 by American Car & Foundry.

Pullman expanded into freight car production after building his new plant in Chicago. In 1884, using a streamlined assembly process employing 29 gangs of 4 men each, it produced 100 flatcars for the Vicksburg, Shreveport & Pacific Railroad in an eight-hour shift. By 1925 the company, which three years earlier had acquired Haskell & Barker, was building twice as many freight cars as passenger vehicles.[12]

The availability of large tracts of relatively cheap land devoid of neighboring residential development was a factor in the decision of car builders to choose remote sites instead of the central cities. This was a factor in Pullman's decision to build his plant in the Lake Calumet area as well as the decision of Standard Steel Car Company of Butler, Pennsylvania, to open a factory in Hammond in 1907. Chicago lumberman Turlington W. Harvey chose a remote south suburban site for a factory and company town for his American Fireproof Steel Car Company. The company produced only 100 cars before it closed following the Panic of 1893.[13]

The reluctance of the railroads to build specialized cars that would carry loads in only one direction led to the creation of fleets of cars owned by individual shippers, especially refrigerator, livestock, and tank cars that by the late 1800s collectively accounted for something like 10 percent of the total of railroad cars in the U.S. By the end of the twentieth century, fleets owned by shippers and independent car companies accounted for nearly half of the nation's rail fleet.[14]

Private car companies began in the East in the 1850s and quickly spread to Chicago. The United States Rolling Stock Company organized in 1871 in the East but in 1884–1885 found it necessary to build a large plant south of Chicago in Hegewisch. Henry C. Hicks developed stock cars in Minneapolis in 1881 but moved to Chicago in 1884 to establish his Hicks Humane Live Stock Car Company. Likewise, George H. Hammond, a Detroit meatpacker, found it necessary to establish a slaughterhouse in Hohman, Indiana, just southeast of Chicago and later renamed in his honor, to get better rail connections to markets in the East as well as to western livestock sources. Hammond also developed a refrigerated car to transport dressed beef to the East, and by 1885 his company owned 600 such vehicles.[15]

Other Chicago-area meatpackers quickly realized the advantages of owning their own fleets and began acquiring them. Beginning in 1872 in a plant in south suburban Blue Island, Ferdinand E. Canda built refrigerator cars for various customers. Gustavus Swift, who was using refrigerator cars developed by others in 1878, hired an engineer to design his own vehicles and three years later had 200 of them in operation. Philip D. Armour bought his first cars in 1883 and by 1900 had a fleet of 12,000.[16]

The necessity of bringing livestock from the West also required specialized cars. Hicks and Canda developed such vehicles earlier, but interest in the humane treatment of animals in transit was the impetus behind cars developed by Chicago wholesale clothing merchant Alonzo C. Mather

in the 1880s. Mather had witnessed the fatal goring of some cattle by a large steer while on a train trip in 1881 and was determined to build a car with interior pens to confine the animals as well as facilities to feed and water them en route. By 1895 he operated a fleet of 3,000 cattle cars. Shortly after Mather started in the railcar business, fellow Chicagoan J. W. Street got into it as well by acquiring other lines, including Hicks's, and controlled 9,000 cars just after the turn of the century.[17]

Car Leasing

The conception of the private freight car—a vehicle owned by someone other than a railroad corporation—dates almost from the inception of railroads in America, and in the mid-nineteenth century as much as 10 percent of the freight business was handled by private cars. Some early shippers simply leased cars from the railroads, but some major shippers, like Chicago's meatpackers and J. D. Rockefeller's oil company, owned their own fleets for their specialized operations and sometimes leased cars to other shippers with similar needs. Privately owned cars and cars leased by outside companies enabled the railroads to avoid the expense of building fleets of specialized vehicles that might sit idle for months at a time and were dedicated to hauling traffic in only one direction. The advantage of such vehicles is that they could be used by their shipper-owners on any railroad, not just the line that happened to own the freight car. By 1900 Philip D. Armour leased many of his 12,000 refrigerated cars to other businesses, including produce shippers.[18]

Before the end of the century some companies sprang up specifically to lease freight cars to firms that could not afford or did not want to bother with their own fleets. Like the private refrigerator fleets, these companies tended to congregate in Chicago, which because of its central location and concentration of railroads, provided a huge market. Even the tank car leasing industry, which had originated with the American oil industry in Pennsylvania after the Civil War, eventually gravitated to Chicago. By the end of the twentieth century, the leased car business in the United States was huge: the nation's three major leasing firms (GATX, Union Tank Car, and GE Capital Rail Services), all based in Chicago, had a combined fleet of more than 400,000 of the nearly 1,400,000 freight cars in service in North America. In addition, TTX Company, the firm the railroad industry established as Trailer Train Company in 1956 in Chicago to provide it with a pool of freight cars so as to relieve regional and seasonal spot shortages of cars, had 129,000 railcars.[19]

Max Epstein was not the first person to buy and lease freight cars, even in Chicago, but he became one of the most successful, and his GATX (General American Transportation Corporation) survived into the twenty-first century by expanding into airplanes and ships as well as railroad cars. Epstein, an enterprising young employee of a Chicago stockyards provision company, in 1898 heard that a Pittsburgh brewing company was considering buying 20 used refrigerator cars and brokered the deal between the owners, a meatpacker that had intended to scrap the cars, and the brewery at $50 per car. He impressed the brewery executives who had come to inspect the cars by repainting one in the company's logotype. The meatpacker then asked Epstein if he could unload another 28 surplus reefers, which he himself bought on contract for $1,000 down with the $10,200 balance to be paid in installments.[20]

By the time he incorporated as Atlantic Seaboard Dispatch in 1902, Epstein was leasing out a fleet of 32 cars, including five tank cars used to haul lard. Within five years his fleet had swelled to 400 rail vehicles, mainly tank cars, and he had begun manufacturing his own at a factory in East Chicago, Indiana. Mainly by acquiring four tank car leasing companies in Penn-

sylvania and Oklahoma and a refrigerator line in Wisconsin, General American, as the company had been renamed in 1927, had more than 30,000 cars in its fleet. By the beginning of the twenty-first century GATX's lease fleet consisted of 71,000 tank cars, 58,000 specialized freight cars, and 900 locomotives.[21]

The railroad tank car was developed during the Civil War by various inventors but was first developed as a practical vehicle by James and Amos Densmore to haul Pennsylvania oil to market. They soon had plenty of competition. J. J. Vandergrift in 1866 founded the Star Tank Line to haul oil from Pennsylvania to Chicago, and he sold the company to Rockefeller's Standard Oil Company in 1873. From then until the dissolution of the Standard Oil Trust in 1911, Union Tank Car Company, as it was renamed in 1878, was an exclusive hauler of Standard Oil products. The dissolution of the trust by the 1920s forced the company, by then renamed UTCC and headquartered in Chicago, to find other customers by leasing its fleet. By 1931 it had branched into the hauling of chemicals.[22]

In 1981 Union Tank Car was acquired by the Marmon Holdings Inc., the private company owned by the descendants of Nicholas J. Pritzker. As the twenty-first century dawned, the company leased 64,539 tank cars, many of them built in its East Chicago, Indiana, factory and 16,491 other freight cars.[23]

North American Car Company, founded in 1907 in Chicago, was the third surviving firm specializing in railcar leasing. It eventually was acquired by Tiger International Inc., the global air freight company, but when that company wound up in financial difficulty during the recession in the early 1980s, North American was forced into bankruptcy in 1984. Its fleet of 55,000 cars and its management operation was bought in 1986 by General Electric Railcar Services Corporation, a General Electric Company subsidiary based in Chicago.[24]

The Decline

The decline of the car-building industry in Chicago parallels that of the railroads and occurred for many of the same reasons. As competition from automobiles and airlines, in the case of passenger service, and motor trucks, barges, and pipelines, in the case of freight, all increased after 1930, the nation's railroad system began to shrink, and with it the market for railcars. The general decline and migration of heavy manufacturing from the Rust Belt was another factor, as was the commensurate increase in the size of freight cars that enabled the railroads to carry more freight with fewer cars. The average freight car capacity increased from 46.3 tons in 1929 to almost 90 tons by the end of the century.

The automobile and airplane captured most of the railroads' intercity passenger traffic, and the automobile also cut into the commuter rail market of both the steam and the interurban carriers, less so in Chicago than in other cities. The motor truck, pipelines, and barge lines made substantial inroads into the railroads' freight markets. For trucks, this was especially true in the less-than-carload shipments that formerly traveled in rail boxcars. Agricultural commodities shifted from rail to barge. The substantial investments made by the federal, state, and municipal governments in highways, airways, and waterways after World War I and the absence of any investment in railroads until the 1970s took its toll. The nation's railroad system shrank from 233,670 miles in 1940 to 136,642 miles in 1995, while over the same span the U.S. highway system tripled from 311,378 miles to 953,009 miles and the airway system increased tenfold from 36,947 miles to 394,000.[25]

Railroads in 1929 carried about three-quarters of the nation's freight tonnage, but that had declined to 40 percent by the end of the century (see Table 9-1). Rail passenger traffic collapsed in spectacular fashion after World War II. Rail accounted for 27 percent of the nation's passenger miles traveled in 1945, but less than 1 percent in 1970 when the federal government came to the rescue with Amtrak, and only 0.6 percent in 1996 when Amtrak was teetering on the edge of insolvency. The effect on the rail supply industry was dramatic: U.S. locomotive production, which averaged more than 1,000 a year until 1974, averaged slightly more than 600 annually in the decade of the 1990s. Passenger car production fluctuated widely but had declined to an average of only about 50 a year in the late 1990s from a level of hundreds of cars a year in the 1950s.[26]

TABLE 9-1 **U.S. Freight Transportation Distribution** (percentage of ton-miles)

Year	Rail	Truck	Pipeline	Water	Air
1916	77.2%	——	4.4%	18.4%	——
1930	74.3	3.9	5.3	16.5	——
1940	61.3	10.0	9.6	19.1	0.01
1950	56.1	16.3	12.1	15.4	0.03
1970	39.8	21.3	22.3	16.5	0.17
1996	40.0	27.7	17.7	14.2	0.37

Sources: Interstate Commerce Commission, *Transport Economics,* Annual Reports for the years indicated in the table. U.S. Army Corps of Engineers, *Waterborne Commerce of the U.S.,* Part 5, annual reports for the years indicated. U.S. Department of Transportation, *Air Carrier Traffic Statistics,* All Services, for the years indicated. Eno Transportation Foundation Inc., *Transportation in America, 1997* (Lansdowne, Va., 1997), Domestic Intercity Ton-Miles by Mode, 46.

The rail supply business became highly cyclic: the railroads bought freight cars when the economy was good but made do with older equipment during the economic downturns. During those recessions, many railroads also deferred track maintenance. As is typical in declining industries, the surviving rail supply companies tended to consolidate into ever-larger enterprises to reduce competition, which, because of their huge overhead became more vulnerable to downturns and competition from smaller companies better able to control costs.

The case histories of several Chicago companies illustrated the phenomenon. The giant Pullman, once the nation's largest builder of both passenger and freight cars, simply imploded. Thrall Car Manufacturing Company was acquired by another firm in a merger. Johnstown

America Industries, the Pennsylvania company that was spun off from Bethlehem Steel in 1991, moved its headquarters to Chicago, diversified by acquiring other transportation companies, and sold off the rail car operation in 1999. North American Car Company filed for bankruptcy and was acquired by General Electric. The pattern of railroad industry companies' use of the assets of their core business to diversify into less cyclic and more profitable businesses in other industries before selling off the core was relatively common in the second half of the twentieth century.[27]

The demise of the once-great Pullman empire was less of a bang than a whimper. The company's first major setback occurred in 1947 when it lost an antitrust case to the federal government and had to divest itself of its railcar operating subsidiary that owned, staffed, and

Eventually as the demand for railroad cars slowed to a trickle in the last quarter of the twentieth century, Pullman quietly faded from existence. A single abandoned car sat rusting in Pullman's empty South Side factory yard in 1996 when this photograph was snapped.

maintained sleeping cars for the railroads. Ironically, the government's victory came just as the railroad passenger business was entering its dramatic decline that led to government ownership through Amtrak. The Budd Company, a rival builder, had complained to the U.S. Justice Department about the Pullman monopoly as early as 1935 when Pullman used its corporate muscle to undermine a sale of Budd cars to the Chicago, Burlington & Quincy Railroad. The Justice Department on July 12, 1940, filed a civil suit against Pullman for violation of the Sherman and Clayton antitrust acts. The court ruled in the government's favor in 1944 and ordered Pullman to divest either its operating or car-building divisions. Pullman chose the former and in 1947 completed the sale of 6,000 sleeping cars staffed by 30,000 employees to a consortium of 57 railroads.[28] The black porters featured in advertisements were no longer employees of Pullman but of the railroads.

The postwar U.S. market for passenger cars was split roughly in half between the railroads and mass transit systems, and neither segment of the industry was in particularly good financial shape by the 1960s. Although commuter railroad ridership had held up relatively well, intercity traffic had been in free fall since World War II. Federal subsidies began to flow to the nation's mass transit systems in the 1960s although not on a regular basis until the 1970s. In four of the seven years in the period 1973–1979 there were fewer than 100 rail passenger cars built in America, the most highly industrialized nation on earth. Punctuating the highly cyclic rail passenger car market were huge orders for rapid transit cars placed by cities like New York and Chicago, and the few remaining car builders bid furiously for that business, often bidding projects under their costs to keep production lines running.[29]

Pullman was the successful bidder at $210 million for a huge order for 754 subway cars for New York City but ultimately lost $44.8 million on the deal. In 1975 it was the successful bidder for 284 bi-level Superliner cars for Amtrak, and it reopened its Hammond plant because the Chicago factory was still busy with the New York order. The Amtrak project quickly ran into trouble: technical difficulties with the initial cars slowed production, and a 27-week strike in 1977–1978 put the project hopelessly behind schedule. When Pullman in 1979 failed to win an order for 600 cars for the Chicago Transit Authority, Samuel B. Casey, Jr., its chairman, announced his company was withdrawing from the passenger car business after 120 years.[30]

The company tried to continue to compete in the freight car business, but that, too, was doomed. Its huge plants in Butler and Bessemer were designed to mass-produce freight cars and proved to be too expensive to operate when the freight car market precipitously collapsed during the recession in the early 1980s. Annual freight car production in the United States dropped from 95,836 in 1979 to only 5,772 in 1983 and despite some recovery by the end of the decade was only a third of what it had been earlier. Pullman was acquired by Wheelabrator Frye, which closed the Butler and Bessemer plants in 1983 and sold them to Trinity Industries the following year. Portions of the giant Chicago plant ultimately wound up in the hands of Morrison Knudsen and finally Amerail before shutting down in 1998.[31]

The decline of the railroad industry also affected other rail supply companies. Portec Incorporated in 1997 sold off its railroad supply division, a manufacturer of rail maintenance products dating back to 1905. Varlen Corporation, which also made railroad components, was acquired by Amsted Industries, another Chicago company, in 1999. Johnstown America Industries sold its railcar building division in 1999 and changed its name to Transportation Technologies Industries. In 2001, Trinity Industries acquired through merger the privately owned Thrall Car Manufacturing Company based in suburban Elmhurst.[32]

Changing Technology

Technological changes in the twentieth century also had a substantial effect on the rail supply industry in Chicago. Some companies adapted by incorporating the new innovations in their products, and others successfully found new markets outside of the railroad industry. Western Railroad Supply Company, under a variety of names, was one of a handful of companies making signals to survive for a century and a half the cyclic nature of the railroad business; numerous acquisitions, mergers, and divestitures; and the expansion and contraction of the railroad industry. Over the years the company founded as American Signal Company changed its name to Railroad Supply (1895), Western Railroad Supply (1932), and Western-Cullen-Hayes (1977). Over the same span it acquired four other companies making railroad signals and track equipment (Chicago Railroad Signal and Supply, L. S. Brach Manufacturing, Bryant Zinc, and Hayes Track Appliance); was acquired by three other companies (J. Patrick Lannon in 1953, Federal Signal Corporation in 1968, and an investment group in 1977); and finally was spun off as an independent company again in 1990.

To a great extent the company's longevity was attributable to its willingness to adapt to new electronic technology. As early as 1889 it developed an automatic rail-highway-crossing warning device activated by a locomotive passing over and activating an electric relay. In 1912 it obtained in the acquisition of L. S. Brach an automatic "wave light" signal for crossings, and two years later in the Bryant Zinc acquisition it got the rights to the "wig wag" signal developed by that company. In 1936 it developed in house an automatic crossing warning barrier. The company also built and sold the now familiar automatic alternating crossing signals and gates as those devices were developed.[33]

Two other rail supply companies survived in a changing world by abandoning the railroad industry and adapting their technologies to other markets. National Aluminate Corporation, which came into existence as a result of a merger in 1929, traced its origins to a company that made and sold aluminum sulfate to treat water used in railroad locomotive boilers. That market dried up when the railroads converted to diesel electric locomotives in the 1950s, but Nalco survived by producing chemicals for other types of water treatment and in 1999 was acquired by Suez Lyonnaise Des Eaux, a French corporation.[34]

One of the most unusual firms in Chicago's railroad supply industry was Rand McNally & Co., which began in 1856 as a job printshop owned by William Rand and Andrew McNally and by 1864 had branched into railroad timetables and tickets. The company produced its first map, a product for which it was to become well known, in the 1872 Railway Guide. Early in the twentieth century Rand McNally began producing photoguide books for motorists, and as the nation's highway system was built it began producing road atlases. Ultimately maps and atlases became the company's major business as railroad passenger volume declined later in the century. Rand McNally survived a bankruptcy and was still producing maps into the twenty-first century.[35]

The conversion from steam to diesel power began with switching locomotives and did not spread to mainline service until the new technology proved itself. The principal beneficiary of the locomotive conversion from steam to diesel was the Electro-Motive Division of General Motors Corporation, based for much of its existence in a Chicago suburb. Electro Motive Engineering Corporation had been founded in Cleveland in 1922 to build railroad vehicles. These vehicles had an internal combustion engine that drove a generator to provide electrical power to motors that applied traction directly to the axles. Steam engines typically transferred power from the pistons to the driving wheels by means of steel driving rods.

Perhaps the most famous of the self-propelled streamliners of the 1930s powered by GM's Electro-Motive Division to usher in the diesel age were the stainless steel zephyrs introduced by the Burlington. This was the Silver King pictured in Galesburg, Illinois. (J. Michael Gruber)

General Motors, a corporation assembled from existing companies by William Durant and Alfred P. Sloan, acquired Electro-Motive in 1930 and began actively promoting the new technology to the railroad industry. In 1933 it built the engines for the Union Pacific's *M-10000* and the Burlington's *Pioneer Zephyr,* both of which were sets of self-propelled trains. GM decided to build a huge new plant for diesel locomotive production and chose as the site the western Chicago suburb of McCook to be closer to the center of the railroad industry in the U.S. The first locomotive produced there was a 100-ton switch engine that came off the line in 1936, but EMD executives realized that they needed to build larger units to compete with steam engines in freight service. In 1939 the company produced a demonstration unit and sent it on an 83,764-mile test on American railroads.[36]

The Depression and World War II retarded adoption of diesel power by the railroads, but following World War II the railroads rapidly replaced their fleets of steam locomotives with diesels. Although old-line steam locomotive builders like American Locomotive Company (ALCO), Montreal Locomotive Works, Baldwin Locomotive Works, and Fairbanks-Morse converted to diesel production, EMD was the prime beneficiary of the conversion. The company during the height of the diesel conversion employed more than 11,000 workers to grind out as many as 10 locomotives a day and accounted for as many as 80 percent of the locomotives in use on American railroads.[37]

However, production declined after the diesel conversion was completed, new competition from General Electric Company appeared in the 1970s, and a recession hit the industry in the early 1980s. By 1978 EMD was producing about half the locomotives it had in the 1950s, and in both 1983 and 1987 the division was forced to shut down its plant for several months because of the lack of orders. GE passed EMD in locomotive production in 1884, and in the 1990s EMD shifted its final assembly to a London, Ontario, plant. It kept the McCook plant as its corporate headquarters and the place to build components, a task that required only about 2,400 employees, about 1,000 of them on the production line. However, it utilized only about a third of the 3 million square feet of manufacturing space it had at that location. EMD began searching for other companies to buy portions of the facility.[38]

It was not long after the American

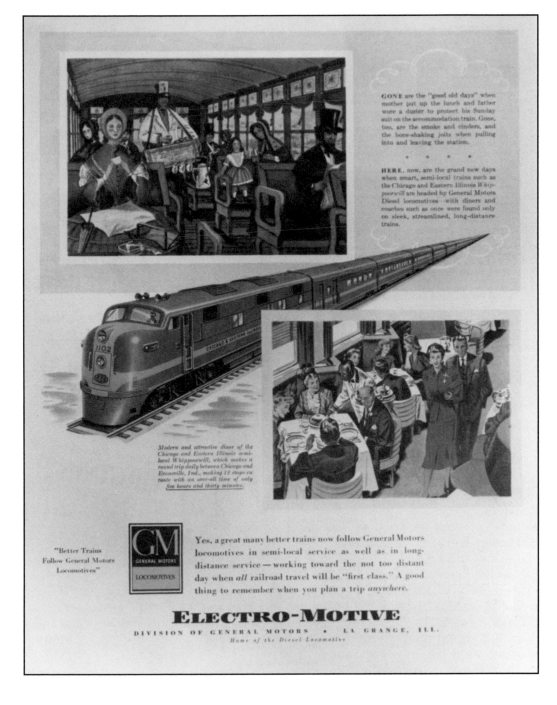

Another shrunken giant of Chicago's railroad supply industry is the Electro-Motive division of General Motors Corporation based in the western suburb of Mc-Cook. For a time after World War II, it became the dominant manufacturer of diesel-electric locomotives as the railroads converted from steam to oil.

Railroads had an effect on the commercial music industry. Songs like the "Ballad of Casey Jones" and "Rock Island Line" did much to popularize railroading. However, this "The Chicago Express" march two-step has been largely forgotten.

railroad industry began its decline in the middle of the twentieth century, dragging with it the rail supply industry, that the industry's apologists began to blame government for much of their troubles. Not only had government built the highways, locks and dams, and airports used by competitors of the railroad industry, but government regulation was strangling the railroad corporations, making it difficult for them to compete. The U.S. Justice Department had forced the bifurcation of Pullman just as the rail passenger business was on the verge of a precipitous decline. Rail-

road proponents in particular singled out the Interstate Commerce Commission as a regulatory dinosaur that treated the railroads as if they still had a monopoly on transportation.

It had taken the nation's railroads barely a century to be transformed from an unregulated industry ruthlessly putting its nineteenth-century competitors out of business, so powerful it could dictate to the rest of the country how to set its clocks, to an atrophying giant being strangled by competition and government rules.

Dominance, Reform, and Regulation

10

Almost from the inception of the iron horse, state and local governments felt it necessary to attempt to impose some sort of regulation on the mechanical beasts that were chugging and clanging across the landscape, striking awe into children and frightening livestock. The federal government did not get involved in the business of regulating railroads until much later in the nineteenth century, so early laws were left to a patchwork of state and local governments. Congress finally acted late in the nineteenth century after it be-

llatedly recognized that local controls on interstate commerce not only made it difficult for common carriers to operate across state lines but were almost impossible to enforce.

The earliest rules dealt primarily with safety. The mixing of fast-moving trains with slow, horse-drawn drays at crossings, equestrians, pedestrians, and children playing along the tracks was sufficiently dangerous that states and municipalities almost from the beginning mandated the sounding of locomotive whistles and bells

By 1941, Michigan Avenue had become a palisade of steel, stone, and glass overlooking the IC's Panama Limited destined to head south for New Orleans. The Art Institute is visible in the distance. (Alan R. Lind, Transport History Press)

Despite the existence of federal safety regulations and a signal system, a rear-end crash of two IC commuter trains in 1972 caused the deaths of 45 persons. Most of the deaths in the wreck were concentrated in the lightweight bi-level car that was crushed like an eggshell by heavier steel cars in the second train. (See Appendix C.)

to warn people of the approach of trains. The courts, using English common law as a precedent, also began to deal with the issue of torts—the liability for bystanders and railroad employees maimed and killed by trains.

Surprisingly, the issue of railroad operating safety except at crossings was left to the carriers themselves. Federal safety regulations did not appear until late in the nineteenth century. By then the railroad industry itself had addressed safety by installing telegraph lines and wayside signals, and was contemplating replacing wooden passenger cars with less flammable steel vehicles.

The first attempts at what would later be recognized as the economic regulation of railroads showed up in the 1830s in

state charters and municipal franchises that granted the railroads their powers to operate over designated rights-of-way. Thus Illinois by means of the granting of charters attempted to determine that Alton, not St. Louis, would be the beneficiary of its new railroad network. Chicago, in turn, by means of franchises tried to dictate which railroads would operate within its borders and where they would run.[1]

There was some enlightened self-interest involved. New York State for some years required the railroads built parallel to the Erie Canal to pay the canal tolls on the freight they hauled. In Illinois, the February 7, 1851, amendment to the charter of the Rock Island & La Salle Railroad permitting its extension east to Chicago required it to pay tolls to the Illinois and Michigan

Canal for freight traffic hauled between La Salle and Chicago and presumably lost to the parallel canal. However, the railroad was able to avoid that provision when the canal trustees blundered and failed to comply with a technicality in the law.[2]

The railroads by the end of their first three decades of existence had become the sufficiently dominant form of transportation in America so that state governments, absent any interest in Washington, found it increasingly necessary to impose some form of economic regulation on them. The federal government used its wartime powers during the Civil War to control railroads, but after the war ended in 1865 the railroads regained freedom, and within a few years farmers and shippers dependent upon them for transportation began to agitate local and state government for some sort of regulation, especially of rates. A number of states in the Midwest followed with granger laws to regulate railroads within their borders.

By the 1880s, the railroads had exploited the Commerce Clause of the U.S. Constitution to free themselves from state regulation to the point that Congress was finally forced to create an agency to deal with the railroads on a national basis. By then the era of the robber barons was under way, and while the manipulations of those controversial investors may or may not have made sense in the financial world of the late nineteenth century—a topic debated by scholars at considerable length over the years—they certainly contributed to a popular sentiment that the railroad industry needed regulation. Yet it took the newly created Interstate Commerce Commission, Congress, and the courts the better part of two decades to create an effective program of economic regulation of the railroads.[3]

Passenger traffic was the first to be monopolized by the railroads in the 1830–1860 period, followed quickly by mail and merchandise freight. It was largely a matter of speed, reliability, and economics: canal boats had a top speed of 2 to 3 miles an hour and stagecoaches 4 to 6 mph, but railroads averaged 15 mph. Canals and turnpikes, unless they were adjacent to each other, generally did not compete for traffic, but when canals were built alongside existing roads they quickly captured most of the freight business at the expense of the wagons. Passengers for the most part preferred the more comfortable travel by water over dusty, bumpy stagecoach rides. The railroads had a devastating effect on both those modes, especially for passengers and package freight, but were somewhat slower to capture the canals' bulk freight business that was more sensitive to price than time.[4]

The highways were another matter;

The second worst train wreck in Illinois history occurred in 1946 when a Chicago, Burlington & Quincy intercity train rear-ended another at high speed in west suburban Naperville despite the existence of signals designed to prevent such accidents. Forty-five persons were killed and 69 were injured. The Interstate Commerce Commission, which had begun regulating railroad safety, ruled that the mixture of cars of differing weights and strengths in each train was a factor in the high death toll.

The locomotive of this train in the 1946 Naperville crash was impaled by steel from the cars in the train it rear-ended, but the engineer survived. He was blamed for blowing a red signal just before the crash. (See Appendix C.)

long-haul wagons were unable to compete with the railroads and disappeared within a few years, as did the passenger stagecoach. The wagon operators who survived did so by transforming themselves into local distributors to and from railroad freight stations, and the stagecoach, at least in Chicago, devolved into the omnibus, hauling travelers between railroad depots and hotels.[5]

The steamboat was a potentially more formidable competitor but, unlike the railroads, was a slave to geography. The steaming time between any two cities on the lakes or rivers was determined by the circuity of the route. A trip between Chicago and Detroit is 283 miles by rail but more than 600 by lake around the

northern tip of the Michigan peninsula, a journey that in the 1850s translated into 36 1/2 hours by rail and 120 hours by steamship—an average speed of just under 8 miles an hour by rail and 5 miles an hour by water. A river steamboat journey from Pittsburgh to St. Louis, like the one taken in 1842 by Charles Dickens, was 1,164 miles, but when the two cities were finally linked by railroad after 1857, the distance between them was nearly cut in half to 612 miles.

The comparative reliability of railroads over steamboats and lake ships was another major factor in the early diversion of passenger traffic to the new mode. Weather was disruptive to maritime traffic, but for the most part it was only an annoyance to railroads. The fierce storms that lashed the Great Lakes each autumn disrupted shipping not only by delaying schedules but by causing shipwrecks. The existence of such weather-dictated shipping seasons gave the railroads their first toehold in the northern transportation market. New York in the 1830s tolerated the building of seven independent railroads end-to-end along the length of the Erie Canal not only to feed traffic to the canal but to provide transportation during the winter months when it was closed.[6]

By 1880 railroads had exploited their advantages of time and speed to the point that they effectively had a monopoly on intercity passenger traffic in America. They dominated freight haulage to the extent that they had driven the steamboat industry out of business, forced the closing of most of the canals and all the turnpikes, and had taken away from the Great Lakes all but its bulk ore, grain, and coal business and some cross-lake packet traffic. As late as 1929 the railroads still controlled as much as 75 percent of the nation's intercity revenue freight as measured in ton-miles. The Great Lakes were second at 16 percent, followed by oil pipelines at 4.4 percent, motor trucks at 3.2 percent, and rivers and canals at only 1.4 percent.[7]

Railroad Time

There is probably no more dramatic example of the influence the railroads had on America in the 1880s than the Chicago Time Convention of 1883. It is an example of regulation in reverse: an industry imposed its regulation—in this case standard time—on the rest of the nation. Such a system was necessary because the ever-tighter scheduling requirements of railroads could not tolerate local deviations of even a few minutes. The practice common then was for each city to independently set local clocks by the rules of astronomy, so that noon was determined when the sun was directly overhead, which might be 12:18 p.m. in Detroit, 11:50 a.m. in Chicago, 11:38 a.m. in St. Louis, and 11:27 a.m. in St. Paul.[8]

Individual railroads over the years had tried with varying degrees of success to standardize times along their routes. British railroads standardized time as early as 1847, but the United Kingdom was, and still is, in a single time zone. In the United States as late as 1883 there were still 100 different railroad times. C. F. Dowd, principal of a Saratoga Springs, New York, seminary some years earlier had proposed the division of the United States into four arbitrary time zones to provide some standardization while at the same time taking astronomical time into account. The idea gained proponents until the delegates at the railroads' General Time Convention in October 1881 directed convention secretary William F. Allen, managing editor of the Official Guide of the Railways and a proponent of time zones of the type proposed by Dowd, to come up with an acceptable plan.[9]

Allen's plan for four time zones to be divided along the 75th, 90th, 105th, and 120th meridians was adopted by the Railroad Time Convention in Chicago in October 1883, to take effect on Sunday, November 18, 1883. On that day, conductors, engineers, and other railroad employees gathered, watches in hand, in Chicago's Union Station when at 11:45 a.m. the depot

manager stopped the master clock, restarting it only after a telegraph connection with an observatory in Allegheny, Pennsylvania, indicated it was noon in the central time zone. The effect was to move clocks in Chicago back by 9 minutes and 33 seconds, but St. Louis was relatively unaffected.

News of the new standard was greeted with some derision, but it was rather passively and quickly accepted by the public. An international conference the following year established 24 time zones worldwide. Congress finally, in 1918, officially recognized the railroad time zones as the national standard.

Torts and Courts

The late nineteenth century was also the era of the robber barons, those speculators and financiers mostly based in New York who manipulated railroad securities and the railroads themselves to amass great personal wealth. By the end of the century, the bulk of the railroad trackage in the United States was concentrated in the hands of seven groups, although the railroads themselves were still organized as capital stock companies ostensibly under the control of thousands of individual shareholders. The robber barons were simply the most visible aspect of the increasing monopoly that the industry they controlled exerted over American transportation. Inevitably, the cry began to arise to place the industry under government regulation.

Somewhat surprisingly, some of the first regulation of railroads, absent any effective action by the legislatures, occurred in the courts and gave rise to a body of law known as torts as persons injured by trains and the estates of people killed by them began to sue the railroads. Legal scholar Lawrence M. Friedman put the role of the railroads in tort law in perspective:

> Almost every leading case in tort law was connected, mediately or immediately, with this new and dreadful presence. In this first

generation of tort law, the railroad was the prince of machines, both as symbol and as fact. It was the key to economic development. It cleared an iron path through the wilderness. It bound cities together, and tied the farms to the cities and the seaports. Yet trains were also wild beasts: they roared through the countryside, killing livestock, setting fire to crops, smashing passengers and freight. Railroad law and tort law, then, grew up together. In a sense, the two were the same.[10]

The cases did not result in any sweeping regulation of railroads but were decisions on liability made in individual personal injury cases in local and state courts across the country. Often the courts simply determined which party was liable for the accident, or whether the victim contributed to his own fate by being negligent in failing to watch for trains before he crossed the tracks. Employees could sue the railroads for injuries if their employers caused them by negligent misconduct, but not if another employee was negligent. Gradually the courts began to shift more of a burden to the railroads, and eventually in the twentieth century federal laws regulating safety began to preempt the state tort laws.[11]

The charters granted by states to early railroad corporations also included some regulatory provisions, and the railroads were an early force in shaping American corporate law. Illinois, for example, created its railroad corporations by means of special acts, or charters, passed on behalf of each railroad applicant. The charters invariably imposed some conditions, such as where (between which cities) the railroad could run. To protect the public, Illinois also designated many of its early railroads as common carriers available to the entire traveling or shipping public. In fact, the Constitution of 1870 declared railroads to be public highways. The demand for railroad charters had increased to the point in the late 1840s that the Illinois legislature in 1849 passed an "Act to provide for a general system of railroad incorporations."

Besides providing for the administrative chartering of corporations by the state in addition to charters granted by special acts of the legislature, it allowed railroads to cross the rights-of-way of canals and toll highways so long as they did not disrupt traffic on the other mode. Railroads were also given the power of eminent domain to obtain rights-of-way from recalcitrant landowners.[12]

That provision illustrated a general characteristic of railroad law before 1870 in Illinois: most prior legislation was intended to promote the building of railroads. Railroads, albeit privately owned, were seen by legislatures and the courts as tools for economic development that could be rendered ineffective by excessive regulation. But after the Civil War, as consolidations resulted in ever-larger railroad corporations, that attitude began to change.[13]

The Granger Laws

Although other states had made some modest attempts at railroad regulation earlier, the movement to regulate railroads in Illinois began on the farm, and its most obvious target was Chicago, the big city rail junction that increasingly had come to dominate the midwestern grain trade. Chicago in 1852, when it had but one railroad in operation for the entire year, shipped almost 5.5 million bushels. By 1859 with 10 railroads in operation, that volume of grain had more than doubled to 13 million bushels, most of it received by rail and shipped by sea, and by 1871 it exceeded 64 million bushels. By then the trunk railroads had begun to make some inroads into the Great Lakes' ship traffic and hauled almost 7.7 million bushels eastward.[14]

The mechanization of grain elevators and the standardization of the grading of grain gave Chicago a substantial advantage over its rival river ports. A single Illinois Central elevator could simultaneously unload 12 railroad cars, and Chicago's 12 railroad elevators combined had the capacity to handle 500,000 bushels every 10 hours—a quarter of the volume St. Louis moved over its levee to and from steamboats in all of 1854. The resulting efficiencies meant Chicago could transload grain at a cost of half a cent per bushel, contrasted to five cents in St. Louis.[15]

As the railroads spread west and hauled grain in ever-greater quantities to Chicago from newly settled farms in eight states in the years after the Civil War, many farmers in Illinois became increasingly embittered at the marginal existence they were living. New machinery and new farmland resulted in larger crops with the resulting drop in price that farmers could get for their grain or cattle. Their disenchantment focused on Chicago, the sprawling, rowdy, and often bawdy agricultural emporium where the "livestock ring" of commission agents at the Union Stock Yards and commodities merchants at the Board of Trade bought and sold cattle and grain by telegraph and increasingly set the standards that determined the price the farmers could get. The railroads, in which many farmers had invested in the 1850s to get an outlet for the crops and which increasingly had been absorbed into ever-larger corporations controlled by the moneymen in New York, also came in for criticism by the farm groups. For example, the railroads in collusion with many warehouses in which they had financial interests enacted a 20-day warehouse storage charge of two cents per bushel regardless of whether the grain ever wound up in a grain elevator, and an eight-cent-per-bushel charge on grain shipped to warehouses that were not involved in the collusive ring.[16]

Since the states could not retroactively amend railroad charters to include controls, there was little that farm groups could do to correct the perceived problem. The early charters in the Midwest, since they were intended to encourage the building of railroad lines to spur development, contained few, if any, provisions to regulate the lines once they were built.

Measures taken in the East earlier proved to be woefully inadequate for the problem in the Midwest after the Civil War. States in the Northeast, as early as 1839 in Rhode Island, began creating special agencies or commissions primarily to impose safety restrictions but also to ensure that the railroads complied with their charters. Probably the best-known such agency was created in Massachusetts in 1869, and although it had few real legal powers, its chairman, Charles Francis Adams, Jr., used the power of public opinion effectively to force some compliance.[17]

The railroads' control of grain elevators was a major factor in the decision by Illinois in 1871 to begin regulating both industries. However, by 2003 when this photograph was taken, the grain traffic had shifted elsewhere and the Santa Fe elevator next to the Sanitary and Ship Canal at Damen Avenue on the Southwest Side sat vacant. The rail spur continued to serve other industries in the area.

The farmers in Illinois, who began organizing locally in 1860s, after 1867 formed secret chapters, or Granges, of the Patrons of Husbandry—an organization founded in Washington in 1867 by a U.S. Agriculture Department clerk. The agenda of the "granger movement," as it came to be known, was to provide some sort of equity to farmers by regulating the rates they were charged for hauling agricultural products. The Grangers in 1870 in Illinois found a solution to their quandary by amending both the state constitution and statutes to permit the state to regulate common carrier commerce with a device that spread to every state in the union and the federal government—the public utility or commerce commissions. The prototype born in Illinois after 1870 dealt only with railroads and warehouses, which included grain elevators.[18]

Because the National Grange for the Patrons of Husbandry was the principal proponent of regulation, the resulting legislation in Illinois and other states collectively became known as the granger laws. The Illinois Grange wisely chose to avoid the state legislature, which up until then had been known to favor the cause of railroads, and took its case directly to a far more democratic body, the state's constitutional convention. Grangers and other agrarian interests met in April 1870 in downstate Bloomington and approved several resolutions to influence the impending constitutional convention.

One of the more powerful voices for reform at the time was Joseph Medill, one of the principal stockholders of the *Chicago Tribune* and a constitutional convention delegate. One of Medill's goals for the new constitution was to provide for state improvement of the Illinois River and canal connections in order to restrain the railroads' control of rates. The constitutional article that emerged empowered the state to regulate warehouses—but only in Chicago—and to enact legislation to protect "producers, shippers, and receivers" of grain. It also directed the General Assem-

bly to "correct abuses and prevent unjust discrimination in the rates of freight and passenger tariffs on the different railroads in the state."[19]

The next year (1871) the legislature complied by enacting legislation creating a Board of Railroad and Warehouse Commissioners, set limits on passenger fares, established maximum rates for grain storage, and determined that freight rates be based on the distance hauled. In 1873 the act was amended to require the commission to prepare a schedule of reasonable freight charges.

Since Illinois was at the core of the nation's rail network, its legislation was rapidly followed by similar laws in Wisconsin, Minnesota, and Iowa. The railroads had no choice but to fight the legislation in court. This led to a succession of U.S Supreme Court rulings known collectively as the "Granger Cases" that reached Washington for argument in 1875. By then the Panic of 1873, overexpansion, and the manipulations of the robber barons had left much of the railroad industry in serious financial shape, if not bankruptcy.

In the principal Granger Case, *Munn v. Illinois,* the court ruled that grain elevators in the prior 20 years had become an almost monopolistic business in the seven or eight states of the Midwest and could be regulated in the public interest. In an equally important ruling in separate Granger Cases involving four railroads—*Chicago, Burlington & Quincy Railroad v. Iowa; Peik v. Chicago & North Western Railway; Chicago, Milwaukee & St. Paul Railroad v. Ackly;* and *Winona & St. Peter Railroad v. Blake*—the Supreme Court sustained the validity of the Illinois, Wisconsin, Iowa, and Minnesota laws fixing maximum rates for passengers and freight within their jurisdictions absent any federal regulation under the interstate commerce clause of the U.S. Constitution. However, the Supreme Court in later rulings restrained considerably the sweeping powers of states to regulate rail rates, which they thought they had won in the Granger Cases.[20]

Despite the subsequent decisions, the Granger Cases were of enormous importance not only because they established the theory of economic regulation of transportation but because they gave momentum to a growing movement for national regulation of railroads. Although Congress was slow to react, interstate regulation of commerce would become a reality before the end of the century, but only after financial abuses by the railroads and their owners infuriated more of the public than just farmers.

Interstate Commerce

In the decades after the Civil War, cutthroat competition resulted in fluctuating rates that angered shippers, as did rebates the railroads granted to major shippers, like John D. Rockefeller's Standard Oil Co., and attempts by railroad cartels to divide traffic. As early as 1870, Burlington, North Western, and Rock Island created what was known as the Iowa Pool, an agreement to split traffic evenly three ways on their Chicago-Omaha lines.[21]

Contributing to the predatory rate wars were the economics of the new industry, a factor only poorly understood by many of the critics calling for regulation. Because railroads were the first transportation systems to build and own everything associated with their service, they had relatively high capital costs that translated into high fixed costs of operation. As much as two-thirds of the costs of railroads were attributable to overhead expenses that had to be met—such things as the mortgage, track maintenance, locomotives, cars, bridges, stations, fuel, and personnel costs of managers, maintenance, and clerical staffs that had to be paid whether or not trains moved. The remaining costs, including for train crews, varied with traffic.[22]

Those high fixed costs made the railroads more vulnerable to competition than earlier transportation systems and forced the rail companies to cut rates to generate traffic. The assumption was that even reduced revenue was better than none at all, that a seat sold at a discount for one dollar is better than an empty one that generates no revenue. The cartels that emerged after the Civil War were the result of an effort to divide up traffic to eliminate the cutthroat competition.

The existence of high fixed costs also encouraged railroad rate makers to favor large shippers over small because the big shippers could guarantee predictable and large volumes of traffic to help the railroads cover their fixed costs. When Gustavus F. Swift found that the principal eastern trunk lines were resisting his attempts to ship dressed beef and because of their financial interest in various stockyards were giving discounts to shippers of live cattle, he began shipping meat to the East Coast through Canada over the Grand Trunk. By 1885 the Grand Trunk was handling 292 million pounds of dressed beef, or 60 percent of Chicago's output.[23]

On the other hand, the manipulation of railroads by the so-called robber barons, while it created a public distrust that contributed to regulation of the industry, often tended to keep freight rates down by making the industry more competitive. One robber baron would cut rates to gain market share, forcing the others to follow suit to keep traffic on their railroads. For example, Jay Gould, despite his stock manipulations with the Erie Railroad, managed the railroad well enough and initiated enough rate wars to make it difficult for the other eastern trunk lines to successfully operate a cartel.[24] A railroad with no competition in an area, however, could charge almost anything it wanted.

Federal regulation of interstate commerce was slow to develop despite the commerce clause in the constitution. The U.S. Supreme Court did not in its first 35 years of existence have to deal with the commerce clause, and its first ruling on the subject in 1824 in the *Gibbons v. Ogden* case involved the Fulton-Livingston steamboat monopoly. The court in 1822 gave

President James Monroe an unofficial written opinion supporting his veto of a bill extending federal power over turnpikes within the borders of individual states. By the term of Chief Justice Morrison Remick Waite (1874–1888), cases involving attempts to regulate railroads were common largely because of the phenomenal growth of the industry.[25]

The nation's railroad system, which grew by only 3,303 miles during the Civil War, exploded in growth after the war ended. The national rail plant more than doubled from 35,085 miles at the war's end to more than 70,600 miles in 1873. For the first time, there was an indication that the railroads may have been expanding too quickly. *Poor's Manual of Railroads in the United States* warned in its 1877 and 1878 editions that although railroads needed a population base of 850 people per square mile to operate profitably, that ratio had declined from 1,026 per square mile in 1860 to 730 in 1870 and 590 in 1873. Some western lines were supported by populations of only 471 people per square mile.[26]

Even the regional granger railroads based in Chicago joined the track-laying orgy. The North Western reached the Wyoming state line in 1886 and within two years had pushed on another 120 miles to Casper. The Burlington built far beyond the agricultural belt of the Midwest to Billings, Montana; the Rock Island extended to Tucumcari, New Mexico; and the Milwaukee Road was considering a transcontinental line to Seattle.

Long before that happened, the railroad ledgers began to indicate problems were developing. Gross railroad earnings dropped from $9,000 per mile in 1870 to $7,933 three years later, and during the Panic of 1873, half the railroads, including the new Union Pacific were forced into bankruptcy. That, the subsequent depression of 1884–1885, and the Panic of 1893, after which 156 railroads collapsed financially, had the effect of causing another wave of railroad consolidations as weaker carriers were absorbed by their stronger

competitors. By 1906, nearly two-thirds of the U.S. rail mileage—about 225,000 miles of railroad—was under the control of just seven groups of investors. The groups included Vanderbilt's New York Central and North Western (22,500 miles); the Pennsylvania Railroad, Baltimore & Ohio, and Chesapeake & Ohio (20,000 miles); J. P. Morgan's Erie and Southern (18,000 miles); Jay Gould's empire (17,000 miles), which included the Missouri Pacific; William H. Moore's 15,000-mile system that included the Rock Island; James J. Hill's network of the Great Northern, Northern Pacific, and Burlington (21,000 miles); and Edward Harriman's Union Pacific, Southern Pacific, and Illinois Central group (25,000 miles).[27]

The effect of both the consolidations and expansion was to make the task of state regulators impossible. Bills for federal regulation of the railroads had appeared in Congress as early as 1871, but it was not until 1883 that President Chester A. Arthur urged Congress to act to prevent further railroad abuses.

In 1886, a special committee headed by Senator Shelby M. Cullom, a Springfield lawyer, friend of Lincoln, former governor of Illinois, and critic of railroad services, reported back to the full Senate that the accounts of rail abuses were true. Earlier in his political career Cullom had suggested a second railroad be built across southern Illinois parallel to the Baltimore & Ohio because the B&O's monopoly rendered its service atrocious, and as speaker of the Illinois House in 1873 he was instrumental in passage of the granger reform law regulating rail rates.[28]

As is often the case in legislative reform campaigns, the courts intervened to give the legislature an even greater incentive. Following the Cullom report in 1886, the U.S. Supreme Court, in another Illinois case *(Wabash, St. Louis & Pacific Ry. v. Illinois),* watered down much of its earlier rulings in the Granger Cases and said states could not regulate rates in interstate commerce beyond their borders. After the

Wabash decision, the only legal mechanism remaining to curb the railroads was the interstate commerce clause of the U.S. Constitution. "As a result of this decision, the railroad question became truly national, and there rose an imperative demand for national regulation," constitutional historian Charles Warren noted.[29]

Congress got the message. Cullom's bill in the Senate and a companion piece in the U.S. House emerged from conference committee as the Interstate Commerce Act, which was signed by President Cleveland in 1887. Incredibly, the law contained no enforcement provisions, so the newly created Interstate Commerce Com-

mission had to resort to the courts to correct each abuse it detected. Cease-and-desist orders were often disobeyed, and appeals delayed the proceedings. The U.S. Supreme Court in the 16 cases on the Interstate Commerce Act it heard between 1887 and 1905 ruled in favor of the railroads 15 times.[30]

A succession of laws passed after the progressives and President Theodore Roosevelt were elected was intended to expedite ICC regulatory proceedings, broaden the powers of that agency, and tighten loopholes. For example, the Hepburn Act of 1906 gave the ICC the power to set maximum rates, and the Mann-Elkins Act

Except for a continuing battle to eliminate railroad crossings, Chicago was not successful in imposing many regulations on the interstate railroads. An exception was the relocation of Baltimore & Ohio tracks south of Grand Central Station as part of a massive project, shown here in 1929, to straighten the south branch of the Chicago River. (Krambles-Peterson Archive)

of 1910, among other things, prohibited rate discrimination against short-haul shippers. The issue culminated in 1913 when Congress, upset that the ICC favored the railroads, effectively disbanded the agency by cutting off its funding and passed Wisconsin senator Robert La Follette's Railroad Validation Act. It required the ICC to evaluate the assets of all railroad property and review the financial history of each line to enable the agency to establish rates based on the railroads' true value instead of using the inflated valuation and watered-down stock claimed by the railroads.

Effective federal regulatory control, ironically, came almost on the eve of the high watermark of railroad industry. After the federal government was forced to federalize an almost paralyzed industry in World War I, railroads began a long slide that lasted for most of the rest of the twentieth century.

Local Regulation

Federal regulation did not put an end to attempts by the state and city to impose controls on railroads locally, however. Switching rates, intrastate passenger fares, safety (especially at grade crossings), and what could perhaps be described as environmental concerns were all the subject of state and local laws after 1890 and well into the twentieth century. Again, the massive railroad network within Chicago was the target.

Since local switching rates did not fall under the category of interstate commerce to be regulated by the Interstate Commerce Commission and the railroads in Chicago priced their switching services as high as the market would bear, often higher, to discourage short hauls within the city, which were often money-losing propositions, the Illinois Railroad and Warehouse Commission in 1909 tried to set a limit on switching charges. That forced the railroads in Chicago to get together in 1911 and form what was known

as the Lowrey Agreement to set uniform rates for switching.[31]

By that time public disenchantment with the failures of the state's regulatory system had switched from the steam railroads to Chicago's mass transit system, the street and elevated railways. The City Council in 1907 had approved franchise extensions known as the Traction Settlement Ordinances, which imposed an income tax on the street railways and capped fares at five cents. To bypass similar attempts to economically regulate his elevated railway lines, Samuel Insull, the utilities magnate who had come into control of the city's Ls because they could not pay their electric bills, turned to the state legislature. In 1911 it created the Public Utilities Commission among other things to regulate intrastate railroad fares, including many of the interurban railways as well as the street and elevated systems. The new commission replaced the obsolete and largely ineffective Illinois Railroad and Warehouse Commission and shifted the task of economic regulation from the city to the state.[32]

The Public Utility Commission at first refused to raise fares, causing the street railways to resort to the courts for relief. When it finally caved in to reality, public outrage over the commission's decision to raise fares in 1920 caused the state legislature the following year to abolish it and replace it with the Illinois Commerce Commission, a regulatory body with essentially the same powers. That agency continued to set intrastate fares until Chicago's mass transit system was publicly acquired by the Chicago Transit Authority after 1945, the interurban railroads went out of business in the 1950s and 1960s, and the Regional Transportation Authority was created in 1974 to regulate the commuter railroads. After that the ICC concentrated on the telephone, natural gas, and power industries, although it continued to regulate grade crossing safety on railroads. The RTA then used the contractual device called purchase of service agreements with railroads to set fare and service standards on the commuter lines.[33]

(above) Chicago used franchises and ordinances to impose some regulation on railroads before the federal government assumed that role. The city required the Illinois Central to build its downtown line in a causeway in the lake. As the water between the causeway and the shore was filled in, the city wound up with a railroad in its front yard. This view from Van Buren Street looking north toward the Art Institute shows the railroad at grade in 1896 as work was just beginning to lower the tracks below ground level. Note the grain elevators along the Chicago River in the distance. (Norm Carlson Collection)

(below) In this view looking south from Van Buren, IC commuter trains continued to run at grade (left) as crews dug the trench into which the railroad would be moved. (Norm Carlson Collection)

By the 1880s, the proliferation of both steam railroads and street railways in Chicago caused the city to look for solutions to what was becoming an intolerable problem of traffic congestion, pollution, and safety caused by the mixing of wagons, carriages, pedestrians, trains, and horse and cable cars at street level. The steam railroads ran on their own rights-of-way, but as the city grew rapidly after the Civil War the number of rail-street cross-

ings proliferated and with it the number of casualties from accidents at those crossings. By one estimate, the city had 1,500 railroad-street grade crossings in 1890, and the toll at them was approaching 100 deaths and 300 injuries annually.[34]

Although safety was the issue used as the justification for what the city did next, the underlying reason was to relieve what had become intolerable traffic congestion at the grade crossings. Faced with similar street

This photo of the IC at Van Buren Street was taken in 1900 after the track-lowering project had been completed. (Norm Carlson Collection)

congestion resulting from heavy maritime traffic on the Chicago River that caused the bridges to be open for long periods to allow ships to pass, the city 30 years earlier had decided to grade-separate the river and street traffic by digging two vehicular tunnels beneath the river.

Since the city did not have the wherewithal to finance a massive track elevation program, it resorted to the simple expediency of requiring the railroads to do it. It was one of two programs Chicago attempted to impose that in retrospect illustrated there are limitations on regulation: a body politic cannot impose on private enterprise costs it cannot afford. Chicago over a period of four decades (1890–1930) attempted to require the railroads to elevate all their tracks in the city and to electrify their operations. The track elevation program was the more successful of the two before the Great Depression put an end to it.

Only one line, the Illinois Central commuter division, was ever converted from steam to electricity. The Lake Front Ordinance of 1919 among other things required the Illinois Central to replace all steam-powered locomotives on its freight and passenger lines in the city by February 20, 1935. The IC's commuter division was electrified in 1926, but the Depression, World War II, and the adoption of the diesel locomotive to replace steam engines after the war put an end to any further attempts at electrification by the city.[35]

From a century of hindsight, it is now obvious that it was impossible for a municipality like Chicago to impose economic regulation on common carriers whose lines extended far beyond the city limits. In the nineteenth century the only regulatory mechanism available to the city was the franchises it granted, which enabled the carriers to use or cross its streets. So the role of regulator of rates and fares shifted to the state and federal governments. The lone exception was the issue of public welfare and safety.

In the case of the city's track elevation program, the overriding public issue was safety, although Chicago's ulterior motive was to reduce street traffic congestion at rail crossings. With the demise of the track elevation program in the Great Depression those two issues continued to plague the city and its suburbs into the twenty-first century.

Local safety regulations contributed to the demise of this railroad. For the most part the interurban lines serving Chicago did not have the funds to replace their fleets of cars with new equipment. These wooden coaches shown at the Aurora & Elgin's Glen Ellyn station in 1950 ran until the railroad failed eight years later. Chicago had banned the use of wooden cars in its new subways as a fire safety measure, which meant the CA&E couldn't use the new Dearborn Subway after the Garfield Park elevated line was razed. (Norm Carlson Collection)

11 Railroad Crossings

Grade separation—placing railroads above or below street level—was a solution to the crossing safety question in Chicago in the 1890s. The IC began raising its tracks in 1892 to prepare for the Columbian Exposition. This photograph, taken that year, shows the existing tracks crossing 57th Street, with the new tracks being elevated just to the west. (Norm Carlson Collection)

Railroad grade crossings rarely get much attention until someone is killed at one, and then they make the news for only a day or two. But collectively the hundreds of crossings in the Chicago area have played a major, often negative, role on metropolitan development—probably more so than in any other American city. As the railroads flocked to Chicago, they cut up the city into a spiderweb of neighborhoods and rural settlements whose only connections to the rest of the city were over street-rail crossings that punctuated the landscape at intervals. Street traffic was funneled to those crossings, and as

the density of development increased they became traffic bottlenecks.[1]

Probably because the great train wrecks produced images of piles of shredded railway cars and mangled corpses, and the accidents at grade crossings infrequently resulted in more than a single casualty, crossing accidents generally received less conspicuous display in the daily press than the wrecks. They got scant mention in both academic and popular railroad literature. Nevertheless, the greatest carnage on America's railroads occurred at the nation's highway and street crossings. In fact, the first efforts to regulate railroad safety in the U.S.

in the 1830s dealt with the crossing problem, which persisted into the twenty-first century despite substantial efforts of government and the railroads to reduce the toll. Grade-crossing accidents by the end of the twentieth century accounted for 45 percent of all fatalities on U.S. railroads—an annual average of 441 deaths.[2]

Illinois, the nexus of much of the nation's rail network, understandably had a large number of crossings and a resulting high toll. Of the approximately 260,000 railroad crossings in the United States (159,000 public and 101,000 private) at the end of the twentieth century, 13,348 were in Illinois. The six-county Chicago metropolitan area had 2,517 crossings, or less than 20 percent of the total in the state, but in 2002 it accounted for 60 (almost 39%) of the state's 155 crossing collisions between trains and vehicles. Only 12 crossing collisions, or 7.7 percent of the state total, were in Chicago.[3]

The relatively low toll in the city was attributable to its program in the late nineteenth and early twentieth centuries to elevate railroads to eliminate crossings. But even as Chicago eliminated them, railroad-induced urban sprawl across northeastern Illinois resulted in the building of ever-more crossings in the suburbs. The growth of automobile use and the building of hard roads only exacerbated the problem by creating a demand for more crossings. In 1892 before the track elevation program began there were an estimated 1,000 to 1,500 grade crossings in Chicago alone. Although the track elevation program eliminated hundreds of them, suburban sprawl created more, and as late as 2002 there were 1,953 rail-highway crossings in the Chicago metropolitan area.[4]

Ironically, the motivating issue behind the crossing improvement programs in both 1892 and 2000 was the reduction of traffic congestion on the roads; safety was only the secondary issue although it was often sold to the public as the main reason. The highway traffic delays caused by the high volume and relatively slow speed

of freights in the metropolitan area was a problem from the 1850s onward. As late as 2002, the Metropolitan Planning Council, a civic group, recommended that the federal, state, and local governments begin a crash program to build highway bridges to eliminate the 40 worst crossings in Chicagoland.[5]

The increase in volume of highway traffic in the second half of the twentieth century was accompanied by an increase in the size of commercial vehicles, which proved to be an ominous portent for railroad safety. It was rare when a dray or Model T Ford caused a derailment or casualties to anyone but the road vehicle occupants, but a train traveling at 79 miles an hour, the legal limit, smashing into an 80,000-pound tractor trailer or a loaded school bus was another matter. Thirteen persons aboard an Amtrak train in 1999 died when it smashed into a truck carrying steel and derailed in Bourbonnais, Illinois.[6]

Perhaps because the crossing deaths occurred singly or in pairs as trains crashed into buggies and wagons in the nineteenth century and automobiles and motor trucks in the twentieth century, they evoked less of a public demand for action than had the steamboat explosions of the first half of the nineteenth century in which hundreds of passengers had died in a single blast. Pedestrians were frequent victims at railroad crossings in both centuries, as were trespassers—the railroad industry term for nonemployees wandering across the tracks at somewhere other than public crossings. By one enumeration in the late nineteenth century, trespassers accounted for more than half of the pedestrians killed on railroad tracks.

The increase in the number of trains and their speeds in the late 1800s was certainly a factor in a commensurate increase in the crossing death toll, as was an increase in the volume of traffic on the highways. As motor vehicles were added to the mix in the 1900s, the toll at grade crossings increased sharply. Four hundred eight persons died in U.S. crossing accidents in

Collisions between trains and highway vehicles date back to the inception of railroads, and usually the wagon, automobile, or motor truck got the worst end of the deal. This car was hit by a Nickel Plate Road train in Plymouth, Indiana, in 1943. (Thomas R. McKee)

1890, but in 1937 the toll climbed to 1,607. Only an aggressive safety campaign forcing the railroads and governments at all levels to spend considerable sums of money to equip the crossings with warning signals and gates, and to experiment with such things as crossing barriers and enforcement devices, including remote television cameras, reduced the toll.[7]

The federal government was very slow to get into the issue of regulation of railroad safety, although as early as 1837 Congress began to pay attention to the problem of steamboat safety. Despite passage in 1852 of the Steamboat Inspection Act requiring regular boiler inspections and licensing of pilots and engineers on the waterways and the increased severity of railroad accidents beginning in the 1850s,

Congress left the issue of railroad safety to local and state governments and the carriers for more than 40 years. It did not tackle that issue on a national basis until 1893 when it adopted the Safety Appliance Act. The law for the first time mandated the use of air brakes and automatic couplers on railroads engaged in interstate commerce, but it left enforcement up to the new Interstate Commerce Commission. In 1908 it adopted the Federal Employer's Liability Act setting national standards to cover the liability of railroads to their employees. The ICC continued to investigate and regulate railroad safety on a limited basis until 1970 when Congress created the Federal Railroad Administration with broad powers to create and enforce rules relating to railroad safety.[8] (See

Appendix C for a list and synopsis of railroad disasters in the Chicago area.)

Railroads had been on the scene only a few years when it became obvious some sort of crossing regulation was needed. In England, the Railway Clauses Consolidation Act of 1845 required the building at railroad expense of overpasses or underpasses at all public crossings, but in America where the railroads were built through sparsely settled areas and the roads of the time had little traffic, grade crossings were the norm. The earliest crossing safety laws in America generally required only that locomotive engineers give highway users some warning by ringing bells or blowing whistles. After the 1834 accident on the Boston & Worcester, the nation's first grade-crossing incident, when a train hit a buggy and killed the horse, the Massachusetts legislature enacted a law requiring all locomotives to have bells to be rung as trains approached crossings, a practice that spread across the nation and is still in effect, and the railroad posted warning signs at crossings.[9]

In 1849 when Illinois had only three railroads in operation, it followed the lead of Massachusetts and other eastern states and passed a law requiring locomotive engineers to sound either a bell or whistle "80 rods" (1,320 feet) from a public crossing, which had to be identified with a posted sign that said "Railroad crossing—look out for cars when the bell rings or whistle sounds." However, the distinction between what was publicly accessible and what was the exclusive domain of the early railroads was sometimes cloudy, and determining the relative degrees of negligence in grade-crossing accidents occupied Illinois courts for the last half of the nineteenth century.[10]

Early Accidents

Many of the earliest grade-crossing accidents involved carriages and wagons, and because of the relatively slow speed of trains in the 1850s they were not always fatal. Children fascinated by the new mode of transportation or playing on the tracks were another matter. In the days when fields were not commonly fenced and the potential lethality of trains was poorly understood by the public, livestock were the most common victims of railroad trains all along the rights-of-way, not just at crossings. Most roads in the 1850s were little more than dirt tracks occasionally graded by the local townships, and the public that used them was unused to having to yield the right-of-way to trains.

Perhaps the first documented crossing accident in the Chicago area, or at least the first one that wound up in litigation, occurred in December 1850, when a Galena & Chicago Union train spooked the horses of Abner Loomis at a railroad crossing in western Cook County and dumped him and his wagon into a ditch. The horses ran off, never to be seen again. Loomis sued the railroad for $200 for the loss of the horses, claiming the locomotive engineer had failed to sound his whistle or ring his bell when approaching the crossing. He won in the trial court but lost the case on appeal.[11]

Failing to give the warning required by the 1849 law was also an issue in the suit John C. Dill filed against the Galena Railroad after his buggy was hit by a train on St. Charles–Elgin Road near Elgin on December 23, 1854. He survived the mishap and sued to be reimbursed $500 for the buggy, $300 for boarding and nursing care after the accident, and $500 for medical care for his injuries. The attitude of the railroad was that Dill was responsible for his own troubles. A witness testified that he later approached John Bice Turner, president of the Galena, and suggested the railroad pick up the destitute victim's hospital expenses. "Captain Turner said he could do nothing for him," a conclusion to which the Illinois Supreme Court concurred because of errors made during the trial.[12]

The newly arrived railroads in the 1850s bisected neighborhoods and separated farms, and the walking public was not always willing to go out of their way to a public grade crossing to get across the tracks. The proclivity of pedestrians to use the most direct route to their destinations, regardless of whether a railroad had been built in the way, by the middle of the decade had forced some railroads to fence their rights-of-way in urban areas. That was not always an effective deterrent.

In 1856, four-and-a-half-year-old Frederick Jacobs climbed several fences some distance from his home in western Cook County, opened a gate to a small settlement of shanties housing Galena Railroad employees, was struck by a locomotive, and lost his arm. Probably because the accident did not occur at a public crossing, the engineer had not sounded his bell or whistle as he approached. Jacob's family won a verdict of $2,000—a considerable sum in those days—but the railroad appealed, and the Illinois Supreme Court, in reversing the earlier award, opined in 1858, among other things, that railroads were private property and persons should cross them only at public crossings.[13]

The legal distinction between private rights-of-way and public crossings took a while to sink into the public consciousness. As early as 1851 Jacob Grimes, a lumber dealer in west suburban Batavia, sued the Aurora Branch Railroad to collect $110 after his horse fell into a railroad-owned well while Grimes was using the animal to pull a loaded freight car down the tracks rather than wait for the railroad to deliver the car. The railroad detached several cars from a train and had parked the car containing Grimes's shipment on a siding to await a switch engine. The courts ruled the railroad had not given him permission to be on the tracks.[14]

The lack of fencing was a constant problem for railroads in rural areas because of wandering livestock. Robert Jones, a Will County farmer who had deeded the Joliet & Northern Indiana Railroad a right-of-way across his land with the stipulation that it also build a fence, sued after the railroad failed to do so and he lost 25 sheep to a train. A man identified only as A. Rockafellow sued the Central Military Tract Railroad (later Chicago, Burlington & Quincy) for $150 because a train killed his ox, which had wandered onto the tracks in 1855 in Arlington, Bureau County.[15]

The courts in the nineteenth century generally held that just as railroads had the responsibility to have their engineers sound bells or whistles on the approach to crossings, the public had an obligation to exercise care by listening for those warning sounds and keeping a look out for trains—"ordinary care and prudence," the courts called it. Thus the courts held that Ruby Van Patten was unable to collect from the Chicago, Burlington & Quincy Railroad after her husband was killed by a train while walking over a crossing in Farmington, Illinois, in 1871. He was bundled up against the cold weather and apparently did not see or hear the train. However, beginning in the 1960s the appeals courts began upholding jury awards against the railroads in grade-crossing cases on the assumption the carriers and their insurers had the financial resources to compensate victims of crossing accidents regardless of who was at fault.[16]

As train speeds increased during the second half of the nineteenth century, so did the likelihood that crossing accidents would prove fatal to the public. The train that hit and injured Charles Gretzner in 1866 in Chicago was traveling at only about five miles an hour, but the Illinois Central Railroad express passenger train that killed William Partlow, his brother-in-law, and their two horses in the downstate hamlet of Humbolt on November 12, 1891, was traveling between 40 and 50 miles an hour.[17]

By the 1860s, both railroad and highway traffic in the Chicago area had grown to the point that the city required the railroads to post flagmen at the busiest crossings to warn equestrians and pedestrians of approaching trains. In 1869, the state legislature gave counties the power to mandate flagmen, but not before Charles Gretzner sued the Chicago & Alton Railroad for injuries suffered in an 1866 accident in which he was hit by a backing train at Van Buren and Canal streets in Chicago. The testimony by witnesses and railroad employees was conflicting as to whether the flagman at the crossing was at his post and whether Gretzner was trying to beat the train to the crossing.[18]

Crossing Safety Regulations

The proliferation of railroads in Illinois following the Civil War forced the state to address the issue of safety at public crossings, though somewhat vaguely given the technology of the time. In 1869 and again in 1874, the Illinois General Assembly required railroads in unincorporated areas to build public crossings "so that at all times they shall be safe to persons and property." The Cities and Villages Act of 1872 made that provision applicable to crossings in municipalities as well. That resulted in a proliferation of local ordinances restricting train speeds, often to 10 miles an hour within municipalities, and requiring the use of running lights for nighttime operation.[19]

The courts also took on an increased role in the issue of grade-crossing safety. Although pedestrians and equestrians were expected to exercise some care in crossing tracks, the Illinois Supreme Court in 1873 ruled that the railroads had a broad duty "to provide the proper safeguards, and the degree of diligence must be in proportion to the hazard." The railroads in the late nineteenth and early twentieth centuries were under considerable public scrutiny because of the perceived abuses of the robber barons and monopolistic practices, and in Illinois and elsewhere the courts of that time generally upheld the insistence of local governments that the cost of improvements, whether it be gates or bridges, was the responsibility of the railroads. Only later in the twentieth century when the railroad industry was in financial distress did the courts relent and shift the burden of crossing improvements to the public highway programs.[20]

As a practical matter the technology of the time meant that there was little the railroads could do to comply with the state acts except to post warning signs at crossings and continue to require train crews to use their locomotive bells and whistles to warn pedestrians and equestrians. At heavily trafficked urban crossings they could post flagmen to warn the public, but the flagmen were alerted to approaching trains only by bells and whistles. The flagmen were often railroad employees injured in the line of duty on other jobs. The telegraph had been in use on railroads since the 1850s primarily for train dispatching, and it was of little use at crossings near rail yards where train traffic was heaviest because of switching operations.

The obvious solution was to provide some sort of barrier that could be lowered at crossings that could prevent the public from crossing in front of trains—the now familiar crossing gates. They came into widespread use in Chicago in the 1880s. Originally they were manually lowered by flagmen, but gates that a gateman could operate by crank or air pressure from a tower for better visibility quickly came into use.[21]

However, gates alone did not eliminate the carnage at the increasing number of crossings in Chicago and its suburbs. Although by some reports as many as two persons a day were being killed by trains in Chicago in 1893, subsequent reports by the Railroad and Warehouse Commission of Illinois and the Cook County Coroner's office indicated a much lower toll. The commission in its report for the fiscal year ending June 30, 1900, by which time Illinois had more than 13,000 railroad-highway crossings, indicated that 105 persons were killed and 135 injured at crossings in the entire state. However, the coroner for the calendar year ending December 31, 1900, reported 88 persons killed in Chicago at rail-highway crossings.[22]

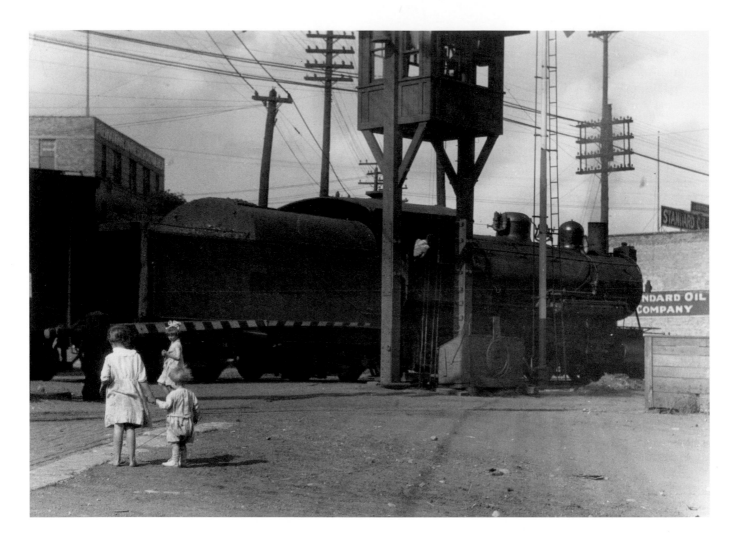

Chicago forced the railroads to post flagmen at the busiest crossings even before the Civil War, but as technology improved they were replaced by mechanical gates. These gates operated by a man in the tower were photographed in Aurora in 1919. (A. W. Johnson Photo, Krambles-Peterson Archive)

The differing railroad death tolls arose not only from difficulties in identifying the cause of death for persons who died much later from injuries suffered along railroads but also the location and circumstances in which the injuries were suffered. For example, Alfred Swan was hit by a Pennsylvania Railroad train at 47th Street on January, 10, 1888, but did not die until the following March 20. The attending physician attributed his death to complications from "Bright's Disease," a kidney ailment, although his lawyer argued in court later that the "complications" were due to the accident.[23]

Local authorities sometimes characterized as "railroad crossing accidents" incidents in which a person was crossing the tracks between highways, but the railroad industry classified them as "trespassing accidents" separate from the highway-crossing toll. Besides the 105 persons killed at crossings, the Railroad and Warehouse Commission reported in 1900 that 84 persons were killed and 300 injured at railroad stations, and 388 were killed and 1,430 injured due to "other causes," which included trespassing accidents along the right-of-way other than at crossings. The coroner's data for 1906 indicated that 100 persons were killed at crossings in Chicago and 371 at other points along the railroads, but the latter number apparently included railroad employees killed in the line of duty.[24]

However, the public outcry for improved rail crossing safety in the late nineteenth century did not always differentiate between where and how people were killed. Various published reports listed the annual railroad death toll in Chicago as between 200 and 300 persons in 1891, but examination of the individual Cook County Coroner's reports on each fatality indicates only about 37 percent occurred at crossings. A list of all 166 railroad fatalities in Chicago during the first six months of 1892 showed 62 persons died at crossings and 72 were killed while walking along the tracks, 15 of the victims were railroad employees killed while performing their duties, 1 was a suicide, 13 were passengers killed at stations, and 3 died of other or unknown causes.[25]

The failure of gates to solve Chicago's crossing problem was the result of several factors, including the great number of crossings and tracks in the city; their cost, which made the railroads reluctant to in-

stall them at all but the busiest crossings; and the public's tendency to walk or drive around them when it appeared they could beat a train to the crossing—a problem that persisted into the late twentieth century in the suburbs. By one late nineteenth-century estimate it cost a railroad $1,075 to build a crossing protected by gates and $1,061 a year to maintain it. The estimate included $960 per annum for salaries for the gate-keepers on a 24-hour basis. As a result, gates were often left unmanned at night when traffic was slight, a factor cited as a cause of the injuries to Alfred Swan in 1888 and the death of Elida Hansen at 48th Avenue on July 29, 1894.[26]

The existence of multiple tracks at crossings, in some instances as many as 22 at yards, was a factor that undermined confidence in gates at many crossings.

A type of crossing warning signal in the early twentieth century was the wigwag—an automatic mechanical device that emulated the human flagman waving a lantern. Wigwags ultimately were replaced by flashing signals, although this one in Galena survived into the twenty-first century. (Steve Smedley)

Eight-year-old John J. P. Theobald on April 5, 1892, was distracted watching one train on the Milwaukee Road at the Division Street crossing to the point that he did not notice a train approaching from the opposite direction. He had stepped around the downed gates to get a better look when he was hit and killed by the second train. A couple of years earlier Adolph Harbaum was killed when he ignored the gates and a watchman who gave him a verbal warning at Polk Street—a crossing with nine tracks. He had watched a Rock Island passenger train pass and began to cross the tracks, only to be hit by a backing Lake Shore & Michigan Southern train concealed by some parked railroad cars on the seventh track. The next year William Clough, a butcher delivering meat, was confronted by 22 tracks at the Lake Shore's 43rd Street crossing of a railroad yard. He was hit by a passenger train, the approach of which on one of the center express tracks had been concealed by trains parked on other tracks.[27]

Such accidents made it obvious to both the railroad industry and local government that as improved technology made feasible automatic devices to provide crossing protection, they would have to be installed in great numbers in Illinois, a state in which a person was barely able to travel more than 10 miles without encountering railroad tracks. The cost of posting flagmen around the clock at every crossing in the state was prohibitive, so much so that the railroads eventually acceded to a series of mandates by Chicago beginning in the late nineteenth century to elevate their tracks above the street level in an effort to reduce traffic congestion caused by slow and frequent trains. The measure had the added benefit of greatly reducing the number of grade crossings and the accidents that occurred at them. Grade separation, as elevation or depression of the tracks is called, effectively eliminates crossing accidents but is very expensive, costing an estimated average of $5 million per crossing in 1995 contrasted to $150,000 for automatic crossing signals and gates.[28]

Grade Separation Program

By the 1880s, the proliferation of both steam railroads and street railways in Chicago caused the city to look for solutions to what was becoming an intolerable traffic congestion and safety problem caused by the mixing of wagons, carriages, pedestrians, trains, and horse and cable cars at street level. The steam railroads ran on their own rights-of-way, but as the city grew rapidly after the Civil War the number of rail-street crossings proliferated and with it the number of casualties at those crossings.

The other and perhaps more compelling argument the city officials used to force the railroads to raise their tracks was the impact that slow-moving trains had on street traffic. A survey of 36 crossings on eight railroads between 6 a.m. and 7 p.m. on one day in 1892 showed that the tracks at those locations were crossed by a total of 68,375 vehicles, 9,145 streetcars carrying 261,942 passengers, and 119,181 pedestrians. A total of 3,031 delays averaging about two minutes apiece were experienced at the crossings.[29]

Two decades earlier, faced with similar street congestion resulting from heavy maritime traffic on the Chicago River, the city decided the only solution was to grade-separate the river and street traffic by digging vehicular tunnels beneath the river. It was an expensive solution, but in 1871 Chicago had completed a vehicle and pedestrian tunnel under the main stem of the river at LaSalle Street and a similar one under the south branch of the river at Washington Street. The LaSalle tunnel had cost the city $566,276—an enormous sum at the time. Both were converted to cable car tunnels in the late 1880s.[30]

Despite the fact that several schemes were proposed to build subways and elevated lines principally for mass transit service, one as early as 1869, the cost of raising the tracks of the privately owned steam railroads and streetcar lines was beyond the financial capacity of the city or at least the willingness of the taxpaying voters to pay for such schemes. The obvious solution, at least to the city, was to induce private industry to pay for track elevation, and the Columbian Exposition scheduled for 1893 in Jackson Park became the catalyst to get the program rolling. The Chicago City Railway, the major street railway operator on the South Side, had already concluded it needed to become the principal investor in an elevated railway line to the fairgrounds. Thus the city's first L was built.[31]

The city's first target for steam railroad track elevation was the Illinois Central Railroad, whose mainline was adjacent to the fairgrounds in Jackson Park. Forcing the elevation of those existing and heavily used tracks was a more difficult problem that the city solved by the simple expediency of passing an ordinance requiring the railroad to undertake and finance the project because "public interests imperatively require" it. On May 23, 1892, the City Council approved an ordinance that required the IC to elevate to a height of 18 feet above street level its tracks between 51st and 67th streets in the Hyde Park neighborhood adjacent to the fairgrounds. The railroad completed the task in 1893.[32]

Even before the fair opened that year, some Chicagoans were circulating a proposal to elevate and electrify all steam railroad tracks within 20 miles of the center of the city. The idea had gained sufficient political momentum that Mayor Carter H. Harrison II in 1897, with City Council approval, appointed a special commission on track elevation.[33]

Over the next two decades a succession of ordinances required the railroads to elevate their tracks at their expense in much of the city. In 1894, the Rock Island and Lake Shore were required to elevate part of their lines, and the following year the North Western was told to raise its Galena line between the river and Hamlin Avenue. In 1896 sections of the North Western's north line and the Pittsburgh, Ft. Wayne & Chicago line on the

South Side were ordered elevated. An ordinance adopted October 23, 1899, required four railroads to elevate assorted lines on the South and Southwest sides. On February 4, 1901, the City Council approved an ordinance requiring three railroads to elevate 100 miles of track on the West Side and on November 11, 1901, passed an ordinance to require four railroads to elevate 16 miles of track on the South Side. The following April 2, the council adopted another ordinance requiring six railroads on the West Side to elevate 88.5 miles of track, and on June 30 of that year three railroads were ordered to raise 40 miles of tracks.[34]

There were some questions about the legality of the track elevation program and some resistance on the part of the railroads. Although compliance by the railroads turned out to be voluntary on the assumption that the elimination of congestion would increase the speed of trains and the efficiency of railroad operations, the city at various times resorted to threats to force compliance. The Illinois Central, which was a supporter of the Columbian Exposition and served it with commuter trains, voluntarily agreed to raise its tracks on the South Side near the fairgrounds, but other railroads were a little more recalcitrant. At one point the City Council threatened to post police at grade crossings to stop trains on the Pennsylvania and Baltimore & Ohio railroads and to unilaterally build the necessary causeways and viaducts and bill the railroads for the work.[35]

The track elevation program initially accomplished its safety goal of reducing the number of crossing fatalities from 99 in 1899 to only 20 in 1908, but afterward the crossing death toll began creeping upward again, probably because of the increased automotive traffic on the streets and growth of the city into areas in which the tracks still ran at grade. After 1906, fatalities from street traffic accidents in Chicago regularly exceeded the number of persons killed at grade crossings.[36]

Federal regulation of general railroad safety did not begin until very late in the nineteenth century. Signal systems were developed by the railroads without any government regulation to control trains and prevent wrecks. An IC commuter train is shown beneath a signal bridge at Kensington. The two men sitting on the bridge maintained the signals. (Alan R. Lind, Transport History Press)

By the end of the 1919 construction season the railroads collectively had spent nearly $95 million elevating nearly 550 miles of track and eliminating 963 grade crossings. The program continued through the 1920s but ultimately fell victim to the Depression of the 1930s, as did the city's collateral attempt to force electrification of the steam railroads. The effect was that some outlying areas of the city and most suburbs still had grade crossings, although some inner suburbs, like Evanston and Oak Park, had piggybacked their own track elevation programs onto Chicago's. Despite some interest by the Illinois Commerce Commission in track elevation projects during the Depression, after World War II most grade-separation projects were handled on an individual crossing-by-crossing basis with the bulk of the money for vehicular underpasses or bridges coming from public highway funds.[37]

The State Acts on Crossings

In the late 1800s the state also began to attack the problem of general railroad safety. Illinois in 1889 empowered its Railroad and Warehouse Commission to require that railroads install "safety appliances" to prevent collisions at rail-rail diamond crossings similar to Grand Crossing, the site of the 1853 disaster. Some of the technology employed in those signal systems could be transferred to highway crossings. The history of crossing safety appliances is poorly documented, but manually operated crossing gates appeared by 1870, and within 10 years the industry had developed automatic gates activated by tripping mechanisms along the tracks.[38]

The rapid advance in electronic technology in the late nineteenth century made automatic signaling possible as train speeds increased and automobiles began to appear on the scene. William Robinson's 1872 invention of the direct current track circuit, initially to operate wayside signals to control trains, by 1889 was adapted to operate warning bells at crossings when a locomotive passed over and activated an electric relay. As motor vehicles on the highways proliferated in the early twentieth century, the railroad industry found it necessary to develop automatic visual warnings to augment the bells.

An automatic banjo signal in which a flashing red light and large red disk indicated the approach of a train appeared in 1913 in Plainfield, New Jersey; a signal in which a series of six lights flashed in sequence to emulate a flagman waving a lantern was installed the same year in Searen, New Jersey; and the wigwag, a crossing signal that automatically waves a red light back and forth in the manner of a flagman, appeared in 1914. By 1922, vehicle and train speeds had increased to the point that the signal section of the American Railway Association established 20 seconds as the minimum warning time for motorists at crossings—a standard that still stands. The contemporary signal in which two red lights flash alternatively was developed in the 1930s. The modern gate and signal combination was developed in 1936 by Harry C. Sampson of the Chicago & Alton and manufactured by Western Railroad Supply Co. of Chicago.[39]

The Illinois General Assembly wisely turned the grade-crossing protection issue over to a statewide regulatory body. The Illinois Commerce Commission, successor to the Railroad and Warehouse Commission and the Public Utilities Commission, was given the power in 1921 to regulate crossings "to promote public safety" by requiring lighted stop signs to be posted at crossings. The law stipulated that the commerce commission's powers on crossing protection also superseded those of any local jurisdictions.[40]

Despite the new signal technology, by the middle of the twentieth century the death toll at crossings far exceeded that of train wrecks. The state of Illinois as early as 1955 empowered the Illinois Commerce Commission to begin a crossing safety program—two decades before the federal government got into the act. By 1976, before the effects of federal, state, and local safety programs began to show some results,

164

Railroads and government have experimented over the years, not very successfully, with foolproof crossing barriers to obviate the problem of drivers ignoring signals and driving around gates. Their inherent flaw was that they could trap drivers on the tracks. This one was tried on the North Shore in the 1920s and worked by lowering a mesh screen to stop the car before it crossed the tracks. (Norm Carlson Collection)

This crossing barrier was an unsuccessful experiment by federal and Illinois officials near Chenoa, Illinois, in the 1990s. (Steve Smedley)

more than 1,000 persons died at highway crossings nationally, more than 100 of them in Illinois. However, in the last five years of the century the nation's crossing death toll had been reduced to an average of 441 a year, 36 per year in Illinois.[41]

The safety program begun in 1955 in Illinois had two very important provisions. One was the creation of the grade-crossing safety fund—a commitment by the state to use public funds to pay for crossing protection instead of dumping the problem onto the railroads which by then were suffering the financial consequences of competition from motor trucks, automobiles, and airplanes, as well as regulatory strangulation by the Interstate Commerce Commission. Between 1955 and 1996, Illinois plowed more than $241 million into the crossing protection fund. The other provision was the empowerment of the Illinois Commerce Commission to close unnecessary and dangerous crossings. Ultimately, 715 such crossings were closed statewide from the passage of the act through 1996.[42]

Grade-Crossing Disasters

Despite the best efforts of government and the railroads to improve crossing safety, the increase in the size of commercial motor vehicles and their proliferation on the roads posed a new threat in the second half of the twentieth century. Larger buses and state laws mandating the busing of schoolchildren put more such vehicles on the road, and an increase in the size and number of trucks on the road increased the likelihood of train derailments in crossing accidents.[43]

The increased complexity of the highway system and the signals needed to control vehicular traffic were also factors in a number of grade-crossing accidents, including a 1995 collision of a train with a school bus in suburban Fox River Grove. In the last three decades of the twentieth century, the growth of Chicago's northwest suburbs had resulted in substantial increases in traffic on the Northwest High-

way (U.S. Highway 14) that ran parallel to and in some cases adjacent to a Union Pacific Railroad (formerly Chicago & North Western) commuter line through the area. The growth in traffic over the years had forced the Illinois Department of Transportation to install increasingly complex signal systems for traffic at various streets that intersected both the Northwest Highway and the tracks, which were protected by independently operated crossing signals maintained by the railroad and under the jurisdiction of the Illinois Commerce Commission.

The traffic signals that had been installed on U.S. 14 in Fox River Grove 5 years earlier and upgraded 12 months before the accident were supposedly electronically controlled to take highway, pedestrian, and crossing traffic all into account. As a train approached, the crossing signals were supposed to override the highway signals 30 seconds before the train's arrival to give any motorists stopped on the tracks time to get out of harm's way. However, the system was also programmed to give any pedestrians in the intersection the right-of-way for 21 seconds to cross. That effectively delayed the get-out-of-harm's-way time for motorists on the crossing to a maximum of just nine seconds, although the average margin because of differing train speeds may have been more like four to six seconds.

That recipe for disaster came to a boil on October 25, 1995, when a bus carrying local high school students was stopped by a red light at Northwest Highway with its rear end hanging out over the crossing. The bus failed to clear the crossing after the light turned green and was hit by a commuter train, killing seven students and injuring 24. After the accident, the various regulatory agencies required the re-timing of all highway signals on highways parallel and adjacent to railroad lines to allow greater time for motor vehicles to clear the crossings.[44]

The greater danger to railroad trains was the heavy trucks that appeared on highways

The development of
progressively heavier trucks
increased the risk to trains at
crossings. This Amtrak train
bound from Chicago to
Springfield was derailed
when it hit a heavy truck
carrying road construction
materials near Braidwood,
Illinois, in the 1970s. Fortunately, no deaths resulted.
(Steve Smedley)

in increasing numbers after World War II, a phenomenon Robert B. Shaw, the chronicler of U.S. railroad safety, noted as early as 1978 in his epic *A History of Railroad Accidents, Safety Precautions and Operating Practices*. Although the 1930 wreck of two Chicago, North Shore & Milwaukee Railroad trains at a crossing near Kenosha, Wisconsin, is an exception, automobiles rarely caused train wrecks, and the typical victims of such accidents were the occupants of the cars. However, heavy trucks, especially those carrying volatile liquids, posed a serious danger to trains. The first such accident in Chicago was the 1950 collision between a streetcar and gasoline truck on the South Side of Chicago that immolated 33 persons.[45]

The February 23, 1930, North Shore wreck occurred when the driver of an automobile passed another stopped at the crossing signals on Wisconsin Highway 43

for an approaching North Shore freight and went around the signals in an attempt to beat the freight over the crossing. However, a passenger train was simultaneously approaching from the other direction at 75 miles an hour. It hit the car, killing both occupants; then the two cars, still swaying from the impact, sideswiped the passing freight, derailing both trains. A total of 12 persons died in the resulting wreck and 95 were injured.[46]

Train wrecks resulting from truck collisions increased in number and severity beginning in the 1950s. Of the 3,502 grade-crossing accidents reported nationally in the year 2000, a total of 851 involved heavy trucks, including 446 trailer trucks. Although the January 24, 1970, collision between the City of New Orleans and a loaded oil truck at an Illinois Central Railroad crossing in Loda about 94 miles south of Chicago caused no major injuries to

The destruction of a train after it collided with a truck in Bourbonnais, Illinois, in 1999 raised the question of grade separation once again, especially given concerns about whether high-speed railroads similar to those in Europe and Japan could ever be built in the United States.

passengers, the resulting fireball immolated the locomotive, three crewmen, and the truck driver. Less than three years later a trailer truck crashed through crossing gates in a heavy fog in northwest suburban Bartlett and smashed into a Chicago, Milwaukee, St. Paul & Pacific Railroad commuter train. No passengers died in the November 23, 1973, accident, but the locomotive engineer and truck driver were killed. Two years later an Amtrak turboliner bound from Chicago to Springfield was hit by a truck carrying asphalt paving material near Elwood, a Will County community southwest of Chicago, derailing the train and injuring 41 persons.[47]

Truck-train accidents continued with some frequency. On June 18, 1998, a two-car South Shore commuter train operated by the Northern Indiana Commuter Transportation District rammed a trailer truck carrying steel coils at a private crossing operated by a steel mill in Portage, Indiana. One 19-ton coil was hurled into one of the passenger cars, killing three occupants. The National Transportation Safety Board put a large share of the blame on federal, state, and private agencies for failing to provide adequate protection at a crossing known to be dangerous.[48]

The worst of the truck-train collisions in the general Chicago area occurred on March 15, 1999, when Amtrak train Number 59 carrying 207 passengers and 21 crewmen bound from Chicago to New Orleans on the Illinois Central Railroad slammed into a trailer truck carrying steel in Bourbonnais, Illinois, about 50 miles south of Chicago. The impact derailed both locomotives and 11 passenger cars, which also hit two freight cars parked on a siding before catching fire from the diesel fuel spilling from the locomotives. Eleven persons were killed and 122 injured in the accident that National Transportation Safety Board investigators blamed on the truck driver, who had tried to race across the crossing after the lights had started flashing but before the gates lowered. The agency said the driver's judgment was impaired by fatigue because before the accident he had worked more hours than allowed by federal regulations.[49]

The propensity of some motorists, like the Bourbonnais truck driver, to try to beat trains over crossings, even those protected by signals and gates, caused federal, state, and local governments to adopt a different approach to safety before the end of the century. They began to emphasize the enforcement of traffic laws to deter errant motorists. Just before the century ended, the governments began experimenting with "cop in the box" methods of enforcing grade-crossing safety by automatically monitoring crossings with television and computers.

Even so, grade-crossing safety remained an issue in Chicago's suburbs as well as in Illinois generally. The Metropolitan Planning Council in 2003 recommended a program to replace the 40 worst grade crossings in the Chicago area with bridges. However, in Chicago the number of fatal crossing accidents had by then dwindled to the point that the police department in its annual report on traffic safety no longer listed them as a separate category but lumped them together with such incidents as fatal bicycle accidents in a category called "other." There were 6 such "other" fatal accidents in 1999 and 20 in 2000.[50]

The inability of government and the railroads to solve the grade-crossing safety problem was another symptom of the phenomenon of decentralization that occurred in the Chicago area during the twentieth century. Every time Chicago eliminated a grade crossing with a viaduct, two new ones sprang up in the suburbs. *Decentralization* is the polite term for what its detractors call *urban sprawl*, and although metropolitan planners usually blamed it on the proliferation of expressways and automobiles after World War II, its roots went back to the railroads in the nineteenth century.

Decline and Decentralization

Steel sheeting covered the old-style locomotive to make it look sleek and modern—the railroads' version of the art deco style popular in the 1930s—as a response to competition from airlines and autos. (J. Michael Gruber)

The collective decline of the American railroad industry in the twentieth century had less of an effect on Chicago than on other areas of the nation. The nation's railroad system continued to expand up until World War I, declined until about 1980, and finally stabilized in the last two decades of the century. Not all railroads followed that scenario; indeed, some strong carriers grew stronger as the century progressed, but others withered and died. Some merged into rail giants, and others were dismembered. The industry willingly turned over both its commuter and intercity passenger service to government control.

The railroad network overall shrank from a high of 254,037 miles in 1916 to 97,817 miles in 2001, and its share of the freight market (as measured in ton-miles) declined from 77 percent in 1916 to 40 percent at the end of the century, although the volume of freight carried by rail over that span tripled. Thus the railroads settled into the role of long-haul carriers and abandoned to motor trucks the lightly trafficked markets. The shrinkage of the system resulted in the loss of railroad service to hundreds of communities across the United States, an event that has not proved to be as calamitous as it sounds because of the development of motor vehicles and the building of paved highways.[1]

The effect of the general railroad decline in Chicago, the center of the system, was not nearly as dramatic as what happened in much of the rest of the country. Metropolitan Chicago had too many miles of track to begin with, and the abandonment of some of them provided space for other development. However, the volume of freight traffic through the Chicago gateway remained substantial despite the loss of much of the city's heavy, smokestack industries, so much so that early in the twenty-first century a civic group known as the Metropolitan Planning Council began agitating for a public-private project to eliminate many railroad diamond crossings and to speed up freight trains.

Passengers were the first traffic the railroads captured from the waterways and highways in the nineteenth century and were the first to desert the railroads in the twentieth. The decline of railroad passenger service in America was dramatic, but again, Chicago survived in considerably better shape than most cities outside the Boston–New York–Philadelphia-Baltimore-Washington corridor. Aside from the municipal transit systems, there were three somewhat distinct types of railroad passenger service in America, and their fates were somewhat different: the electric interurban railways with one exception simply went out of business, the intercity railroads suffered a near-fatal decline in business and ultimately transferred their surviving passenger operations to the federal government, and the commuter railroads fared the best of all. There was some shrinkage of the commuter system, but it survived largely intact and with substantial ridership until federal, state, and local grants became available to subsidize it.

Nationally, intercity passenger travel on railroads declined from 1.2 billion persons in 1920 to only 289 million in 1970 when the railroads' passenger fleet of 11,378 cars was a fifth the size it had been 50 years earlier. The following year the federal agency that had been created to take over the intercity passenger trains acquired only 1,190 of those cars.[2] By 1980 when the Chicago, South Shore & South Bend commuter line ordered new cars, there effectively were no U.S. car builders left in business. They all had been victims of the decline of the railroad passenger car market, and the vehicles had to be ordered from a Japanese company.

The creation of the National Railroad Passenger Corporation (Amtrak) in 1971 and the consolidation of all intercity passenger trains in one depot allowed the abandonment and redevelopment of three of the city's six Victorian intercity train stations and their adjacent yards and substantial modification of a fourth. Three depots survived in one form or another as downtown commuter terminals. The survival of and post–World War II modernization of the city's commuter railroads with diesel locomotives and high-capacity, bi-level gallery cars enabled them to become more efficient and to survive competition from the automobile and expressway. The commuter railroad system shrank in size after the war but after coming under public control began to expand once again in the final decades of the century.

The commuter railroads and the city's rail transit system, perhaps more than any other factors, enabled Chicago to avoid the blight in the 1960s and 1970s that plagued urban downtowns in other midwestern cities, like Detroit and St. Louis, and somewhat ameliorated automobile-induced suburban sprawl. The freight railroads never found a successful bypass to avoid Chicago, perhaps because of geography, the critical mass the city's rail plant had attained, and the fact that other east-west gateways like St. Louis and Memphis offered no better solutions than the congestion of the Windy City's yards. Efforts by the state Transportation Department in

The commuter railroads successfully modernized to survive in Chicago, first by buying high-capacity, bi-level coaches. The Burlington Route was the first to reequip its fleet with bi-levels, which were pulled by steam engines until the line dieselized in the 1950s.

The North Western bought new bi-level cars and dieselized its commuter trains just after the Burlington. (Steve Smedley)

the early 1980s to revamp and consolidate the railroad yards in East St. Louis, Illinois, to revitalize that blighted community and improve the rail gateway there ended in failure when the railroads could not agree on sharing the cost of the program.

At the end of the twentieth century Chicago was still the dominant railroad center in the nation, and by one count a third of the nation's total rail shipments and half its container traffic moved through the metropolitan area annually. The Chicago Terminal District handled 500 freight trains a day hauling 37,500 cars over 893 miles of track—more than existed in six states. The tracks were shared by 700 trains a day operated by Metra and Amtrak. The rail freight traffic was evenly split between terminating, originating, and through trains.[3]

That volume of rail traffic in itself was a problem because trains that sped across the Great Plains were forced to creep through the rail maze in Chicago at speeds ranging from 6.8 to 12 miles an hour. A freight car that took 24 hours to get from the East Coast to Chicago typically took two days to negotiate the metropolitan rail plant before continuing to the West Coast. The competitiveness of the surviving six trunk railroads—the CSX and Norfolk Southern from the East, Burlington Northern Santa Fe and Union Pacific from the West, and Canadian National and Canadian Pacific from the North—was an impediment to attempts to consolidate and streamline the scores of separately owned yards and tracks that crisscrossed Chicagoland.

Shifts in freight patterns also caused changes in Chicago's rail plant. As many branch lines were abandoned in the metropolitan area, their signals were ripped out and the tracks were torn up to be sold for scrap. Many of the ties, however, were left to rot in the ground.

The decentralization of the meatpacking industry to rural locations caused the Chicago Union Stock Yards and their huge rail yard to close in 1971, for example. The loss of the grain trade to the western rivers by 1990 idled not only the city's huge grain elevators but their yards as well. The advent of motor trucks rendered largely obsolete the once ubiquitous boxcar and the freight stations it served in Chicago. Although boxcars had once been the most common type of freight cars, by the end of the twentieth century the eight largest (Class I) railroads in the United States owned only 1,324 of them. The stock car, a boxcar with slatted sides for hauling live animals, had disappeared entirely.

The worldwide container revolution in transportation greatly reduced the role of the boxcar and the assorted freight houses, loading docks, and sidings needed to service it. In the 1950s railroads began to adapt flatcars to carry both truck trailers and marine shipping containers. The major breakthrough came in 1961 when the transportation industry agreed on standard 20- and 40-foot shipping containers with common

The shrinkage and financial troubles of the railroad industry in the 1900s resulted in many changes, including the creation of Amtrak, one of whose trains is shown here on the West Side headed for Union Station, and the abandonment of railroad freight houses. A long-abandoned Milwaukee Road freight house can be seen beyond the Amtrak train.

fittings that could be transferred from ship to train to truck. The concept was so successful and aggressively pursued by the railroads that intermodal traffic increased from a negligible amount in the 1950s to more than 8.7 million units (containers and trailers) by 1998. About 5 million of them passed through Chicago that year. That presented problems at rail gateways like Chicago, where the yards and freight facilities were designed for a different mix of traffic. Such piggyback freight required large, open, and paved rail yards accessible to trucks and mobile gantry cranes, not the constricted freight houses of the past.

The decentralization of cities, or urban sprawl, is usually associated with the development of efficient motorized vehicles and paved roads after World War I. California is often cited as the prime example of the phenomenon of decentralization and the havoc it wrought on the railroads, especially those hauling commuters. But California was never much of a railroad state: it is almost three times the size of Illinois and has almost triple the population, but its railroad plant at 5,604 miles is considerably smaller than Illinois's 8,063-mile system.[4]

In Chicago, a linear decentralization process began along railroad lines shortly after the fire of 1871, more than two decades before the first automobile, an electric, made its appearance on Chicago streets. The fire caused a considerable relocation of both people and industry to outlying areas, but always along railroad lines because there were no transportation alternatives. The outward movement accelerated just after the turn of the century when a system of electric interurban railroads were built into Chicago's hinterlands, some extending 90 miles from the Loop. The interurban railroads ultimately fell victim to Chicago's post–World War II expressway-building program, but the outlying growth both they and the steam lines caused enabled the latter to survive as a viable transportation system into the twenty-first century.

The decline of railroad traffic in the twentieth century, primarily because of competition from motor trucks, rendered obsolete the industry's once plentiful downtown freight houses. This Burlington freight house just south of Roosevelt Road was demolished in 1976. (Steve Smedley)

The Interurbans

The first victims of the general decline of the railroad industry in the twentieth century were the last to appear on the scene—the electric interurbans. Although largely forgotten except by a segment of rail fans, the interurbans played a substantial role in the suburban population growth spurt before the onset of the Great Depression. The mainline commuter railroads that had created suburbia in the first place continued to influence city suburban

The South Shore, the nation's last interurban, limped along with 1920s vintage steel cars until it was publicly acquired in 1991. This train was photographed operating on the streets of Michigan City, Indiana, in true interurban fashion in 1938. (Norm Carlson Collection)

development through the second half of the twentieth century. Between 100,000 and 150,000 suburbanites a day used those railroads to commute to downtown Chicago in the second half of the century even during the height of the automobile- and expressway-building boom.[5]

The adaptation of electric traction to railways by Frank J. Sprague in 1888 led to the development of streetcars and elevated lines in urban areas and interurban railroads in the suburbs and rural areas on the eve of the Motor Age. The interurban-building frenzy in the United States hit the Chicago area after 1900 when 12 independent interurban railroads that collectively operated nearly 600 miles of track were built in the metropolitan area and extending as much as 90 miles from the city. Most of them disappeared during the De-

pression, but the three that survived did so because they developed into commuter railroads.[6] (See Table 12-1.)

The survivors' common characteristic was that they all obtained access to downtown Chicago over other railroads and thus were able to offer a high-speed, one-seat service to commuters. However, the Chicago, Aurora & Elgin folded in the late 1950s (1957 for passenger service and 1959 for freight) after it lost its access to the Loop when the Garfield Park elevated line was razed to make room for an expressway, and the Chicago, North Shore & Milwaukee went out of business in 1963 (1955 on the Shore Line route and 1963 on the remainder of the railroad) because of declining business in competition with the automobile and the motor truck. The availability of excellent commuter service on the Chicago & North Western, which had lines parallel to both the North Shore and Aurora & Elgin, was also a factor in the demise of those interurbans. The sole interurban to survive into the twenty-first century—the Chicago, South Shore & South Bend—did so because it had a healthy freight service in industrial northwest Indiana and its commuter operations were publicly acquired beginning in 1990. The freight service remained in private hands.[7]

Although the weaker interurban railroads disappeared even before the Depression without leaving a trace, those with high-speed commuter service left an indelible mark on the metropolitan area. In the first three decades of the twentieth century, the corridors in which the North Shore and Aurora & Elgin were built parallel and adjacent to existing commuter railroads showed a considerably higher rate of population growth than other corridors served only by steam railroads. In the 22.7-mile corridor in the northern suburbs from Evanston to North Chicago where the North Shore ran alongside a North Western, the population of the incorporated municipalities more than quadrupled between 1900 and 1930. The corridor gained more than 100,000 residents in that period, an average of 3,335 a year. However, a few miles inland along the 24.2-mile corridor from the Chicago city limits to Libertyville, served exclusively by the Milwaukee Road, the growth was only a tenth that of the interurban corridor—an average population growth of only 393 a year.

The growth pattern in western suburbs where the Aurora & Elgin interurban was built parallel and adjacent to another North Western commuter line was even more dramatic. The 25-mile corridor from Oak Park to Geneva gained more than 146,000 residents in the 1900–1930 period, an average of 4,891 per year. Conversely, growth in the flanking rail corridors served exclusively by the Milwaukee Road and Burlington Route was more modest. The Burlington's corridor from Berwyn to Naperville gained an average of 2,930 residents a year, and the Milwaukee Road from Elmwood Park to Bartlett showed a growth of only 542 persons annually over the same 30-year plan (see Appendix B and Table 12-2).

The North Shore interurban line responded to its competitors' streamlining of their trains with the articulated Electroliner, used between Chicago and Milwaukee. These trains got their power from overhead wires by means of trolley poles. (William D. Middleton)

TABLE 12-1 **Chicago Area Interurban Railroads**

Railroad (Terminals)	Mileage	Year Opened	Year Closed
Chicago, North Shore & Milwaukee (Chicago to Milwaukee)	106	1895	1963
Chicago, Aurora & Elgin (Chicago to Fox River valley)	61	1902	1957
Chicago & Interurban Traction (79th Street to Kankakee)	54	1907	1927
Chicago & Joliet Electric (Archer and Cicero avenues to Joliet)	37	1901	1933
Chicago, South Shore & South Bend (Randolph Street to South Bend)	90	1903	——
Aurora, Plainfield & Joliet (Aurora to Joliet)	20	1901	1925
Joliet & Eastern Traction (Joliet to Chicago Heights)	20	1909	1923
Aurora, Elgin & Fox River (Carpentersville to Yorkville)	37	1906	1935
Elgin & Belvidere (Elgin to Belvidere)	36	1906	1930
Chicago, Ottawa & Peoria (Joliet to Princeton)	95	1902	1934
Chicago, Harvard & Geneva Lake (Harvard to Lake Geneva, Wisc.)	11	1899	1930
Chicago, Aurora & DeKalb (Aurora to DeKalb)	25	1906	1923

Sources: George S. Rogers, *Chicago Area Interurban Systems: 1892–1963,* unpublished report in files of Chicago Regional Transportation Authority. George W. Hilton and John F. Due, *The Electric Interurban Railways in America* (Stanford, Calif., 2000 ed.), 335–43.

Commuter Railroads in the Automobile Age

The influence of both types of railroads on the growth of suburbia is indisputable. In 1900, the population of those portions of the six counties outside of Chicago served by commuter railroads constituted less than 20 percent of the population of the metropolitan area. By 1940, the last decennial census before the automobile began to make a big impact on outlying growth, suburbia accounted for 26 percent of the metropolitan population. By the end of the twentieth century, the suburbs collectively had 64 percent of the population, although the bulk of that growth in the second half of the century was attributable to automobility (see Table 12-3).

Commuting, like the intercity passenger

TABLE 12-2 **Growth in Commuter Rail Corridors, 1900 to 1930**

Corridor (No. of suburbs)	Corridor Length	Population* 1900	Population* 1930	Increase	Average Growth Per Year
CNW North** (10)	22.7	32,960	133,023	100,063	3,335
MR North(7)	24.2	1,972	13,762	11,790	393
CNW Northwest (6)	18.4	6,568	30,768	24,200	806
MR West(10)	19.9	1,644	17,920	16,276	542
CNW West**(14)	25.0	18,370	165,090	146,720	4,891
CBQ West (11)	18.9	14,603	102,513	87,910	2,930

*Includes only incorporated municipalities in each corridor. Satellite cities (Aurora, Elgin, and Waukegan) and incorporated townships (Cicero) are excluded.

**Interurban railroad corridors

trains, was not a particularly profitable market for the railroads, however. The commuter lines that survived the onslaught of the automobile and motor truck did so primarily because their corporate parents had substantial overland freight traffic that could subsidize, or at least bear the bulk of the cost of, the physical plant shared with commuter and intercity passenger operations at least until such time as local, state, and federal governments began subsidizing passenger operations beginning about 1970. Freight provided the revenue that enabled the railroads to maintain the tracks and signals over which commuter service could be operated. For example, between 1947 and 1956, freight accounted for between 85 and 90 percent of the revenues of the Chicago & North Western, by then the Chicago region's largest commuter carrier. Conversely, the Chicago, Rock Island & Pacific and Chicago, Milwaukee, St. Paul & Pacific disappeared in bankruptcy because they lacked sufficient overland freight traffic to remain competitive with the other granger railroads. Their Chicago-area commuter operations, which constituted only a fraction of the freight railroads' costs, were absorbed into the Regional Transportation Authority in the 1980s.[8]

Despite cross subsidies from freight traffic, the mainline or steam railroads began to pare their commuter operations as early as the 1930s, although the Wisconsin Central abandoned its suburban service to Antioch as early as 1897. The most vulnerable were the lightly used lines. Thus the Illinois Central, which had begun running a limited number of commuter trains in 1893 on its Iowa line as far west as suburban Addison in anticipation of Columbian Exposition traffic, discontinued the service during the Great Depression in 1931. The Grand Trunk Western line from Dearborn Station to Valparaiso, Indiana, was discontinued in 1935, as was the Chicago & Eastern Illinois service from the same station to south suburban Crete. The Erie Railroad commuter service to Rochester, Indiana, also ended in the 1930s. The Wabash, which ran as many as eight round-trips to the southwest suburbs in the early twentieth century, by the 1970s had reduced the schedule to one daily round-trip, and the New York Central Railroad commuter line between LaSalle Street Station and Elkhart, Indiana, was discontinued in the early 1960s. The Pennsylvania Railroad's commuter service to Valparaiso, Indiana, after successively being passed to the Penn Central, Conrail, and Amtrak, was finally abandoned by the latter in 1991.

TABLE 12-3 **Chicago Metropolitan Area Population Distribution**

Year	Metropolitan	Chicago	Suburbs*
1890	1,391,890	1,099,850	292,040
1900	2,084,750	1,698,575	386,175
1910	2,702,465	2,185,283	517,182
1920	3,982,123	3,212,000	770,123
1930	4,449,646	3,367,438	1,082,208
1940	4,569,643	3,369,608	1,200,035
1950	5,177,600	3,620,962	1,556,638
1960	6,220,913	3,550,404	2,670,509
1970	6,977,267	3,369,367	3,607,900
1980	7,102,328	3,005,072	4,097,256
1990	7,180,235	2,783,726	4,396,509
2000	8,091,720	2,896,016	5,195,704

*Those portions of Cook, Du Page, Kane, Lake, McHenry, and Will counties outside of Chicago.
Source: U.S. Census for the years indicated.

Some of the region's strongest commuter railroads also pared their systems somewhat. In stages between 1966 and 1980, the North Western abandoned the outer end of its commuter line between McHenry, Illinois, and Williams Bay, Wisconsin, primarily because of the state of Wisconsin's failure to provide subsidies for the little-used service. In 1982 the Milwaukee Road for much the same reason dropped commuter service between Fox Lake, Illinois, and Walworth, Wisconsin.

Public Control of Passenger Trains

The strategy of the freight railroads beginning in the 1950s was to abandon their money-losing passenger trains, both commuter and intercity, and transfer the remainder to some sort of public agency that could subsidize them. The railroads' share of intercity passenger market had declined from 75 percent at the end of World War II to 18.5 percent in 1965 as long-distance travelers shifted to automobiles and the airlines. By 1958 the Interstate Commerce Commission reported in a study that the nation's railroads collectively were losing about $750 million a year on passenger operations. Ultimately, Congress in 1970 passed and President Richard M. Nixon signed the Rail Passenger Service Act law creating the National Railroad Passenger Corporation, which became popularly known as Amtrak.[9]

The railroads serving Chicago in the 1960s decided to try the same strategy with their commuter lines. Led by the Chicago & North Western's general counsel, Richard M. Freeman, they formed what they called the passenger and law committee to induce Illinois to create what in 1975 became the Regional Transportation Authority to subsidize their commuter lines. The creation of the agency and the taxing authority to support it were narrowly approved by Chicago-area voters by a 684,266 to 671,287 vote on March 19, 1974.[10]

Despite an intense lobbying effort by the railroads, the vote was a clear indication of the declining influence of those carriers in the very suburbs they had created. The issue carried by a three-to-one margin in Chicago primarily on the basis of anticipated subsidies for the city's mass transit system but lost by a two-to-one margin in the by then auto-dominated suburbs. In the outlying counties of Du Page, Kane, Lake, McHenry, and Will, the "no" vote varied from four-to-one to ten-to-one.[11]

After considerable political and financial turbulence in its formative years, the RTA, after being reformed in 1983, provided the commuter railroad system with financial stability in the form of reliable subsidies. However, that did not occur until after the RTA, bordering on insolvency in 1981, made the unfortunate decision to double commuter fares, an action that

caused a substantial drop in ridership, reversing a long trend. Suburban rail patronage did not fully recover to its pre-1980 levels until the end of the century.[12]

Intercity Trains

The decline of the railroad passenger train incongruously coincides with an explosive growth in personal travel in the United States. In 1920 annual per capita intercity travel was only 500 miles—50 by auto and 450 by train. Ten years later it was nearly 2,000 miles—only 219 miles by train and 1,691 by auto. By 1950 intercity travel was more than 3,300 miles per person per year, 5,808 miles by 1970, and

As deficits became a problem, the commuter lines continued to use hand-me-down locomotives until the 1970s when government subsidies started. This Rock Island locomotive shown at 99th Street in Chicago was an older diesel downgraded from intercity service. The bankrupt Rock Island commuter line ultimately was bought by the Regional Transportation Authority. (Michael Brown)

8,014 miles by 1990. Per capita train travel was almost the same in 1950 (215.7 miles) as it had been in 1930. After 1970 it rapidly declined to 53.6 miles annually and remained at that level. The airplane as well as the interstate highway system were the obvious culprits in the postwar decline in rail travel. Per capita air travel increased from 61.7 miles in 1950 to 538.6 miles in 1970 and 1,390.8 miles in 1990.[13]

The falloff in train travel was a mixed blessing. As early as the first decade of the twentieth century when the steam railroads still held a monopoly on passenger traffic, there were indications that it was not a particularly profitable business for the railroad industry as a whole, a problem that had become obvious by World War I. The passenger train peaked in importance in California as early as 1910 and began to slip thereafter. The decline of the interurban railways in the Midwest probably began about the same time, although the failures did not accelerate until the 1920s.[14]

The shift away from passenger trains occurred first in rural areas, along marginal branch lines, first as electric interurban railroads were built, and later as farmers found that automobiles could be used for trips between towns as well as between farm and town, even on the unimproved roads of the day. The building of paved highways after the Great War, the development of intercity motor buses in the 1920s, the result of the Depression in a decline in business travel that was the mainstay of the railroad passenger train, and finally the introduction of longer-range and higher-capacity aircraft after World War II all accelerated the erosion. The relatively high rail passenger fares in the 1920s and the slowness of the railroads to take countermeasures to halt the desertion of commercial travelers during the Depression may also have contributed to the ridership slippage.[15]

Automobiles made their first impact on railroad ridership on branch lines in rural areas early in the twentieth century. The railroads responded by downsizing trains to self-propelled vehicles capable of being operated by small crews. This self-propelled gas electric shown in 1956 was used in rural mail service.

Self-propelled motor trains, like the Chicago to Iowa Land O' Corn, were used by the railroads on lighter-density mainline routes. (Alan R. Lind, Transport History Press)

The development of more reliable and more comfortable automobiles after World War I was the first factor to have an impact on rail passenger travel at least 25 years before the airplane became a reliable competitor. The decline in first-class travel on Pullman cars began in the 1920s, and by the end of the Depression it was less than half of what it had been two decades earlier. The number of Pullman Company passengers declined from 39.3 million in 1920 to 29.4 million in 1930 and 14.8 million in 1940. After World War II, the introduction of larger aircraft with longer ranges and the introduction by the airlines of coach fares that made travel affordable to the middle class accelerated the decline of long-distance train travel to the point that rail's share of the intercity market (as measured in passenger miles) declined from 27.1 percent in 1945 to 2.8 percent in 1960.[16]

The effect on Chicago was substantial. More than 25.4 million passengers boarded or embarked from intercity trains in Chicago in 1913, but by 1993 that had declined to only 2.48 million. It is no coincidence that over the same span auto registrations in Chicago increased from less than 30,000 to more than a million and the number of passengers using the city's airports increased from zero to almost 72 million. The first commercial airline flights date from 1926.[17]

The creation of Amtrak had a substantial effect on Chicago: the quasi-governmental corporation not only preserved a core of intercity passenger service in the Midwest with Chicago as its dominant hub but managed to quickly consolidate long-distance passenger operations at the city's six railroad depots into a single operation at Union Station. This was a project the city had been dreaming about for most of the century. Wabash Railroad president Frederic A. Delano as early as 1906 had suggested an arrangement of six depots side by side south of the Loop, and Daniel Burnham in his 1909 Plan of Chicago proposed the consolidation of downtown freight terminals at the mouth of the Chicago River, then still a busy lake port, but not the passenger depots. Subsequent plans by engineer Bion J. Arnold for the City Club of Chicago (1913), the Chicago Plan Commission (1914), John F. Wallace for the Chicago City Council (1915), consulting engineer Edward Noonan for the City Council Committee on Railway Terminals (1933), and V. V. Boatner in compliance with the U.S. Emergency Railroad Transportation Act of 1933 (1936) all recommended some terminal consolidations, but except for the relocation of North Western station above street level (1911) and the construction west of the Chicago River of a new Union Station with its yards depressed below street level (1926), few of their recommendations became reality.[18]

The practical effect of having three major railroad stations (Grand Central at Harrison and Wells streets, LaSalle at LaSalle and Van Buren streets, and Dearborn at Dearborn and Polk streets) and their coach yards just south of the Loop was to block southward expansion of Chicago's central business district. As a result, commercial and retail development beginning in the 1920s occurred to the north of the main stem of the Chicago River. The widening of Pine Street, later renamed Michigan Avenue, into a broad thoroughfare had been proposed by Burnham in his 1909 Chicago Plan but was not completed until 1920.[19]

The project resulted in an immediate explosion of high-rise construction on both sides of the river along Michigan Avenue in what had once been the city's port, warehouse, and industrial district. The Wrigley Building and London Guarantee Building (later Stone Container Building) were completed north and south of the river, respectively, in 1923; Tribune Tower was finished north of the river in 1925; the 333 N. Michigan Avenue building opened just south of the river in 1928; and the Medinah Athletic Club at 505 N. Michigan Avenue (later used as a hotel) was finished on the North Side in 1929. Ultimately North Michigan Avenue between the river and Oak Street was transformed into what became known as the "magnificent mile"—a strip of upscale retail stores that to a large extent displaced State Street in the Loop as the city's prime downtown shopping area.[20]

One major drawback to plans to consolidate and modernize the city's depots was that none of the projected increases in intercity passenger traffic that had been used to justify the project in fact occurred. Increased use of automobiles and the building of hard roads after World War I shifted some of the passenger market from trains to cars. The other problem with any attempted consolidation was the commuter traffic that also used the stations. In 1913 according to Arnold's station-by-station head count, Chicago's six major depots, without significant competition from any other mode, were handling about 70,000 intercity passengers a day on nearly 600 trains—a passenger count that would compute to roughly 25.5 million annual riders, a volume of traffic Chicago's two major airports did not attain until 1967. However, nearly 64 percent of the passenger traffic at the six downtown stations in 1913 was commuters. Only Grand Central and Dearborn stations did not have appreciable commuter traffic[21] (see Table 7-2).

As intercity rail passenger traffic began a dramatic decline after World War II when the airline industry emerged as a major competitor, additional proposals were made to consolidate Chicago's depots. The South Side Planning Board submitted one in 1957, followed by a state law creating a railway terminal authority later that year, and a proposal by Mayor Richard J. Daley in 1956 to consolidate stations to free up land for a new University of Illinois Chicago campus. Nothing came of them until Amtrak soon after its creation consolidated the surviving intercity operations at Chicago Union Station on March 6, 1972. The consolidation was not the result of any deference to Chicago to eliminate underutilized and aging stations but the desire by Amtrak to reduce operating expenses by eliminating duplicate facilities.[22]

By then intercity passenger traffic in Chicago had shrunk to a fraction of what it had been earlier in the century. The daily Amtrak trains serving Union Station as the new century dawned collectively carried an average of less than 6,000 passengers a day—only about 8 percent of the traffic handled by Chicago's six stations when Arnold did his daily count in 1913. The decline in the number of trains was even more dramatic, from 591 a day in 1913 when 21 railroads competed for passengers to only 46 in 2001 when Amtrak was the sole surviving intercity rail passenger carrier.[23]

Although the Illinois Central's Randolph Street station east of the Loop, the Rock Island's LaSalle Street station south of the Loop, and the North Western's depot west of the river remained open for commuter operations, the Amtrak consolidation enabled the railroads to close and sell off their Grand Central, Dearborn, and 12th Street (Central) terminals for other development. Union Station, which ultimately passed to Amtrak's ownership, handled that agency's trains as well as the commuter services of the Burlington Route and Milwaukee Road and several smaller commuter operations. The Grand Central and 12th Street terminal buildings were demolished, in 1971 and 1974, respectively. The LaSalle Street station was razed in 1981 for an office building, and the Rock Island commuter depot moved to a smaller building to the south. The North Western's 1911 depot was demolished in 1984 and replaced with an office tower incorporating a station on the lower floors. The Dearborn head house, as the terminal building is referred to in railroad parlance, was remodeled into a shopping center as an anchor for a housing development built on the site of its former train shed and yards to the south. The red sandstone terminal with its massive clock tower was the only landmark from Chicago's golden age of railroads to survive into the twenty-first century.

Freight

The shrinkage and consolidation of the U.S. railroad industry that occurred in the last half of the twentieth century had effects that were less obvious to the Chicago public but were important nonetheless. U.S. railroads lost a considerable share of the freight market to competing modes and by the end of the century were carrying less than half of the nation's freight. However, those data are somewhat misleading because the number of ton-miles carried by railroads had more than tripled to 1.53 trillion in 2000 from 455 billion in 1929. The trains got longer, heavier, and faster even though the number of railroads and the mileage operated shrank.[24]

In Chicago, which at the end of the twentieth century was still unchallenged as the nation's largest rail hub, the changes resulted in a busier freight railroad system. The city's railroad plant saw a steady growth in traffic: from about 12,600 freight cars a day in 1929, traffic grew to 17,000 cars daily during World War II, and by the end of the century it exceeded 28,500 cars every 24 hours. That volume of freight cars required an average of 413 daily trains into and out of the metropolitan area.[25]

Despite the growth in traffic volume, changes in the nature of the commodities carried resulted in substantial changes in the city's railroad plant. Older and obsolete freight yards in the center of the city—a necessity when there was substantial freight transferred between the Great Lakes ships and trains—were abandoned or used for storage, and bigger classification yards were built on huge parcels of cheap land in the suburbs. Freight stations, the equivalent of the downtown passenger depots used to transfer small shipments (less-than-carload freight in railroad parlance), were abandoned and replaced by intermodal yards. As old industries moved to new sites in the suburbs without rail access, old industrial sidings were torn up or left to rot. The migration of the meatpacking industry to rural locations doomed the massive Chicago Union Stock Yards by midcentury although it did not close until 1971, and the demise of much of the city's steelmaking industry in the second half of the century reduced the amounts of raw materials and finished steel hauled to and from Chicago.

The Chicago area had as many as 160 freight yards as late as World War II. But by the end of the century only 49 remained—6 of them hump-equipped classification yards in which incoming trains were broken up and reassembled into outbound trains by the process of pushing them over an artificial hill, or hump as it is known in the industry. The cars then would coast onto various destination tracks on which new outbound trains were formed. In flat yards, the sorting is done by switch engines—a much slower process.[26]

Nothing more clearly shows the changes in Chicago's freight railroads than the growth of what is known in the industry as intermodal, or "piggyback," traffic in which loaded truck trailers and marine shipping containers are transferred to and from railroad flatcars. The railroad industry began to experiment with techniques of handling intermodal traffic, principally truck trailers, in the 1920s but did not begin to attack the market on a large scale until the 1950s. By the end of the century America's railroads hauled more than 9 million such trailers and containers. Moreover, the Chicago area by virtue of the fact that it handled 5.97 million such trailers and containers in the year 2000 was the world's third largest port for such traffic, behind only Hong Kong and Singapore.[27]

From the beginning, Chicago's railroads had tackled the problem of gathering and distributing merchandise by means of team tracks, essentially short spur lines on which boxcars could be parked for loading and unloading to and from wagons, and somewhat later by freight stations or freight houses, as they were sometimes called. The first of the city's freight houses, a 7,500-square-foot structure, dates from 1850 on the Galena & Chicago Union. They were essentially linear warehouses with doors along both sides—one for access from railroad cars and the other from wagons and, somewhat later, from motor trucks. By the early part of the twentieth century there were as many as 76 such freight houses scattered about the city along rail lines. The Chicago Tunnel Company's 60-mile freight subway system beneath downtown Chicago also connected to various steam railroad facilities, including the massive freight house operated by the Soo Line at 507 W. Roosevelt Road. But as motor trucks improved in range and size, the railroads found they did not have to maintain large freight houses near the downtown area to serve the Loop. The development of piggyback freight after World War II doomed the freight houses.[28]

Although freight wagons had been carried on trains as early as 1848 in Chicago, the first sustained piggyback service did not appear until 1926 on the North Shore. That interurban could not haul freight cars over the elevated line it used as access to the Loop, so it used trucks to pick up and deliver at its Montrose Avenue freight house about 5.5 miles north of the Loop. Eventually the railroad ordered flatcars specially designed to haul truck trailers to put an end to the costly process of having to load and unload truck trailers and rail cars at the terminal. The trailers could simply be ramped off the train, hooked to a truck tractor, and driven to their destination. The North Shore handled a peak of 18,000 trailers in 1943, but after the war, traffic dropped off quickly and the service was abandoned in 1947.[29]

The major railroads quickly picked up on the idea and in 1960 hauled 550,000 piggyback flatcars. By then the marine shipping container was making an appearance. The first container ship, the Ideal X, dates from 1956, but the market did not take off until 1961 when shippers agreed on standard 20- and 40-foot containers with common fittings to permit their transfer between ships, trains, and motor trucks. In 2000, America's railroads hauled more universal containers (6.29 million) than truck trailers (2.89 million).[30]

The effect of the intermodal revolution on Chicago, aside from the city's inability to develop a marine intermodal port at 95th Street because of the constraints the St. Lawrence Seaway placed on the size of ships, was to force the railroads to convert many existing yards to intermodal facilities. At the end of the twentieth century there were 47 such intermodal yards scattered around the metropolitan area, some converted from classification yards, like the Burlington's Clyde yard in Cicero and the North Western's Proviso yard near Northlake. Others were built on prairies beyond the fringe of the metropolitan area. The Burlington Northern and Santa Fe Railway dubbed its 621-acre intermodal yard on the former Joliet Army Arsenal site about 40 miles southwest of the Loop a "logistics park." The yard, which opened October 14, 2002, handled autos shipped by rail as well as truck trailers and marine containers. Not to be outdone, the Union Pacific Railroad beginning in late 2001 built a 750-acre intermodal yard near Rochelle about 65 miles west of the Loop. The railroad had considered sites closer to Chicago, including one in West Chicago about 30 miles west of the Loop, but could not overcome local objections to increased truck traffic such a facility would generate. The UP yard was intended to take some of the pressure off the railroad's existing intermodal yards at Proviso and on the West Side of Chicago.[31]

The development of intermodal facilities was the railroad industry's response to its shrinking share of the freight market because of competition from motor trucks. Those vehicles had begun making inroads into railroad traffic in the 1930s but as late as 1950 handled only about a third of the volume of traffic. In the next 20 years, the railroads' share declined from 56 percent of the total domestic intercity ton miles in the U.S. to less than 40 percent, and trucks increased their share from 16 percent to more than 21 percent. Over the same two decades, much of the American railroad network in the Northeast and stretching west to Chicago, as well as some granger railroads west of Chicago, were sliding toward bankruptcy. The causes of that financial collapse were much more complicated than simply competition from highway trucks.[32]

Liquidation, Consolidation, and Diversification

These marine shipping containers destined for the Far East are shown being stacked by gantry cranes on flatcars at the North Western's Wood Street yard in Chicago. The eagle logo on several of the containers indicated they belonged to American President Lines, a major Pacific Ocean ship operator between the West Coast and Asia. (Michael Brown)

The nineteenth century had been the era of growth for America's railroads; most of the twentieth century was one of contraction, consolidation, and turmoil. Major factors in the twentieth century included economic regulation, competition from other and in many cases newer and more efficient modes of transportation, federal and state subsidies to competitors, gerontic management, and the relative wealth of the nation that enabled the population and much of its industry to afford individual transportation at the expense of com-

mon carriers. New technologies also combined to take their toll on the iron horse as investors flocked to newer industries that promised greater growth. Their collective effect on the Chicago-based granger railroads was particularly severe: none survived. One by one they were acquired by someone else, sold off in pieces, merged into a bigger system, or simply liquidated.

All but one of the interurban railroads were liquidated. Both the Rock Island and Milwaukee Road were dismembered in bankruptcy. The Burlington was merged into Jim Hill's northern lines (Great Northern and Northern Pacific) under the name Burlington Northern and then merged with the Santa Fe. The Union Pacific grabbed up the North Western, and the Illinois Central was acquired by the Canadian National and merged with the Grand Trunk Western. So Chicago, which had 22 independent railroads calling it their headquarters in 1900, by 2000 had only one—the Wisconsin Central. In 2001 it was acquired by the Canadian National.

Yet for the most part the granger roads' trackage and physical plant in and around the Chicago area survived under different ownership because the nation's rail junction was too valuable for any railroad to wholly abandon. By the final decade of the century the railroad industry had been sufficiently rationalized with its surviving markets and had developed enough new business, principally intermodal traffic and low-sulphur coal that met tightened federal environmental standards, that it was stable and for the most part profitable. Intermodal traffic, including both truck trailers and marine shipping containers carried on railroad flatcars, did much to revive the railroad industry in the final decades of the twentieth century.

The path the railroads took in the twentieth century was in many ways typical of the patterns followed by obsolescing industries. There were waves of consolidations as management attempted to merge their way out of financial trouble, followed by periods of contraction as the consolidated carriers tried to achieve cost savings by shedding unprofitable subsidiaries. Heavy-handed regulation, a legacy of the era of the robber barons, made any quick turnaround almost impossible for the railroad industry although some individual carriers prospered. For a time there was also a great deal of diversification into new non-transportation ventures as the railroads used their assets, principally surplus land, to acquire cash cows.

The Chicago & North Western Railway is as good an example as any of what hap-

pened. The railroad, which had begun its existence in 1848 as a 10-mile strap-iron line operating a secondhand locomotive between Chicago and Oak Park, ended the nineteenth century as a 9,000-mile line fanning out across the Midwest as far west as Wyoming. However, by the time the twentieth century was drawing to a close, the North Western had not only shrunk to 5,419 miles but had been acquired by the Union Pacific Railroad as its transcontinental link to Chicago.

As late as 2002 it was still possible to see an occasional North Western locomotive, mixed with diesels painted in UP and Southern Pacific livery, pulling a Union Pacific train through the western suburbs of Chicago, but that would last only until the surviving railroad got around to repainting its locomotives in its standard yellow and gray scheme. The trains also contained fading freight cars painted with the logotypes of such prior UP acquisitions as the Missouri Pacific and Denver & Rio Grande Western—vestigial reminders of the great wave of mergers that swept the railroad industry in the last quarter of the twentieth century and reduced the number of class one railroads in the United States to only seven—two of them foreign owned.[1]

Perhaps because the decline of America's railroads began shortly after the federal government began to regulate them, not only by means of the Hepburn Act of 1906 that empowered the Interstate Commerce Commission to set rates but the Sherman Antitrust Act of 1890 as well, there has been a tendency by many historians to associate the two phenomena as cause and effect. Historians also tend to attribute the decline of railroads to the appearance of the motor vehicles and hard roads. In fact, the nation's railroad system in the twentieth century underwent a process of rationalization as the newer technologies appeared to compete; thus the airplane replaced the streamliner on long passenger trips, the motor truck replaced the boxcar for package freight, and

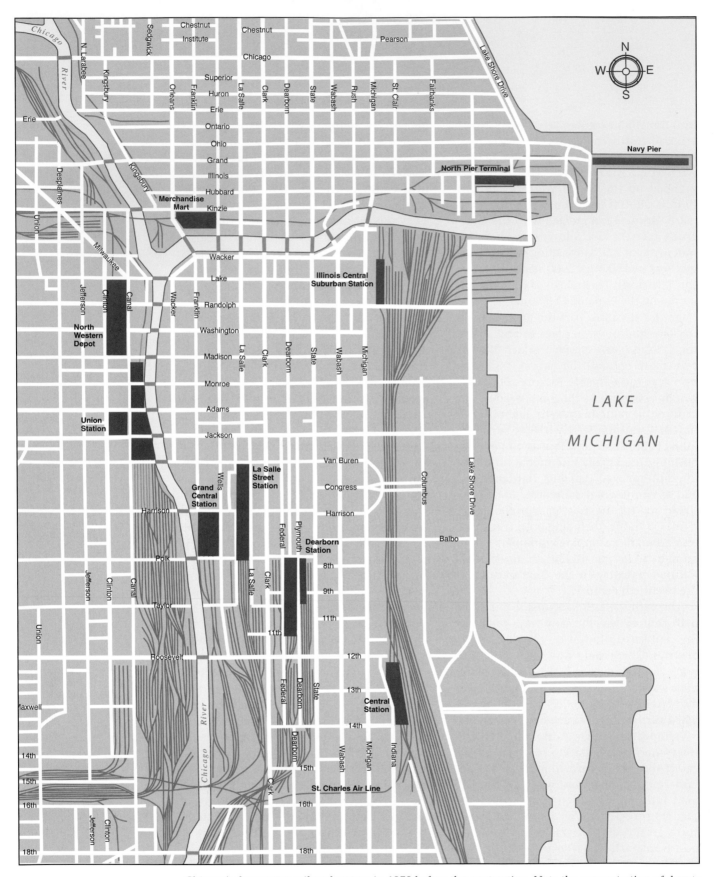

Chicago's downtown railroad system in 1970 before the contraction. Note the concentration of depots and yards to the west and south that had the effect of restricting the growth of the central business district in those directions.

the pipeline replaced the tank car as the principal vehicle for transporting oil.[2]

The Chicago region wasn't hit as hard by the rail bankruptcies as the industry as a whole, which hit bottom sometime in the 1970s when a wave of bankruptcies in the East and Midwest awoke the public and Congress to the problem. The industry was deregulated between 1970 and 1980 with a succession of federal laws that nationalized the railroad passenger service, consolidated the railroads of the Northeast into a single carrier, and nullified the economic regulatory powers of the ICC for the remainder of the industry. Railroad historian Albro Martin argued that deregulation actually began with the 1965 U.S. Supreme Court decision overturning a 1963 ICC ruling against a petition by the Southern Railway to offer special rates for grain hauled in new, 100-ton jumbo covered hopper cars from farms in the Midwest to southern poultry and livestock producers. The Southern argued it needed the lower rates to compete with the unregulated barge-truck combinations that had captured two-thirds of the market.[3]

The timing of railroad regulation early in the twentieth century could not have been worse for the industry, coming as it did just as inflation appeared on the American scene. Inflation was poorly understood at the time (1896–1916) and raised costs faster than the regulators would allow rate increases. Raising capital also became a problem for railroads. New industries that appeared in the twentieth century captured the interest of investors at about the same time as regulation began to retard the rate of return on railroad earnings, which meant that the capital-intensive railroads had a difficult time competing for money. By 1917 the rail situation had deteriorated to the point that the railroads were so overwhelmed by World War I military traffic that the federal government was forced to temporarily take control of them, although it never attempted to nationalize the system by buying it.[4]

The timing of regulation also coincided to a great extent with the emergence of an unregulated competitor—the horseless carriage in all its forms. By the end of World War I, not only was the automobile beginning to take away passengers in rural markets, but motor trucks had proved their feasibility as midrange carriers and motor buses had appeared on the scene. World War I restrictions on shipping because of the congestion on the U.S. railroads forced many companies to begin to use trucks, which previously in their brief existence had been confined to the role of urban delivery vehicles. By the time the war ended motor trucks had begun to compete successfully at distances of as much as 250 miles against both Lake Michigan packet ships and railroads in the Michigan-to-Chicago fruit and vegetable trade, for example.[5]

Although travelers were the first to shift their allegiance from rail to road (and later air), the decline of passenger traffic alone would not prove fatal to the railroads, except the electric interurbans. In 1916, freight accounted for approximately three out of every four dollars of railroad revenue, and the nation's Class I railroads collectively had freight revenues of $2.4 billion and expenses of $1.7 billion for an operating ratio (percentage of operating revenues consumed by operating expenses) of 71.7 percent. On the passenger side, the railroads had revenues of $846.5 million and expenses of $626.9 million for a ratio of 74.1 percent. However, by 1965 freight accounted for 86.5 percent of railroad operating revenues and in 1970, the year before Amtrak was created, it accounted for 91 percent.[6]

Operating ratios—statistics that only financial officers, stock analysts, and economists can love—are considered one of the most important measurements of the financial health of railroads. Generally, operating ratios below 70 percent, which means 70¢ out of every dollar in revenue is eaten up by operating costs and 30¢ is operating profit, are considered excellent. Ratios above 80 percent, or operating costs of 80¢

The wave of bankruptcies that hit the eastern railroads in the 1970s caused a boom at the scrap yards. Here an Erie Lackawanna diesel is demolished in McCook, a western suburb of Chicago. (Steve Smedley)

or more per dollar of revenue, are poor. Between 1890 and 1910, operating ratios for the industry as a whole had averaged a healthy 66.6 percent but skyrocketed during the government takeover in World War I to a high of 94.3 percent in 1920. They recovered somewhat during the 1920s, skyrocketed again during the Depression, recovered during World War II, and began to increase again after hostilities ended. By 1970 when much of the industry was on the verge of financial collapse, the operating ratio for Class I railroads in the U.S. was almost 96 percent.[7]

The Bankruptcies

The financial troubles of the U.S. railroad system did not become painfully obvious to the public until more than two decades after World War II when much of the system in the Northeast and Midwest

lapsed into insolvency. When the collapse finally occurred, three of the four original trunk carriers serving the market between Chicago and the eastern ports were forced into bankruptcy. Only the Baltimore & Ohio, which had merged with the Chesapeake & Ohio in 1963, was unaffected. The Norfolk & Western, which got to Chicago only in 1964 with the acquisition of the Wabash and Nickel Plate Road, also remained profitable.

The Erie, which merged with the Delaware, Lackawanna & Western in 1960, did not survive. However, the most spectacular and the best documented of the collapses was that of the Penn Central Transportation Co. It filed for bankruptcy in 1970, just 2 1/2 years after being created in the merger of the venerable New York Central and Pennsylvania railroads. The Penn Central collapse, coming on the heels of the decision by the federal government to take over the nation's railroad passenger system, resulted in a succession of laws reforming the railroad regulatory system, requiring the consolidation of the railroads in the Northeast into a single carrier, and authorizing substantial federal subsidies to correct years of deferred maintenance.

There were a number of underlying reasons for the financial deterioration of northeastern railroads, including the decline in heavy manufacturing in a belt from the Atlantic seaboard around the southern end of the Great Lakes to Chicago. Manufactured goods as late as 1951 accounted for a third of the Pennsylvania Railroad's traffic and under normal circumstances were considerably more profitable to carry than commodities like coal and grain.[8] However, manufactured goods, especially less-than-carload (LCL) merchandise carried in boxcars, proved to be more vulnerable to competition from trucks than were bulk commodities like coal and grain. Railroad LCL traffic, which paid a lucrative rate of $40 per ton in the 1960s, had declined from 53 million tons in 1920 to 15 million in 1940 and 3 million in 1960.[9]

Trucks were not the only competition. The construction of oil pipelines over the years had caused the tank car fleet of the railroads to shrink to 5,000 by 1968—about a fifth of what it had been in 1925. The dispersal of the meatpacking industry to smaller plants closer to the source of livestock had caused the extinction of the railroad stock cars. Those losses in the 1950s and 1960s had not yet been offset by increased intermodal traffic.

The financial collapse of the Penn Central and Erie was not nearly as threatening to Chicago's economy as it had been in the Northeast, where the Jersey Central, Reading, New Haven, and Lehigh Valley railroads also failed at about the same time, effectively forcing Congress to fund a federal bailout and deregulate the railroad industry. In Chicago, some track was abandoned, but Union Station and its yards were transferred to Amtrak, and the Penn

Central freight facilities were acquired by the new Consolidated Rail Corporation, the name for the railroad Congress created to absorb the bankrupt systems. The old Lake Shore (later New York Central) mainline between Chicago, Toledo, Cleveland, and New York became Conrail's principal line to the East. The Erie's redundant mainline was largely abandoned, and the old Pennsylvania Railroad mainline (Pittsburgh, Fort Wayne & Chicago) was downgraded to a single track.

Within a few years the railroad financial crisis had migrated to the midwestern granger railroads, resulting in the bankruptcy of two carriers and the abandonment of thousands of miles of track over a period of two decades. Probably because the effect of the rail crisis in the Midwest varied considerably from carrier to carrier, the railroads there did not get the political, financial, or media attention that was lavished on the railroads of the Northeast.

At one extreme the Chicago, Burlington & Quincy, because it was absorbed into the Burlington Northern transcontinental system, was unaffected by the troubles of the other lines. On the other hand, both the Chicago, Rock Island & Pacific and the Chicago, Milwaukee, St. Paul & Pacific were bankrupted and disappeared from the scene. The Chicago Great Western was swallowed up by the Chicago & North Western in 1968 on the eve of the crisis, and the Chicago & Alton, which had been absorbed by the Gulf, Mobile & Ohio in 1947, was in turn merged into the Illinois Central in 1972 after the Penn Central collapse and the rail crisis was in full swing. The North Western and IC ultimately survived by means of aggressive track abandonment programs, the creation of conglomerates that in effect sold off surplus railroad land to finance diversification, and some federal subsidies. The earnings of the newly acquired subsidiaries then sustained the two railroads at least long enough to ensure they would survive the shakeout, and both were eventually absorbed by other carriers.

The Granger Bankruptcies

The United States Railway Association, which drew up the plan to consolidate the northeastern railroads and funneled $2 billion in subsidies to the resulting Conrail, took a different approach with the midwestern lines. Although the Rock Island and Milwaukee Road were granted some limited federal financial assistance to keep them operating for a few years and upgrade a few of their more important mainlines, they were eventually left to die. The Rock Island, in fact, was the first bankruptcy liquidation of a Class I railroad in United States history. The Milwaukee Road suffered a less ignominious fate by having its ill-fated transcontinental line liquidated and its various midwestern lines sold to the highest bidder at what amounted to a court-sponsored auction.[10]

The failures of both the Rock Island and Milwaukee were the result of a complex set of problems that beset the railroad industry as a whole in the twentieth century, not the least of which was excess trackage and too much competition. The Rock Island and Milwaukee Road were able to survive competition from other railroads in the nineteenth century, although they

Even as the airlines and the automobile took away the intercity passenger traffic from the railroads after World War II, some politicians used trains on election campaign swings. Here Richard M. Nixon, campaigning for vice president, rides an IC train in 1951. (Alan R. Lind, Transport History Press)

TABLE 13-1 **U.S. Intercity Freight Distribution** (in billions of revenue ton-miles)

Year	Railroads	Trucks	Great Lakes	Rivers and Canals	Oil Pipelines	Air	Total
1929	455	20	97	9	27	——	608
1939	339	53	76	20	56	——	544
1950	597	173	112	52	129	——	1,063
1960	579	285	99	121	229	1	1,314
1970	771	412	114	205	431	3	1,936
1980	932	555	96	311	588	5	2,487
1990	1,071	735	87	377	583	10	2,863

Source: Smith, *Transportation in America* (1992 ed.).

were forced to resort to such anti-competitive measures as the Iowa Pool to do so, but they increasingly found themselves unable to compete in the twentieth century as barges, trucks, airplanes and automobiles eroded their market share.

Throughout its history the Rock Island was never particularly strong financially relative to its competitors, and it had been in and out of bankruptcy intermittently during the twentieth century. The Milwaukee Road survived as a granger carrier in the nineteenth century but failed as a transcontinental line in the twentieth. Both the Rock Island and Milwaukee Road served a Midwest market in direct competition with the other granger railroads, including not only the Illinois Central and North Western but in places the Burlington, Santa Fe, Chicago Great Western, and Soo Line. Both competed for traffic with the Burlington, North Western, and IC in the transcontinental link between Chicago and Omaha, from where the Union Pacific carried the traffic to the West Coast. The Rock Island also had competition from the North Western, IC, Santa Fe, and Burlington in the Chicago–Kansas City market, and the Milwaukee Road competed with the North Western, Burlington, and Soo between Chicago and Minneapolis–St. Paul. The grain traffic that helped sus-

tain the two railroads despite the competition during much of the nineteenth century suffered some erosion with the successful federal effort during and after World War I to rebuild the barge industry on the rivers. The federal and state programs to build hard roads and resulting competition from trucks took away much of the lucrative package freight and less-than-carload business (see Table 13-1).

Rail competition was particularly acute for the Milwaukee Road. Unlike the other granger railroads, which relied on the transcontinental lines for connections to the West Coast, it belatedly built its own transcontinental line to Seattle in 1906 through one of the more sparsely populated sections of the nation in direct competition with the Great Northern, Northern Pacific, and Union Pacific. The line proved to be a financial drain on the Milwaukee Road from its inception. Obtaining capital for the 1,500-mile extension to the Pacific Coast, which was completed in 1909, required some creative financing, first by establishing the Puget Sound Company to build the line, then by issuing $100 million in new stock to existing shareholders to raise cash that could be paid in installments to Puget Sound with a collateral of $100 million in bonds issued to the railroad. Because construction costs were ultimately $155 million, the Puget Sound Company was forced to issue additional bonds to the public after inflating its reported book value to $269 million to make the investment seem safe.[11]

Such a beginning was ominous, and the transcontinental line quickly became a financial albatross. Despite the fact that it was the only northern tier railroad to offer through service between Puget Sound and Chicago on its own tracks, the Milwaukee Road never seriously challenged its competitors, who had to rely on connections with other railroads to get to the Windy City. In any event, the Milwaukee was forced into bankruptcy receivership three times during the century—in 1925, 1935, and 1977. The Rock Island, although unburdened by a transcontinental line, had a similar record with bankruptcies in 1915, 1933, and 1975.[12]

By the 1960s, both the Rock Island and Milwaukee, which had only emerged from bankruptcy after World War II, were once again struggling to survive and began fishing about for merger partners. Chicago financier Henry Crown had made a substantial investment in the Rock Island just before its postwar reorganization when he was able to buy the railroad's bonds at a substantial discount and, hoping to profit by the transaction, prodded the railroad to find a strong merger partner. The Crown family interests in the railroad included $9 million of the $47.5 million in the railroad's outstanding first mortgage bonds, $20 million of the $50.3 million in debentures, and 270,000 shares of common stock, or about 10 percent of the total outstanding.[13]

However, within a decade Crown was attempting to cash out his investment by means of merging the Rock Island with another railroad. He first approached the North Western about a merger in 1962, but the two carriers could not reach an agreement, and he then sought out the Southern Pacific. The SP suggested a three-way merger also involving the Union Pacific, which nearly a century after it had

begun operations and unlike its two principal competitors, the Santa Fe and Great Northern–Northern Pacific–Burlington, still did not own a route to Chicago. The Union Pacific by that time had also decided it needed direct links to both the Chicago and St. Louis gateways, and only the Rock Island had direct links between Kansas City and St. Louis and from both Kansas City and Omaha to Chicago.[14]

The agreement that resulted in June 1963 was for the Union Pacific to acquire the bulk of the Rock Island in exchange for Union Pacific stock. The Southern Pacific, which connected to the Rock at Tucumcari, New Mexico, was to receive the Rock Island's southwestern lines from Kansas City.[15]

The intention of Crown, who was continuously a member of the railroad's board of directors from 1949 to 1975 and was chairman of its finance committee from November 13, 1961, until September 9, 1974, was to obtain Interstate Commerce Commission approval within two years, but other railroads, especially Ben W. Heineman and the North Western, fought the merger so aggressively that the case dragged on for 12 years before the ICC issued its ruling. During that time the Rock Island's financial position deteriorated to the point that it began deferring maintenance to reduce operating losses that from 1965 to 1975 totaled $129 million. By the time the ICC approved the merger on December 3, 1974, the Rock Island's deferred maintenance amounted to an estimated $600 million to $700 million, and the Union Pacific was no longer interested.[16]

The Rock Island, by then running short of cash, applied for a $100 million federal loan essentially from funds designated by Congress to keep the northeastern railroads operating until a solution could be found to the crisis. After the United States Railway Association (USRA) denied the application in early 1975, the Rock Island filed for bankruptcy protection on March 17. The USRA gave as a principal reason for its denial the redundancy of the Rock

This Milwaukee Road engine was left rusting on a siding after that carrier filed for bankruptcy in 1977.

Island: 80 percent of its routes were served by other railroads.[17]

The railroad thus was excluded from significant federal financial assistance and became embroiled in a running court dispute between Crown, who wanted the railroad sold off to recoup his investments; trustee William Gibbons and president John Ingram, who wanted the railroad reorganized; and the federal government, which wanted the railroad sold off in pieces to competitors. It limped along, borrowing $200 million until 1979, when a succession of events doomed it. A strike by the Brotherhood of Railway and Airline Clerks reduced traffic to a trickle despite efforts by management to keep the railroad running, and General Motors Corporation within a week switched to the North Western a daily train carrying parts between Detroit and its West Coast plants, costing the Rock Island $50,000 a day in revenue.[18]

Within a couple of weeks the Interstate Commerce Commission, at the suggestion of the Carter administration, ruled that the Rock Island did not have cash to oper-

ate and issued an order directing the Kansas City Terminal Railroad to temporarily operate it. Federal Judge Frank McGarr ended the matter January 25, 1980, when he ordered trustee William Gibbons to liquidate the railroad. Portions of the Rock Island survived, including its commuter division, which was purchased by Chicago's Regional Transportation Authority, and its original line from Blue Island to Bureau, Illinois, which was sold to the Chessie System, but a substantial part of the railroad was scrapped.[19]

The fate of the Milwaukee Road was similar. The railroad was very weak financially for much of the twentieth century, but when the ICC in 1970 approved the merger of the rival and parallel Great Northern, Northern Pacific, and Burlington railroads, the Milwaukee Road's cash position deteriorated rapidly. Several petitions by the Milwaukee Road for inclusion in the resulting Burlington Northern were denied by the ICC.[20] By 1977, much of its transcontinental line west of the Dakotas was in such poor condition it was under a

10-mile-per-hour slow order, and the Milwaukee Road did not have sufficient cash to operate and pay contingent interest on its mortgage bonds and debentures. The railroad's parent holding company, Chicago Milwaukee Corporation, reported losses attributable to rail operations in five of the seven years leading up to the bankruptcy. The Milwaukee Road lost $23.6 million in 1975, $8.8 million in 1976, and $14.9 million for the first three quarters of 1977. Then on December 19, 1977, a week before payments were due on first mortgage bonds and debentures, the Milwaukee Road filed for bankruptcy.[21]

The proceedings in Federal District Court before Judge Thomas R. McMillen moved at a somewhat faster pace than those of the Rock Island, which were protracted by the dispute among Crown, the federal government, and the railroad's management team. As in the Rock Island case, the critical factor leading to the dismemberment of the Milwaukee Road was the position of the federal government that the Milwaukee Road was largely redundant. Washington was therefore reluctant to plow money into a failing railroad competing with solvent carriers. Washington was also unwilling to absorb the costs of labor protection in the Rock Island and Milwaukee cases by using money that it had mandated for the Penn Central merger to financially compensate employees who lost their jobs.[22]

In early 1980, McMillen, based on a recommendation of the ICC, ordered service terminated on the western half of the 9,800-mile railroad west of Miles City, Montana—the western section of the transcontinental line that had caused the carrier so much financial difficulty. Traffic on that section of the Milwaukee Road had deteriorated to the point that only one train a day was being operated across Montana.[23] By 1982, a bidding war between two Canadian railroads had developed for the surviving eastern half of the Milwaukee Road, forcing the North Western to join the bidding for defensive purposes.

The Grand Trunk Western, a subsidiary of the Canadian National, was rejected because it was owned by the Canadian government, but the Soo Line, a subsidiary of the Canadian Pacific, ultimately outbid the North Western.[24]

Even before the Rock Island and Milwaukee Road filed for bankruptcy, it had become obvious to the management of most railroads, especially the granger lines, that they needed to shrink their companies by getting rid of unprofitable lines, especially the rural branch lines that were built in the nineteenth century to encourage development but a century later did not have enough traffic to justify their existence. The North Western already had a well-developed abandonment program, but the Rock Island and Milwaukee Road were forced to hurriedly put together plans to justify their reorganization in bankruptcy court. The Rock Island, which began bankruptcy as a 7,500-mile railroad, in late 1979 was proposed for reorganization as a 1,934-mile line.[25] The Milwaukee Road was 9,221 miles long when it filed for bankruptcy in 1977, and within two years its reorganization plan envisioned survival of a core railroad of only 3,200 miles.

Diversification

Neither of the bankrupt carriers proved adept at diversification—a financial tactic that helped some of their granger competitors survive the shakeout in the railroad industry. The Milwaukee attempted to diversify, creating the Chicago Milwaukee Corporation as a shell of a holding company, but failed. The carrier's principal nonrail asset, the Milwaukee Land Company that at its height owned 300,000 acres of prime timberland in Washington, Idaho, and Montana, had for years been subsidizing the railroad with the proceeds of timber sales. However, by the 1970s the railroad's losses and physical condition ($70 million in deferred maintenance) had become so great that the parent Chicago Milwaukee holding company began to sell off land to increase the size of the subsidies and to provide cash for diversification. By 1972 the land company was half the size it had been at its height.[26]

The diversification programs of both the North Western and IC produced better results although, aside from any subsidies available to cover railroad losses, their long-term benefits to the core railroads were debatable. The managements of the conglomerates were responsible to the shareholders of their holding companies, not the underlying railroads from which the holding companies sprang. In both cases the conglomerates that resulted from diversification programs eventually adopted as their goals the disposal of the underperforming railroads.

The North Western, in 1955 probably the weakest of the four granger railroads based in Chicago, was the first to act to get its financial house in order. Ben W. Heineman, a Chicago lawyer and investor, got control of the railroad in 1956, aggressively moving to cut passenger deficits by getting rid of money-losing intercity trains and modernizing the Chicago-area commuter lines. He also acquired several smaller railroads to increase the North Western's penetration in the Midwest.

His strategic plan for the North Western was to create a giant granger railroad by acquiring the Milwaukee Road, Rock Island, and Chicago Great Western. Nothing came of the proposed mergers with the other two big railroads, but the 1,500-mile Great Western once described as "a mountain railroad in a prairie country serving a traffic vacuum"—an x-shaped system with Omaha, St. Paul, Kansas City, and Chicago at the four corners—was having an increasingly difficult time competing with the bigger railroads around it.[27]

As merger mania gripped the railroad industry in the 1950s, the Great Western began looking for a stronger partner, a goal that became urgent in 1963 after the Union Pacific announced it wanted to acquire the Rock Island. Such a combination was potentially lethal to a small

bridge line like the CGW. The Kansas City investment group that controlled the railroad after a Chicago-based group lost control during the Depression had hoped to merge the CGW variously with the Kansas City Southern, Rock Island, Soo Line, and St. Louis–San Francisco (Frisco). Finally, Robert F. McAteer, a CGW outside director, negotiated the merger with Heineman's North Western in 1964. The merger cleared the regulatory hurdles four years later, and by 1983 the North Western had retired 75 percent of the old CGW trackage.[28]

Heineman, meanwhile, had become involved in a diversification program with the creation of Northwest Industries—a venture in which the assets of the railroad were used to assemble a conglomerate that could then dispose of the railroad because of its marginal earnings potential. Beginning in 1965, the holding company got control of the Velsicol Chemical Company and in 1968 became a full-fledged conglomerate by buying an existing one—consisting of the Philadelphia & Reading Company, a former anthracite coal firm that had diversified by acquiring Acme Boot; Fruit of the Loom, Imperial Reading, and Union Underwear, all clothing manufacturers; an oil pipeline builder called Lone Star Steel; and Universal Manufacturing, which made ballasts for fluorescent lights. A bid to take over B. F. Goodrich, the rubber company, failed in 1969.[29]

The problem remained the railroad, which by 1969 was reporting operating losses after several years of modest profitability. Heineman's solution was relatively simple, although other railroads like the IC were unable to emulate it: he cut the railroad adrift from the holding company and sold it to an investment group of employees in 1972. Without the financial backing of a parent, the railroad was forced to aggressively cut branch lines while at the same time seeking transcontinental bridge traffic between the Union Pacific and eastern railroads. In fact, North Western executives joked in the 1970s that

Increased real estate values in downtown Chicago also claimed the North Western's main depot on Madison Street. The old station was demolished to make way for a new office tower that incorporated the commuter station on its first two floors. (Steve Smedley)

their initials, C&NW, stood for "Cheap and Nothing Wasted," a variation on the moniker the riders of their passenger trains had given them years before—"Can't and Never Will." The North Western, which exceeded 9,000 miles in 1975, was down to 5,419 by 1993.[30]

The failure of both the Rock Island and Milwaukee Road and the merger of the CB&Q into the rival Burlington Northern left the UP with no choice but to try to acquire the North Western to reach Chicago, although it had obtained a more circuitous route via St. Louis as a result of its 1982 merger with the Missouri Pacific, which had reached the Windy City earlier by acquiring the Chicago & Eastern Illinois. As the only transcontinental carrier with no direct connection to Chicago, the UP increasingly was forced to use the North Western for high-speed piggyback freight. By the 1990s, the Union Pacific, which as

recently as 1982 had owned 2.1 million shares of stock in IC Industries (a holding company incorporated in 1962) that it was forced to divest as a result of the ICC ruling in the Illinois Central Gulf merger case, began buying a stake in the North Western. The recapitalization of the North Western on April 7, 1992, resulted in the issuance of more than 20 million shares of common stock—9.9 million to the public and 10.2 million nonvoting shares to UP Rail Inc. By then, 62 percent of all C&NW traffic was being interchanged with the UP.[31]

Like many railroads, the mix of traffic that sustained the North Western changed dramatically in the second half of the twentieth century as competition from other modes of transportation took its toll, traditional manufacturing industries declined in importance, new international trade patterns arose, and environmental protection laws took effect. After a long dispute with the Burlington North-ern over access to the low-sulphur coal-fields in the Powder River Basin of Wyoming, the North Western finally won its case with UP assistance and in the 1990s became for the first time in its exis-tence a coal-hauling railroad.

By the 1990s, coal had replaced grain as the railroad's principal revenue commod-ity, followed by agricultural products, automotive-steel-chemicals, and inter-modal containers and trailers. By 1992 coal accounted for $267.3 million in revenue and 638,000 carloads; agricultural products $218.1 million and 320,600 carloads; auto-motive-steel-chemicals $190.9 million and 318,000 carloads; and intermodal $116.4 million and 689,200 carloads.[32]

The Illinois Central was a modestly profitable railroad that was conservatively managed by chairman and chief executive Wayne A. Johnston. In 1962 its board de-cided that to survive it needed to diversify on the assumption that a conglomerate would spread the financial risk, stabilize earnings, and reduce the cost of capital. The principal assets available to finance such diversification were large tracts of railroad land, including more than 100 acres on Chicago's lakefront that once served as a railroad yard, and the carrier's substantial tax loss carry forwards that could nullify the tax liabilities of merger partners. William B. Johnson, the former Pennsylvania Railroad (1947–1959) lawyer, said that when he was hired in 1966 to succeed Johnston, the board of directors agreed that his task was to modernize and merge the railroad, develop its real estate, and diversify.[33]

In fact, the holding company called IC Industries had been incorporated to act as the corporate shell for diversification, which began in 1965 with the acquisition of a St. Louis firm (Chandeysson Electric Company) that specialized in the rewind-ing of electric traction motors for diesel lo-comotives. Thereafter, Johnson moved quickly to further diversify. In 1968 he ac-quired a Wisconsin foundry and later in

the year merged with Abex Corporation (formerly American Brake Shoe and Foundry Company). But it was in 1969 that Johnson took his first step outside the railroad industry with the purchase of Pepsi-Cola General Bottler. By 1980 when IC Industries failed in its hostile takeover bid of Sunbeam Corp., an appliance manu-facturer, it had already acquired a life in-surer, Midas International (auto mufflers), Pet Inc. (food), and Hussman Inc. (refriger-ation equipment), and it had operated a combination shopping center and amuse-ment park (Old Chicago).

In 1980, the railroad accounted for only 24 percent of IC Industries' operating prof-its, and the conglomerate, following the lead of Heineman's Northwest Industries, was looking for a way to dispose of the car-rier whose assets had made the diversifica-tion possible. That presented another problem: the railroad, already picked clean of its nonrail assets and tax benefits, was an unlikely candidate for acquisition un-less it could be reduced in size by shedding many of its financially marginal lines.[34]

The principal hurdle to the disposal of the land, which included substantial sites in New Orleans, Memphis, and Chicago, where an office complex called Illinois Center rose on the former downtown yards, was legal. The IC, the original land grant railroad, had been built on land do-nated for the purpose of a railroad by the federal government, the state, and Chicago, which originally allowed it access on a breakwater-trestle in the lake that only became part of the shoreline after it was used as a landfill for debris from the Chicago Fire. Although many interests ob-jected to the railroad's disposal of what had originally been public land, the sale of un-used railroad land as well as air rights over active railroad tracks was made possible by a 1919 Chicago ordinance and several amendments to it in the 1920s. The air rights provision was first utilized in 1955 for construction of the Prudential Building on air rights over the IC's active commuter line, and by 1966 IC Industries had cleared up court challenges to the sale or development of the other unused property.

At the same time the railroad began selling land for development it gained a merger partner. The 6,461-mile Illinois Central was shaped something like a fan spreading west and south from Chicago to Omaha on the Missouri River and New Orleans on the Gulf of Mexico. The merger partner Johnson chose was a north-south parallel line—the 2,766-mile Gulf, Mobile & Ohio that had been competing with the IC between Chicago and ports on the Gulf since 1947 when it had acquired the Chicago & Alton.[35]

It was not long after the ICC approval of the Illinois Central Gulf merger was ratified in federal court in 1971 that IC Industries began to publicly discuss disposal of the railroad, however. There was also some irony in the fact that at about the same time, even though IC Industries had used land grant assets to fund diversification into nonrail enterprises, it began to use newly available federal subsidies to upgrade its track. The federal Railroad Revitalization and Regulatory Reform Act of 1976, commonly known as the 4R Act and passed to provide badly needed capital for the rebuilding of the railroads of the Northeast under the newly formed Consolidated Rail Corporation, made some subsidies available to marginal railroads in other parts of the country. In 1977 the Illinois Central Gulf, as the railroad was then called, issued $12.4 million in redeemable preference shares for track rehabilitation and the following year borrowed an additional $83.9 million under the same program.

IC Industries first publicly raised the issue of divestiture of the railroad in its 1976 annual report, and by 1980 divestiture had been added to the holding company's strategic plan.[36] Reforms of the regulatory process in the federal Staggers Rail Act of 1980 effectively freed the holding company of ICC interference in its program to pare down the railroad to make it saleable, and Johnson announced at the IC Industries annual meeting in 1984 in Chicago

that the goal was to slim down the railroad from more than 9,000 miles to a core of 3,000 miles by 1990. Harry Bruce, the railroad's chairman and chief executive, suggested in a meeting with Johnson in 1983 that the railroad had too many unprofitable branches to make it saleable as a whole and should be reduced in size to interest buyers. Although the railroad in 1979 had begun a program to abandon 283 miles of branch lines, the sale of secondary mainlines began in earnest in 1984. That year it sold off 686 miles of former Gulf, Mobile & Ohio lines to the newly created Gulf & Mississippi Railroad and 686 miles of other lines, principally the Chicago-Omaha line completed in 1899, to the new Chicago, Central & Pacific Railroad. The railroad, in addition to the dividend of 50 percent of earnings all IC Industries subsidiaries were required to pay, also was required to turn over to the holding company as quarterly dividends the proceeds of such sales of lines.[37]

IC Industries, which continued to sell mainlines as fast as buyers could be found, reported its best financial results in history in 1985 with an operating profit of $264 million on revenues of $4.4 billion. The 284-mile Paducah to Louisville line was sold the following year, and the 631-mile former GM&O lines from Chicago to St. Louis and Kansas City were peddled a year later to the newly created Chicago, Missouri & Western Railway, a corporation put together by a soon-to-fail holding company called Venango River Corporation, whose principal asset was the Chicago, South Shore & South Bend interurban railroad. The lines eventually wound up in the hands of the Southern Pacific.[38]

But by 1988, IC Industries was coming apart as a conglomerate. Still unable to find a buyer for what was left of the renamed Illinois Central Railroad (from Illinois Central Gulf), the holding company decided to spin off the railroad as a separate corporation in a stock distribution to IC Industries shareholders, then abruptly changed its name to Whitman Corpora-

tion after a line of candy one of its subsidiaries sold. The railroad survived as a 2,732-mile carrier between Chicago and New Orleans until it was in turn acquired by the Canadian National at the end of the century.

The shrinkage of the Illinois Central and other railroads in the second half of the twentieth century made available for other uses thousands of acres of land on which mainlines, sidings, branch lines, yards, and facilities had been located. In the 50 years following the end of World War II, U.S. railroads abandoned more than 175,000 miles of track, which translates to more than 200,000 acres of land. Some of the land in areas with fragile environments, such as the marshes southeast of Chicago, had limited value. But other parcels, like the vast coach yards south of Chicago's Loop, were a veritable gold mine for the departments the railroads set up to dispose of the surplus property. Other land in suburban or rural areas was sold or donated to public agencies and turned into nature trails or linear parks.

The IC still had considerable freight traffic in downtown Chicago as late as the 1960s. It ultimately shifted it elsewhere to make room for the redevelopment of the prime lakefront land that had become too valuable to be used for a railroad.
(Michael Brown)

14 Redevelopment

The only railroad tracks that remained south of the Loop as the twentieth century closed were used by the Rock Island commuter line operated by Metra, a publicly owned agency.

Long before the American rail system began to shrink, creating a huge pool of surplus property no longer needed for railroad operations, the city covered by more miles of track than any other began to look for creative ways to reuse portions of its railroad plant. Thus the redevelopment of railroad land in Chicago predates by half a century what happened in most of the rest of the nation, where programs to reuse abandoned rail property were more of an afterthought. The concentration of high-density development in downtown Chicago, as was also the case in some eastern cities, by the late nineteenth century put pressure on the city to find ways to redevelop railroad land, even tracks still in active use. In his 1909 Plan of Chicago, Daniel Burnham suggested that much of the city's rail plant could be consolidated for greater efficiency and to free up land covered by tracks and depots for redevelopment for business uses.[1]

Chicago's first efforts at rail redevelopment actually predated Burnham's plan by nearly two decades. The earliest programs dated at least from the 1890s when the railroad system was still expanding nationally but decentralizing locally to outlying areas, freeing some railroad property near the central city for redevelopment. By the 1950s, the use of air rights over active railroad lines in the central city was well established. As the abandonment of rail land accelerated with the decline of railroads in the twentieth century, Chicago after 1970 became the beneficiary of hundreds of acres of prime downtown land for redevelopment.

Ultimately the city and its suburbs learned to use former rail lines, depots, freight houses, and yards in some very creative ways. As planned unit developments arose on former yards near the Loop, abandoned lines in the suburbs were converted into linear parks—hiking and biking trails stretching for miles. Using the same theory, the state converted the abandoned Illinois & Michigan Canal into a canoe and hiking trail across northern Illinois. Other abandoned rail lines were converted to use as rapid transit lines for Chicago's elevated railway system. Even where railroad operations continued, the city used air rights over tracks to allow office towers to rise. New skyscrapers incorporating passenger terminals into their lower floors were built where the city's Victorian depots once stood, and a number of surviving depots in Chicago and the suburbs were converted into offices and shops.

Perhaps the most exciting and innovative rail redevelopment in Chicago involved the city's lakefront. The tracks that once ran on a causeway in the lake were buried in an open cut, creating an unobstructed view of that body of water, and the shallows were filled to create a park. Some of the city's museums were then built upon the filled land.

Much of the great railroad land selloff in the last half of the twentieth century involved unused freight houses or vacant parcels in small towns across the nation. In some cases lines owned by major railroads were sold to newly formed short-line railroad companies that could operate them less expensively. In other cases, as parallel mergers took their toll, entire mainline rights-of-way were suddenly declared to be surplus, abandoned, and put up for sale. Such was the eventual fate of much of the Erie-Lackawanna line across northern Indiana to Chicago and the Chicago Great Western line from Iowa across northern Illinois to Chicago.

Such wholesale mainline abandonments beginning in 1963 in Chicago's suburbs and shortly thereafter in west central Wisconsin were the origins of the national Rails-to-Trails movement as superfluous rights-of-way were acquired by public agencies and converted into linear parks. The Illinois Prairie Path in suburban Cook, Du Page, and Kane counties was created from the Chicago, Aurora & Elgin Railroad right-of-way, and the Elroy-Sparta trail in Wisconsin, notable for its long tunnels, came into being at about the same time on a section of abandoned Chicago & North Western mainline.

The sheer size of the railroad plant in Illinois, which throughout the twentieth century ranked second only to Texas in mileage, and Chicagoland, which had more trackage than any other metropolitan area, was a problem in itself and one that took the region half a century to solve. It was one thing for cities like Indianapolis or St. Louis to find ways to reuse their single downtown depots that they had determined to preserve and quite another for Chicago to find alternative uses for six. Besides the depots, the 400-square-mile Chicago switching district at the end of World War II contained more miles of track than all but 16 states and accounted for about 47 percent of the Illinois rail system.

Rail Abandonments

Illinois's position at the center of America's railroad system with two of the nation's three largest rail centers—Chicago in the north and St. Louis (the bulk of whose rail yards were east of the Mississippi River in Illinois) in the south—meant the state suffered somewhat less than the nation as a whole once the wholesale abandonment of lines began. Illinois was covered with mainlines aimed at Chicago or St. Louis, while many other states—Iowa, for example—had a much higher proportion of branch lines and secondary mainlines.

Between 1920 and 1975, before assorted federal deregulation laws passed in the wake of the Penn Central bankruptcy made abandonment easier, Illinois lost about 3,145 miles of rail lines. That amounted to about a quarter of its rail system, about the same as the national average. However, about a third of that loss in

Portions of the former Chicago Great Western right-of-way in the metropolitan area were left to nature after the line was abandoned.

Illinois was electric interurban railways, which, for the most part, served small markets and went out of business before or during the Great Depression.[2]

After 1975, largely as a result of the federal government trying to pare down the amount of trackage in the Northeast to reorganize a viable system under Conrail and the railroads in other areas following suit, the number of abandonments accelerated both nationally and in Illinois. Almost half of the national system but less than a third of the railroad routes in Illi-

nois disappeared after deregulatory legislation made it easier to abandon them. However, a relatively small proportion of track was abandoned in the Chicago area. In the 11-year period between 1976 and 1986, a total of 3,180 miles of line were abandoned in Illinois, but only 195.8 miles, or 6 percent of the total, were in the Chicago metropolitan area.[3]

After 1990, by which time the nation's rail system was stabilized, the abandonments slowed considerably. Between then and the end of 2000, only about 400 additional miles of track were ripped out in Illinois. Thus the system of railroads in Illinois, which had peaked at more than 12,000 miles early in the twentieth century, by the end of the century had shrunk to approximately what it had been in 1880[4] (see Table 14-1).

The bulk of the abandonments in Illinois in the 1970s and early 1980s were lines in rural areas resulting from the 1973 federal Regional Rail Reorganization Act, or the 3R Act as it is commonly called, that reorganized the Penn Central, as well as from efforts by the Baltimore & Ohio Railroad to pare its branch line system in Illinois. The Penn Central reorganization plan alone called for the elimination of 2,600 miles of lines in Illinois. However, the Rail Passenger Service Act of 1970, which created Amtrak, resulted in the eventual abandonment of Dearborn, Central (12th Street), and Grand Central stations and their considerable coach yards in Chicago as well as other passenger facilities there. LaSalle Street Station was replaced with a smaller commuter facility nearby. Other reductions did not involve wholesale abandonment of routes but simply a reduction in the number of tracks to adjust the rail line to the volume of traffic it was carrying; for example, the Illinois Central ripped out the second track on its north-south mainline through much of Illinois.[5]

Although the first major commercial redevelopment of active railroad property in Chicago began in the late 1920s with the

Merchandise Mart and Chicago Daily News buildings, the Great Depression and World War II delayed other redevelopment until the second half of the century. By then, changes in traffic patterns from rail to truck, railroad mergers that instantly created surplus yards, the continued decline of traditional industries like meatpacking, and the collapse of rail passenger traffic made idle a vast acreage of rusting railroad track. The largest single abandonment of railroad property in Chicago occurred in 1971 when Amtrak consolidated the city's surviving intercity passenger operations at Union Station, effectively rendering superfluous four depots and their yards south of the Loop.

TABLE 14-1 **Railroad Mileage**

	1880	1920	1965	1995
Illinois	7,583	12,188	10,956	7,663
U.S.	93,200	253,000	212,000	108,264

Source: Stove, *The Routledge Historical Atlas of American Railroads,* 40, 116, 129.

Early Redevelopment

Perhaps the first major redevelopment of railroad property in Chicago occurred beginning in the 1890s when Marshall Field I, founder of the department store, indicated he wanted the city to build a new natural history museum in what was then known as Lake Park (later Grant Park) along the lakeshore. But Aaron Montgomery Ward, founder of the catalogue house and civic champion of keeping the lakeshore open for public use, was opposed to any such development. Field, who died in 1906, made a behest in his will of $8 million for the museum, but Ward blocked the project with litigation that twice wound up in the state Supreme Court (1909 and 1911). Finally, the Illinois Central Railroad agreed to donate to the South Park Commission two square blocks

of filled land along the lake south of 12th Street and east of its right-of-way. The act was not entirely gratuitous: the railroad had been under pressure from the city for years to give it filled land along the lake for use as a park. The railroad had intended to use it as the site for a new depot. The Field Museum was built, and the area surrounding it later in the century was redeveloped as a museum campus that included the Shedd Aquarium, Adler Planetarium, and the Soldier Field stadium.[6]

Marshall Field & Company was also involved in the first major commercial redevelopment of active railroad land in the city. The Merchandise Mart project had its origins in the desire by James Simpson, president of the company (1923–1930) as well as successor to Charles H. Wacker as chairman of the Chicago Plan Commission (1926–1935), to find a site to consolidate at a single location his company's 13 different warehouses scattered around the city. He settled on an underutilized railroad yard just north of the Chicago River at Wells Street that had served, until the Chicago & North Western Railway built a new station along Canal Street west of the river in 1911, as that railroad's downtown passenger yard and station. Simpson's company in 1927 acquired most of the property and was granted air rights by the North Western over the rest, a compromise that enabled the railroad to maintain service on a branch freight line to industry along the north side of the river as far east as the lake at the eventual site of Navy Pier on the lake. The operation of the line, which originated with the Galena Railroad in the 1850s, continued through the end of the twentieth century.

Marshall Field & Company erected on the two-block site a mammoth 25-story building containing 4.2 million square feet of space that, as the structure's boosters boasted, was the largest building in the world until the Pentagon was completed in Washington during World War II. The warehouse was later converted to showrooms for wholesalers and was known as the Merchandise

Union Station's yards, shown here in the 1950s, survived the downsizing of Chicago's railroad plant because they were taken over by Amtrak and continued to be used by various commuter operations. (Michael Brown)

Mart. In 1977 the 1.5-million-square-foot Apparel Mart was built over C&NW air rights immediately to the west.[7]

The Chicago Daily News building, a 26-story structure later known as 2 North Riverside Plaza, was completed in 1929 on air rights above the Chicago, Milwaukee, St. Paul & Pacific Railroad tracks leading to and from Union Station. The massive Union Station construction project,

which was anticipated in Burnham's 1909 Plan of Chicago and required 12 years to complete, also required the demolition of a Butler Brothers warehouse on the west bank of the Chicago River in 1913 to route Milwaukee Road tracks to the new station. The resulting station and yards occupied six blocks of prime riverfront land, and the air rights above them were used in the second half of the century for a succession of office towers known collectively as Riverside Plaza.[8]

The necessity to redevelop railroad land was abruptly forced on Chicago's suburbs following the collapse of two electric interurban railways in the two decades after World War II; the modernization of the commuter railroad system, which involved the replacement of some outlying coach yards with new facilities; and the abandonment of several branch lines. Prior to that there was apparently little interest in saving the rights-of-way and facilities of assorted interurban railroads that had failed in the years before and during the Depression, and certainly no concerted effort on the part of suburbs to do so. But the explosive growth of suburbia after World War II changed the equation. The suburbs served by the electric interurbans suddenly found themselves with unsightly, abandoned rail lines stretching for miles through their

downtown districts and residential subdivisions. Such rights-of-way were usually no more than a hundred feet wide and had limited capacity for redevelopment. The solution ultimately discovered was to convert the rights-of-way into linear parks; larger parcels where the yards had once sat were redeveloped into a variety of projects, everything from municipal structures to apartment buildings. In a few instances sections of the abandoned railroads were converted into railway museums.

Suburban Redevelopment

A small section of traction engineer Bion J. Arnold's defunct Elgin & Belvidere electric interurban railway near the hamlet of Union in McHenry County was purchased in 1962 by the Illinois Railway Museum to house its small but growing collection of interurban cars. The electric

Union Station's yards remained a busy place in the twenty-first century. The tracks at the right would normally be occupied by commuter trains but were empty on the Sunday in 2003 when this photograph was taken.

The office tower in the background replaced a portion of Union Station, but the old 1920s-era train-shed roof can be seen in the foreground.

Kane County. The railway had stopped passenger service in 1934 and freight service in 1971.[9]

One of the first postwar redevelopment projects involving a steam railroad was the Chicago & North Western's suburban coach yard in West Chicago about 30 miles west of the Loop. The eight-acre yard in the middle of the suburb's central business district was abandoned in 1956 when the railroad moved its commuter yard to a site west of town. The track was ripped out in 1961, and the land was subsequently sold for use as a scrap metal yard and a gas station. The suburb acquired a portion of the old yard and in 1993 built a public library on it.[10]

The nearby suburb of Aurora, actually a satellite city, was faced with the problem of what to do with an abandoned 1855 limestone roundhouse that the Burlington Northern had closed in 1974. Although the abandoned structure on the edge of the city's downtown area deteriorated over the subsequent 20 years, the city blocked attempts by the railroad to raze the landmark, perhaps the oldest such structure in the nation. Finally a development group headed by Chicago Bears football star Walter Payton used financial and tax incentives from the city to rehabilitate and convert the structure into an entertainment center featuring a restaurant and brew pub. A portion of the old structure was used as a commuter station and railroad offices.[11]

In other suburbs, rather than abandoning obsolete facilities, railroads adapted them to serve changing traffic patterns, especially growing intermodal traffic. Thus older classification yards operated by the Burlington Northern in Cicero and the North Western in Proviso Township were converted in part or in total to intermodal interchange facilities for the transfer of long-haul truck trailers and shipping containers between road and rail. This typically involved paving the yards and installing gantry cranes to lift trailers and containers to and from rail flatcars.

In west suburban Wheaton after the

railway had gone out of business in 1930, and much of its mainline had remained fallow since then. Likewise, an investment group that would later become known as the Fox River Trolley Museum bought some cars in 1961 from the failed Chicago, Aurora & Elgin to save them from the scrap heap and acquired a 1.5-mile section of the 40-mile Aurora, Elgin and Fox River Electric Company line at South Elgin in abandonment and scrapping of the Aurora & Elgin interurban in the early 1960s, the line's 20-acre yard and mechanical shop on the western edge of the city's central business district became a concern for successive municipal administrations. One city council approved the erection of five 20-story apartment complexes, but the next council, concerned about the density of development, reneged after two of the towers were completed on 13 acres in 1975. The balance of the site was developed as police station, municipal storage yard, and commuter parking lot for the nearby North Western commuter station.[12]

The North Shore Railroad yard and shops in Highwood, after their abandonment in 1963, were redeveloped as the Moraine Hotel complex, a strip shopping center, a fast food outlet, and a parking lot for North Western commuters. An early development instigated by the North Shore was Ravinia Park in the suburb of Highland Park. Before the advent of the automobile, suburban interurban railroads often opened public parks as a way to generate traffic on the assumption that Chicago residents would like to spend a day in the country. Ravinia was opened in 1904 but sold off by the railroad in 1909 and became the site of outdoor summer-long music festivals drawing crowds after Chicago's opera and symphony seasons ended each year. The park continued in operation into the twenty-first century, long after the railroad had shut down.[13]

Other sections of the North Shore's Shore Line were split up and sold to developers for stores and apartment buildings after the railroad's demise, and some of the line, which ran on the street in many suburbs, was paved over for auto traffic. However, a major portion of the route wound up as bicycle paths, and sections of the Skokie Valley route farther inland were used as a utility easement and by the North Western and its successor Union Pacific as a freight line.[14]

There were assorted proposals to save both the Aurora & Elgin and North Shore as

mass transit systems, but the only electric interurban to escape the scrap heap was the Chicago South Shore & South Bend, and only because it was acquired in 1991 by a public agency called the Northern Indiana Commuter Transportation District. By then, federal, state, and local subsidies were available to mass transit systems like the South Shore. Such subsidies came too late for the Aurora & Elgin and North Shore, only small portions of which were saved as mass transit lines because they were converted to extensions of the Chicago Transit Authority's rapid transit system.[15]

Thus at the end of the twentieth century only 84 miles survived in mass transit service of what in 1925 had been a 537-mile interurban network serving the Chicago metropolitan area as far north as Milwaukee, as far east as South Bend, and as far west as Belvidere, Illinois. When the South Shore was removed from the calculations, the two CTA extensions combined comprised only about 8 miles of the combined 167-mile North Shore and Aurora & Elgin systems. The demise of those two railroads and the ability of a public transit agency to save small sections of them coincided with and was the result of the national movement to provide public subsidies to mass transit.[16]

The antebellum Burlington roundhouse in Aurora was saved by preservationists and converted into a combination commuter station, brew pub, and restaurant.

(facing page) The development of a biking-hiking trail system in the Chicago area was made possible beginning in the 1960s by the conversion of abandoned railroad rights-of-way. The I&M Canal Trail used that abandoned waterway.

The first of the two fragments to be retained in mass transit service was a three-mile section of the former CA&E mainline west of Laramie Avenue in Chicago. The line was not preserved intact; in fact, the original right-of-way was used for construction of the Congress (later Eisenhower) Expressway. However, the Chicago Transit Authority's Garfield Park (later Congress) line that had ended at Laramie was extended on a new right-of-way about three miles west to a new terminal at Desplaines Avenue in Forest Park. That extension, which utilized the median strip of the expressway, a short subway, and property adjacent to the expressway, opened in 1958, almost a year after the CA&E had suspended passenger service.[17]

The CTA had considered taking over operation of the entire CA&E and had made several public proposals to do so. But it lacked the operating funds to keep the system running; moreover, no state or federal operating subsidies were then available, and Chicago was unwilling to subsidize suburban riders. The cost of construction of the replacement of the Garfield L because of its displacement by the Congress Expressway was born by Chicago and federal highway funds as part of the road construction project.[18]

Acquisition of the five-mile-long Skokie Swift branch of the CTA between Howard Street on Chicago's northern municipal limits and Dempster Street in north suburban Skokie was precipitated by the demise of the North Shore in 1963. In 1961 the U.S. Congress had passed the National Housing Act, which for the first time made available limited funds for experimental mass transit projects, "demonstration projects" as they were called in the language of the federal bureaucracy. Because the CTA was taking over an existing electric interurban line, the capital costs were minimal—$340,000 for such things as electrical work, building a temporary station with parking, and adding pan trolleys to enable the fleet of assigned cars to make their electrical pickup from the overhead wires used on

the North Shore instead of the third rails used on the rest of the CTA system. During the two-year demonstration project in 1964–1966, the Skokie Swift actually turned a $216,717 operating profit.[19]

Rails to Trails

Most of the rest of the CA&E and portions of the North Shore became the prototype for what evolved into an innovative national program to convert abandoned rail rights-of-way into publicly owned linear parks, or nature trails. Typically, the portions of the abandoned rights-of-way were improved with a crushed stone or asphalt path atop the former roadbed for use by pedestrians or cyclists. The remaining fringe was allowed to revert to nature or was landscaped as parks. Where possible the railroad's original bridges were used to span highways or streams, or pedestrian bridges were built to replace them. In some cases, as in the case of the Sparta-Elroy trail in Wisconsin, the original railway tunnels were incorporated into the trails.

Although abandoned railroads had been converted to nature trails before World War II—most notably the Cathedral Isle Trail in the privately owned Hitchcock Woods forest preserve in Aiken, South Carolina, established in 1939 on the long-abandoned South Carolina Canal and Rail Road Company right-of-way—the national Rails-to-Trails movement traces its origins to the conversions in the 1960s in Chicago's western suburbs and Wisconsin. Promoters of the Elroy-Sparta Trail, which was developed in 1965 from a former Chicago & North Western right-of-way in west central Wisconsin, claim it was the first such rail-to-trail conversion in the United States, but there is substantial evidence that the Illinois Prairie Path in Chicago's western suburbs, built on the abandoned Aurora & Elgin right-of-way was contemporaneous and may have predated it.[20]

The origin of the Prairie Path dates to September 30, 1963, six years after the railroad abandoned passenger service and four

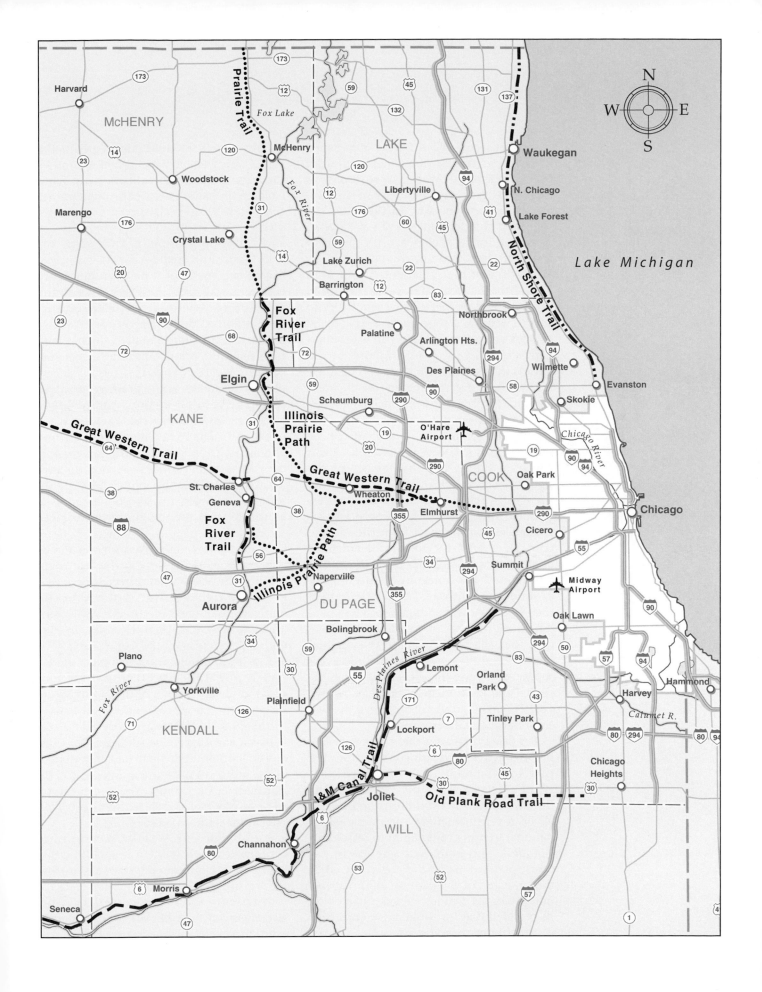

years after it ran its last freight train, when the *Chicago Tribune* published a letter by May Theilgaard Watts, a resident of Naperville and retired naturalist at the Morton Arboretum in Lisle. In the letter she suggested the dormant Aurora & Elgin be converted into a public footpath similar to those in Great Britain, the Long Trail in Vermont, and the Appalachian Trail from Maine to Georgia. The letter prompted other interested persons in the Chicago area to write, and they staged a walk by 80 persons on October 19, 1963, in west suburban Wayne to drum up support for the idea. Early the next year a citizen's committee was formed to raise money for the cause and promote the idea to the public.[21]

One of the major obstacles to the creation of the Prairie Path and many of the rails-to-trails projects that followed was the legal tangle over ownership of the right-of-way, which reflected the manner in which the railroad organizers had assembled their lines in the first place. Although railroads almost from their inception were granted powers of eminent domain to buy land, they often resorted to quicker and less antagonistic measures to acquire rights-of-way. Those alternatives included easements, long-term leases, and donations of land, often with the stipulation that the land revert to the original owner should it cease to be used as a railroad. Untangling the ownership issues occupied the Prairie Path promoters for two years after the group incorporated in 1964 as a not-for-profit corporation.

For years thereafter the promoters were preoccupied with clearing debris from the trail and surfacing the pathway portion. What emerged was a partnership of the Illinois Prairie Path volunteers and all levels of government from the municipal to national to bring the trail up to reasonable standards and permit its safe use by cyclists, pedestrians, and equestrians. After the surfacing of the pathway with crushed limestone, the various agencies had to restore old bridges or build new ones over various highways and streams.[22]

The success of the Prairie Path in Du Page County encouraged agencies in other suburban counties to emulate it. In Kane County on the western edge of suburbia, the Forest Preserve District not only acquired and extended sections of four CA&E lines to Aurora, Batavia, Geneva, and Elgin, but created the 37-mile Fox River Trail, much of it on abandoned rail rights-of-way right between Algonquin and Aurora. After the North Western in 1968 absorbed the Chicago Great Western Railway, it abandoned much of that carrier's mainline across northern Illinois and various western suburbs, which acted quickly to add it to the growing trail system. The result was the 12-mile Great Western Trail from Villa Park to West Chicago in Du Page County and an unconnected 18-mile trail of the same name between St. Charles in Kane County and Sycamore in DeKalb County. The eight-mile gap between the two remained as a North Western branch line to serve local industry.[23]

The Rails-to-Trails movement was somewhat slower to develop in the northern suburbs, in part because there were fewer available rights-of-way and the North Shore abandonment occurred several years after the Aurora & Elgin. However, by the end of the century Lake County and several of its municipalities operated the 9-mile North Shore Bike Trail over the former Mundelein branch of the North Shore between that suburb and Lake Bluff as well as the 24-mile Robert McClory Bike Path between the Lake-Cook line and the Wisconsin border. That path had functioned as the railroad's mainline to Milwaukee. In northern Cook County, the North Shore right-of-way was converted to Green Bay Trail as far south as Wilmette.[24]

An abandoned 7.5-mile section of a Chicago & North Western branch line between Algonquin and Crystal Lake in the far northwest suburbs became the nucleus for McHenry County's Prairie Trail. The last major rail line to join the metropolitan trail system was the former Penn Central Railroad (originally the Joliet & Northern Indiana) line across southern Cook and Will counties. The line was abandoned in the 1970s after the Consolidated Rail Corporation, the successor to the bankrupt Penn Central, deemed it superfluous, and a coalition of local governments cooperated to acquire it. The 20-mile line was renamed Old Plank Road Trail and officially opened in 1997.[25]

By the end of 2003, the Rails-to-Trails Conservancy, a national organization founded in 1986 and based in Washington, D.C., claimed there were in the U.S. 12,648 miles of nature trails converted from old railroad lines. Of the two pioneering states, Illinois had 44 trails collectively stretching for 519 miles and Wisconsin had 63 trails that combined were 1,328 miles long. Illinois's totals, despite an aggressive program by state and local officials, reflected the fact that many abandonments, especially those in highly developed urban areas, were unsuitable for conversion.[26]

Stockyards

One of the best examples of a metropolitan rail site unsuitable for conversion to parkland was the Chicago stockyards. The development of the motor truck and especially the federal highway system doomed the big central stockyards in places like Chicago and Kansas City. Chicago's Union Stock Yards had been designed by Octave Chanute essentially as a railroad yard surrounded by livestock pens and abattoirs, although the entire complex eventually became known as the stockyards. The shipment of livestock on the hoof to Chicago's central facility and dressed meat to markets around the nation worked well for the better part of a century, but after World War II development of refrigerated trucks and the federal highways on which to operate them resulted in the decentralization of the meatpacking industry to rural areas closer to the source of livestock.

The Union Stock Yards about four miles

southwest of the Loop accordingly declined in importance. In 1955 Wilson and Company was the first meatpacker to close its operations in Chicago, followed by the others in the next few years, and in 1971 the stockyards were shut down. That left Chicago with the problem of what to do with an abandoned square mile rail yard, which, it turned out, was as much a blessing as a curse. Like many industrial cities of the Northeast and Midwest, Chicago in the postwar period began hemorrhaging industry as older factories needed replacement and the companies that owned them were unable to find suitable sites in the

A major section of the abandoned CGW rail line was redeveloped as the Great Western Trail, a linear park for hikers and bikers. This section, photographed in 2003, is near the suburb of Carol Stream.

city and moved onto cheaper land in the suburbs. The city and a community organization called the Back of the Yards Neighorhood Council, which had been co-founded in 1939 by legendary urban activist Saul Alinsky, came up with a plan to turn the site into an industrial park that eventually became home to 110 companies employing 15,000 workers.[27]

Illinois Center

The stockyards was a joint venture by all the railroads serving Chicago, but the first individual railroad to begin a systematic plan to dispose of its surplus railroad property in Chicago after World War II was the Illinois Central, which by virtue of state legislation, land grants, and city ordinances in the 1850s and 1860s, owned a sizeable portion of the city's lakefront between Hyde Park and the Chicago River. Once the IC's board of directors in the early 1960s decided to sell off surplus land to pay for diversification, it hired William B. Johnson as chief executive to get the project under way.[28]

One of Johnson's first tasks was to convince Chicago's Mayor Richard J. Daley of the merit of the railroad's plan to use the air rights over an abandoned freight yard east of the Loop and south of the river as a site for skyscrapers. At the time the air rights issue was being challenged in court by shareholders and taxpayers, and the railroad did not want the city and state to intervene on the side of the opponents of development. Keeping the lakefront east of the Loop free of development had been a contentious issue in Chicago since Montgomery Ward's one-man, 20-year campaign in the late 1800s.[29]

Those opposed to lakefront development based their arguments on a federal land grant of 20 acres for a park east of Michigan Avenue between Madison and Randolph streets and the 1836 decision by the Illinois-Michigan Canal Commission, which had platted Chicago to keep as a public open space "forever open, clear, and free of any buildings, or other obstructions" the lakefront land east of Michigan Avenue between Madison and 12th streets. However, the commissioner's mandate soon came under pressure from all manner of people, companies, and agencies intent upon developing the land. Although much of the disputed land ultimately became the lakefront Grant Park between 12th and Randolph streets, the railroad wanted to redevelop its remaining holdings north and south of the park.[30]

The most valuable of those was 83 acres east of the Loop and south of the river that included the original Fort Dearborn military reservation. This area had been granted to the railroad in the 1850s and a century later was covered with an unsightly rail yard used for storage of rusting and unused freight cars. Over the years that tract and the lakefront right-of-way connecting it to the rest of the railroad had been the subject of a continuous if unfull-filled campaign by the city to beautify the lakefront by lowering the tracks below street level to give an unobstructed view of the lake and electrifying the IC commuter line. The tracks were depressed and the commuter line electrified pursuant to a 1919 city ordinance, and another ordinance in 1929 permitted the railroad the use of the air rights over its tracks, which it exercised after the war to permit construction of the Prudential Building in 1954 and the 40-story Outer Drive East apartment building in 1964. In 1968, IC Industries sold 3 1/2 acres of the site to Standard Oil of Indiana for its 83-story tower. Those three buildings were all along Randolph Street, which left the bulk of the site to the north for redevelopment once the lawsuits were resolved in the railroad's favor.[31]

After that happened, IC Industries in 1969 induced the City Council to zone the site for a planned unit development (retail, office, hotel, and residential) to allow the construction south of the river and east of Michigan Avenue of what is known as Illinois Center. Between then and the end of the century, 11 separate structures were

(above) The IC's yards at Central (12th Street) Depot, shown in the 1930s, were ripe for redevelopment after the collapse of intercity passenger traffic and the creation of Amtrak in 1970. Soldier Field can be seen in the upper right. (Alan R. Lind, Transport History Press)

(below) The Central Station development, shown here in 2003, arose on the old IC 12th Street yards. The Prudential and Standard Oil (later Aon) buildings seen in the distance were developed using air rights over IC property.

At the start of the twenty-first century, Dearborn Station was the sole survivor of Chicago's six grand depots dating from the 1800s. The rest had been demolished or redeveloped. Dearborn wound up as a combined shopping and office complex anchoring new residential development to the south.

built in Illinois Center beginning in 1970 with a 29-story steel and glass box designed by Mies Van der Rohe.[32]

Johnson was not finished, however. The railroad still owned considerable surplus property along the lake south of the Loop and sold a chunk of it to the city for the expansion of the McCormick Place exhibition center. Another prime piece of real estate was the railroad's 1893 intercity passenger station, yard, and general offices east of Michigan Avenue between 11th and 13th streets. The decision by Amtrak to consolidate at Union Station left the IC facilities without any tenants, and the depot was closed in 1972 and demolished two years later. The 80-acre site was developed in the 1990s as Central Station, a

mixed residential, retail, hotel, commercial, and office development that included three high-rise buildings.[33]

Dearborn Park

The development of Dearborn Park on the former railroad yards serving Dearborn Station at Dearborn and Polk streets and collateral redevelopment of the adjacent Grand Central Station at Harrison and Wells streets, both south of the Loop, may not have been the most ambitious of the rail redevelopment projects in Chicago, but they were probably the most difficult to accomplish politically. Dearborn Station, built in 1885, had served more railroads than any other, including passenger trains operated by the Atchison, Topeka & Santa Fe, Wabash, Erie, Grant Trunk Western, Chicago & Eastern Illinois, Monon, and Chesapeake & Ohio railroads. Grand Central, built in 1890, had handled the Baltimore & Ohio, Pere Marquette, Chicago Great Western, and Soo Line. Once Amtrak moved its surviving trains to Union Station in the 1970s, both Dearborn and Grand Central and their coach yards, which covered a total of 600 acres, became vacant overnight and available for development.

The abandonment of such large parcels of land immediately south of the Loop and the effect that the resulting urban blight would have on downtown business concerned some of the city's commercial leaders to the point that they formed an organization to start a private-public drive to redevelop the property as a residential city within a city. The organization, headed by Thomas G. Ayers, president of the Commonwealth Edison Company utility, included executives from the major banks, utilities, and Sears, Roebuck & Company, as well as Philip M. Klutznick, the developer of the planned south suburban community of Park Forest and several suburban shopping centers.[34]

Despite the emergence of a rival group headed by architect Bertrand Goldberg, the developer of the Marina City towers

Grand Central Station, whose tower with the B&O logo can be seen in the background (at left beyond the train), was along the river just south of the Loop. Though not as busy as the other downtown depots, it served B&O passenger trains and had an adjacent freight terminal. Its commuter traffic was negligible, which made it vulnerable to demolition once Amtrak moved its trains to Union Station.

just north of the Loop, and an interest in the property by George Halas, owner of the Chicago Bears who was looking for the site for a new football stadium, Ayer's organization prevailed and was able to start construction on the first phase that included apartments, townhouses, and single-family homes in 1977. The railroads, Chessie (corporate successor to the Baltimore & Ohio and Chesapeake & Ohio), the bankrupt Penn Central Transportation Company, and the local Chicago & Western Indiana were only too willing to sell, and by then most major railroads had established land subsidiaries to dispose of surplus property.[35]

Dearborn Park was built on the Dearborn Station yards to a relatively low density for Chicago. Although it was originally proposed to contain 25,000 housing units on 250 acres, it was actually confined to 1,696 units on 51 acres. Goldberg's nearby River City on the Grand Central Station yards was proposed to have a considerably

More than two decades after Grand Central had been razed, the site, shown in 2003, was only partially redeveloped. The Sears Tower is in the background.

higher density—six 72-story towers containing 6,000 units—but only one building, containing 450 units, was built. The lone holdout against redevelopment of the south Loop rail yards was the Regional Transportation Authority's commuter rail subsidiary, Metra, which held on to the former Rock Island Railroad mainline yard serving the LaSalle Street commuter station.[36]

In the early 1990s, a surplus Atchison, Topeka & Santa Fe Railroad yard about a mile south of downtown Chicago attracted the attention of business leaders in the adjacent Chinatown neighborhood. They began developing that site as 32-acre Chinatown Square, a mixed-use retail mall, office, and residential development.[37]

Station Redevelopment

Developers also began to covet Chicago's three surviving train depots on the fringe of the central business district—North Western, Union, and LaSalle Street—long before Amtrak was created. However, all three served a substantial and growing commuter market, as well as intercity trains in the case of Union Station, and could not be abandoned. But all three were eventually redeveloped. The old LaSalle Street station, which also held the offices of the defunct Rock Island Railroad, was razed in 1981 to be replaced by the Chicago Board Options Exchange, and a new but smaller station was built a block to the south. Preservationists were unable to save the 1911 North Western Station at Canal and Madison streets, but the 42-story Citicorp Center that arose in its place in 1987 contained new station facilities on its first few floors. The train shed and access yards to the north were not affected by the project.[38]

Union Station, which sprawled for six prime blocks along the south branch of the river, was the subject of the greatest redevelopment. Four separate Gateway Center office buildings varying between 21 and 35 stories were built over the Union station concourse and tracks north of the depot between 1965 and 1983. The original station had consisted of two buildings, the concourse and the head house, the latter of which contained railroad offices and a cathedral-like main waiting room called the Great Hall. Although the head house was left intact primarily because of the efforts of preservationists, the Commission on Chicago Landmarks in early 2002 approved a plan to redevelop the office portion of the building, raising it in height from the existing 8 stories to 26 stories but preserving the Great Hall.[39]

By the end of the twentieth century, Chicago's downtown railroad plant had been reconfigured to one that more nearly recognized the realities of the contemporary transportation situation and the need for the city to expand high-density business and residential development in its downtown area. There was less economic, public, and political pressure to force rail redevelopment in outlying areas, despite congestion on the railroad system itself. The surviving downtown railroad system consisted of three major passenger corridors and two primarily serving freight. The passenger corridors were the sunken Illinois Central and South Shore commuter line between the Loop and the lake, the tracks west of the Chicago River serving Union and North Western stations, and a third, smaller corridor south of the Loop that gave Rock Island commuter trains access to a scaled-down LaSalle Street Station.

The two surviving downtown rail freight corridors flanked the Loop to the north and south. The below-grade North Western line north of the main stem Chicago River had lost its industrial customers and was unused, and the city was agitating for the railroads to abandon the elevated St. Charles Air Line south of the Loop at 16th Street. The North Western line, which at one time served Navy Pier on the lake but over the years had been truncated at Rush Street as industries along it relocated, had been suggested as a corridor that needed to be preserved for future use as a mass transit line. The use of air rights over the line for both buildings and streets had already transformed it into more of a subway than an open-air railroad.[40]

In the 1990s the St. Charles Air Line, the one-mile stretch of railroad built in 1856 to connect the Illinois Central and Michigan Central with the western railroads, came under pressure for abandonment. The line, which had been elevated and was not an obstruction to street traffic, had no shippers along its short route and served strictly as a connector. It still carried as many as 16 daily trains, but its right-of-way had become more valuable for redevelopment than it was as a railway. Thus the pressure to abandon the line came not from the railroads but from other interests in the city. Municipal officials, residents of the area, and developers, claiming that there were other connections between the Illinois Central and the western railroads, suggested it was time to close down the line.[41]

As the new century dawned, the redevelopment of superfluous railroad property was a work in progress. For one thing, the fate of Amtrak's huge passenger yards south of Union Station had become a vague question to be dealt with at some time in the future. The agency required substantial federal subsidies to cover its operating deficits, and the yearly appropriations debates in Congress became an annual battle for survival in the last quarter of the twentieth century. Several successive Amtrak administrations suggested that if its subsidies were substantially reduced, the agency would have to reduce its operations in the West, including Chicago. Congress inevitably relented and renewed the subsidies, if at a lower level, but the threat of a shutdown of intercity passenger service outside the Boston-Washington Northeast Corridor seemed to arise every few years. Of course, such a shutdown would have made Amtrak's Chicago coach yards superfluous and available for redevelopment so long as a proposed compact of midwestern states did not step in to operate intercity train service out of Chicago.

The suitability of railroad lines for redevelopment, especially the elevated tracks in areas away from the central business district, was something of an enigma. For example, redevelopment of the abandoned

The colonnaded train shed (foreground) was all that remained of the 1911 North Western Depot after the head shed was demolished and an office tower (background) was built in its place in 1987. Even the station was renamed Ogilvie Transportation Center after a former governor who had nothing to do with the railroad.

Milwaukee Road Bloomingdale line across Chicago's North Side was also being discussed, albeit without much progress, as the new century dawned. The line looked something like an overgrown linear jungle atop a causeway wandering through a rapidly gentrifying urban landscape, and pressure by the affluent arrivals in the neighborhood began to increase to convert the line to public use from a haven for homeless derelicts, miscreants, and teenagers looking for a private place to get drunk.

Reuse of other surplus rail property will probably have to await markets for its redevelopment, however. Although areas of the North Side and south Loop area gentrified in the last two decades of the twentieth century, blighted sections of the city were unlikely to attract private capital for redevelopment. The availability of railroad land was also contingent upon the needs of the transportation industry, although as the millennium ended some civic organizations were discussing construction of a rail bypass similar to the port-to-downtown Alameda Corridor in Los Angeles as a way to reduce both train traffic and automobile traffic congestion. It remained to be seen what effect such a corridor, if it were ever built, would have on the rest of the region's railroad plant, however.

Epilogue

Chicago at the dawn of the new millennium was still North America's railroad capital although no railroads called it home. Their tracks all still pointed in its direction, however. It was no longer a hog butcher or stacker of wheat, and the travelers crossing the continent were far more likely to pause in transit to change conveyances at O'Hare or Midway airports than Union Station. On the other hand, a shipping container of merchandise from Germany to Singapore was likely to pass through the Windy City on its long trip.

The deregulation of much of the nation's transportation system in the final decades of the twentieth century produced mixed results. The post-deregulation financial distress of the trunk airlines and many trucking companies, depending upon one's viewpoint, can be interpreted as a blessing as those industries weeded out their inefficient members, or as a curse proving that some things can never be totally regulation free. However, there was general agreement as the century ended that deregulation of the railroad industry had been a success.

It is true that the number of railroad companies and the size of the nation's rail system shrank dramatically, a process that had begun long before deregulation. The miles of railroad in the United States on December 31, 2000—the official end of the century and millennium—was approximately 40 percent of what it had been before World War I. The number of major U.S. and Canadian railroads serving substantial portions of the U.S. through merger, consolidation, and liquidation shrank from 132 on the eve of the Great Depression to only 7 at the end of the century—8 if Amtrak is included.

The extent of the decline, especially in Illinois, is somewhat illusory. Chicago, which at the beginning of the century was home to the headquarters of 22 independent railroads of any size, at the end of the century had none. The head sheds of the major railroads with lines to Chicago were scattered in such diverse places as Montreal, Calgary, Jacksonville, Norfolk, Fort Worth, Kansas City, and Omaha.

Despite the consolidations, Illinois still had 52 railroad companies operating within its borders, although only 7 of them rated as Class I carriers—the 5 surviving major U.S. lines (Burlington Northern Santa Fe, Union Pacific, Norfolk Southern, Kansas City Southern, and CSX), plus Amtrak and 2 Canadian transcontinental railroads (Canadian National and Canadian Pacific). There also were the 17 switching and terminal companies that had been around for more than a century, as well as 8 regional railroads of at least 350 miles and 20 shorter lines. As the big railroads shucked their least profitable branches to concentrate on mainline traffic, the regional and short-line carriers were formed to take over and operate those lesser lines.[1]

Despite the shrinkage in railroad plant, American railroads at the dawn of the twenty-first century originated more tons of traffic (1.74 billion) than they had in 1929 (1.34 billion), when the system was more than twice as large, and they hauled it greater distances. The increased volume of traffic meant that Chicago was as inundated with railroad trains in 2001 as it had been a century earlier.[2]

The situation reached the point that the city, various business groups, civic organizations, and the railroads banded together in 2003 and came up with a plan to alleviate some of the congestion. Despite Chicago's massive railroad network, the lack of adequate connections between railroads required at least 3,500 trucks on a daily basis to transfer shipping containers and truck trailers between railroad yards. Although much of the plan dealt with building new bridges to eliminate 25 highway-rail grade crossings at which congestion was the worst, the coalition also proposed 6 flyover bridges to separate train traffic and eliminate rail-to-rail crossing diamonds.[3]

Whether the project will ever get off the ground is problematic. Almost before the press conference announcing the plan had ended, political sniping over how much the railroad industry would contribute to the $1.5 billion plan had become an issue. U.S. representative William Lipinski, a Chicagoan and member of the House Committee on Transportation and Infrastructure, suggested that the railroad industry's $212 million share of the project was too low. However, Chicago mayor Richard M. Daley warned that increasing the rail industry's share might cause them to back out of the program. Just such financing problems doomed the state's MARGE plan to rehabilitate the East St. Louis rail network and caused a premature

end to Chicago's track elevation in the late 1920s before it was completed.[4]

An added problem was that Amtrak, which would have been a major beneficiary of the plan in that some of the improvements would eliminate freight interference with its passenger trains, was in financial distress. The quasi-government agency had been limping along with government subsidies and was rescued from periodic shutdowns only by emergency appropriations from Congress. On July 28, 2003, the U.S. Transportation Department sent to Congress a proposed Amtrak reform act that among other things would shift operations outside of the Washington-Boston corridor, including Chicago-based trains, to a new corporation that would run them under contract with the affected states.[5]

Whatever becomes of the federal, state, and local plans to streamline the Chicago rail infrastructure, it seems likely that Chicago will remain the nation's busiest rail center for the foreseeable future if for no other reason than the most obvious: all the tracks go there.

Appendix A

Suburban Population Growth, 1850–1900 (by railroad corridors)

Town	1850	1860	1870	1880	1890	1900
Lake Shore — Chicago & North Western (Chicago to Winthrop Harbor)						
Evanston	——	831	3,062	4,400	9,000	19,259
Wilmette	——	——	——	419	1,458	2,300
Kenilworth	——	——	——	——	——	339
Winnetka	——	——	——	584	1,079	1,833
Glencoe	——	——	*	387	569	1,020
Highland Park	——	——	*	1,154	2,163	2,806
Lake Forest	——	——	*	877	1,203	2,215
Lake Bluff	——	——	——	——	——	490
North Chicago	——	——	——	——	——	1,150
Waukegan	——	3,433	4,507	4,012	4,915	9,426
North Central — Chicago, Milwaukee & St. Paul (Chicago to Fox Lake)						
Niles	——	——	——	——	——	544
Morton Grove	——	——	——	——	——	564
Glenview	——	——	——	——	——	450
Libertyville	——	——	——	——	550	864
Northwest — Chicago & North Western (Chicago to Harvard)						
Des Plaines	——	——	*	818	986	1,666
Arlington Hts.	——	——	——	——	1,424	1,380
Palatine	——	——	*	731	891	1,020
Barrington	——	——	*	410	848	1,162
Woodstock	——	1,327	1,574	1,475	1,683	2,502
Northwest — Chicago, Milwaukee & St. Paul (Chicago to Elgin)						
River Grove	——	——	——	——	287	333
Franklin Park	——	——	——	——	——	483
Bensenville	——	——	——	——	——	374
Itasca	——	——	——	——	——	256
Elgin	——	2,797	5,441	8,787	17,823	22,433
West — Chicago & North Western (Chicago to Geneva)						
River Forest	——	——	——	*	*	1,539
Maywood	——	——	——	——	*	4,532
Melrose Park	——	——	——	——	——	2,592
Elmhurst	——	——	——	——	——	1,728
Lombard	——	——	*	378	515	590
Glen Ellyn	——	——	——	——	——	793
Wheaton	——	645	998	1,160	1,622	2,345
Geneva	——	——	*	1,239	1,692	2,446

Suburban Population Growth, 1850–1900 (cont.)

Town	1850	1860	1870	1880	1890	1900
Southwest — Chicago, Burlington & Quincy (Chicago to Aurora)						
Cicero	——	——	1,545	3,294	5,433	16,310
Riverside	——	——	——	450	*	1,551
Brookfield	——	——	——	——	——	1,111
LaGrange	——	——	——	531	2,314	3,969
Western Springs	——	——	——	——	451	662
Hinsdale	——	——	——	819	1,584	2,578
Downers Grove	——	——	——	586	960	2,103
Naperville	——	2,599	1,713	2,073	2,216	2,629
Aurora	——	6,011	11,162	11,878	19,688	24,147
Southwest — Chicago & Alton (Chicago to Joliet)						
Summit	——	——	——	——	*	547
Lemont	——	——	——	2,108	2,278	2,449
Lockport	——	2,822	1,772	1,679	2,449	2,659
Joliet	2,659	7,104	7,263	11,657	23,264	29,353
Southwest — Chicago & Rock Island (Chicago to Joliet)						
Blue Island	*	*	*	1,542	3,329	6,114
Tinley Park	——	——	——	——	——	300
Joliet	2,659	7,104	7,263	11,657	23,264	29,353
South — Illinois Central (Chicago to Homewood)						
Riverdale	——	——	——	——	——	558
Harvey	——	——	——	——	——	5,395
Homewood	——	——	——	——	——	352

*Population not reported separately.

Suburban Rail Corridor Population Growth, 1850–1900

	1850	1860	1870	1880	1890	1900
Lake Shore (CNW)* [to Winthrop Harbor]	——	831	3,062	7,821	15,472	31,412
North Central (MR) [to Fox Lake]	——	——	——	——	550	2,422
Northwest (CNW) [to Harvard]	——	1,327	1,574	3,434	5,832	7,730
Northwest (MR)** [to Elgin]	——	——	——	——	287	1,446
West (CNW) [to Geneva]	——	645	998	2,777	3,829	16,565
Southwest (CBQ)*** [to Aurora]	——	2,599	3,258	7,753	12,958	30,913
Southwest (C&A)**** [to Joliet]	2,659	2,822	1,772	3,787	4,727	5,655
Southwest (RI)***** [to Joliet]	——	——	——	1,542	3,329	6,414
South (IC)***** [to Homewood]	——	——	——	——	——	6,305

*Excludes Waukegan
**Excludes Elgin
***Excludes Aurora
****Excludes Joliet
*****Excludes those suburbs annexed to Chicago prior to 1900

Appendix B

Suburban Population Growth, 1900–2000 (by railroad corridors)

West Central Corridor (Oak Park to Geneva)
[Chicago & North Western, Chicago, Aurora & Elgin, 1901–1957]

MP*	Suburb (incorporated)	1900	1920	1940	1960	1980	2000
8.5	Oak Park (1901)	——	39,858	66,015	61,093	54,887	52,524
9.7	River Forest (1880)	1,539	4,358	9,487	12,695	12,392	11,635
10.5	Maywood (1881)	4,532	12,072	26,648	27,330	27,998	26,987
11.3	Melrose Park (1893)	2,592	7,147	10,933	22,291	20,735	23,171
14.3	Berkeley (1924)	——	——	724	5,467	5,137	5,245
12.6	Bellwood (1900)	——	1,881	5,220	20,729	19,811	20,535
15.7	Elmhurst (1882)	1,728	4,594	15,458	40,329	44,276	42,762
17.8	Villa Park (1914)	——	854	7,235	23,294	23,155	22,075
19.9	Lombard (1869)	590	1,331	7,075	25,296	38,879	42,322
22.4	Glen Ellyn (1892)	793	2,851	8,055	15,972	23,743	26,999
25.0	Wheaton (1859)	2,345	4,137	7,389	26,263	43,043	55,416
27.5	Winfield (1921)	——	——	567	2,452	4,422	8,718
29.8	West Chicago (1873)	1,877	2,594	3,355	6,854	12,550	23,469
35.5	Geneva (1867)	2,446	2,803	4,650	7,646	9,811	19,515
	Total	**18,442**	**84,480**	**172,811**	**297,711**	**340,839**	**381,373**
	20-year pop. gain	——	+66,038	+88,331	+124,900	+43,128	+40,534
	Avg. gain/year	——	+3,302	+4,417	+6,245	+2,156	+2,027

Southwest Corridor (Cicero to Aurora)
[Chicago, Burlington & Quincy]

MP*	Town (incorporated)	1900	1920	1940	1960	1980	2000
7.0	Cicero (1867)	16,310	62,238	64,712	69,130	67,058	85,616
9.6	Berwyn (1901)	——	18,856	48,451	52,224	46,849	54,016
11.1	Riverside (1875)	1,551	2,532	7,935	9,750	9,236	8,895
12.3	Brookfield (1893)	1,111	3,589	10,817	20,429	19,395	19,085
13.8	LaGrange (1879)	3,969	6,525	10,479	16,326	15,693	15,608
15.5	Western Springs (1886)	662	1,258	4,856	12,408	12,876	12,493
16.9	Hinsdale (1873)	2,578	4,042	7,336	13,400	16,726	17,349
18.3	Clarendon Hills (1924)	——	894	2,181	5,885	6,870	7,601
19.5	Westmont (1921)	——	——	3,044	5,997	17,353	24,554
21.2	Downers Grove (1873)	2,103	3,543	9,526	21,154	42,691	48,724
24.5	Lisle (1956)	——	——	4,219	13,638	19,584	21,182
28.5	Naperville (1857)	2,629	3,830	5,272	16,091	49,215	128,358
37.5	Aurora (1853)	24,147	40,254	47,170	63,715	81,293	142,990
	Total	**55,060**	**147,561**	**225,998**	**320,147**	**404,839**	**586,471**
	20-year pop. gain	——	+92,501	+78,437	+94,149	+84,692	+181,632
	Avg. gain/year	——	+4,625	+3,922	+4,707	+4,235	+9,082

Northwest Corridor (Elmwood Park to Elgin)
[Chicago, Milwaukee, St. Paul & Pacific]

MP*	Town (incorporated)	1900	1920	1940	1960	1980	2000
10.2	Elmwood Park (1914)	——	1,380	13,689	23,866	24,016	25,405
11.4	River Grove (1888)	333	484	3,301	8,464	10,368	10,668
13.2	Franklin Park (1893)	483	914	3,007	18,332	19,507	19,434
17.2	Bensenville (1894)	374	650	1,869	11,057	16,106	20,703
19.1	Wood Dale (1928)	——	——	738	4,424	11,251	13,535
21.1	Itasca (1890)	256	339	787	3,930	7,129	8,302
23.9	Roselle (1922)	——	——	695	4,827	17,683	23,115
26.5	Schaumburg (1956)	——	——	——	3,296	57,555	75,386
28.4	Hanover Park (1958)	——	——	——	3,713	28,848	38,278
30.1	Bartlett (1891)	——	371	608	2,291	13,254	36,706
36.6	Elgin (1854)	22,433	28,291	38,333	49,447	63,668	94,487
	Total	**23,879**	**32,429**	**63,027**	**133,647**	**269,385**	**366,019**
	20-year pop. gain	——	+8,550	+30,598	+70,620	+135,738	+96,634
	Avg. gain/year	——	+428	+1,530	+3,531	+6,787	+4,832

Lake Shore (Evanston to Winthrop Harbor)
[Chicago & North Western]

MP*	Town (incorporated)	1900	1920	1940	1960	1980	2000
11.0	Evanston (1872)	19,259	43,883	65,389	79,283	73,706	74,239
14.4	Wilmette (1872)	2,300	7,814	17,226	31,685	28,221	27,651
15.2	Kenilworth (1896)	339	1,188	2,935	2,959	2,708	2,949
16.6	Winnetka (1869)	1,833	6,694	12,430	13,368	12,772	12,419
19.2	Glencoe (1869)	1,020	3,381	6,825	10,472	9,200	8,762
23.0	Highland Park (1869)	2,806	6,167	14,476	25,532	30,599	31,365
24.5	Highwood (1901)	1,575	1,146	3,707	4,499	5,455	4,143
28.3	Lake Forest (1861)	2,215	3,657	6,885	10,687	15,245	20,059
30.2	Lake Bluff (1895)	490	819	1,729	4,345	4,434	6,056
33.7	North Chicago (1895)	1,150	5,839	8,465	22,938	38,774	35,918
35.9	Waukegan (1852)	9,426	21,014	34,241	61,784	67,653	87,901
42.1	Zion (1902)	——	5,580	6,355	14,106	17,865	22,866
44.5	Winthrop Harbor (1901)	——	473	785	3,484	5,427	6,670
	Total	**42,413**	**107,655**	**181,448**	**285,142**	**312,059**	**340,998**
	20-year pop. gain	——	+65,242	+73,793	+103,694	+26,917	+28,939
	Avg. gain/year	——	+3,262	+3,690	+5,185	+1,346	+1,447

North Central (Niles to Fox Lake)
[Chicago, Milwaukee, St. Paul & Pacific]

MP*	Town (incorporated)	1900	1920	1940	1960	1980	2000
12.5	Niles (1899)	544	1,258	2,168	29,497	30,363	30,068
14.3	Morton Grove (1895)	564	1,079	2,010	25,154	23,747	22,451
16.2	Golf (1928)	——	——	158	409	482	451
17.4	Glenview (1899)	——	760	2,500	22,364	33,131	41,847
21.1	Northbrook (1923)	——	554	1,265	15,204	30,778	33,435
24.2	Deerfield (1903)	——	610	2,283	14,318	17,432	18,420
35.5	Libertyville (1882)	864	2,125	3,930	9,241	16,520	20,742
41.0	Grayslake (1895)	416	736	1,182	4,347	5,260	18,506
44.0	Round Lake (1908)	——	251	359	997	3,175	5,842
49.5	Fox Lake (1906)	——	467	1,110	3,886	6,831	9,178
	Total	**2,388**	**7,840**	**16,965**	**125,417**	**167,719**	**210,118**
	20-year pop. gain	——	+5,452	+9,125	+108,452	+42,302	+42,399
	Avg. gain/year	——	+273	+456	+5,423	+2,115	+2,120

*Miles from Chicago terminal

Appendix C

Railroad Disasters

The Chicago area, as might be expected because of the huge size of the railroad plant there and volume of traffic it carries, has had its share of rail disasters over the years, although the toll has not been as high as might otherwise be expected because trains traveling through the congested rail plant do so at relatively slow speeds. In fact, contrasted to some of the city's other disasters, the toll on the railroads has been relatively light. For instance, the number of fatalities resulting from the 1905 Iroquois Theater fire and the 1915 *Eastland* capsizing each exceeded the combined death toll for all railroad disasters in the Chicago area. Because the federal government and railroads themselves regulate safety on their lines, the influence of those disasters on the Chicago area, while attracting great attention in the press, has not been as great on the region as a whole as has been the grade-crossing problem.

The nation's first railroad disaster (as defined as an accident causing the death of 10 or more persons) occurred just south of Chicago in 1853. A synopsis of it and the subsequent disasters is given below. A couple of other infamous disasters are included for reference. Grade-crossing accidents are consigned to Chapter 11, and rail accidents involving the mass transit system are summarized in *Chicago Transit*.[1]

The Nation's First Train Disaster

April 25, 1853 The race between the first two eastern railroads to reach Chicago had been concluded barely a year earlier when their rivalry reaped a tragic result—a collision between trains at a diamond crossing at Grand Crossing south of Chicago that killed an estimated 21 persons, mostly German immigrants. The Michigan Southern and Northern Indiana (later renamed the Lake Shore) had first built its tracks into the area to connect to the Rock Island to gain access to downtown Chicago, and the Michigan Central shortly thereafter began building its line into Illinois to connect to the Illinois Central for access to Chicago. However, to get to the IC, the Michigan Central had to cross the newly laid tracks of the Michigan Southern by means of what in the industry is called a "diamond"—an at-grade crossing of two railroads. Since the first railroad to arrive at a crossing site holds squatter's rights, the second railroad must build either a diamond or a bridge spanning the first railroad's tracks.

The Michigan Southern opposed a diamond crossing because its president, John B. Jervis, believed a bridge would be safer. His subordinates even stationed a work gang in the area to prevent a diamond from being built; however, Michigan Central crews one night cut the Michigan Southern tracks, installed a diamond, and the next day notified the Michigan Southern of what they had done. According to one account, Roswell B. Mason, the IC's builder and later mayor of Chicago, had the Michigan Southern guard kidnapped one night, and when the sun rose the next morning the diamond was in place.

The two railroads then worked out a set of operating rules to avoid any conflict between their trains. Unfortunately, the rules were confusingly written, stipulating southbound Michigan Southern trains must "avoid," or yield the right-of-way to, all trains on the Michigan Central but giving all northbound Michigan Southern trains the right-of-way. In fact, Michigan

Southern engineer Edward Davis testified at an inquest after the crash that he had not understood them.

Davis drove his Michigan Southern train at 25 miles an hour into the side of a Michigan Central eastbound express at 10:15 p.m. Ironically, Thomas Rockham, the Michigan Central engineer, had slowed his train from a speed of 20 miles an hour to only 5 miles an hour as he approached the crossing. At the slower speed he could have stopped in time to avoid a collision with the other train, which he saw coming but assumed would stop because by the rules Rockham had the right-of-way. Had he continued at 20 miles an hour instead of slowing down he probably would have cleared the crossing before Davis's train arrived.

The fact that Rockham was running in the dark without a headlight contributed to the accident. He had reported the defective light to the superintendent of the railroad's Michigan City shops two trips earlier, but it had not been repaired. As a precaution, he posted his fireman with a small hand lantern on the front of the locomotive as he approached the crossing. Davis claimed he did not see the darkened train in time to materially slow his train, which he hit at exactly the wrong place. The Michigan Central consisted of a locomotive, followed by 5 freight cars, 2 immigrant passenger cars sandwiched in mid-train, and 17 more freight cars at the end. Davis's locomotive struck the first of the two wooden passenger cars, derailing and splintering them and throwing many of their occupants who survived the impact into an adjacent marsh, where they drowned. Davis and his fireman had jumped from the locomotive before impact, and the only fatalities were the occupants of the two cars.[2]

The South Bend Washout

June 28, 1859 A washout destroyed some Michigan Southern track in South Bend, Indiana, and 34 persons were killed in the resulting train wreck.

Illinois's Worst Wreck

August 10, 1887 The collapse of a small bridge over a nameless drainage ditch was the cause of the wreck near Chatsworth, Illinois, of a Toledo, Peoria & Western excursion train carrying 500 persons from Peoria to Niagara Falls, but the fragile wooden coaches that disintegrated on impact and caught fire caused most of the 85 deaths. The bridge was afire when the train approached, but the engineer was unable to stop in time. The cause of the fire was never determined, although a track crew had been burning brush along the TP&W right-of-way about nine hours before the wreck.[3]

Lady Elgin *Sinking*

September 8, 1860 The steamship *Lady Elgin* sank after a collision with a schooner on Lake Michigan off north suburban Glencoe, Illinois, causing the death of 279 persons.

The Chicago Fire

October 8–9, 1871 The Great Chicago Fire that consumed much of the city destroyed 17,450 buildings covering 2,100 acres and claimed an estimated 250 lives.

The Iroquois Theater Fire

December 30, 1903 The fire that swept Chicago's newly opened but as yet unfinished Iroquois Theater during a matinee performance of a play caused the deaths of 602, of which 150 were children.

The Glenwood Wreck

July 13, 1904 A special 12-car excursion passenger train on the Chicago & Eastern Illinois Railroad and packed with children from the Sunday school of the Doremus Congregational Church in Chicago on a return day trip from Momence, Illinois, slammed into the rear of a freight train in south suburban Glenwood, killing 18 children. The crew of a freight train, which was backing down the mainline to reach a siding, failed to post a flagman at the rear to warn other trains. The brakeman, who had only five months' experience in that capacity, and the engineer, who had only four months' experience on the railroad and disappeared the day after the crash, were blamed for the accident.[4]

The Miller, Indiana, Crash

June 19, 1909 Two Chicago, Lake Shore & South Bend (later Chicago, South Shore & South Bend) trains collided head-on east of Miller, Indiana, killing 12 and injuring 52 persons. The Indiana Railroad Commission investigation concluded that the motorman of the eastbound train failed to follow written orders to wait on a siding for the other train to pass.[5]

The Western Springs Wreck

July 14, 1912 A Chicago, Burlington & Quincy Railroad express mail and baggage train roared past an erroneously set green signal and slammed into the rear of the *Overland Express* stopped in west suburban Western Springs, killing 13. The disaster was the result of confusion between station operators who set the signals. The signals on the Burlington in those days had only two aspects, as they are known in the railroad industry—danger (red, or stop) and clear (green, or go)—and their operation required the constant relay of information by telephone back and forth between stations along the railroad.

The operators in stations were required to manually set the signals to danger as trains passed; however, they could reset the signals to clear (green) only after being advised by phone by the operator in the next station that the train had passed it. However, the operator in Western Springs misunderstood a request by an operator in Congress Park 14 miles to the east and set her signal to stop the *Overland Express* pas-

senger train. The Western Springs operator and brakeman on the train gave somewhat conflicting versions of what happened next, but the brakeman with his flag was only 1,200 feet behind his train, and the next signal at West Hinsdale was clear, or green, when an express mail and baggage train roared past it and slammed into the rear of the *Overland Express*.[6]

The Eastland Disaster

July 24, 1915 The steamship *Eastland* capsized on the Chicago River, drowning 844 persons.

The Circus Train Wreck

June 22, 1918 An empty troop train of 21 steel Pullman cars slammed into the rear of a stopped train of wooden cars pulling the Hagenbeck Wallace circus show bound for a performance in Hammond, Indiana, just to the west, killing 68 circus employees and performers but none of the menagerie. Because of an overheated hot box (railroad parlance for the box containing the axle bearings) on one of the cars, the 26-car circus train had stopped on a siding with its rearmost cars still on the mainline. Despite the fact that the line was protected by an automatic block signal system, the conductor sent a brakeman walking back along the line with a lantern to protect the rear of the train.

However, the engineer of the second train had fallen asleep at the throttle and blew a caution signal two miles behind the circus train, a stop signal a mile back, and soon thereafter the brakeman, who was frantically waving a red lantern. The brakeman later testified he also threw a lighted fusee (flare) through the locomotive cab window trying to awaken its crew. The troop train hit the rear of the circus train with such force that the rearmost cars were splintered, and the pile of wooden wreckage was ignited by kerosene lamps, roasting alive many of those who had survived the impact. Rescue crews later found 20 mangled bodies beneath the troop train locomotive, the crew of which survived without serious injury. The bodies of many of the victims were burned beyond recognition and buried in a mass grave in the circus showmen's section of Chicago's Woodlawn Cemetery.[7]

Kenosha Crossing Wreck

February 23, 1930 The driver of an automobile passed another car, which was stopped at the railroad crossing signals on Wisconsin Highway 43 to wait for an approaching North Shore freight, and went around the signals in an attempt to beat the freight over the crossing. However, a passenger train was simultaneously approaching from the other direction at 75 miles an hour. It hit the auto, killing both occupants, but its cars swaying from the impact caused it to sideswipe the passing freight, derailing both trains. A total of 12 persons died in the crash, and 95 were injured in what still stands as the worst grade-crossing accident in the Chicago area.[8]

Granville Avenue Wreck

November 24, 1936 A Chicago, North Shore & Milwaukee interurban train consisting of three steel cars plowed into the rear of an eight-car Chicago Rapid Transit Company elevated train that had cars of mixed wooden and steel construction and was stopped at the Granville Avenue station on the Howard line. The North Shore train plowed through 35 feet of the 40-foot wooden car at the end of the CRT train, killing 10 persons in the car and injuring 59. The steel CRT car immediately in front of the demolished one suffered only minor damage.[9]

The Naperville Wreck

April 25, 1946 The engineer aboard the Chicago, Burlington & Quincy's *Exposition Flyer* passenger express at 80 miles an hour blew a caution yellow signal about 1.2 miles behind the *Advance Flyer* stopped in Naperville, a red signal 934 feet behind the stopped train, and a brakeman waving his flag 800 feet behind the train. The *Exposition Flyer* plowed into the rear of the *Advance Flyer* at about 45 miles an hour, killing 45 persons and injuring 69.

Despite admonitions dating back to 1938 by the Interstate Commerce Commission against the mixing of cars of different weights and strengths in trains, just such a mixing of cars of differing construction contributed to the death toll. The last two cars of the 13-car *Advance Flyer* were of heavyweight steel construction, weighing 160,300 and 169,800 pounds, respectively, but the antepenultimate car was a relatively lightweight steel diner (115,800 pounds) of a type that had become popular on railroads in the 1930s. Although the heavyweight car in front of it suffered relatively light damage, the lightweight diner was bent into a U-shape by the force of the collision. Most of the casualties were in that car and the last car on the train, which had been demolished by the locomotive. The accident caused the railroad to upgrade its signal system further to display caution lights for two signal blocks behind trains and to adopt a standard of 1,250,000 pounds of buffing strength requiring, in effect, a double center sill, or keel, on all of its passenger cars. The Association of American Railroads standard for buff strength at the time was 800,000 pounds.[10]

Wilson Avenue Collision

November 5, 1956 An eight-car Chicago Transit Authority train slammed into the rear of a six-car North Shore limited stopped in the Wilson Avenue elevated station. The front of the first aluminum CTA car was crushed against the rear of the steel North Shore car, and eight persons died in the accident, which a Cook County Coroner's jury blamed on the CTA motorman.[11]

The Illinois Central Commuter Crash

October 30, 1972 An Illinois Central Gulf Railroad commuter train smashed into the rear end of another commuter train at a station just south of Chicago's Loop, killing 45 and injuring 300 in what was the worst railroad disaster in history within the Chicago city limits. The death toll would have been higher, but the accident occurred at the station serving Michael Reese Hospital and a block from Mercy Hospital, and emergency medical assistance was available within minutes.

The accident occurred when a four-car train consisting of new bilevel cars overshot the ICG's 27th Street station platform by 600 feet, forcing the motorman to back up to board and discharge passengers. He did so without having the conductor post a flagman to the rear, but in the process of backing up that distance he reset the automatic block signals from green to red. Unfortunately, an express train following by a few minutes had passed the signal tower before the signals changed from yellow to red, and it slammed into the stopped train at 45 miles an hour.

The express, which had not been scheduled to stop at 27th Street, was made up of single-level heavyweight steel cars manu-factured in the 1920s. They telescoped through the recently delivered, lighter-weight cars on the first train, causing the bulk of the fatalities.[12]

The DC-10 Crash at O'Hare

May 25, 1979 The city's worst aviation disaster occurred when an American Airlines DC-10 jumbo jet lost an engine on takeoff and crashed at O'Hare International Airport, killing 273 persons.

The Truck-Train Collision in Bourbonnais

March 15, 1999 An Amtrak train carrying 207 passengers and 21 crewmen bound from Chicago to New Orleans on the Illinois Central Railroad slammed into a trailer truck carrying steel in Bourbonnais, Illinois, about 50 miles south of Chicago, killing 11 persons on the train and injuring 122. The impact derailed both locomotives and 11 passenger cars, which also hit 2 freight cars parked on a siding before catching fire from the diesel fuel spilling from the locomotives. The accident was blamed on the truck driver, who had tried to race across the crossing after the lights had started flashing but before the gates had lowered.[13]

Notes

1—Before the Iron Horse

1. The French term *bateaux,* meaning *boats,* referred to both canoes and double-ended, planked rowboats that could be powered by oar, pole, or sail on relatively calm waters. The term was often confused with large canoes such as the *Canot du Maitre* favored by fur traders. Claiborne Adams Skinner, "The Sinews of Empire: The Voyageurs and the Carrying Trade of the *Pays d'en Haut*" (Ph.D. diss., University of Illinois, Chicago, 1990), 178–81.

2. James William Putnam, *The Illinois and Michigan Canal: A Study in Economic History* (Chicago, 1918), 20–21. Bucklin in his "Report to the Board of the Canal Commissioners," 1833, 17, estimated the cost of the canal at $4,107,440.43 and the railroad at $1,052,488.10.

3. Milo M. Quaife, *Chicago's Highways Old and New: From Indian Trail to Motor Road* (Chicago, 1923), 58–59. June Skinner Sawyers, *Chicago Portraits: Biographies of 250 Famous Chicagoans* (Chicago, 1991), 127–28.

4. Lottie E. Jones, *History of Vermillion County, Illinois* (Chicago, 1911), 148–71. Richard S. Simons and Francis H. Parker, *Railroads of Indiana* (Bloomington, Ind., 1997), 139–41. Bessie Louise Pierce, *A History of Chicago* (Chicago, 1937), 1:114.

5. Milo Milton Quaife, *Chicago and the Old Northwest, 1673–1835* (1913; reprint, Urbana, Ill., 2001), 262–84, and *Chicago's Highways Old and New,* 58–65. Gurdon Saltonstall Hubbard, *The Autobiography of Gurdon Saltonstall Hubbard: Pa-pa—ma-ta-be, "The Swift Walker"* (1889; reprint, Chicago, 1911). Sawyers, *Chicago Portraits,* 127–28. A. T. Andreas, *History of Chicago from Earliest Times to the Present Times* (Chicago, 1884), 1:110–11.

6. John F. Stover, *The Routledge Historical Atlas of the American Railroads* (New York, 1999), 12–13. For biographies of John Frink, see Quaife, *Chicago's Highways Old and New,* 157–61, and *Album of Genealogy and Biography,* Cook County, Ill., Chicago, 1897, 139–40. *Chicago Daily Democrat,* May 25, 1858. *Oswego Ledger-Sentinel,* August 9, 2001.

7. *Weekly Chicago Democrat,* May 25, 1847, and July 14, 1847. Quaife, *Chicago's Highways Old and New,* 157–58.

8. Andreas, *History of Chicago* 1:258, 377. *Album of Genealogy and Biography,* Cook County, Ill. (Chicago, 1897), 139–40. *Chicago Daily Democrat,* May 25, 1858.

9. Jones, *History of Vermillion County,* 148–71. Abraham Lincoln, letter published in Sangamo Journal, March 15, 1832, and reprinted in Roy P. Basler, ed., *Collected Works: The Abraham Lincoln Association, Springfield, Illinois* (New Brunswick, N.J., 1953), I:5–6. Robert P. Howard, *Illinois: A History of the Prairie State* (Grand Rapids, Mich., 1972), 197–98.

10. Abbott Payson Usher, *A History of Mechanical Inventions* (1929; reprint, New York, 1988), 356–57. Eugene S. Ferguson, *Oliver Evans: Inventive Genius of the American Industrial Revolution* (Greenville, Del., 1980), 9–13, 35. Robert H. Thurston, *A History of the Growth of the Steam Engine* (1878; reprint, Ithaca, N.Y., 1939), 151–52, 157–60. Grenville and Dorothy Bathe, *Oliver Evans: A Chronicle of Early American Engineering* (Philadelphia, 1935), 100. Eugene S. Ferguson, "The Steam Engine before 1830," Melvin Kranzberg and Carroll W. Russell, eds., *Technology in Western Civilization: The Emergence of Modern Industrial Society, Earliest Times to 1900* (Oxford, UK, 1967), 1:258–60.

11. Ludwig Klein, preface to Franz Anton Ritter Von Gerstner, *Early American Railroads* (Stanford, Calif., 1997), 39–40, originally published as *Die innern Communicationen der Vereingten Staaten von Nordamerica,* Germany in 1842–1843.

12. John F. Stover, *The History of the Baltimore & Ohio Railroad* (1987; West Lafayette, Ind., 1995), 32–33. James E. Vance, Jr., *The North American Railroad: Its Origin, Evolution, and Geography* (Baltimore, 1995). See John H. White, Jr., *American Locomotives: An Engineering History, 1830–1880,* rev. ed. (Baltimore, 1997), for the development of steam locomotives. John Reynolds, *My Own Times* (Chicago, 1879), 321–22. Donald J. Heimberger, *Wabash* (Forest Park, Ill., 1984), 14 (supplement). Howard, *Illinois,* 200–2.

13. Vance, *The North American Railroad,* 11, 125. D. W. Meinig, *The Shaping of America: A Geographical Perspective on 500 Years of History* (New Haven, Conn., 1993), 2:323–27.

14. Howard, *Illinois,* 193–202. Putnam, *The Illinois and Michigan Canal,* 115–17. Louis C. Hunter, *Steamboats on the Western Rivers: An Economic and Technological History* (1949; reprint, Mineola, N.Y., 1993), 585–605. David M. Young, *Chicago Maritime: An Illustrated History* (DeKalb, Ill., 2001), 145, using navigation tables and railroad timetables, noted that the distance between Chicago and Detroit is more than 600 miles by lake but only 283 miles by rail, and the route between Pittsburgh and St. Louis was 1,164 miles by river but only 612 miles by rail.

15. Gerstner, *Early American Railroads,* 389, 415. J. B. Mansfield, *History of the Great Lakes* (1899; reprint, Cleveland, 1972), 1:439.

16. Gerstner, *Early American Railroads,* 505–6.

17. Reynolds, *My Own Times,* 324.

18. Gerstner, *Early American Railroads,* 506–7. Reynolds, *My Own Times,* 322. H. Roger Grant, *"Follow the Flag": A History of the Wabash Railroad Company* (DeKalb, Ill., 2004), 12, noted that a 3.5-mile animal-powered railway line was built in 1837

and operated briefly between Naples, Illinois, a town just south of Meredosia on the Illinois River, and Bluffs, a community to the east that was situated in a natural gap in the palisades that dominated the river valley. A decade later that abandoned right of way was reused by the Sangamon & Morgan Railroad, which was later incorporated into the Wabash system.

19. Gerstner, *Early American Railroads,* 483–505. Andreas, *History of Chicago,* 1:246. Howard, *Illinois,* 193–202.

20. George M. McConnel, "Recollections of the Northern Cross Railroad," *Transactions of the Illinois State Historical Society,* XIII (Springfield, 1908), 145–52.

21. Stover, *Routledge Historical Atlas,* 10–11. Average stage-coach travel times computed from contemporary accounts, including Charles Dickens, *American Notes for General Circulation* (1842; reprint, New York, 1985), 201–45, and J. H. Buckingham's letters in Harry E. Pratt, ed., *Illinois as Lincoln Knew It: A Boston Reporter's Record of a Trip in 1847* (Springfield, Ill., 1938).

22. Wayne C. Temple, *Lincoln's Connections with the Illinois and Michigan Canal, His Return from Congress, and His Invention* (Springfield, Ill., 1986), 75–80. Quaife, *Chicago's Highways Old and New,* 162–67, offers some examples of the travails of stagecoach travel. A particularly humorous account of a stagecoach trip in Ohio was recounted by Dickens, *American Notes,* 201–45.

23. Note that horse-drawn freight vehicles of the period varied considerably in size. Among the most popular in long-distance commerce were the Conestoga wagon, with a capacity of five to six tons, and the Prairie Schooner, a covered wagon of about half that size. Assorted other wagons were also used in overland trade. Jack D. Rittenhouse, *American Horse-Drawn Vehicles* (New York, 1948), 47, 72–97. White, *American Locomotives,* 71.

24. Quaife, *Chicago's Highways Old and New,* 141–53. James E. Vance, Jr., *Capturing the Horizon: The Historical Geography of Transportation since the Sixteenth Century* (Baltimore, 1990), 178, 338.

25. Meinig, *The Shaping of America* 1:325, 362. Pierce, *A History of Chicago,* 1:11–12. See Quaife, *Chicago's Highways Old and New,* for an extensive discussion of the Indian trails serving Chicago.

26. Skinner, "Sinews of Empire," 162, 177–79. Sawyers, *Chicago Portraits,* 144–45.

27. Andreas, *History of Chicago,* 1:142. Pierce, *A History of Chicago,* 1:44.

28. Theodore J. Karamanski and Deane Tank, Sr., *Maritime Chicago* (Chicago, 2000), 17. Kenan Heise and Michael Edgerton, *Chicago: Center for Enterprise* (Woodland Hills, Calif., 1982), 1:49–50.

29. Gersten, *Early American Railroads,* 419–20. Hunter, *Steamboats on the Western Rivers,* 374–75, 442–43, 483–84, 572–74. Mansfield, *History of the Great Lakes,* 1:184–88.

30. Quaife, *Chicago's Highways Old and New,* 122–37.

31. Rolf Achilles, *Made in Illinois: A Story of Illinois Manufacturing* (Chicago, 1993), 20–21. Pierce, *A History of Chicago,* 1:144.

2—Arrival of the Railroads

1. William Z. Ripley, *Railroads: Finance and Organization* (New York, 1915), 4–5. William Cronon, *Nature's Metropolis: Chicago and the Great West* (New York, 1991), 81–83.

2. Harold M. Mayer, "The Railway Pattern of Metropolitan Chicago" (Ph.D. diss., University of Chicago, 1943), 14. Cronon, *Nature's Metropolis,* 60–61. Albro Martin, *Railroads Triumphant: The Growth, Rejection, and Rebirth of a Vital American Force* (Oxford, UK, 1992), 240.

3. Howard, *Illinois,* 198. John F. Stover, *History of the Illinois Central Railroad* (New York, 1975), 8. Pierce, *A History of Chicago,* 1:61. Theodore Calvin Pease, *The Frontier State, 1818–1848* (1918; reprint, Urbana, Ill., 1987), 208. Reynolds, *My Own Times,* 321–22.

4. H. Roger Grant, *The North Western: A History of the Chicago & North Western Railway System* (DeKalb, 1996), 8–9. W. H. Stennett, *Yesterday and To-day: A History of the Chicago & North Western Railway System* (Chicago, 1905), 7–8.

5. Pierce, *A History of Chicago,* 1:116, n. 214, citing the *Chicago Democrat* of January 20, 1846. Stennett, *Yesterday and To-day,* 10, citing Richard P. Morgan's 1847 report to Ogden.

6. Stennett, *Yesterday and To-day,* 10. William B. Ogden, railroad president, *Galena & Chicago Union Company Annual Report of 1848* (Chicago, 1848), 10. F. Howe, railroad secretary and treasurer, *Galena & Chicago Union Annual Report of 1848,* 20. Andreas, *History of Chicago,* 2:260.

7. Andreas, *History of Chicago,* 2:247. Grant, *The North Western,* 8–9. Ralph William Marshall, "The Early History of the Galena and Chicago Union Railroad" (Master's thesis, University of Chicago, 1937), 59–65. *Chicago Democrat,* October 5, 1847.

8. Andreas, *History of Chicago,* 2:247.

9. Andreas, *History of Chicago,* 2:247. Pierce, *A History of Chicago,* 2:35. *Galena & Chicago Union Railroad, Second Annual Report to Stockholders* (Chicago, March 5, 1849), 10. *Chicago Journal,* October 26, 1848.

10. Stennett, *Yesterday and To-day,* 14, 9–10, citing Richard P. Morgan, Galena & Chicago Union Stock Prospectus of Aug. 10, 1847, 14, 21. Andreas, *History of Chicago,* 2:262.

11. Ripley, *Railroads,* 5–11. He notes (p. 4) the interest of European investment in American railroads began at the time of the California gold rush in 1849. Stover, *History of the Illinois Central,* 37, attributes the meetings held in England to the formation of protective committees there after the IC, because of higher than expected construction costs, levied additional charges on stockholders in 1854–1857.

12. Alfred D. Chandler, Jr., *The Visible Hand: The Managerial Revolution in American Business* (Cambridge, Mass., 1977), 90, 92. Ripley, *Railroads,* 11–14.

13. Stennett, *Yesterday and To-day,* 17, 23, 48, 63.

14. Ibid, 7, 13, 16, 42.

15. Richard C. Overton, *Burlington Route: A History of the Burlington Lines* (New York, 1965), 4. Stephen James Buck, "Political and Economic Transformation in the Civil War Era: Du Page County, Ill., 1830–1880" (Ph.D. diss., Northern Illinois University, 1992), 52.

16. Overton, *Burlington Route,* 4–12.

17. John Lauritz Larson, *Bonds of Enterprise: John Murray Forbes and Western Development in America's Railway Age* (1984; reprint, Iowa City, Iowa, 2001), 48–49. Overton, *Burlington Route,* 8–9, noted that the first train operated September 2, 1850, between Batavia and Junction, but regular service between Aurora and Chicago over Galena Railroad tracks east of Junction did not commence until the following October 21.

18. William Edward Hayes, *Iron Road to Empire: The History of 100 Years of the Progress and Achievements of the Rock Island Lines* (Chicago, 1953), 3–7. Ronald Tweet, "The Continuing Journey of the Hennepin Canal," in the *Illinois and Mississippi Canal: History of the Rock Island District Corps of Engineers, 1866–1975,* internal report of the U.S. Army Corps of Engineers, Rock Island, Ill. (undated reprint by the Illinois Department of Natural Resources). Young, *Chicago Maritime,* 159–61.

19. Hayes, *Iron Road to Empire,* 10–15. F. Daniel Larkin, "Chicago & Rock Island Railroad," *Encyclopedia of American Business History and Biography: Railroads in the Nineteenth Century,* ed. Robert L. Frey (New York, 1988), 45–46.

20. Larson, *Bonds of Enterprise,* 49–52. Overton, *Burlington Route,* 11–38.

21. Grant, *The North Western,* 14–15. Stover, *History of the Illinois Central,* 11–12.

22. Hunter, *Steamboats on the Western Rivers,* 334–35, 585–86, 661, notes that annual steamboat arrivals at St. Louis from the Upper Mississippi increased from 656 in the 1845–1848 period to 947 in the 1866–1870 period before beginning a long decline.

23. Putnam, *The Illinois and Michigan Canal,* 110–11. Pierce, *A History of Chicago,* 2:492–99, tables citing *The Daily Democratic Press, Annual Review,* 1952 (Chicago, 1852), 10–11; Chicago Board of Trade, *Second Annual Statement, 1859* (Chicago, 1859), 83–104; *Seventh Annual Statement, 1864–1865,* 74–104; and *Fourteenth Annual Report, 1871* (Chicago, 1871), 86–109.

24. Illinois Central Railroad, Annual Report to Stockholders (Chicago, March 19, 1856), no page number, addendum table of passengers transported to and from each station during the year of 1856.

25. Wyatt Winton Belcher, *The Economic Rivalry between St. Louis and Chicago, 1850–1880* (New York, 1947), 63–64. James Neal Primm, *Lion of the Valley: St. Louis, Missouri* (Boulder, Colo., 1981), 294.

26. Grant, *The North Western,* 14–15. Stennett, *Yesterday and To-day,* 27. Stover, *History of the Illinois Central,* 135–36.

27. Stennett, *Yesterday and To-day,* 26–27.

28. Cronon, *Nature's Metropolis,* 267–68, 309.

29. Vance, *Capturing the Horizon,* 304.

30. Ibid.

31. Howard, *Illinois,* 199–200.

32. Putnam, *The Illinois and Michigan Canal,* 12–22, 34, 56. Pierce, *A History of Chicago,* 2:65, 70–72, 119–22.

33. Carlton J. Corliss, *Main Line of Mid-America: The Story of the Illinois Central* (New York, 1950), 2–10. Stover, *History of the Illinois Central,* 11–12.

34. Gregory S. Rose, "Extending the Road West," *The National Road,* Carl Raitz, ed. (Baltimore, 1996), 160–61. Corliss, *Main Line of Mid-America,* 16–20. Stover, *History of the Illinois Central,* 20–22.

35. Corliss, *Main Line of Mid-America,* 50.

36. Andreas, *History of Chicago,* 2:251–52. Vernon Carstensen, ed., *The Public Lands: Studies in the History of the Public Domain* (Madison, Wis., 1968), 139–46. David M. Ellis, "The Forfeiture of Railroad Land Grants, 1867–1894," *Mississippi Valley Historical Review,* June 1946, 27.

37. Corliss, *Main Line of Mid-America,* 124–28. Andreas, *History of Chicago,* 2:252–53.

38. Roswell B. Mason, letter of October 12, 1883, to C. C. P. Holden, reprinted in Andreas, *History of Chicago,* 2:253–55.

39. Pierce, *A History of Chicago,* 2:48–49. Lois Wille, *Forever Open, Clear, and Free: The Struggle for Chicago's Lakefront,* 2nd ed. (Chicago, 1991), 26–31. Stover, *History of the Illinois Central,* 43. Donald L. Miller, *City of the Century: The Epic of Chicago and the Making of America* (New York, 1996), 99–103.

40. Wille, *Forever Open, Clear, and Free,* 26–31.

41. Grant, *The North Western,* 25–28. Stennett, *Yesterday and To-day,* 35, 42.

42. Robert J. Casey and W. A. S. Douglas, *Pioneer Railroad: The Story of the North Western System* (New York, 1948), 76–80. Stennett, *Yesterday and To-day,* 34, 39–40. Grant, *The North Western,* 25.

43. Grant, *The North Western,* 25–27. Stennett, *Yesterday and To-day,* 42–43. Michael H. Ebner, *Creating Chicago's North Shore: A Suburban History* (Chicago, 1988), 21–22.

44. Ebner, *Creating America's North Shore,* 21–22. Stennett, *Yesterday and To-day,* 42–43.

3—Critical Mass

1. Alvin F. Harlow, *The Road of the Century: The Story of the New York Central* (New York, 1947), 70. Vance, *The North American Railroad,* 84–88.

2. Harold M. Mayer and Richard C. Wade, *Chicago: Growth of a Metropolis* (Chicago, 1969), 28–30.

3. Railroad classes are determined by gross operating revenues, which vary by the size of the individual carriers. Although the standards over the years have changed to reflect inflation, Class I railroads at the beginning of the twenty-first century were those with annual revenues of $261.9 million or more; Class II railroads had annual revenues of $21 million to $261.9 million; and Class III had annual revenues of under $21 million, according to the Association of American Railroads (www.aar.org). The data on railroads with Chicago in their names were culled from an admittedly incomplete list of North American railroads maintained by Carter S. Pawlus for the Sheboygan (Wisconsin) Society of Scale Model Railroad Engineers on March 3, 2003, best located by using a search engine instead of the cited URL of www.geocities.com/Vienna/Choir/6820.

4. Meinig, *The Shaping of America,* 2:259. Vance, *The North American Railroad,* 143.

5. Putnam, *The Illinois and Michigan Canal,* 20–25. James D. Dilts, *The Great Road: The Building of the Baltimore & Ohio, the Nation's First Railroad, 1828–1853* (Stanford, Calif., 1993), 212–13, citing the *Baltimore American* of March 11, 1836.

6. Stover, *History of the Baltimore & Ohio Railroad,* 113.

7. Ibid., 148, 150. Baltimore & Ohio Railroad, Fiftieth Annual Report (Baltimore, 1876), 14.

8. F. Daniel Larkin, "New York Central Railroad" and "Erie Railroad," *Encyclopedia of American Business History,* 282–85, 115–17.

9. Vance, *The North American Railroad,* 85. John F. Due, "Lake Shore & Michigan Southern Railway," *Encyclopedia of American Business History,* 220–21. Maury Klein, *The Life and Legend of Jay Gould* (Baltimore, 1986), 99–136, gives an account of the Erie Wars.

10. George H. Burgess and Miles C. Kennedy, *Centennial History of the Pennsylvania Railroad Company* (Philadelphia, 1946), 16–25. Thomas C. Cochrane, *Pennsylvania: A Bicentennial History* (New York, 1978), 90–94.

11. Cochrane, *Pennsylvania,* 99–100. Burgess and Kennedy, *Centennial History of the Pennsylvania Railroad,* 74–79, 176–78.

12. Edward Hungerford, *Men of Erie: A Story of Human Effort* (New York, 1946), 158–70, 180–99. William Reynolds, *European Capital, British Iron, and an American Dream: The Story of the Atlantic and Great Western Railroad* (Akron, Ohio, 2002), 43–60.

13. John A. Rehor, *The Nickel Plate Story* (Waukesha, Wis., 1965), 17–31.

14. Robert J. Parks, *Democracy's Railroads: Public Enterprise in Jacksonian Michigan* (Port Washington, N.Y., 1972), 43–60, 84–86, 134–39, noted that four separate canals were proposed between 1827 and 1830, but only two were approved in the Internal Improvements Act of 1837—the Allegan, Clinton & Kalamazoo Canal across the central portion of the state between Lake St. Clair just north of Detroit and Lake Michigan at the future site of Saugatuck, and a short, 14-mile canal between the Saginaw and Maple rivers that would permit cross-state navigation between Port Huron on Lake Huron and Grand Haven on Lake Michigan. Both projects were abandoned in the 1840s because of the state's deteriorating financial condition. Larson, *Bonds of Enterprise,* 32–33.

15. Parks, *Democracy's Railroads,* 43–49, 80–87, 95–96, 154–81.

16. David McClellan and Bill Warrick, *The Lake Shore & Michigan Southern Railway* (Polo, Ill., 1989), 9–12, 17–23, 25–34.

17. Larson, *Bonds of Enterprise,* 34–40.

18. John W. Brooks, *Report on the Merits of the Michigan Central Railroad* (Detroit, 1846), no page. Larson, *Bonds of Enterprise,* 40.

19. Due, "Lake Shore & Michigan Southern Railway," 220–21. Larson, *Bonds of Enterprise,* 48.

20. Andreas, *History of Chicago,* 2:156. Stover, *The History of the Illinois Central,* 34–35.

21. John Lauritz Larson, "Michigan Central Railroad," *Encyclopedia of American Business History,* 254–55, and *Bonds of Enterprise,* 40. McClellan and Warrick, *The Lake Shore & Michigan Southern,* 25–34.

22. Cleland B. Wyllie, "The History of the GTW Port Huron to Chicago Main Line," *Inside Track,* September 1972. *Durand Express,* May 18, 1961. Dale Berry, RRHX, "Railroad History Timeline" (Michigan Internet Railroad History Museum). www.michiganrailroads.com.

23. G. R. Stevens, *History of the Canadian National Railways* (New York, 1973), 34–40.

24. Ibid., 109–16. Wyllie, "The History of the GTW Port Huron to Chicago Main Line." *Durand Express,* May 18, 1961. Patrick C. Dorin, *The Grand Trunk Western Railway* (Seattle, 1977), 11–12.

25. George W. Hilton, *The Great Lakes Car Ferries* (Berkeley, Calif., 1962), 35. The Pere Marquette Historical Society, "A Condensed Time Line of the Pere Marquette," January 9, 2002, posted on www.railroadxing.com.

26. Quaife, *Chicago's Highways Old and New,* 66–67, 141–43. Pierce, *A History of Chicago,* 52–53.

27. Ronald E. Shaw, *Canals for a Nation: The Canal Era in the United States, 1790–1860* (Lexington, Ky., 1990), 138–43. James Rogers Taylor, *The Transportation Revolution, 1815–1860* (New York, 1951), 47–48.

28. Richard S. Simons, "Indiana's Lifeline: The Monon Railroad," Indiana State Historical Society (Indianapolis, 2003). George W. Hilton, *Monon Route* (Berkeley, Calif., 1978), 11, 21, 27, 39–47. Simons and Parker, *Railroads of Indiana,* 129–33. Maury Klein, *History of the Louisville & Nashville Railroad* (New York, 1972), 517–18.

29. Vance, *The North American Railroad,* 130–31. John F. Stover, *Iron Road to the West: American Railroads in the 1850s* (New York, 1978), 130–31. New York Central Railroad System, "History of the Cleveland, Cincinnati, Chicago & St. Louis Railway Company," annual report for the year 1913. George H. Drury, *The Historical Guide to North American Railroads* (Waukesha, Wis., 1992), 213. Edward A. Lewis, *American Shortline Railway Guide* (Waukesha, Wis., 1991), 132.

30. Hunter, *Steamboats on the Western Rivers,* 39, 326. Simons and Parker, *Railroads of Indiana,* 139–43.

31. Drury, *The Historical Guide to North American Railroads,* 64–69. Richard Saunders, Jr., *Merging Lines: American Railroads, 1900–1970* (DeKalb, Ill., 2001), 309–12. Klein, *History of the Louisville & Nashville Railroad,* 517–18. H. Craig Miner, *The Rebirth of the Missouri Pacific, 1956–1983* (College Station, Tex., 1983), 58–81. Elmer G. Sulzer, *Ghost Railroads of Indiana* (1970; reprint, Bloomington, Ind., 1998), 9–11, points out that 1,069 miles of mainline trackage in Indiana was ultimately abandoned, including the Chicago, Attica & Southern (1941–1950) and sections of the Big Four, Monon, Wabash, and Chicago & Eastern Illinois.

32. Pei-Lin Tan, "The Belt and Switching Railroads of the Chicago Terminal Area" (Ph.D. diss., University of Chicago, 1935), 34–35. August Derleth, *The Milwaukee Road: Its First Hundred Years* (1948; reprint, Iowa City, 2002), 206–7. Simons and Parker, *Railroads of Indiana,* 143, 216–19. Thomas H. Ploss, *The Nation Pays Again* (1983; reprint, Chicago, 1991), 19–20, 92–100. Ploss, a Milwaukee Road lawyer at the time, wrote (92–100) a

colorful description of the deteriorated condition of the line based on a trip he made over it in 1970 and was of the opinion the Milwaukee Road should never have acquired it.

33. Derleth, *The Milwaukee Road,* 15, 23.

34. Ibid., 56, 92, 288–89. *Milwaukee Free Democrat,* June 21, 1858.

35. Derleth, *The Milwaukee Road,* 98–99. Grant, *The North Western,* 29.

36. R. Milton Clark, "Chicago, Milwaukee, & St. Paul Railway," *Encyclopedia of American Business History,* 49–50. For some reason the Milwaukee Road has been one of the best documented of all American railroads. Other general histories of the railroad include Arthur Borak, *Financial History of the Chicago, Milwaukee & St. Paul Railway* (Minneapolis, 1929); John W. Cary, *The Organization and History of the Chicago, Milwaukee & St. Paul Railway Company* (Milwaukee, 1892); H. H. Field, *History of the Milwaukee Railroad* (Chicago, 1941); Herbert William Rice, *Early History of the Chicago, Milwaukee & St. Paul Railway* (Iowa City, 1938); Stanley W. Johnson, *The Milwaukee Road Revised* (Moscow, Idaho, 1997); and Jim Scribbens and Bob Hayden, *Milwaukee Road Remembered* (Milwaukee, 1990).

37. James Lydon, "History of the Wisconsin Central Railway," unpublished manuscript ca. early 1960s in the files of the Portage County (Wisconsin) Historical Society, Chapter 15 (no pages indicated). Vance, *The North American Railroad,* 278.

38. Maury Klein, *Union Pacific: The Rebirth, 1894–1969* (New York, 1989), 2:96–100. Saunders, *Merging Lines,* 20–24.

39. Frank N. Wilner, *Railroad Mergers: History, Analysis, Insight* (Omaha, Neb., 1997), 234–39, 252–53.

40. James Marshall, *Santa Fe: The Railroad that Built an Empire* (New York, 1945), 43–44. Keith L. Bryant, Jr., *History of the Atchison, Topeka & Santa Fe Railway* (New York, 1974), 23, 75, 134–35. William S. Greever, "Cyrus K. Holliday," *Encyclopedia of American Business History,* 183.

41. Marshall, *Santa Fe,* 202–5. Bryant, *History of the Atchison, Topeka & Santa Fe Railway,* 136–38, 157–58.

4—Bypassing Chicago

1. Primm, *Lion of the Valley,* 160, 210–38, noted that Missouri put up $7 million in bonds to capitalize Pacific Railroad across that state. Belcher, *The Economic Rivalry Between St. Louis and Chicago,* 89–91, 167–68. Carl W. Condit, *The Railroad and the City: A Technological and Urbanistic History of Cincinnati* (Columbus, Ohio, 1977), 7, 20, 23.

2. Stover, *Iron Road to the West,* 116 (table), 120–21 (table).

3. Shaw, *Canals for a Nation,* 126–34. Condit, *The Railroad and the City,* 7–11, 16, 23, 61–63, 99–119. Primm, *Lion of the Valley,* 233.

4. Belcher, *The Economic Rivalry Between St. Louis and Chicago, 1850–1880,* 72–74, 75–77. Primm, *Lion of the Valley,* 111–13.

5. Belcher, *The Economic Rivalry Between St. Louis and Chicago,* 75–78. Primm, *Lion of the Valley,* 215–20.

6. Belcher, *The Economic Rivalry Between St. Louis and Chicago,* 82–85.

7. Ibid., 89–91. Primm, *Lion of the Valley,* 217–18, 229.

8. *Sangamo Journal,* March 15, 1832. Pease, *The Frontier State, 1818–1848,* 205. Gene V. Glendinning, *The Chicago & Alton Railroad: The Only Way* (DeKalb, Ill., 2002), 9, citing the *Sangamo Journal* of November 14, 1834. "Bill Introduced in the Illinois Legislature Supplemental to Charter of the Springfield and Alton Turnpike Company" (Feb. 24, 1841), and 395–398, "Open Letter on the Springfield and Alton Railroad," dated June 30, 1847, and published in the *Sangamo Journal,* July 6, 1847, both reprinted in Basler, *Collected Works: Abraham Lincoln,* 1:250–52, 1:395–98.

9. "Report on the Alton and Springfield Railroad," reprinted in Basler, *Collected Works: Abraham Lincoln,* 1:398–405; Glendinning, *The Chicago & Alton Railroad,* 14.

10. Glendinning, *The Chicago & Alton Railroad,* 14, 16–17.

11. Thomas Ford, *A History of Illinois* (Chicago, 1945), 288–89. John H. Krenkel, *Illinois Internal Improvements, 1848–1848* (Cedar Rapids, Iowa, 1958), 72. Paul Simon, *Lincoln's Preparation for Greatness: The Illinois Legislative Years* (Norman, Okla., 1965), 76–105. Howard, *Illinois,* 198–99. Pierce, *A History of Chicago,* 1:44.

12. Heimburger, *Wabash,* 14 [supplement].

13. Klein, *The Life and Legend of Jay Gould,* 100, 233–34.

14. *New York Times,* August 7, 1941.

15. Grant, *"Follow the Flag,"* 133–90, discusses in detail in chapters 6 and 7 the Wabash's financial troubles and its relationship with the Pennsylvania Railroad.

16. Klein, *The Life and Legend of Jay Gould,* 251–55. Heimburger, *Wabash,* 21.

17. Paul H. Stringham, *Toledo, Peoria & Western: Tried, Proven & Willing* (Peoria, 1993), 1.

18. Pennsylvania Railroad, "Corporate Genealogy, Toledo, Peoria & Western," filed as a valuation report of June 30, 1918, with the Interstate Commerce Commission (Washington, D.C., January 1929), 23:958, 964–65, 974–77. Stringham, *Toledo, Peoria & Western,* 48.

19. Drury, *The Historical Guide to North American Railroads,* 324–26. Robert G. Lewis, *The Handbook of American Railroads* (New York, 1956), 230–31. Stringham, *Toledo, Peoria & Western,* 58–59.

20. Grant, *The North Western,* 189–99. Drury, *The Historical Guide to North American Railroads,* 193.

21. U.S. Railroad Retirement Board, "Employer Status Determination, Delaware Otsego Corp." (Chicago, April 24, 2002), B.C.D. 02-32.

22. Rail America Inc. (Boca Raton, Fla.), press releases of June 29 and September 7, 1999. U.S. Department of Transportation, Surface Transportation Board, "SF&L Railway Inc.—Acquisition and Operation Exemption—Toledo, Peoria & Western Railway Corporation between La Harpe and Peoria, Ill." STB Finance Docket No. 33996 (Washington, D.C., October 15, 2002), and "SF&L Railway Inc.—Abandonment Exemption—In Hancock, McDonough, Fulton, and Peoria Counties, Ill., STB Docket

No. AB-448 (Sub-No. 2X) (Washington, D.C., January 31, 2003).

23. Stringham, *Toledo, Peoria & Western*, 58–59. Lewis, *The Handbook of American Railroads*, 230–31. Rail America Inc., press release of June 29, 1999.

24. John Swartz, president of the Santa Fe Railway, press release of Feb. 3, 1989. Simons and Parker, *Railroads of Indiana*, 104.

25. Reynolds, *European Capital, British Iron, and an American Dream*, 24–25, 53–54.

26. Vance, *The North American Railroad*, 113–17, notes that other popular gauges on early American railroads were 5 feet in the South and 5 feet 6 inches in Canada and Maine. Most American railroads adopted the standard 4-feet-8 1/2-inch gauge between the end of the Civil War and 1896. Reynolds, *European Capital, British Iron, and an American Dream*, 224–28.

27. Howard, *Illinois*, 246. OPRT Management Commission, Forest Preserve District of Will County, "Old Plank Road Trail," History (Joliet, 2003), www.oprt.org.

28. Derleth, *The Milwaukee Road*, 206–7. Richard Saunders, Jr., *Main Lines: Rebirth of the North American Railroads, 1970–2002* (DeKalb, Ill., 2003), 162–63. Ploss, *The Nation Pays Again*, 94–95. Illinois Department of Transportation, Bureau of Railroads, "Rail Line Abandonments in Illinois" (Springfield, Ill.), 1978, 1979, 1980.

29. George W. Hilton and John F. Due, *The Electric Interurban Railways in America* (Stanford, Calif., 1960), 338–42. George S. Rogers, "Chicago Area Interurban Systems (1892–1963): A Brief History" (Chicago Regional Transportation Authority, 1976), 1, 3–5. The railroads, their terminals, mileage, and dates of operation, included the Chicago & Interurban Traction Co., from 79th Street in Chicago 54 miles to Kankakee, 1907–1927; the Joliet & Eastern Traction Co., from Chicago Heights 20 miles to Joliet, 1909–1923; the Aurora, Plainfield & Joliet Railway, from Joliet 20 miles to Aurora, 1901–1924; and the Aurora, Elgin & Fox River, from Aurora 37 miles to Elgin, 1906–1935.

30. Hilton and Due, *The Electric Interurban Railways in America*, 339, 346–49. Drury, *The Historical Guide to North American Railroads*, 160–62. Thomas R. Bullard, *Interurban Empire Builders* (Oak Park, Ill., 1989, unpublished manuscript), 32–35.

31. Frank P. Donovan, Jr., *Mileposts on the Prairie: The Story of the Minneapolis & St. Louis Railway* (New York, 1950), 13, 22.

32. Ibid., 63–64, 152.

33. H. Roger Grant, *The Corn Belt Route: A History of the Chicago Great Western Railroad Company* (DeKalb, Ill., 1984), 1–33, 176–85, 209–10, 3–7, 173–96.

34. Michael W. Blaszak, "Belt Railway of Chicago: Back from the Brink," *Trains*, July, 1993, 46–47.

35. Michael Krieger, *Where Rails Meet the Sea: America's Connections Between Ships & Trains* (New York, 1998), 77–83.

36. Hilton, *The Great Lakes Car Ferries*, 1–3, 55–56, 69–82.

37. Ibid., 68, 111–20, 262–63.

38. Krieger, *Where Rails Meet the Sea*, 81. Karl Zimmermann, *Lake Michigan's Railroad Car Ferries* (Andover, N.J., 1993), 19–28, indicates that by the time the C&O petitioned the Interstate Commerce Commission on March 18, 1975, to abandon service, its car ferry fleet had been reduced from eight ships to three and was losing $4 million a year.

5—Shaping Chicago

1. Milo M. Quaife, *Lake Michigan* (Indianapolis, 1944), 116, 119.

2. Donald F. Wood and James C. Johnson, *Contemporary Transportation* (Upper Saddle River, N.J., 1996), 100–1, 133–34, 252–63, 408–11.

3. Cronon, *Nature's Metropolis*, 55, 82, 90–93.

4. Mayer and Wade, *Chicago*, 40–42.

5. Achilles, *Made in Illinois*, 29. John Moses and Joseph Kirkland, *The History of Chicago, Illinois* (Chicago, 1895), 1:240–41.

6. Andreas, *History of Chicago*, 1:571, 3:733.

7. Stennett, *Yesterday and To-Day*, 13. Hunter, *Steamboats on the Western Rivers*, 362. Mansfield, *History of the Great Lakes*, 1:439.

8. Ripley, *Railroads*, 69–88, discusses railroad earnings in the nineteenth and early twentieth centuries.

9. Putnam, *The Illinois and Michigan Canal*, 104–13.

10. Cronon, *Nature's Metropolis*, 371–85.

11. Stennett, *Yesterday and To-Day*, 10. Pierce, *A History of Chicago*, 2:492, citing the *Chicago Democratic Press, Annual Review*, 1852, 10–11.

12. Chicago Board of Trade, *Second Annual Statement* (Chicago, 1859), 83–104.

13. Lewis Coe, *The Telegraph: A History of Morse's Invention and Its Predecessors in the United States* (Jefferson, N.C., 1993), 38–42, notes that in 1861 the telegraph rate between San Francisco and Chicago was $5.60 for the first ten words and 50¢ a word thereafter; 134, cites the Erie Railroad in 1851 as the first to use telegraph for train dispatching; and 133–39, discusses the railroads and telegraph in general.

14. Chicago Board of Trade, *Second Annual Statement* (Chicago, 1859), 83-104.

15. Cronon, *Nature's Metropolis*, 106–20.

16. Ibid., 112.

17. Martin, *Railroads Triumphant*, 168.

18. Putnam, *The Illinois and Michigan Canal*, 92, 112–15. Martin, *Railroads Triumphant*, 240. Cronon, *Nature's Metropolis*, 209–59.

19. Miller, *City of the Century*, 205–16. Cronon, *Nature's Metropolis*, 209–10. Chicago Board of Trade, *Fourteenth Annual Report* (Chicago, 1871), 86–109. John H. White, Jr., *The American Railroad Freight Car* (Baltimore, 1993), 31.

20. White, *The American Railroad Freight Car*, 31. Cronon, *Nature's Metropolis*, 225–32.

21. Sawyers, *Chicago Portraits*, 16–17, 240–41, contains short biographies of Armour and Swift. See also Louis Carroll Wade, *Chicago's Pride: The Stockyards, Packingtown, and Environs in the Nineteenth Century* (Urbana, Ill., 1987). Harper Leech and John Charles Carroll, *Armour and His Times* (New York, 1938); and Louis F. Swift, with Arthur Van Vlissingen, Jr., *Yankee of the Yards: The Biography of Gustavus Franklin Swift* (Chicago, 1927).

22. Cronon, *Nature's Metropolis*, 232. White, *The American Railroad Freight Car*, 284.

23. Cronon, *Nature's Metropolis*, 239.

24. International Harvester Co., *Roots in Chicago* (Chicago, 1947), centennial corporate history, 12.

25. Heise and Edgerton, *Chicago*, 1:86–87. Wayne G. Broehl Jr., *John Deere's Company: A History of Deere and Company and its Times* (New York, 1984), 122. Stewart H. Holbrook, *Machines of Plenty: Pioneering in American Agriculture* (New York, 1955), 47.

26. Andreas, *History of Chicago*, 3:387, 471–75. Pierce, *A History of Chicago*, 2:114–15.

27. Martin, *Railroads Triumphant*, 218. Chicago Board of Trade, *Fourteenth Annual Report*, 86–109

28. White, *The American Railroad Freight Car*, 19–24, 122. Corliss, *Main Line of Mid-America*, 73–75. The conversion occurred between 1855, when the IC began testing the fuel, and 1866.

29. International Harvester Co., *Roots in Chicago*, 12.

30. Ibid., 17–18.

31. Chandler, *The Visible Hand*, 217.

32. Mayer and Wade, *Chicago*, 118. Perry R. Duis, *Challenging Chicago: Coping with Everyday Life, 1837–1920* (Urbana, Ill., 1998), 193.

33. Mayer and Wade, *Chicago*, 118–22, 234. Duis, *Challenging Chicago*, 193.

34. Chandler, *The Visible Hand*, 16.

35. Ibid., 188.

36. Ibid., 17, 41, 79–80.

6—The Suburbs

1. Ann Durkin Keating, *Building Chicago: Suburban Developers and the Creation of a Divided Metropolis* (Columbus, Ohio, 1988), Map 2, 210, and 98–119 for a detailed analysis of Chicago's annexations of suburbs in the nineteenth century. Metra, "1999 Weekday Outlying Station Ranking of Total Boardings," statistical tables in the files of Metra's Chicago offices, shows the IC's 59th Street station at the University of Chicago with 1,571 daily boardings, and the North Western's north line stations at Ravenswood with 1,246 boardings and at Rogers Park with 1,072 boardings, ranking those stations, respectively, as 22nd, 40th, and 56th among the commuter railroad agency's 235 stations in terms of ridership.

2. U.S. Census of 1880, 1890, and 1900. Illinois Secretary of State, *Blue Book*, Incorporated Municipalities (Springfield, Ill., 1905). Keating, *Building Chicago*, 183–84 (table 8), 197 (table 20).

3. Rufas Blanchard, *History of Du Page County, Illinois* (Chicago, 1882), no page indicated.

4. Keating, *Building Chicago*, 13–14, 178 (table 4), 209 (map 1).

5. Ibid., 13–14, 178 (table 4), 209 (map 1).

6. Ibid., 180–81 (table 6), 182 (table 7).

7. Ibid., 180–81, Homewood, 23 miles south of Chicago on the Illinois Central, and Matteson, 28 miles south, were still predominantly agricultural in 1860; and, 30, indicates Wright's Grove, although it had no railroad depot, had a commuter economy.

8. Joseph P. Schwieterman and Martin E. Toth, *Shaping Contemporary Suburbia: Perspectives on Development Control in Metropolitan Chicago* (Chicago, 2001), 5–10.

9. Mileages from Chicago to various suburbs vary considerably depending upon how the route is measured. For example, Riverside can be described as being 12 miles from Chicago as measured in a straight line from State and Madison in Chicago's Loop to the geographical center of the village as measured on DeLorme Mapping, *Illinois Atlas and Gazetteer* (Freeport, Maine, 1991), 29; 11 miles from Union Station along the route of the Burlington Railroad; or 13 miles by automobile using the most direct route via Roosevelt Road and Ogden Avenue. An 1883 Burlington timetable gives the distance as 12 miles from Central Station at the lakefront to Riverside. The distance cited in the text and subsequent references for distances to suburbs are railroad route miles from downtown depots as cited by Metra, "1999 Weekday Outlying Station Ranking of Total Boardings," a table that includes the MP, or milepost, of every commuter railroad depot from its respective downtown terminal.

10. Kenneth T. Jackson, *Crabgrass Frontier: The Suburbanization of the United States* (New York, 1985), 61–67, 79–81. Robert Fishman, *Bourgeois Utopias: The Rise and Fall of Suburbia* (New York, 1987), 122–33. Catharine Beecher, *Treatise on Domestic Economy, For the Use of Young Ladies at Home and School* (New York, 1847). Andrew Jackson Downing, *Cottage Residences* (1842; reprint, New York, 1981).

11. Fishman, *Bourgeois Utopias*, 126–33.

12. Quaife, *Chicago's Highways Old and New*, 76. Chicago, Burlington & Quincy Railroad, *Chicago-Aurora Centennial: 1864–1964* (Chicago, 1964), 7.

13. Walter L. Creese, *The Crowning of the American Landscape* (Princeton, N.J., 1985), 219–40. Keating, *Building Chicago*, 73–74. Jackson, *Crabgrass Frontier*, 79–81.

14. Keating, *Building Chicago*, 172–75, table 1.

15. Ebner, *Creating Chicago's North Shore*, 16–18, 40.

16. C. W. Richmond and H. F. Valette, *A History of the County of Du Page, Illinois* (Chicago, 1857), no page indicated. Buck, "Political and Economic Transformation in the Civil War Era," 52.

17. Joseph P. Schwieterman, *When the Railroad Leaves Town: American Communities in the Age of Rail Line Abandonment* (Kirksville, Mo., 2001), 64–65.

18. Jean Moore, *Wheaton: A Pictorial History* (St. Louis, 1994), 8–13.

19. The populations cited here and in subsequent paragraphs are from the decennial federal censuses for 1850, 1860, 1870, 1880, 1890, and 1900. Buck, "Political and Economic Transformation in the Civil War Era," 59–67.

20. Schwieterman, *When the Railroad Leaves Town*, 64–65. Buck, "Political and Economic Transformation in the Civil War Era," 499.

21. The data are for the suburbs of Riverside, Brookfield, La Grange, Western Springs, Hinsdale, Downers Grove, and Naperville, but they exclude Cicero and Berwyn because they were also served by street and elevated railways by the turn of the century, distorting the effect steam railroads had on population

growth. Aurora was also excluded because in the nineteenth century it was an industrial satellite city and did not acquire suburban characteristics until later in the twentieth century. Chicago, Burlington & Quincy Suburban Time Table (Chicago, 1883), outbound trains.

22. The corridor included the communities of River Forest, Maywood, Melrose Park, Elmhurst, Lombard, Glen Ellyn, Wheaton, West Chicago, and Geneva, but not Oak Park, which had street and elevated railway service.

23. Blanchard, History of Du Page County, Ill., 280–81, 291–92. Buck, "Political and Economic Transformation in the Civil War Era," 386–87. The data refer to the suburbs of River Grove, Franklin Park, and Bensenville, all in existence in 1900, but not Elgin, an industrial satellite city in Kane County served by several railroads.

24. Alan R. Lind, Limiteds Along the Lakefront: The Illinois Central in Chicago (Park Forest, Ill., 1986), 54, 129–31.

25. Population data here, as elsewhere, were taken from the U.S. censuses for 1860, 1870, 1880, 1890, and 1900. Illinois Secretary of State, Blue Book (Springfield, Ill., 1905), 438–55, includes the dates of incorporation of the various municipalities.

26. Pierce, A History of Chicago, 2:143–44. Isaac N. Arnold, William B. Ogden and Early Days in Chicago (Chicago, 1881), 6–8. Grant, The North Western, 8–9. Ebner, Creating Chicago's North Shore, 21–23.

27. Ebner, Creating Chicago's North Shore, 21–23.

28. Wisconsin Central Railroad passenger time table, January 31, 1887. Charles Stats, "Wisconsin Central Lines: Suburban Service at Chicago, 1887–1897," The Soo, 6, 1 (January, 1984), Soo Line Historical and Technical Society Inc., Neenah, Wis., 8–20.

29. Stats, "Wisconsin Central Lines: Suburban Service at Chicago," 1887–1897, The Soo, 6, 2 (April 1984), 14, 19, 8–33.

30. Ebner, Creating Chicago's North Shore, 114–24.

31. Chicago, Milwaukee & St. Paul Railway, "Time Table of Suburban Trains, Evanston Division, July 24, 1895." Bruce G. Moffat, The L: The Development of Chicago's Rapid Transit System, 1888–1932, Central Electric Railfans' Bulletin No. 131 (Chicago, 1995), 210–16.

32. William D. Middleton, North Shore: America's Fastest Interurban (San Marino, Calif., 1964), 15–17. Moffat, The L, 210–16.

33. Everett Chamberlin, Chicago and Its Suburbs (Chicago, 1874), 204–5. U.S. Census of 1860. Illinois Secretary of State, Blue Book, Incorporated Municipalities (Springfield, Ill., 1905). Atlas of Du Page County (Elgin, Ill., 1874), in the Du Page County Historical Society, Wheaton, Ill.

34. Richard P. Morgan in the Galena & Chicago Union stock prospectus of August 10, 1847, as cited by Stennett, Yesterday and To-Day, 10, projected that the proposed Galena & Chicago Union would produce $393,000 in total revenue in its first year of operation between Chicago and Galena, of which less than half ($150,000) would be from passengers.

35. Stennett, Yesterday and To-Day, 42–44. Ebner, Creating Chicago's North Shore, 16–18, 40.

7—Travelers and Terminals

1. Putnam, The Illinois and Michigan Canal, 111. Hunter, Steamboats on the Western Rivers, 484–88.

2. Duis, Challenging Chicago, 35–36.

3. Robert B. Shaw, A History of Railroad Accidents, Safety Precautions and Operating Practices, 2nd ed. (Potsdamn, N.Y., 1978), 1–12. Martin, Railroads Triumphant, 102–6. John F. Stover, American Railroads (1961; reprint, Chicago, 1997), 155, 156. See also Oliver Jensen, The American Heritage History of Railroads in America (Avenel, N.J., 1975), 178–89, for a concise, illustrated history of some of the more famous train wrecks.

4. Shaw, A History of Railroad Accidents, 474–80, enumerates on a year-by-year basis major accidents on American railroads between 1831 and 1900. George W. Hilton, Eastland: Legacy of the Titanic (Stanford, Calif., 1997), 137 (table 3).

5. Shaw, A History of Railroad Accidents, 9–10.

6. David M. Young, Chicago Transit: An Illustrated History (DeKalb, Ill., 1998), 15–16, 35.

7. Parmelee Transportation Company, An Essential Link in American Transportation, 1853–1953 (Chicago, 1953), 7–14. Robert G. Parmelee, "The Fight for Chicago's Railroad Transfer Business," undated manuscript ca. 1996 in author's collection, 1–3, notes that "The Parmelee Transportation Company by 1930 was owned by Morris Markin, principal in the Checker Cab Manufacturing Company, who formed Continental Air Transport Company to haul passengers to and from Chicago Municipal (later Midway) Airport."

8. Chicago City Council, Special Ordinances of Chicago (Chicago, 1898), X:265 (p. 527); Chicago & Galena Union Railroad Co. (July 17, 1848), X:278 (p. 544); Chicago & Rock Island Railroad Co. (May 26, 1851), X:329 (p. 642); Illinois Central Railroad Co. (June 7, 1852), X:358 (p. 710); Pittsburgh, Fort Wayne & Chicago Railroad Co. (Feb. 13, 1854), X:344 (p. 682); Illinois & Wisconsin Railroad Company (Oct. 4, 1852), VIII:197 (p. 406); Chicago & Alton Railroad Company (April 11, 1853), VIII:206 (p. 419); Pittsburgh, Ft. Wayne & Chicago Railroad Company (February 13, 1854), X:358 (p. 710), (August 16, 1858), X:363 (p. 717); and Chicago, Burlington & Quincy Railroad Company (Dec. 15, 1862), VIII:206 (p. 419).

9. Carl W. Condit, Chicago, 1910–1929: Building, Planning and Urban Technology (Chicago, 1973), 39. Moffat, The L, 166–85; Brian J. Cudahy, Destination Loop: The Story of Rapid Transit Railroading in and Around Chicago (Brattleboro, Vt., 1982), 19–34; and Young, Chicago Transit, 59–62, all contain discussions of the Loop L.

10. Chicago City Council, Special Ordinances of Chicago, X:265 (p. 527); Chicago & Galena Union Railroad Co. (July 17, 1848), X:278 (p. 544); Chicago & Rock Island Railroad Co. (May 26, 1851), X:329 (p. 642); Illinois Central Railroad Co. (June 7, 1852), X:358 (p. 710); Pittsburgh, Fort Wayne & Chicago Railroad Co. (Feb. 13, 1854), X:344 (p. 682); Illinois & Wisconsin Railroad Company (Oct. 4, 1852), VIII:197 (p. 406); Chicago & Alton Railroad Company (April 11, 1853), VIII:206 (p. 419); Pittsburgh, Ft. Wayne & Chicago Railroad Company (February

13, 1854), X:358 (p. 710), (August 16, 1858), X:363 (p. 717); and Chicago, Burlington & Quincy Railroad Company (Dec. 15, 1862), VIII:206 (p. 419).

11. Ibid.

12. Duis, *Challenging Chicago*, 36–37.

13. Carroll L. V. Meeks, *The Railroad Station: An Architectural History* (1965; reprint, New York, 1995), 81–82, 109.

14. City Council Committee on Railway Terminals, "The Railway Passenger Terminal Problem at Chicago" (Chicago, December 1933), 27–30.

15. Grant, *The North Western*, 21. Corliss, *Main Line of Mid-America*, 50–60. Hayes, *Iron Road to Empire*, 19–20.

16. Ira J. Bach and Susan Wolfson, *A Guide to Chicago's Train Stations: Present and Past* (Athens, Ohio, 1986), xix–xx.

17. Stennett, *Yesterday and To-Day*, 15, 23; Galena & Chicago Union Railroad company, *Third Annual Report to Stockholders* (Chicago, June 5, 1850), 10; *Ninth Annual Report to Stockholders* (June 4, 1856), 21.

18. Corliss, *Main Line of Mid-America*, 50. Stover, *History of the Illinois Central*, 43–44.

19. *Chicago Daily Democrat*, October 13, 1852. Hayes, *Iron Road to Empire*, 20–21.

20. Chicago City Council, *Special Ordinances of Chicago*, X:278 (p. 544) Chicago & Rock Island Railroad Co. (May 26, 1851). X:329 (p. 642), Illinois Central Railroad Co. (June 7, 1852).

21. *Chicago Tribune*, December 18, 1866. Hayes, *Iron Road to Empire*, 81–85.

22. Glendinning, *The Chicago & Alton Railroad*, 51–52, 117–18. Burgess and Kennedy, *Centennial History of the Pennsylvania Railroad Company*, 123. Bach and Wolfson, *A Guide to Chicago's Train Stations*, 8–9.

23. Hunter, *Steamboats on the Western Rivers*, 529–33, notes that Congress in 1852 passed the Steamboat Inspection Act to put some teeth into the regulations originally imposed in 1837 in the Steamboat Act. See Young, *Chicago Maritime*, 97–14, for Chicago maritime disasters.

24. Shaw, *A History of Railroad Accidents*, 99–102. David McLellan and Bill Warrick, *The Lake Shore & Michigan Southern Railway* (Polo, Ill., 1989), 119–21.

25. Shaw, *A History of Railroad Accidents*, Appendix.

26. Ibid., 61–64, placed the death toll at 82. Helen Louise Plaster Stoutemyer, *The Train that Never Arrived: A Saga of the Niagara Excursion Train that Wrecked between Chatsworth and Piper City August 10, 1887* (Fairbury, Ill., 1970), 13, 34; and *Chicago Tribune*, August 14, 1887, both said the toll was 85.

27. John H. White, Jr., *The American Railroad Passenger Car* (Baltimore, 1978), 1:116. Rudyard Kipling, *American Notes: Rudyard Kipling's West* (1891; reprint, Norman, Okla., 1981), 129.

28. White, *The American Railroad Passenger Car*, 1:130–31, 2:662.

29. Ibid., 2:661–63, 1:311–42.

30. Miller, *City of the Century*, 177–78. Cronon, *Nature's Metropolis*, 345–50.

31. Karen Sawislak, *Smoldering City: Chicagoans and the Great Fire, 1871–1874* (Chicago, 1995), 74, 49–67. Cronon, *Nature's Metropolis*, 345. Miller, *City of the Century*, 163. Stover, *History of the Illinois Central*, 182. Glendinning, *The Chicago & Alton Railroad*, 93–94. Pierce, *A History of Chicago*, 3:7. J. Seymour Currey, *Chicago: Its History and Its Builders* (Chicago, 1912), 2:219.

32. Bach and Wolfson, *A Guide to Chicago's Train Stations*, 26–28.

33. Ibid., 22–23.

34. Ibid., 24–25.

35. Interstate Commmerce Commission, *Corporate Geneology, Chicago Union Station Company* (Washington, D.C., 1935). Bach and Wolfson, *A Guide to Chicago's Train Stations*, 30–37.

36. Bach and Wolfson, *A Guide to Chicago's Train Stations*, 14–15.

37. Ibid., 16–19. Chicago Association of Commerce, *Chicago Railroad Passenger Statistics* (Chicago, 1931), report in author's collection.

38. Klein, *Union Pacific*, 1:9–10, noted that in the 1840s a 5,250-mile trip by sea from New York to California via the Panama portage took 35 days, and a 2,800-mile journey by stagecoach from St. Louis to San Francisco took 30 days.

39. Charles J. Balesi, *The Time of the French in the Heart of North America* (Chicago, 1996), 156–57. Pierce, *A History of Chicago*, 1:17, 29. Miller, *City of the Century*, 60–61.

40. Andreas, *History of Chicago*, 1:132, 629–35; 2:501–9. Pierce, *History of Chicago*, 2:39n.

41. *Weekly Chicago Democrat*, November 10, 1846, and May 4, June 29, July 6, and July 13, 1847. Pierce, *A History of Chicago*, 1:395–97, 425–28.

42. Heise and Edgerton, *Chicago*, 1:85–87, 89–92.

43. Mayer and Wade, *Chicago*, 60.

44. Hunter, *Steamboats on the Western Rivers*, 585–605. Young, *Chicago Maritime*, 151–54, 187–90. Pierce, *A History of Chicago*, 2:7–10. Ross Miller, *American Apocalypse: The Great Fire and the Myth of Chicago* (Chicago, 1990), 23.

45. Carlton J. Corliss, *The Day of Two Noons*, Association of American Railroads (Washington, D.C., 1952), 1–14. Chicago Railroad Fair, Official Guide Book (Chicago, 1948); The Chicago Fair, Official Guide Book (Chicago, 1950). Cronon, *Nature's Metropolis*, 341–69. Miller, *City of the Century*, 488–532. Illinois Central Railroad Company, *Annual Report to Stockholders* (Chicago, 1894), summary of business for the year ended June 30, 1894.

46. Frank A. Smith, *Transportation in America, 1992: A Statistical Analysis of Transportation in the United States*, Eno Foundation for Transportation (Vienna, Va., 1992), 47, Intercity Travel by Mode. Chicago Convention and Tourism Bureau, Hotel Facts, 1993.

8—The Bottleneck

1. E. L. Corthell, "The Chicago Railway Terminal Problem, From an Engineering Standpoint," in *The Chicago Railway Terminal Problem*, report of the Chicago Terminal Commission to the Mayor and City Council (Chicago, May 12 and July 11, 1892), 69–71.

2. Mayer, "The Railway Pattern of Metropolitan Chicago," 128.

3. Condit, *Chicago, 1910–1929,* 41–42. Mayer and Wade, *Chicago,* 120–22. Cronon, *Nature's Metropolis,* 345–48. Miller, *City of the Century,* 176–78.

4. Putnam, *The Illinois and Michigan Canal,* 116–17. Harold M. Mayer, *The Port of Chicago and the St. Lawrence Seaway* (Chicago, 1957), 13.

5. *Railway Age,* July 12, 1889, 455. Ronald L. Batory, president of the Belt Railway of Chicago, interview with author, February 1998. *Chicago Tribune,* April 7, 1999.

6. Mayer, "The Railway Pattern of Metropolitan Chicago," 42.

7. White, *The American Railroad Freight Car,* 64–65.

8. Overton, *Burlington Route,* 9–13.

9. W. W. Baldwin, *Corporate History of the Chicago, Burlington & Quincy Railroad Company and Affiliated Companies (as of June 30, 1917)* (Chicago, 1917), a report prepared pursuant to the Interstate Commerce Commission Valuation Order No. 20, 32–34.

10. Andreas, *History of Chicago,* 3:335.

11. Cronon, *Nature's Metropolis,* 221–59.

12. *Chicago Tribune,* Transportation Section, March 1, 1998. Tan, "The Belt and Switching Railroads of Chicago Terminal Area," 37–43.

13. Tan, "The Belt and Switching Railroads of Chicago Terminal Area," 52–55. Blaszak, "Belt Railway of Chicago," 46–53. The Belt Railway of Chicago, Annual Report 2000 (Chicago, 2000), 1, selected financial and reporting highlights.

14. Tan, "The Belt and Switching Railroads of Chicago Terminal Area," 58–59. Michael W. Blaszak, "Baltimore and Ohio Chicago Terminal" (unpublished manuscript, 1993), 1–2. CSX Transportation, "Baltimore & Ohio Chicago Terminal," fact sheet prepared by the corporate communications department, Jacksonville, Fla., 1998, 1.

15. Tan, "The Belt and Switching Railroads of Chicago Terminal Area," 58–59. Blaszak, "Baltimore and Ohio Chicago Terminal," 1–3. CSX, "Baltimore & Ohio Chicago Terminal," 1–2.

16. Michael W. Blaszak, "Whither the Indiana Harbor Belt," *Trains,* March, 1986, 22–37. Charles H. Allen, general manager of the Indiana Harbor Belt Railroad Company, interview of February 3, 1998, with the author. Tan, "The Belt and Switching Railroads of Chicago Terminal Area," 55–58.

17. Michael W. Blaszak, "Big Steel's Belt Line," *Trains,* August 1989, 26–35. Tan, "The Belt and Switching Railroads of Chicago Terminal Area," 63–64.

18. *Chicago Tribune,* Transportation Section, March 1, 1998.

19. Lewis, *American Shortline Railway Guide,* 2–3, 61–62, 152. Tan, "The Belt and Switching Railroads of Chicago Terminal Area," 37–43.

20. Bruce G. Moffat, *The Chicago Tunnel Story: Exploring the Railroad "Forty Feet Below."* Central Electric Railfans' Association Bulletin No. 135 (Chicago, 2002), 7–54. Bruce G. Moffat, *"Forty Feet Below"* (Glendale, Calif., 1982), 72, noted that reports on the maximum mileage of the system give conflicting numbers, from 58.63 miles in the case of a Chicago Plan Commission examination of the tunnel company's atlas trackage in 1949 to as

many as 65 miles in company publicity. Tan, "The Belt and Switching Railroads of Chicago Terminal Area," 41–42.

21. Moffat, *"Forty Feet Below,"* 61. Mayer, "The Railway Pattern of Metropolitan Chicago," 104–6.

22. *Chicago Tribune,* June 15, 1992, quoted the Chicagoland Chamber of Commerce as estimating the damage at $800 million, $525 million of that in lost business and wages.

23. Hilton and Due, *The Electric Interurban Railways of America,* 208–39. William D. Middleton, *The Interurban Era* (Milwaukee, 1961), 396.

24. Middleton, *The Interurban Era,* 393. White, *The American Railroad Freight Car,* 3. Hilton and Due, *The Electric Interurban Railways of America,* 119–48 and 346–49, noted that the 400-mile Illinois Terminal Railroad, while it did not serve the Chicago area, was the nation's largest non-metropolitan interurban, stretching from St. Louis to Peoria with lines to other Illinois cities. It discontinued the last of its electric passenger service in 1956 and converted to diesel power as a freight railroad.

25. Aurora, Elgin & Chicago Railway, *Annual Report to the Illinois Railroad and Warehouse Commission, 1905.* Larry Plachno, *Sunset Lines: The Story of the Chicago, Aurora & Elgin Railroad* (Polo, Ill., 1989), 2:232, 279.

26. Plachno, *Sunset Lines,* 2:368–69, citing A. A. Sprague and Bernard J. O'Fallon, bankruptcy receivers of the CA&E for the period 1926–1944.

27. Middleton, *North Shore,* 90–101. Hilton and Due, *The Electric Interurban Railways in America,* 130–31.

28. Middleton, *North Shore,* 92. Hilton and Due, *The Electric Interurban Railways in America,* 134–35, 146. Thomas R. Bullard, *Illinois Rail Transit: A Basic History* (Oak Park, Ill., unpublished manuscript, ca. 1987), 60.

29. William D. Middleton, *South Shore: The Last Interurban,* 2nd ed. (Bloomington, Ind., 1999), 133–51.

30. Chicago, South Shore & South Bend Railroad, *Annual Report for 1971,* 20-year financial summary, 8.

31. Mayer, "The Railway Pattern of Metropolitan Chicago," 48–56.

32. White, *The American Railroad Freight Car,* 106, citing *Railroad Magazine,* August 12, 1912, 513, and *Railway Age,* July 12, 1889, 455.

33. Blaszak, "Belt Railway of Chicago," 46–53. Robert Milton Hill, *A Little Known Story of the Land Called Clearing* (Chicago, 1983), 67–92.

34. Blaszak, "Whither the Indiana Harbor Belt," 22–37. Meyer and Wade, *Chicago: Growth of a Metropolis,* 234–35.

35. Meyer and Wade, *Chicago,* 234.

9—The Railroad Supply Industry

1. John H. White, Jr., "George Mortimer Pullman," in *Encyclopedia of American Business History,* 335–39. White, *The American Railroad Passenger Car,* 1:212–13, 247. Pullman-Standard Car Manufacturing Company, *The Carbuilder* (Chicago, March 1955), 3–7.

2. Horace Porter, "Railway Passenger Travel, 1825–1880," *Scribner's Magazine* (September 1888), 304. Charles Long, "Pio-

neer and the Lincoln Funeral Train: How Honest Abe was used to Create a Corporate Tall Tale," *Railroad History* (Spring 2002), 88–100.

3. White, *The American Railroad Passenger Car,* 1:213, 219–20, citing Charles S. Sweet, "History of the Sleeping Car" (Chicago, 1923, an unpublished manuscript in the possession of his descendants).

4. *The Carbuilder* (Chicago, March, 1955), 6–7. *Chicago Tribune,* March 30, 1868, carried a story about a trip by Pullman and 30 guests on the Burlington Railroad on his new dining car, "Delmonico."

5. Heise and Edgerton, *Chicago,* 1:150–52. White, *The American Railroad Passenger Car,* 1:261.

6. *The Carbuilder* (Chicago, March 1955), 10–31.

7. Sawislak, *Smoldering City,* 49–67.

8. Richard Schneirov, "Chicago's Great Upheaval of 1877," *Chicago History* 9 (Spring 1980), 3–7. Robert V. Bruce, *1877: Year of Violence* (1959; reprint, Chicago, 1989), 237–53. Philip Foner, *The Great Labor Uprising of 1877* (New York, 1977), 139–56. *Chicago Tribune,* July 24–30, 1877. *Chicago Times,* July 27, 1877. Miller, *City of the Century,* 232–33. David O. Stowell, *Streets, Railroads, and the Great Strike of 1877* (Chicago, 1999), 2, 118–19.

9. Susan E. Hirsch, "The Search for Unity among Railroad Workers: The Pullman Strike in Perspective," in Richard Schneirov, Shelton Stromquist, and Nick Salvatore, eds., *The Pullman Strike and the Crisis of the 1890s: Essays on Labor and Politics* (Urbana, Ill., 1999), 7–8, 43–64. White, "George Mortimer Pullman," in *Encyclopedia of American Business History,* 338.

10. Robert E. Weir, "Dress Rehearsal got Pullman: The Knights of Labor and the 1890 New York Central Strike"; and Hirsch, "The Search for Unity Among Railroad Workers: The Pullman Strike in Perspective," in Schneirov, Stromquist, and Salvatore, *The Pullman Strike,* 8–9, 21–86.

11. *The Carbuilder* (Chicago, March 1955), 10–16.

12. White, *The American Railroad Freight Car,* 152. *The Carbuilder* (Chicago, March 1955), 8.

13. White, *The American Railroad Freight Car,* 583–90.

14. Ibid., 129. Association of American Railroads, *Railroad Facts* (Washington, 1999), 50.

15. White, *The American Railroad Freight Car,* 131–32, 261–62, 129. "G. H. Hammond Packing Company," www.hammondindiana.com.

16. White, *The American Railroad Freight Car,* 129–30, 283, 600.

17. Ibid., 261–63.

18. Ibid., 126–30. Cronon, *Nature's Metropolis,* 230–35.

19. General Electric Company, 10-K Annual Report to the U.S. Securities and Exchange Commission (2001), 15. GATX Corporation, 10-K Annual Report to the U.S. Securities and Exchange Commission (2001), 2–3. Union Tank Car Company, 10-K Annual Report to the U.S. Securities and Exchange Commission (2001), 1–2. www.ttx.com/faqs.

20. Ralph C. Epstein, *GATX: A History of General American Transportation Corporation, 1898–1948* (New York, 1948), 1–6.

21. Epstein, *GATX,* 6–14. GATX Corporation, 10-K An-

nual Report to the U.S. Securities and Exchange Commission (2001), 2–3.

22. Union Tank Car Company Records, 1889–1978, Rockefeller University Archive Center, New York, Series I, Boxes 1–2, contain the financial and legal records of the company as well as clippings, reports, and memoranda.

23. Union Tank Car Company, 10-K Annual Report to the U.S. Securities and Exchange Commission (2001), 1–2.

24. *Chicago Tribune,* July 10 and November 20, 1986.

25. Rosalyn A. Wilson, ed., *Transportation in America, 1997,* Eno Transportation Foundation Inc. (Lansdowne, Va., 1997), 64.

26. Ibid., 46–47, 68–69.

27. Johnstown America Industries Inc., 10-K Annual Report filed with the U.S. Securities and Exchange Commission on December 31, 1994, 2. Thomas M. Begel, chairman and chief executive officer of Johnstown America Industries Inc., interview with author July 6, 1995. Transportation Technologies Industries Inc., 10-K Annual Report filed with the U.S. Securities and Exchange Commission on December 31, 1999, 2.

28. *The Carbuilder* (Chicago, March 1955), 2. *United States of America v. Pullman Company* (Civil Action No. 994), U.S. District Court for the Eastern District of Pennsylvania. White, *The American Railroad Passenger Car,* 1:264–65. Samuel B. Casey, Pullman chairman, interview of March 26, 1979, with author. *Chicago Tribune,* March 28, 1979.

29. George M. Smerk, *Urban Mass Transportation: A Dozen Years of Federal Policy* (Bloomington, Ind., 1974), 54, 139, and *The Federal Role in Urban Mass Transportation* (Bloomington, Indiana, 1991), 54. Young, *Chicago Transit,* 129–39, and "Rail Car Industry—Where Is It Going," *Mass Transit,* 8, 3 (September, 1976), 6–13, 37. Wilson, *Transportation in America, 1997,* 48, 68–69.

30. David M. Young, "Pullman and Transit: End of an Era," *Mass Transit,* 7, 6 (July, 1979), 8–11, and "Budd Bounces Back," *Mass Transit,* 3 5 (March, 1978), 20–23, 50. *Chicago Tribune,* March 22, 1979.

31. Wilson, *Transportation in America, 1997,* 68–69. *Chicago Tribune,* November 8, 1991. Thomas M. Begel, chairman and chief executive of Johnstown America Industries and former chief executive of Pullman, interview with author on July 6, 1995.

32. Portec, Inc., 10-K annual reports filed with the U.S. Securities and Exchange Commission on December 31, 1994, and December 31, 1997. Varlen Corporation, Schedule 14D-9 filed with the U.S. Securities and Exchange Commission on May 24, 1999. Transportation Technologies Industries, Inc., 10-K annual report filed with the U.S. Securities and Exchange Commission on December 31, 1999. Trinity Rail Group Inc., Form 8-K A/A (Amendment #2) filed with the U.S. Securities and Exchange Commission October 26, 2001, and 10-K transition annual report filed with the U.S. Securities and Exchange Commission December 31, 2001.

33. Western-Cullen-Hayes Inc. corporate history brochure (Chicago, 2002).

34. Nalco Chemical Company corporate history (Naperville, Ill., 1995), 1–5. Nalco Chemical Company, Schedule 14D-1 filed with the U.S. Securities and Exchange Commission July 1, 1999.

35. Rand McNally & Co., corporate history brochure (Skokie, Ill., 1994). *Chicago Tribune*, January 16, 2003.

36. General Motors Corporation Electro-Motive Division, press release of September 8, 1972.

37. Maury Klein, "The Diesel Revolution," *Invention and Technology* (Winter 1991), 16–22. Jerry A. Pinkepank, "How the 'Home of the Diesel Locomotive' Builds Diesels," *Trains*, December 1968), 10–17. David P. Morgan, "The LaGrange Influence," *Trains* (September 1972), 30–32. *Chicago Tribune*, March 10, 1991.

38. P. K. Hoglund, general manager of EMD, remarks of May 31, 1979, to the Transportation Securities Club in McCook, Ill. P. Michael Smith, director of marketing and commercial administration for EMD, interview of March 6, 1991, with author. "General Motors Unit a Training Ground," *UTU Daily News Digest*, March 29, 2001. Andrew Toppan, "Diesel Production Statistics," *Motive Power Review* (March 25, 2000), 1–27.

10—Dominance, Reform, and Regulation

1. Howard, *Illinois*, 248.

2. Erie E. Parmalee Prentice, *The Federal Power over Carriers and Corporations* (New York, 1907), 94–95. Putnam, *The Illinois and Michigan Canal*, 109–11.

3. A detailed discussion of the financial practices of the men who came into control of many railroads in the second half of the nineteenth century is far beyond the scope of this book. There is an enormous amount of literature on the subject, but railroad industry historians Albro Martin, *Enterprise Denied: Origins of the Decline of American Railroads, 1897–1910* (New York, 1971), and *Railroads Triumphant: The Growth, Rejection, and Rebirth of a Vital American Force* (Oxford, England, 1992), and Klein, *The Life and Legend of Jay Gould*, offer more sympathetic views of such "industrial statesmen." Chandler, *The Visible Hand*, 122–87, has an interesting discussion of the period.

4. U.S. Department of Transportation, *America's Highways 1776–1976: A History of the Federal Aid Program* (Washington, 1976), 12. Stover, *American Railroads*, 36.

5. Young, *Chicago Transit*, 35–36.

6. Vance, *Capturing the Horizon*, 125–28.

7. *Railroad Facts* (Washington, 1991), 32.

8. Cronon, *Nature's Metropolis*, 78–79.

9. David S. Landes, *Revolution in Time: Clocks and the Making of the Modern World* (Cambridge, Mass., 1983), 285–86. William E. Miles, *Chicago Tribune Magazine*, November 13, 1979, 30–32.

10. Lawrence M. Friedman, *A History of American Law* (New York, 1973), 410.

11. Ibid., 412–13. James W. Ely, Jr., *Railroads and American Law* (Lawrence, Kans., 2001), 223–24.

12. "An act to provide for a general system of railroad incorporations," Laws of Illinois, 1849.

13. Ely, *Railroads and American Law*, 41. Friedman, *A History of American Law*, 409–10.

14. J. W. Norris, *General Directory and Business Advertiser for the City of Chicago for the Year 1844* (Chicago, 1844), 77. *Chicago Daily Democratic Press, Annual Review, 1852*, 10–11. Chicago Board of Trade, *Second Annual Statement, 1859*, 83–104, and *Fourteenth Annual Report, 1871*, 87–109.

15. Cronon, *Nature's Metropolis*, 109–19.

16. Belcher, *The Economic Rivalry between St. Louis and Chicago*, 186–92. Howard, *Illinois*, 357–62.

17. Slason Thompson, *A Short History of American Railways, Covering Ten Decades* (Chicago, 1925), 148–49.

18. Solon J. Buck, *The Agrarian Crusade: A Chronicle of the Farmer in Politics* (New Haven, 1920), 19–72. Howard, *Illinois*, 357–62.

19. Lloyd Wendt, *Chicago Tribune: The Rise of a Great American Newspaper* (Chicago, 1979), 226. Charles Warren, *The Supreme Court in United States History* (Boston, 1922, 1926), 2:578–79. Constitution of Illinois, 1870, Art. XI, Sec. 15.

20. *Munn v. Illinois*, 94 U.S. 113 (1877). *Chicago, Burlington & Quincy Railroad v. Iowa*, 94 U.S. 155 (1877); *Peik v. Chicago & North Western Railway*, 94 U.S. 164 (1877); *Chicago, Milwaukee & St. Paul Railroad v. Ackly*, 94 U.S. 179 (1877); and *Winona & St. Peter Railroad v. Blake*, 94 U.S. 180 (1877). Warren, *The Supreme Court*, 2:578–92.

21. Stover, *American Railroads*, 116.

22. Cronon, *Nature's Metropolis*, 85, 139.

23. Ibid., 237–39.

24. Klein, *The Life and Legend of Jay Gould*, 89–97. Chandler, *The Visible Hand*, 141–42.

25. Warren, *The Supreme Court*, 1:595, 2:625–35.

26. Thompson, *A Short History of American Railroads*, 217–18.

27. Stover, *American Railroads*, 135–36.

28. Howard, *Illinois*, 334.

29. *Wabash, St. Louis and Pacific Railway Company v. Illinois*, 118 U.S. 557 (1886). Warren, *The Supreme Court*, 2:632–34.

30. Stover, *American Railroads*, 134.

31. Blaszak, "Whither the Indiana Harbor Belt," 24–25.

32. Chicago City Council, "An Ordinance Authorizing the Chicago City Railway Company to Construct, Maintain, and Operate a System of Street Railways in Streets and Public Ways in the City of Chicago," and "An Ordinance Authorizing the Chicago Railways Company to Construct, Maintain, and Operate a System of Street Railways in Streets and Public Ways in the City of Chicago" (collectively known as the Traction Settlement Ordinances), February 11, 1907, ratified by the voters in a referendum April 2, 1907. Harry P. Weber, *Outline History of Chicago Traction* (Chicago, 1936), 61–79. Young, *Chicago Transit*, 77–78.

33. Young, *Chicago Transit*, 80–81, 108, 133.

34. *Railway Age Gazette*, Vol. 59, No. 15 (August 10, 1915), 634.

35. Journal of the Proceedings of the City Council of Chicago, July 21, 1919, 968–1000. Condit, *Chicago, 1910–1929*, 286. Stover, *History of the Illinois Central*, 297–304.

11—Railroad Crossings

1. Duis, *Challenging Chicago,* 46–47.

2. Federal Railroad Administration, *Safety Data, Highway-Rail Incidents at Public and Private Crossings, 1975–2000* (Washington, D.C., 2001), and *Highway-Rail Casualties at Public and Private Crossings, 1975–2000* (Washington, D.C., 2001). The aforementioned data are available on the Internet site of the agency.

3. Illinois Commerce Commission, "Summary of Highway-Rail collisions at Public Grade Crossings in 2002," working paper 2003-01 (Springfield, Ill., 2003), 13–14.

4. Chicago Terminal Commissions, "The Chicago Railway Terminal Problem" (1892), 20–21, 70, gave conflicting estimates as to the number of crossings ranging from 1,000 to 1,500 "upwards." Metropolitan Planning council, "Critical: A Regional Freight Action Agenda," a report prepared for the Business Leaders for Transportation, a civic group (Chicago, April 2002), 10.

5. Chicago Terminal Commission, *The Chicago Railway Terminal Problem,* 70. Metropolitan Planning Council, "Critical: A Regional Freight Action Agenda" (Chicago, April 2002), 10. Illinois Commerce Commission, "Motorist Delays at Public Highway-Rail Grade Crossings in Northeastern Illinois," working paper 2002-03 (Springfield, Ill., July 2002), 2, estimated that in the six-county metropolitan area the railroads used all crossings for 1,509 hours on "a typical workday," causing 10,982 hours of delay to 463,438 motorists and collectively costing them $330,000. The report estimated the total annual cost of crossing delays at $74 million to $120 million. However, the bulk of the delays were at only 139 of the 1,732 crossings in the study.

6. National Transportation Safety Board, *Collision of Northeast Illinois Regional Commuter Railroad Corporation (Metra) Train and Transportation Joint Agreement School District 47/155 School Bus at Railroad/Highway Grade Crossing in Fox River Grove, Illinois, on October 25, 1995* (Washington, D.C., 1996).

7. Robert W. McKnight, railway signaling historian, "History of Highway-Rail Grade Crossing Warning Devices," text of October 30, 2002, speech to the Lexington Group, in Los Angeles, 5. Jolene M. Molitoris, U.S. Department of Transportation federal railroad administrator, Kenneth R. Wykle, federal highway administrator, joint testimony of March 25, 1999, to the U.S. Senate Committee on Commerce, Science, and Transportation, subcommittee on surface transportation and merchant marine.

8. Hunter, *Steamboats on the Western Rivers,* 529–30. Ely, *Railroads and American Law,* 216–23.

9. Wex S. Malone, "The Formative Era of Contributory Negligence," *Illinois Law Review* 41, no. 2 (July-August 1946), 173–74. Gerstner, *Early American Railroads,* 820 n. 40.

10. "An Act to provide for a General System of Railroad Incorporations adopted November 6, 1849," *A Compilation of the Statutes of the State of Illinois* (Chicago, 1856), vol. 2, secs. 131 and 132, 1071.

11. *Galena & Chicago Union Railroad Company v. Abner Loomis,* 56 Am. Dec. 471, 3 Peck (Ill.) 548.

12. *Galena & Chicago Union Railroad Company v. John C. Dill,* 12 Peck (Ill.) 265.

13. *The Galena & Chicago Union Railroad Company v. Frederick Jacobs,* 20 Ill. 478 (1858).

14. *The Aurora Branch Railroad Co. v. Jacob Grimes,* 13 Ill. 585 (1852).

15. *Joliet & Northern Indiana Railroad Company v. Robert Jones,* 10 Peck (Ill.) 221. *Central Military Tract Railroad Company v. A. Rockafellow,* 7 Peck (Ill.) 541.

16. *The Chicago, Burlington, and Quincy Railroad Co. v. Ruby Van Patten, Admx.,* 64 Ill. 510 (1872). McKnight, "History of Highway-Rail Grade Crossing Warning Devices," 13.

17. *Partlow v. Illinois Central Railroad Co.,* 37 N.E. 663 (1894).

18. Chicago City Council, *Special Ordinances of Chicago,* VIII:203 (p. 413), Chicago, Alton & St. Louis Railroad Company (April 22, 1867). *The Statutes of Illinois: An Analytical Digest of All the General Laws of the State* (Springfield, Ill., 1869), Chap. 86a, para. 124, 558. *Chicago & Alton R.R. Company v. Charles Gretzner,* 46 Ill. 74 (1867).

19. "An Act Relating in relation to fencing and operating railroads," Public Laws 1869, 312, and (1874) 2 Starr & C. Annotated Statutes, 1927. "Cities and Villages Act of 1872, 1 Starr and C. Annotated Statutes," 465. *Pennsylvania Company v. Alfred Swan, et al.* (1890) 37 Ill. App. 83.

20. *Toledo, Wabash & Western Railway Co. v. City of Jacksonville,* 67 Ill. 37, 41, 42 (1873). Ely, *Railroads and American Law,* 125–30.

21. H. G. Prout, "Safety in Railroad Travel," in M. N. Forney, et al., *The American Railway: Its Construction, Development, Management, and Appliances* (1888; reprint, New York, 1972), 216–18.

22. Cronon, *Nature's Metropolis,* 373. Railroad and Warehouse Commission of Illinois, Thirtieth Annual Report (Springfield, 1990), Table XIV, Accidents. *Railway Age,* "Grade Crossing Elimination" (October 15, 1915), 634–35.

23. *Pennsylvania Company v. Alfred Swan, et al.,* 37 Ill. App. 17.

24. Railroad and Warehouse Commission of Illinois, Thirtieth Annual Report (Springfield, 1990), Table XIV, Accidents. *Railway Age,* "Elimination of Grade Crossings in Chicago" (November 14, 1919), 991.

25. E. L. Carthell, "The Chicago Railroad Terminal Problem, From the Engineering Standpoint," Chicago Railroad Terminal Commission, *The Chicago Railroad Terminal Problem,* 70, indicated in 1892 the annual death toll at crossings in Chicago averaged 200. Mayor Hempstead Washburne, letter of February 15, 1892, to the Chicago City Council, *The Chicago Railroad Terminal Problem,* 3, said 300 died at crossings the previous year. *Chicago Sunday Herald,* July 31, 1892.

26. *Pennsylvania Company v. Alfred Swan, et al.,* 37 Ill. App. 17. *Chicago & North Western Railway Company v. Elida Hansen,* by her next friend, 69 Ill. App. 17. *Chicago & North Western Railway Company v. City of Chicago,* 140 Ill. 309, 29 N.E. 1109.

27. *Philip L. Theobald, administrator, v. Chicago, Milwaukee & St. Paul Railway Company,* 75 Ill. App. 208. *Lake Shore & Michigan Southern Railway Company v. William Kuhlman, administrator*

(1885), 18 Ill. App. 222. *Chicago, Rock Island & Pacific Railroad Company v. Clough,* 134 Ill. 586, 25 N.E., 664.

28. Charles Francis Adams, *Notes on Railroad Accidents* (New York, 1879), 159–81, contains a discussion of the signal technology available in the 1870s. National Transportation Safety Board, *Safety at Passive Grade Crossings, NTSB/SS-98-03* (Washington, D.C., 1998), I: Analysis, summary, reflects national average data. Illinois Commerce Commission, *Annual Report on the Use of the Grade Crossing Protection Fund* (Springfield, Ill., 1996), 3, states that the construction of grade separations can range in cost up to $16.9 million.

29. Chicago Railroad Terminal Commission, *The Chicago Railroad Terminal Problem,* 20–21 (table).

30. Frank J. Piehl, "Our Forgotten Streetcar Tunnels," *Chicago History* 4, 3 (Fall 1975), 130–39.

31. Young, *Chicago Transit,* 54–58.

32. Chicago City Council, *Special Ordinances of Chicago,* XI: 381 (p. 771) May 23, 1892.

33. Harvey S. Park, letter of April 10, 1893, published in *Railway and Engineering Review,* April 29, 1893, 267–68. Paul M. Green and Melvin G. Holli, *The Mayors: The Chicago Political Tradition* (Carbondale, Ill., 1987), 24.

34. Chicago City Council, *Special Ordinances of Chicago,* XI: 381, 382, 379, 380, 382 (pp. 771, 775, 740, 749, 822). *Railway and Engineering Review,* October 28, 1899, 603; February 9, 1901, 71; November 16, 1901, 731; April 5, 1902, 293; and July 5, 1902, 517.

35. *Railway Age,* December 2, 1922, 1061. *Railway and Engineering Review,* March 9, 1901, 127, and February 9, 1901, 71.

36. *Railway Age,* October 8, 1915, 634–35; November 14, 1919, 991, quoting Cook County Coroner P. M. Hoffman.

37. *Railway Age,* November 14, 1919, 991; and March 31, 1934, 479.

38. The Revised Statutes of the State of Illinois, Springfield, 1899, Chap. 114, Para. 209–17. McKnight, "History of Highway-Rail Grade Crossing Warning Devices," 6.

39. McKnight, "History of Highway-Rail Grade Crossing Warning Devices," 4–11.

40. "Illinois Commerce Commission Act of May 12, 1905, *Revised Statutes of Illinois* (Chicago, 1929), Chap. 114, para. 61–62.

41. Federal Railroad Administration, *Safety Data, Highway-Rail Incidents at Public and Private Crossings, 1975–2000,* and *Highway-Rail Casualties at Public and Private Crossings, 1975–2000.*

42. Illinois Commerce Commission, *Annual Report on the Use of the Grade Crossing Protection Fund* (Springfield, Ill., 1996), 3.

43. Shaw, *A History of Railrad Accidents,* 280–89.

44. National Transportation Safety Board, *Collision in Fox River Grove, Illinois, on October 25, 1995* (1996), 56–57, also assigned some of the blame to the school districts for failing to adequately train drivers and avoid hazardous crossings on bus routes.

45. National Fire Protection Association, *Fire News,* "Chicago Street Railway Car Fire Preliminary Report" (Boston,

Mass., 1950), 2–4. Report to James O. Dwight, CTA general attorney, June 30, 1950, on the testimony and findings of the Cook County Coroner's inquest concluding June 29, 1950. Shaw, *A History of Railroad Accidents,* 280–89.

46. Middleton, *North Shore,* 105. *Chicago Tribune,* February 24–25, 1930.

47. Federal Railroad Administration, Safety Data, *Highway-Rail Incidents at Public and Private Crossings, 2000. Chicago Tribune,* January 25, 1970; November 24, 1973; and November 20 and 21, 1975. Shaw, *A History of Railroad Accidents,* 285.

48. National Transportation Safety Board, *Collision of Northern Indiana Commuter Transportation District Train 102 with a Tractor Trailer, Portage, Indiana, June, 18 1998,* RAR 99-03 (Washington, D.C., 1999).

49. National Transportation Safety Board, *Collision of National Railroad Passenger Corporation Train 59 with a Loaded Truck Semi-Trailer Combination at a Highway/Rail Crossing in Bourbonnais, Illinois, March 15, 1999, RAR-02-01* (Washington, D.C., 2001).

50. Metropolitan Planning Council, "Getting the Region Moving: A Coordinated Agenda for the 2003 Federal Transportation Debate" (Chicago, 2003), 4. Chicago Police Department, Biannual Report, 1999–2000 (Chicago, 2000), Fig. 16c, 36.

12—Decline and Decentralization

1. Stover, *Routledge Historical Atlas,* 52–53. Wilson, *Transportation in America, 1997,* 44. *Railroad Facts* (1999), 32, 44, and Internet web site, Class I Railroad Statistics, 2001. Scheiterman, *When the Railroad Leaves Town,* xv.

2. *Historical Statistics of the United States,* Washington, D.C., 1975, 2:729. Frank N. Wilner, *The Amtrak Story* (Omaha, Neb., 1994), 61–62.

3. Metropolitan Planning Council, "Critical: A Regional Freight Action Agenda," A report prepared for the Business Leaders for Transportation, a civic group (Chicago, April 2002), 6.

4. Stephen B. Goddard, *Getting There: The Epic Struggle between Road and Rail in the American Century* (New York, 1994), 79–83, 133, 216–17. Stanley I. Fishler, *Moving Millions: An Inside Look at Mass Transit* (New York, 1979), 79–90, 160–85, 186–92.

5. Chicago Department of Streets and Sanitation, Bureau of Street Traffic, "Cordon Count of the Central Business District of Chicago" (Chicago, 1980), Table 2, previous years comparison of passengers entering and leaving the district.

6. Hilton and Due, *The Electric Interurban Railways in America,* and Middleton, *The Interurban Era,* are the two general histories of the industry. Bullard, *Illinois Rail Transit,* 51–116, deals with the interurban industry in Illinois.

7. Hilton and Due, *The Electric Interurban Railways in America,* 335–43. Young, *Chicago Transit,* 142–46. James D. Johnson, *Aurora N' Elgin: Being a Compendium of Word and Picture Recalling the Everyday Operations of the Chicago Aurora & Elgin Railroad* (Wheaton, Ill., 1965), 1–4. Plachno, *Sunset Lines,* 2:383–487. Peter Weller and Fred Stark, *The Living Legacy of the Chicago, Aurora & Elgin: An Illustrated History of the CA&E and Its Transition to the*

Illinois Prairie Path (San Francisco, 1999), 13–22. Middleton, *North Shore,* 63–79. Norman Carlson, ed., *30 Years Later: The Shore Line, Evanston-Waukegan, 1896–1935,* Central Electric Railfans' Association Bulletin (Chicago, 1985), 2–32. Middleton, *South Shore,* 159–74. Norman Carlson, ed., *Chicago, South Shore & South Bend Railroad: How the Medal Was Won,* Central Electric Railfans' Association Bulletin No. 124 (Chicago, 1985), is a history of that line in its formative period.

8. Chicago & North Western Railway Company, 97th Annual Report (Chicago, 1956), 24–27, ten-year revenue and expense summaries.

9. Wilner, *The Amtrak Story,* 14–43. Interstate Commerce Commission, "Railroad Passenger Train Deficit, report proposed by Howard Hosmer (et al.)," Docket No. 31954 (Washington, D.C., 1958). Stover, *American Railroads,* 234.

10. Thomas H. Ploss, *Supplemental Memoirs to The Nation Pays Again* (Antioch, Ill., 1998), 17, 20–21.

11. Joseph A. Tecson, *The Regional Transportation Authority in Northeastern Illinois,* reprint of articles appearing in the *Chicago Bar Record,* May–June and July–August, 1975, 18. John G. Allen, "From Centralization to Decentralization: The Politics of Transit in Chicagoland" (Ph.D. diss., Massachusetts Institute of Technology, 1995), 70–111. Young, *Chicago Transit,* 133.

12. Young, *Chicago Transit,* 135–36. Metra, "Annual Commuter Rail Passenger Trips by Carrier," 1969–2001.

13. Office of the Federal Coordinator of Transportation, *Passenger Traffic Report* (Washington, 1935). U.S. Census decennial reports for the years indicated. Smith, *Transportation in America, 1992,* 47 (table).

14. Martin, *Enterprise Denied,* 29–31. Gregory Lee Thompson, *The Passenger Train in the Motor Age* (Columbus, Ohio, 1993), 152.

15. Thompson, *The Passenger Train in the Motor Age,* 156, 113–14.

16. White, *The American Railroad Passenger Car,* 1.246 (table 3.3) citing his compilation of data from *Poor's Manual of Railroads* and ICC reports. Smith, *Transportation in America, 1992,* 47 (table).

17. Bion J. Arnold, "Report of the Re-arrangement of the Steam Railroad Terminals in the City of Chicago" (Chicago, 1913). National Railroad Passenger Corporation, office of public affairs, for 1993 data for Union Station. Werner Schroeder, "Metropolitan Transit Research Study," 1954, CTA Archives, Chicago. Amtrak department of public affairs data on passenger traffic at Chicago Union Station. Chicago Department of Aviation passenger counts at Midway and O'Hare International Airports, 1993.

18. Frederic A. Delano, "Chicago Railway Terminals: A Suggested Solution for the Chicago Terminal Problem," privately circulated document, Chicago, 1906. Daniel H. Burnham and Edward H. Bennett, *Plan of Chicago* (Chicago, 1909; reprint, New York, 1993), 61–75. Arnold, "Report on the Re-arrangement of the Steam Railroad Terminals in the City of Chicago." John F. Wallace, "Preliminary Report of the Chicago Terminal Railway

Commission," to the City Council Committee on Railway Terminals, March 29, 1915. Edward Noonan, "The Railway Passenger Terminal Problem at Chicago" (Chicago City Council Committee on Terminal Railways, 1933). V. V. Boatner, "Report on Railroad Terminal Co-ordination, Chicago, Illinois, and Vicinity" (Western Regional Co-ordination Committee, Chicago, 1936).

19. Noonan, "The Railway Passenger Terminal Problem at Chicago," 27. Burnham and Bennett, *Plan of Chicago,* 100–1. Mayer and Wade, *Chicago,* 302–3.

20. Mayer and Wade, *Chicago,* 302–3.

21. Arnold, "Report on the Re-arrangement of the Steam Railroad Terminals in the City of Chicago."

22. Condit, *Chicago, 1930–1970,* 250. Wilmer, *The Amtrak Story,* 60. Interviews by the author of Amtrak presidents Paul Reistrup in August 1976, and Alan Boyd in September 1979.

23. Arnold, "Report on the Re-arrangement of the Steam Railroad Terminals in the City of Chicago." Total daily train, car, and passenger movements at Chicago railway stations in 1913. National Rail Passenger Corp., "Amtrak facts, Ten Busiest Train Stations in 2001" (Washington, D.C., 2001). Belt Railway of Chicago, "Chicago Gateway Assessment Study, Summary of Chicago Terminal Assessment Study Information" (Chicago, 1998).

24. *Railroad Facts* (1999), 32, and "U.S. Freight Railroad Statistics" (2002) at www.aar.org.

25. Mayer, "The Railway Pattern of Metropolitan Chicago," 3–5. Ronald L. Batory, cover letter of February 10, 1998, to "Chicago Gateway Assessment Study." "Chicago Gateway Assessment Study," Summary of Chicago Terminal Assessment Study Information (Chicago, 1998). Metropolitan Planning Council, "Critical: A Regional Freight Action Agenda," A report prepared for the Business Leaders for Transportation, a civic group (Chicago, April, 2002), 6, puts the freight traffic in 2002 at a somewhat higher level than the Belt Railway report. MPC in 2002 reported that 37,500 railroad freight cars arrive in, leave, or pass through the city daily and forecast that traffic would nearly double by the year 2020.

26. Mayer, "The Railway Pattern of Metropolitan Chicago," 42. "Chicago Gateway Assessment Study," Summary of Information (1998).

27. Association of American Railroads, "Class I Railroad Statistics, Traffic" (Washington, D.C., 2002), www.aar.org. Mike Stiehl and F. Gerald Rawling, "Chicago Area Transportation Study Working Paper 01-04: Intermodal Volumes: Tracking Trends and Anticipating Impacts in northeast Illinois" (Chicago, May 2001), ii, 1, 6.

28. Stennett, *Yesterday and To-Day,* 13. Mayer, "The Railway Pattern of Metropolitan Chicago," 42. Moffat, *The Chicago Tunnel Story,* 91.

29. Middleton, *North Shore,* 93–95.

30. Stover, *American Railroads,* 208–9. Martin, *Railroads Triumphant,* 242–43. K. Jack Bauer, *A Maritime History of the United States: The Role of America's Seas and Waterways* (Columbia, S.C., 1988), 316–18. Twain Braden, "Maritime Milestones,"

American Ship Review (Portland, Maine), No. 38 (1998): 80. Association of American Railroads, "Class I Railroad Statistics, Traffic" (Washington, D.C., 2002), www.aar.org.

31. Burlington Northern and Santa Fe Railway Co. press release of October 14, 2002. Craig Barner, "Intermodal Center Crews Battle, Defeat Tough Schedule," *Midwest Construction* (New York, November 2002). Union Pacific Railroad press release of May 29, 2002. *Chicago Tribune*, January 26–27 and May 23, 1999, and February 9, 2003.

32. Smith, *Transportation in America, 1992,* 44.

13—Liquidation, Consolidation, and Diversification

1. The Class I railroads in 2002 were Burlington Northern Santa Fe Railway, CSX Transportation, Kansas City Southern Railway, Norfolk Southern Combined Subsidiaries, and Union Pacific Railroad. The Grand Trunk Corporation owned by the Canadian National and the Soo Line Railroad owned by the Canadian Pacific were also Class I carriers. Besides the two Canadian railroads, the Ferrocarril Mexicano (Ferromex), a joint venture involving the UP and Transportation Ferroviaria Mexicana (TFM), partially owned by the KCS, were North American carriers that would qualify as Class I railroads. AAR.org, Class I Railroad Statistics. See Chapter 3, note 3 for the definition of railroad classes.

2. Stover, *American Railroads,* 132–37.

3. Albro Martin, *Railroads Triumphant,* 378–79.

4. Martin, *Enterprise Denied,* 12–18.

5. Goddard, *Getting There,* 86–95. George W. Hilton, *Lake Michigan Passenger Steamers* (Stanford, Calif., 2002), 119–20, 140–48, 107–10.

6. Interstate Commerce Commission, *Statistics of Railways in the United States* (Washington, 1916). *Railroad Facts* (1966), 12. By 1995 after Amtrak had been in operation for 24 years, freight accounted for 97 percent of railroad revenues in the U.S.

7. Stover, *American Railroads,* 162, 177. *Railroad Facts* (1966), 12–14.

8. Stephen Salsbury, *No Way to Run a Railroad* (New York, 1982), 31–32.

9. John F. Stover, *Life and Decline of the American Railroad* (New York, 1970), 235–37.

10. United States Railway Association, *The Revitalization of Rail Service in the Northeast: The Final Report of the United States Railway Association* (Washington, 1986).

11. Ripley, *Railroads,* 34–37.

12. Stover, *American Railroads,* 87. Saunders, *Main Lines,* 160–68, 171, 173. William J. Quinn, chairman and chief executive of the Milwaukee Road at the time of the bankruptcy filing in 1977, in several interviews with the author expressed the opinion that the 1909 transcontinental extension was the cause of the railroad's failure.

13. *Chicago Tribune,* October 5, 1975.

14. Klein, *Union Pacific,* 2:515–18. Grant, *The North Western,* 213. Saunders, *Main Lines,* 152–60.

15. *Chicago Tribune,* October 5, 1975, quoting Henry Crown.

16. Klein, *Union Pacific,* 2:526. Wilner, *Railroad Mergers,* 203–8. Saunders, *Merging Lines,* 328–36, 347–53, 417, 419. Henry Crown, interview of October 1975 with author.

17. *Chicago Tribune,* March 16, 1975.

18. *Chicago Tribune,* September 6, 1979, and February 17, 1981, quoting bankruptcy trustee William Gibbons. Author's notes taken at the court hearing. Saunders, *Main Lines,* 158–59, lays much of the blame on the Rock Island's subsequent failure on Crown.

19. *Chicago Tribune,* January 26, 1980. Author's notes taken at the court hearing.

20. Ploss, *The Nation Pays Again,* 81–92.

21. Chicago, Milwaukee, St. Paul & Pacific Railroad, R-1 Annual Report of 1977, filed with the Interstate Commerce Commission. Chicago Milwaukee Corporation, 10K Annual Reports to the Securities and Exchange Commission for the years 1970–1976. *Chicago Tribune,* December 20, 1977. Author's notes taken at the court hearing.

22. *Chicago Tribune,* February 20, 1980. Author's notes taken at the court hearing.

23. *Chicago Tribune,* March 3, 1980. Author's notes taken at the court hearing.

24. *Chicago Tribune,* May 30, 1982; July 20, 22, and 29, November 13, and December 14, 1983; and April 9, July 27, and October 17, 1984.

25. Plan for reorganization by Trustee William Gibbons, December 26, 1979.

26. Ploss, *The Nation Pays Again,* 101–10.

27. Grant, *The Corn Belt Route,* 155, quoting John W. Barriger III, head of the Depression-era Reconstruction Finance Corp. from which the CGW was forced to borrow $3 million.

28. Ibid., 176–77. Saunders, *Merging Lines,* 336–38.

29. Northwest Industries Inc., *Annual Report to Shareholders,* 1966–1970. Grant, *The North Western,* 214–15.

30. Grant, *The North Western,* 215. Northwest Industries Inc., *Annual Report to Shareholders,* 1972.

31. Chicago & North Western Holdings Corp., *1992 Annual Report to Stockholders,* 23, note 1, and 30, note 12.

32. Ibid., 3–9.

33. Frank Alston, *Con-glom-er-ate: A Case Study of IC Industries under William B. Johnson* (Naperville, Ill., 1992), 83–91, and quoting, 68. William B. Johnson, several interviews with the author, 1976–1983.

34. Alston, *Con-glom-er-ate,* 181.

35. Stover, *Life and Decline of the American Railroad,* 282–83, dates the merger activity from 1955 when the Louisville & Nashville sought to acquire the Nashville, Chattanooga & St. Louis, although the more typical opinion of railroad historians is that the period of consolidation began with the 1959 acquisition by the Norfolk & Western of the Virginian, which was engineered by Stuart Saunders, who later oversaw the Penn Central merger.

36. William B. Johnson, *IC Industries Annual Report to Stockholders,* 1976–1980, management reports. Harry James Bruce, *Mentors & Memories: My Forty Years Inside, Outside, and*

Alongside the Railroad Industry (Wilmette, Ill., 2003), 130–46.

37. Alston, *Con-glom-er-ate*, 216–17, said the dividend policy was intended to make the railroad more attractive to purchasers, but that goal was not widely understood in the financial community.

38. IC Industries, *Annual Report to Stockholders*, 1985.

14—Redevelopment

1. Burnham and Bennett, *Plan of Chicago*, 61–78, 122.

2. John F. Due, "Abandon Railroads? Illinois Replies No," *Illinois Issues* (November 1975), 32. Stover, *Routledge Historical Atlas*, 116. Association of American Railroads, *Railroad Facts* (1996), 44.

3. Illinois Department of Transportation, Bureau of Railroads, "Rail Line Abandonments in Illinois" (Springfield, Ill.), 1976 through 2002. Association of American Railroads, *Railroad Facts* (1996), 44.

4. Illinois Department of Transportation, Bureau of Railroads, "Proposed Rail Improvement Program: FY 2003–2007" (Springfield, Ill., Spring 2002), 4–10.

5. Wilner, *The Amtrak Story*, 60. John F. Due, "Abandon Railroads? Illinois Replies No," 32.

6. Wille, *Forever Open, Clear, and Free*, 79–80.

7. Mayer and Wade, *Chicago*, 41, 123, 126, 312–14. Merchandise Mart Properties Inc., "History of the Mart," Chicago, 2002, www.merchandisemart.com.

8. Mayer and Wade, *Chicago*, 41, 123, 126, 312–14.

9. Illinois Railway Museum, *History of the Illinois Railway Museum* (Union, Ill., 1962), pamphlet. Fox River Trolley Museum, *Fox River Trolley Museum History* (South Elgin, Ill., 2002), pamphlet.

10. *West Chicago Press*, December 20, 1956, and January 12, 1961. Winfield Township Assessor records.

11. National Trust for Historic Preservation, press release of October 7, 1999.

12. Plachno, *Sunset Lines*, 2:501. Skyscrapers.com, "One and Two Wheaton Center."

13. Carlson, *30 Years Later*, 17.

14. Ibid., 8–10, 14, 17, 20, 27.

15. Middleton, *South Shore* (2nd ed.), 159–74.

16. George S. Rogers, Chicago Area Interurban Systems (1892–1963), report in the files of the Regional Transportation Authority, 1980, for data on the mileage of the interurban system. George Krambles and Art Peterson, *CTA at 45: A History of the First 45 Years of the Chicago Transit Authority* (Oak Park, Ill., 1993), 118–19, 125–28.

17. Weller and Stark, *The Living Legacy of the Chicago, Aurora & Elgin*, 133–50. George Krambles, ed., *The Great Third Rail*, Central Electric Railfans Association Bulletin No. 105 (Chicago, 1961), 33–38. Plachno, *Sunset Lines*, 2:45–50.

18. Krambles and Peterson, *CTA at 45*, 118–19. City of Chicago, Department of Public Works brochure of June 22, 1958, commemorating the opening of the Congress line.

19. Krambles and Peterson, *CTA at 45*, 125–28.

20. The Hitchcock Foundation, "The Hitchcock Woods: Points of Interest" (Aiken, S.C., 2002), brochure also available at www.hitchcockwoods.com. South Carolina Department of Parks, Recreation, and Tourism, State Trails Program, "Cathedral Isle," also available at www.sctrails.net. Weller and Stark, *The Living Legacy of the Chicago, Aurora & Elgin*, 63, n.2. Elroy-Sparta State Trail, "History of the Elroy-Sparta State Trail" (Kendall, Wis., 2002), brochure.

21. *Chicago Tribune*, September 30, 1963. Weller and Stark, *The Living Legacy of the Chicago, Aurora & Elgin*, 179–81. Samuel S. and Elizabeth R. Holmes, "Illinois Prairie Path: Trials and Triumphs," transcript of remarks delivered April 12, 1979, in Geneva, Illinois. Jean Mooring, "A Brief History of the Illinois Prairie Path" (unpublished remarks dated January 27, 1981).

22. Weller and Stark, *The Living Legacy of the Chicago, Aurora & Elgin*, 183–211.

23. Illinois Prairie Trail Authority, "Trails: A Guide to Northeastern Illinois Trails" (Wheaton, Ill., 1998), brochure. Philip Elfstrom, president of the Kane County Forest Preserve District, interviews with author in 1984.

24. Ibid.

25. *Joliet Herald-News*, October 31, 1980, and November 17, 1985. *Daily Southtown*, July 7, 1997. *Chicago Wilderness Magazine*, Spring 2000 (no page number indicated).

26. Rails-to-Trails Conservancy, Washington, D.C., data posted as of September 10, 2003, at www.railtrails.org.

27. Robert A. Slayton, *Back of the Yards: The Making of a Local Democracy* (Chicago, 1986). *Chicago Tribune*, January 30 and July 16, 1997. Irving Cutler, *Chicago: Metropolis of the Mid-Continent* (Dubuque, Iowa, 1982).

28. Alston, *Con-glom-er-ate*, 66–73.

29. Wille, *Forever Open, Clear, and Free*, 71–80. Sawyers, *Chicago Portraits*, 259–60, gives a concise account of Ward's life.

30. Wille, *Forever Open, Clear, and Free*, 22–23, 28.

31. Alston, *Con-glom-er-ate*, 79, 82–83.

32. Ibid., 84.

33. Lois Wille, *At Home in the Loop: How Clout and Community Built Chicago's Dearborn Park* (Carbondale, Ill., 1997), 166. Alston, *Con-glom-er-ate*, 101–2.

34. Wille, *At Home in the Loop*, 10, 21.

35. Ibid., 21, 26–27, 85.

36. Ibid., 23, 84.

37. Ibid., 166.

38. Bach and Wolfson, *A Guide to Chicago's Train Stations*, provides a history of each station.

39. Chicago Department of Planning and Development, news release of February 7, 2002. Due, "Abandon Railroads? Illinois Replies No," 327. Stover, *Routledge Historical Atlas*, 40, 116, 129. Illinois Department of Transportation, *Fiscal Year 1999 Annual Report* (Springfield, Ill.), 6. See Bach and Wolfson, *A Guide to Chicago's Train Stations*.

40. *Chicago Sun-Times*, October 19, 1995.

41. *Chicago Tribune*, June 10, 1994; March 1, 1998; and February 19, 1999.

Epilogue

1. Illinois Department of Transportation, Bureau of Railroads, "Proposed Rail Improvement Program: FY 2003–2007" (Springfield, Ill., 2002), 4–5. In 2002 a Class I carrier was defined as a railroad with annual operating revenues in excess of $261.9 million. Regional railroads generally operated 350 miles or more of track, and short lines less than that.

2. *Railroad Facts* (1996), 28, and AAR, Class I Railroad Statistics, 2002. U.S. railroads handled 447.3 million revenue ton-miles in 1929 and 1.495 trillion ton-miles in 2001.

3. Business Leaders for Transportation, "Critical Cargo: A Regional Freight Action Agenda" (Chicago, April 2002, and available from the Metropolitan Planning Council), 1–24. *Chicago Tribune*, June 16, 2003, 1.

4. *Chicago Tribune*, June 17, 2003, 2:4.

5. Norman Y. Mineta, U.S. Transportation secretary, letter of July 28, 2003, to J. Dennis Hastert, speaker of the U.S. House of Representatives. U.S. Transportation Department, "Passenger Rail Investment Reform Act" (A bill to amend title 49, United States Code, to provide for stable, productive, and efficient passenger rail service), Washington, D.C., July 28, 2003.

Appendix C

1. Young, *Chicago Transit*, Appendix B, 177–80.

2. Shaw, *A History of Railroad Accidents*, 99–102. McLellan and Warrick, *The Lake Shore & Michigan Southern Railway*, 119–21.

3. Most accounts place the death toll at 81, but Shaw, *A History of Railroad Accidents*, 61–64, estimated it at 82. Both Helen Louise Plaster Stoutemyer, *The Train that Never Arrived: A Saga of the Excursion Train that Wrecked between Chatsworth and Piper City August 10, 1887* (Fairbury, Ill., 1980), 13, 34, and the *Chicago Tribune*, August 14, 1887, put the toll at 85 because some of the victims died later of injuries.

4. *Chicago Tribune*, July 13–16, 1904. Shaw, *A History of Railroad Accidents*, 180–81.

5. Middleton, *South Shore*, 23–24.

6. *Chicago Tribune*, July 15–18, 1912. Shaw, *A History of Railroad Accidents*, 177–78.

7. *Chicago Tribune*, June 24–25, 1918. Shaw, *A History of Railroad Accidents*, 244–45.

8. Middleton, *North Shore*, 105. *Chicago Tribune*, February 24–25, 1930.

9. Interstate Commerce Commission, Report of the Director of the Bureau of Safety, *Accident on the Chicago Rapid Transit Company, Granville Avenue, Chicago, Ill., November 24, 1936* (Washington, D.C., 1926), 1–8.

10. Middleton, *North Shore*, 105.

11. Interstate Commerce Commission, Investigation No. 2988, *Chicago, Burlington & Quincy Railroad Company, Report In Re. Accident at Naperville, Ill., on April 25, 1946* (Washington, D.C., 1946), 2–14.

12. National Transportation Safety Board, *Collision of Illinois Central Railroad Commuter Trains, Chicago, Illinois, October 30, 1972, RAR-73-05* (Washington, D.C., June 28, 1973). *Chicago Tribune*, Oct. 31, Nov. 1–5, 1972. Shaw, *A History of Railroad Accidents*, 361–63.

13. National Transportation Safety Board, *Collision of National Railroad Passenger Corporation Train 59 with a Loaded Truck Semi-Trailer Combination at a Highway/Rail Crossing in Bourbonnais, Illinois, March 15, 1999, RAR-02-01* (Washington, D.C., 2001).

Selected Bibliography

The following is a list of hardbound publications in general circulation, privately printed works, some unpublished studies, some of the more important articles in periodicals, and significant research papers by scholars on topics relating to Chicago and its railroads. Statistical summaries, most periodicals, government reports, and studies by civic groups are generally cited in the notes.

Achilles, Rolf. *Made in Illinois: A Story of Illinois Manufacturing.* Chicago, 1993.

Alston, Frank, *Con-glom-er-ate: A Case Study of IC Industries under William B. Johnson.* Naperville, Ill., 1992.

Andreas, A. T. *History of Chicago from Earliest Times to the Present Time.* 3 vols. Chicago, 1884–1886.

Arnold, Isaac N. *William B. Ogden and Early Days in Chicago.* Chicago, 1881.

Bach, Ira J., and Susan Wolfson. *A Guide to Chicago's Train Stations: Past and Present.* Athens, Ohio, 1986.

Balesi, Charles J. *The Time of the French in the Heart of North America.* Chicago, 1996.

Basler, Roy P., ed. *Collected Works: The Abraham Lincoln Association, Springfield, Illinois.* 9 vols. New Brunswick, N.J., 1953.

Bathe, Grenville and Dorothy. *Oliver Evans: A Chronicle of Early American Engineering.* Philadelphia, 1935.

Bauer, Jack K. *A Maritime History of the United States: The Role of America's Seas and Waterways.* Columbia, S.C., 1988.

Beecher, Catharine. *Treatise on Domestic Economy, For the Use of Young Ladies at Home and School.* New York, 1847.

Belcher, Wyatt Winton. *The Economic Rivalry between St. Louis and Chicago, 1850–1880.* New York, 1947.

Berger, L. Miles. *They Built Chicago: Entrepreneurs Who Shaped a Great City's Architecture.* Chicago, 1992.

Blanchard, Rufus. *History of Du Page County, Ill..* Chicago, 1882.

Blaszak, Michael W. "Belt Railway of Chicago: Back from the Brink." *Trains,* July 1993.

———. "Big Steel's Belt Line." *Trains,* August 1989.

———. "Whither the Indiana Harbor Belt." *Trains,* March 1986.

Borak, Arthur. *Financial History of the Chicago, Milwaukee & St. Paul Railway.* Minneapolis, 1929.

Bruce, Alfred W. *The Steam Locomotive in America.* New York, 1952.

Bruce, Harry James. *Mentors & Memories: My Forty Years Inside, Outside, and Alongside the Railroad Industry.* Wilmette, Ill., 2003.

Bruce, Robert V. *1877: Year of Violence.* 1959; Chicago, 1989.

Bryant, Keith L., Jr. *History of the Atchison, Topeka & Santa Fe Railway.* New York, 1974.

Buck, Solon J. *The Agrarian Crusade: A Chronicle of the Farmer in Politics.* New Haven, 1920.

Buck, Stephen James. "Political and Economic Transformation in the Civil War Era: Du Page County, Ill., 1830–1880." Ph.D. diss., Northern Illinois University, 1992.

Bullard, Thomas R. *Illinois Rail Transit: A Basic History.* Unpublished manuscript, Oak Park, Ill., ca. 1987.

———. *Interurban Empire Builders.* Unpublished manuscript, Oak Park, Ill., 1989.

Burgess, George H., and Miles C. Kennedy. *Centennial History of the Pennsylvania Railroad Company.* Philadelphia, 1946.

Burnham, Daniel H., and Edward H. Bennett. *Plan of Chicago.* New York, 1993. Originally published by The Commercial Club, Chicago, 1909.

Carlson, Norman, ed. *30 Years Later: The Shore Line, Evanston-Waukegan, 1896–1935.* Chicago, 1985.

Carstensen, Vernon, ed. *The Public Lands: Studies in the History of the Public Domain.* Madison, Wis., 1968.

Cary, John W. *The Organization and History of the Chicago, Milwaukee & St. Paul Railway Company.* Milwaukee, 1892.

Casey, Robert J., and W. A. S. Douglas. *Pioneer Railroad: The Story of the North Western System.* New York, 1948.

Chamberlin, Everett. *Chicago and Its Suburbs.* Chicago, 1874.

Chandler, Alfred D., Jr. *The Visible Hand: The Managerial Revolution in American Business.* Cambridge, Mass., 1977.

Cochrane, Thomas C. *Pennsylvania: A Bicentennial History.* New York, 1978.

Coe, Lewis. *The Telegraph: A History of Morse's Invention and Its Predecessors in the United States.* Jefferson, N.C., 1993.

Condit, Carl W. *Chicago, 1910–1929: Building, Planning and Urban Technology.* Chicago, 1973.

———. *The Railroad and the City: A Technological and Urbanistic History of Cincinnati.* Columbus, Ohio, 1977.

Corliss, Carlton J. *Main Line of Mid-America: The Story of the Illinois Central.* New York, 1950.

Creese, Walter L. *The Crowning of the American Landscape.* Princeton, N. J., 1985.

Cronon, William. *Nature's Metropolis: Chicago and the Great West.* New York, 1991.

Cudahy, Brian J. *Destination Loop: The Story of Rapid Transit Railroading in and Around Chicago.* Brattleboro, Vt., 1982.

Currey, J. Seymour. *Chicago: Its History and Its Builders.* 5 vols. Chicago, 1912.

Cutler, Irving. *Chicago: Metropolis of the Mid-Continent.* Dubuque, Iowa, 1982.

Derleth, August. *The Milwaukee Road: Its First Hundred Years.* Iowa City, Iowa, 2002. Originally published in New York, 1948.

DeRouin, Edward M. *Chicago Union Station: A Look at Its History and Operations before Amtrak.* Elmhurst, Ill., 2004.

Dickens, Charles. *American Notes for General Circulation.* New York, 1985. Originally published in London, 1842.

Dilts, James D. *The Great Road: The Building of the Baltimore & Ohio, the Nation's First Railroad, 1828–1853.* Stanford, Calif., 1993.

Donovan, Frank P., Jr. *Mileposts on the Prairie: The Story of the Minneapolis & St. Louis Railway.* New York, 1950.

Dorin, Patrick C. *The Grand Trunk Western Railway.* Seattle, 1977.

Douglas, George H. *Rail City: Chicago USA.* San Diego, 1981.

Downing, Andrew Jackson. *Cottage Residences.* New York, 1981. Originally published 1842.

Drury, George H. *The Historical Guide to North American Railroads.* Waukesha, Wis., 1992.

Duis, Perry R. *Challenging Chicago: Coping with Everyday Life, 1837–1920.* Urbana, Ill., 1998.

Ebner, Michael H. *Creating Chicago's North Shore: A Suburban History.* Chicago, 1988.

Ely, James W., Jr. *Railroads and American Law.* Lawrence, Kans., 2001.

Encyclopedia of American Business History and Biography: Railroads in the Nineteenth Century. Edited by Robert L. Frey. New York, 1988.

Epstein, Ralph C. *GATX: A History of the General American Transportation Corporation, 1898–1948.* New York, 1948.

Ferguson, Eugene S. *Oliver Evans: Inventive Genius of the American Industrial Revolution.* Greenville, Del., 1980.

Field, H. H. *History of the Milwaukee Railroad.* Chicago, 1941.

Fishman, Robert. *Bourgeois Utopias: The Rise and Fall of Suburbia.* New York, 1987.

Fletcher, William. *English and American Steam Carriages and Traction Engines.* Devon, UK, 1973.

Foner, Philip. *The Great Labor Uprising of 1877.* New York, 1977.

Forney, M. N., et al., *The American Railway: Its Construction, Development, Management and Appliances.* New York, 1972. Originally published in New York, 1888.

Friedman, Lawrence M. *A History of American Law.* New York, 1973.

Gerstner, Franz Anton Ritter Von. *Early American Railroads.* Stanford, Calif., 1997. Originally published in two volumes in Germany 1842–1843 as *Die innern Communicationen der Vereinigten Staaten von Nordamerica.*

Glendinning, Gene V. *The Chicago & Alton Railroad: The Only Way.* DeKalb, Ill., 2002.

Goddard, Stephen B. *Getting There: The Epic Struggle between Road and Rail in the American Century.* New York, 1994.

Gordon, H. Sarah. *Passage to Union: How the Railroads Transformed American Life.* Chicago, 1996.

Grant, H. Roger. *The Corn Belt Route: A History of the Chicago Great Western Railroad Company.* DeKalb, Ill., 1984.

———. *"Follow the Flag:" A History of the Wabash Railroad Company.* DeKalb, Ill., 2004.

———. *The North Western: A History of the Chicago & North Western Railway System.* DeKalb, Ill., 1996.

Green, Paul M., and Melvin G. Holli. *The Mayors: The Chicago Political Tradition.* Carbondale, Ill., 1987.

Grodinsky, Julius. *Jay Gould: His Business Career, 1867–1892.* Philadelphia, 1957.

Hadfield, Charles. *World Canals Inland Navigation, Past and Present.* New York, 1986.

Harlow, Alvin F. *The Road of the Century: The Story of the New York Central.* New York, 1947.

Hayes, William Edward. *Iron Road to Empire: The History of 100 Years of the Progress and Achievements of the Rock Island Lines.* New York, 1953.

Heimberger, Donald J. *Wabash.* Forest Park, Ill., 1984.

Heise, Kenan, and Michael Edgerton. *Chicago: Center for Enterprise.* 2 vols. Woodland Hills, Calif., 1982.

Hill, Robert Milton. *A Little Known Story of the Land Called Clearing.* Privately published, Chicago, 1983.

Hilton, George W. *Eastland: Legacy of the Titanic.* Stanford, Calif., 1997.

———. *The Great Lakes Car Ferries.* Berkeley, Calif., 1962.

———. *Lake Michigan Passenger Steamers.* Stanford, Calif., 2002.

———. *Monon Route.* Berkeley, Calif., 1978.

Hilton, George W., and John F. Due. *The Electric Interurban Railways in America.* Stanford, Calif., 1960.

Hoogenbloom, Ali and Olive. *A History of the ICC: From Panacea to Palliative.* New York, 1976.

Howard, Robert P. *Illinois: A History of the Prairie State.* Grand Rapids, Mich., 1972.

Hubbard, Gurdon Saltonstall. *The Autobiography of Gurdon Saltonstall Hubbard: Pa-pa—ma-ta-be, "The Swift Walker."* Chicago, 1911. Originally published in 1889 under the title of *Gurdon Saltonstall Hubbard, Incidents and Events in the Life of; Collected from Personal Narratives and Other Sources and Arranged by His Nephew, Henry E. Hamilton.*

Hungerford, Edward. *Men of Erie: A Story of Human Effort.* New York, 1946.

Hunter, Louis C. *Steamboats on the Western Rivers: An Economic and Technological History.* Mineola, N.Y., 1993. Originally published in Cambridge, Mass., 1949.

International Harvester Co. *Roots in Chicago.* Chicago, 1947.

Jackson, Kenneth T. *Crabgrass Frontier: The Suburbanization of the United States.* New York, 1985.

Jackson, Robert W. *Rails Across the Mississippi: A History of the St. Louis Bridge.* Urbana, Ill., 2001.

James, Francis. *Walter Hancock and His Common Road Steam Carriages.* Alresford, Hampshire, UK, 1975.

Jensen, Oliver. *The American Heritage History of Railroads in America.* Avenel, New Jersey, 1975.

Johnson, Stanley W. *The Milwaukee Road Revised.* Moscow, Idaho, 1997.

Jones, Lottie E. *History of Vermillion County, Illinois.* Chicago, 1911.

Karamanski, Theodore J., and Deane Tank, Sr. *Maritime Chicago.* Chicago, 2000.

Keating, Ann Durkin. *Building Chicago: Suburban Developers and the Creation of a Divided Metropolis.* Columbus, Ohio, 1988.

Kipling, Rudyard. *American Notes: Rudyard Kipling's West.* Norman, Okla., 1981. Originally published in 1891.

Klein, Maury. *History of the Louisville & Nashville Railroad.* New York, 1972.

———. *The Life and Legend of Jay Gould.* Baltimore, 1986.

———. *Union Pacific: The Rebirth, 1894–1969.* 2 vols. New York, 1989.

Knudsen, C. T. *Chicago & North Western Steam Power: 1848–1956, Classes A–Z.* Chicago, 1965.

Krambles, George, ed. *The Great Third Rail.* Chicago, 1961.

Krambles, George, and Art Peterson. *CTA at 45: A History of the First 45 Years of the Chicago Transit Authority.* Oak Park, Ill., 1993.

Kranzberg, Melvin, and Carroll W. Russell, eds. *Technology in Western Civilization: The Emergence of Modern Industrial Society, Earliest Times to 1900.* Oxford, UK, 1967.

Krenkel, John H. *Illinois Internal Improvements, 1818–1848.* Cedar Rapids, Iowa, 1958.

Krieger, Michael. *Where Rails Meet the Sea: America's Connections Between Ships & Trains.* New York, 1998.

Landes, David S. *Revolution in Time: Clocks and the Making of the Modern World.* Cambridge, Mass., 1983.

Langill, Ellen, and Dave Jensen. *Milwaukee 150: The Greater Milwaukee Story.* Milwaukee, 1996.

Larson, John Lauritz. *Bonds of Enterprise: John Murray Forbes and Western Development in America's Railway Age.* Iowa City, Iowa, 2001. Originally published in Boston, 1984.

Lee, Norman E. *Travel and Transport through the Ages.* Cambridge, UK, 1956.

Leech, Harper, and John Charles Carroll. *Armour and His Times.* New York, 1938.

Lewis, Edward A. *American Shortline Railway Guide.* Waukesha, Wis., 1991.

Lewis, Robert G. *The Handbook of American Railroads.* New York, 1956.

Leydendecker, Liston Edgington. *Palace Car Prince: A Biography of George Mortimer Pullman.* Niwcot, Colo., 1992.

Lind, Alan R. *Limiteds Along the Lakefront: The Illinois Central in Chicago.* Park Forest, Ill., 1986.

MacKay, Donald, and Lorne Perry. *Train Country: An Illustrated History of the Canadian National Railways.* Forest Park, Ill., 1994.

Mansfield, J. B. *History of the Great Lakes.* 2 vols. Cleveland, 1972. Originally published in Chicago, 1899.

Marshall, James. *Santa Fe: The Railroad that Built an Empire.* New York, 1945.

Marshall, Ralph William. "The Early History of the Galena and Chicago Union Railroad." Master's thesis, University of Chicago, 1937.

Martin, Albro. *Enterprise Denied: Origins of the Decline of American Railroads, 1897–1910.* New York, 1971.

———. *Railroads Triumphant: The Growth, Rejection, and Rebirth of a Vital American Force.* Oxford, UK, 1992.

Mayer, Harold M. *The Port of Chicago and the St. Lawrence Seaway.* Chicago, 1957.

———. "The Railway Pattern of Metropolitan Chicago." Ph.D. diss., University of Chicago, 1943.

Mayer, Harold M., and Richard C. Wade. *Chicago: Growth of a Metropolis.* Chicago, 1969.

McClellan, Dave, and Bill Warrick. *The Lake Shore & Michigan Southern Railway.* Polo, Ill., 1989.

Meeks, Carroll L. V. *The Railroad Station: An Architectural History.* New York, 1995. Originally published in 1965.

Meinig, D. W. *The Shaping of America: A Geographical Perspective on 500 Years of History.* 3 vols. New Haven, Conn., 1986, 1993, 1998.

Middleton, William D. *The Interurban Era.* Milwaukee, 1961.

———. *North Shore: America's Fastest Interurban.* San Marino, Calif., 1964.

———. *South Shore: The Last Interurban,* 2nd ed. Bloomington, Ind., 1999.

Miller, Donald L. *City of the Century: The Epic of Chicago and the Making of America.* New York, 1996.

Miller, George H. *Railroads and the Granger Laws.* Madison, Wis., 1971.

Miller, Ross. *American Apocalypse: The Great Fire and the Myth of Chicago.* Chicago, 1990.

Miner, H. Craig. *The Rebirth of the Missouri Pacific, 1956–1983.* College Station, Tex., 1983.

Moffat, Bruce G. *The Chicago Tunnel Story: Exploring the Railroad "Forty Feet Below."* Chicago, 2002.

———. *Forty Feet Below.* Glendale, Calif., 1982.

———. *The L: The Development of Chicago's Rapid Transit System, 1888–1932.* Chicago, 1995.

Moore, Jean. *Wheaton: A Pictorial History.* St. Louis, 1994.

Moses, John, and Joseph Kirkland. *The History of Chicago, Illinois.* 2 vols. Chicago, 1895.

Nordin, S. Swen. *Rich Harvest: A History of the Grange.* Jackson, Miss., 1974.

Oliver, Smith Hemstone. "The First Quarter-Century of Steam Locomotives in America." *United States National Museum Bulletin 210,* Washington, 1956.

Overton, Richard C. *Burlington Route: A History of the Burlington Lines.* New York, 1965.

Parks, Robert J. *Democracy's Railroads: Public Enterprise in Jacksonian Michigan.* Port Washington, N.Y., 1972.

Parmelee Transportation Company. *An Essential Link in American Transportation, 1853–1953.* Chicago, 1953.

Pease, Theodore Calvin. *The Frontier State, 1818–1848.* Urbana, Ill., 1987. Originally published in Springfield, Ill., 1918.

Pierce, Bessie Louise. *A History of Chicago.* 3 vols. Chicago, 1937.

Plachno, Larry. *Sunset Lines: The Story of the Chicago, Aurora & Elgin Railroad.* 2 vols. Polo, Ill., 1989.

Ploss, Thomas H. *The Nation Pays Again.* Chicago, 1991. Originally published in 1983.

Pratt, Harry E., ed. *Illinois as Lincoln Knew It: A Boston Reporter's Record of a Trip in 1847.* Springfield, Ill., 1938.

Prentice, Erie E. Parmalee. *The Federal Power over Carriers and Corporations.* New York, 1907.

Primm, James Neal. *Lion of the Valley: St. Louis, Missouri.* Boulder, Colo., 1981.

Putnam, James William. *The Illinois and Michigan Canal: A Study in Economic History.* Chicago, 1918.

Quaife, Milo M. *Chicago's Highways Old and New: From Indian Trail to Motor Road.* Chicago, 1923.

———. *Lake Michigan.* Indianapolis, 1944.

Raitz, Carl, ed. *The National Road.* Baltimore, 1996.

Reed, Robert C. *Train Wrecks: A Pictoral History of Accidents on the Main Line.* Atglen, Pa., 1996.

Rehor, John A. *The Nickel Plate Story.* Waukesha, Wis., 1965.

Reynolds, John. *My Own Times.* Chicago, 1879.

Reynolds, William. *European Capital, British Iron, and an American Dream: The Story of the Atlantic and Great Western Railroad.* Akron, Ohio, 2002.

Rice, Herbert William. *Early History of the Chicago, Milwaukee & St. Paul Railway.* Iowa City, Iowa, 1938.

Richmond, C. W., and H. F. Valette. *A History of the County of Du Page, Illinois.* Chicago, 1857.

Ripley, William Z. *Railroads: Finance and Organization.* New York, 1915.

Rittenhouse, Jack D. *American Horse-Drawn Vehicles.* New York, 1948.

Rolt, L. T. C. *The Railway Revolution: George and Robert Stephenson.* New York, 1960.

Salsbury, Stephen. *No Way to Run A Railroad: The Untold Story of the Penn Central Crisis.* New York, 1982.

Saunders, Richard, Jr. *Main Lines: Rebirth of the North American Railroads, 1970–2002.* DeKalb, Ill., 2003.

———. *Merging Lines: American Railroads, 1900–1970.* DeKalb, Ill., 2001.

Sawislak, Karen. *Smoldering City: Chicagoans and the Great Fire, 1871–1874.* Chicago, 1995.

Sawyers, June Skinner. *Chicago Portraits: Biographies of 250 Famous Chicagoans.* Chicago, 1991.

Scherb, Jeff. "Moveable Railroad Bridges of Chicago." *Railroad Model Craftsman,* 71:10 and 71:11, March and April, 2003.

Schneirov, Richard, Shelton Stromquist, and Nick Salvatore, eds. *The Pullman Strike and the Crisis of the 1890s: Essays on Labor and Politics.* Urbana, 1999.

Schwieterman, Joseph P. *When the Railroad Leaves Town: American Communities in the Age of Rail Line Abandonment.* Kirksville, Mo., 2001.

Schwieterman, Joseph P., and Toth, Martin E. *Shaping Contemporary Suburbia: Perspectives on Development Control in Metropolitan Chicago.* Chicago, 2001.

Scribbens, Jim, and Bob Hayden. *Milwaukee Road Remembered.* Milwaukee, 1990.

Shaw, Robert P. *A History of Railroad Accidents, Safety Precautions and Operating Practices,* 2nd ed. Potsdam, New York, 1978.

Shaw, Ronald E. *Canals for a Nation: The Canal Era in the United States, 1790–1860.* Lexington, Ky., 1990.

Simon, Paul. *Lincoln's Preparation for Greatness: The Illinois Legislative Years.* Norman, Okla., 1965.

Simons, Richard S., and Francis H. Parker. *Railroads of Indiana.* Bloomington, Ind., 1997.

Skinner, Claiborne Adams. "The Sinews of Empire: The Voyageurs and the Carrying Trade of the *Pays d'en Haut.*" Ph.D. diss., University of Illinois, Chicago, 1990.

Slayton, Robert A. *Back of the Yards: The Making of a Local Democracy.* Chicago, 1986.

Smerk, George M. *The Federal Role in Urban Mass Transportation.* Bloomington, Ind., 1991.

———. *Urban Mass Transportation: A Dozen Years of Federal Policy.* Bloomington, Ind., 1974.

Smith, Frank A., ed. *Transportation in America, 1992: A Statistical Analysis of Transportation in the United States.* Eno Foundation for Transportation, Vienna, Va., 1992.

Solzman, David M. *The Chicago River: An Illustrated History and Guide to the River and Its Waterways.* Chicago, 1998.

Stennett, W. H. *Yesterday and To-day: A History of the Chicago & North Western Railway System.* Chicago, 1905.

Stevens, G. R. *History of the Canadian National Railways.* New York, 1973.

Stoutemyer, Helen Louise Plaster. *The Train That Never Arrived: A Saga of the Niagara Excursion Train that Wrecked between Chatsworth and Piper City August 10, 1887.* Fairbury, Ill., 1970.

Stover, John F. *American Railroads.* Chicago, 1997. Originally published in 1961.

———. *History of the Baltimore & Ohio Railroad.* West Lafayette, Ind., 1995. Originally published in 1987.

———. *The History of the Illinois Central Railroad.* New York, 1975.

———. *Iron Road to the West: American Railroads in the 1850s.* New York, 1978.

———. *Life and Decline of the American Railroad.* New York, 1970.

———. *The Routledge Historical Atlas of the American Railroads.* New York, 1999.

Stowell, David O. *Streets, Railroads, and the Great Strike of 1877.* Chicago, 1999.

Stringham, Paul H. *Toledo, Peoria & Western: Tried, Proven & Willing.* Peoria, Ill., 1993.

Sulzer, Elmer G. *Ghost Railroads of Indiana.* Bloomington, Ind., 1998. Originally published in Indianapolis, 1970.

Swift, Louis F., with Arthur Van Vlissingen, Jr. *Yankee of the Yards: The Biography of Gustavus Franklin Swift.* Chicago, 1927.

Tan, Pei-Lin. "The Belt and Switching Railroads of the Chicago Terminal Area." Ph.D. diss., University of Chicago, 1935.

Taylor, James Rogers. *The Transportation Revolution, 1815–1860.* New York, 1951.

Temple, Wayne C. *Lincoln's Connections with the Illinois and Michigan Canal, His Return from Congress in 1848, and His Invention.* Springfield, Ill., 1986.

Thompson, Gregory Lee. *The Passenger Train in the Motor Age.* Columbus, Ohio, 1993.

Thompson, Slason. *A Short History of American Railways, Covering Ten Decades.* Chicago, 1925.

Thurston, Robert H. *A History of the Growth of the Steam Engine.* Ithaca, N.Y., 1939. Originally published in New York, 1878.

Turner, Frederick Jackson. *The Frontier in American History.* New York, 1996. Originally published in New York, 1920.

U.S. Department of Transportation. *America's Highways 1776–1976: A History of the Federal Aid Program*. Washington, 1976.

Usher, Abbott Payson. *A History of Mechanical Inventions*. New York, 1988. Originally published in Cambridge, Mass., 1929.

Vance, James E., Jr. *Capturing the Horizon: The Historical Geography of Transportation since the Sixteenth Century*. Baltimore, 1990.

———. *The North American Railroad: Its Origin, Evolution, and Geography*. Baltimore, 1995.

Wade, Louis Carroll. *Chicago's Pride: The Stockyards, Packingtown, and Environs in the Nineteenth Century*. Urbana, Ill., 1987.

Warren, Charles. *The Supreme Court in United States History*. 2 vols. Boston, 1922, 1926.

Weber, Harry P. *Outline History of Chicago Traction*. Chicago, 1936.

Weller, Peter, and Fred Stark. *The Living Legacy of the Chicago, Aurora & Elgin: An Illustrated History of the CA&E and Its Transition to the Illinois Prairie Path*. San Francisco, 1999.

Westing, Fred. *The Locomotives that Baldwin Built*. New York, 1966.

White, John H., Jr. *American Locomotives: An Engineering History, 1830–1880*. Rev. ed. Baltimore, 1997.

———. *The American Railroad Freight Car*. Baltimore, 1993.

———. *The American Railroad Passenger Car*. 2 vols. Baltimore, 1978.

Wille, Lois. *Forever Open, Clear, and Free: The Struggle for Chicago's Lakefront*, 2nd ed. Chicago, 1991.

———. *At Home in the Loop: How Clout and Community Built Chicago's Dearborn Park*. Carbondale, Ill., 1997.

Wilner, Frank N. *The Amtrak Story*. Omaha, Neb., 1994.

———. *Railroad Mergers: History, Analysis, Insight*. Omaha, Neb., 1997.

Wilson, Rosalyn A., ed. *Transportation in America, 1997*. Eno Foundation for Transportation, Lansdowne, Va., 1997.

Wood, Donald F., and James C. Johnson. *Contemporary Transportation*. Upper Saddle River, N.J., 1996.

Young, David M. *Chicago Maritime: An Illustrated History*. DeKalb, Ill., 2001.

———. *Chicago Transit: An Illustrated History*. DeKalb, Ill., 1998.

Zimmerman, Karl. *Lake Michigan's Railroad Car Ferries*. Andover, N.J., 1993.

Index

Individual railroads are listed under "railroad companies."

Italicized page numbers indicate maps and tables.